AFRICAN AMERICANS IN CENTRAL TEXAS HISTORY

AFRICAN
AMERICANS
IN
CENTRAL
TEXAS
HISTORY

FROM SLAVERY TO CIVIL RIGHTS

Edited by Bruce A. Glasrud
and Deborah M. Liles

Texas A&M University Press
College Station, Texas

First edition
This paper meets the requirements of ANSI/NISO
Z39.48-1992 (Permanence of Paper).
Binding materials have been chosen for durability.
♻ ∞

Library of Congress Cataloging-in-Publication Data

Names: Glasrud, Bruce A., editor. |
    Liles, Deborah M., editor.
Title: African Americans in central Texas history : from
    slavery to civil rights / edited by Bruce A. Glasrud
    and Deborah M. Liles.
Description: First edition. | College Station, Texas :
    Texas A&M University Press, [2019] | Includes
    bibliographical references and index.
Identifiers: LCCN 2018057927 | ISBN 9781623497477
    (book/hardcover (printed case) : alk. paper) |
    ISBN 9781623497484 (ebook format/all ebooks)
Subjects: LCSH: African Americans—Civil
    rights—Texas—History. | African Americans—
    Texas—Biography. | Civil rights—Texas—
    History. | Slavery—Texas—History. |
    Racism—Texas—History.
Classification: LCC E185.93.T4 A385 2019 |
    DDC 323.1196/0730763—dc23
LC record available at https://lccn.loc.gov/2018057927

CONTENTS

TABLES

ACKNOWLEDGMENTS

African Americans in Central Texas History: From Slavery to Civil Rights began with a discussion between the coeditors—Bruce A. Glasrud and Deborah M. Liles—at an East Texas Historical Association meeting. While talking, we focused on a few aspects of Texas history and black Texans that had not been well researched; we soon concluded that a book on the history of African Americans in the Lone Star State's central region was a must and that we would coauthor/edit such a book. We spoke to Jay Dew, editor in chief at Texas A&M University Press; he, too, thought this a good idea and encouraged us to submit such a manuscript to the press. Thanks for the help and support, Jay.

We also want to thank a number of other individuals. Without the hard work and ability of the authors, of course, the book would not have been feasible. We thank the sixteen authors whose studies are featured in this book and thank the publishers of their works who allowed use of the essays. This collection contains three original articles by Deborah M. Liles, Rebecca Sharpless, and James T. Matthews and a revised article by Martin Kuhlman. We are profusely thankful for these first-rate contributions to our work. The *Southwestern Historical Quarterly* allowed use of four articles; two additional articles were originally published in books by the Texas State Historical Association. For these six articles, we thank Ryan R. Schumacher (managing editor at the Texas State Historical Association) for his help and support. Randal L. Hall (editor) enabled publication of a needed article from the *Journal of Southern History*. Donaly Brice not only allowed us to use his article on black trail hands; he also acquired permission for us from the Genealogical and Historical Society of Caldwell County. Dan Utley, former Texas Historical Commission stalwart, helped us contact the correct individuals in order to secure permission from that august body. Billy Huckaby of the Wild Horse Media Group kindly gave us permission to use a chapter from *Bricks without Straw*, an Eakin Press book. We also received help from overseas; the journal *Slavery and Abolition*, published in England by Taylor and Francis, provided us with permission to use a critical article, thanks to the help of Kendyl Anderson. M. Scott Sosebee, director of the East Texas Historical Association, allowed use of an article previously published in the *East Texas Historical Journal*, and the Texas A&M University Press rights manager, Linda L. Salitros, approved our request to use a chapter from one of that press's books. Also, at Texas A&M University Press, Patricia Clabaugh, associate and project editor, skillfully took the manuscript through the editorial stages. Scribe project manager, Michael Miller, enabled a readable work. Thanks Texas A&M University Press.

What we are also acknowledging is that one of the exhilarating aspects of producing an anthology is the interaction with so many supportive, encouraging, and helpful individuals. This includes two readers who asked pertinent questions, made suggestions, and supported publication; we thank them for their diligence and their favorable recommendations. As an additional case in point, members of the newly formed Central Texas History Association, including but not limited to Charles Swanlund and Kenneth Howell, provided ideas and guidance. Norman Brandenstein graciously allowed us permission to reprint his deceased sister's article. Alex Mendoza created the map of Central Texas counties and Wayne Ludwig created the index. Pearlene Vestal Glasrud critiqued the introduction, Mike Liles critiqued chapter 1, and both provided support throughout this project. Many thanks to them both. Any errors or omissions, however, we realize are our own, for which we remain responsible.

Bruce A. Glasrud, San Antonio, Texas
Deborah M. Liles, Weatherford, Texas

AFRICAN AMERICANS IN CENTRAL TEXAS HISTORY

Betwixt Old Ways and New Freedoms

African Americans in Central Texas

Bruce A. Glasrud and Deborah M. Liles

During the latter years of the nineteenth century, at least sixteen African American males were brutally lynched in Central Texas' Brazos County. Even for the Lone Star State, this was a large, albeit not exceptional, number. However, for five of the lynched black men, an unusual circumstance intruded; as author Cynthia Skove Nevels put it, "European immigrants of different nationalities . . . played crucial roles at the beginning of each" incident. Those immigrants also contributed to the ultimate violent deaths of the black victims.[1] It did not take long for even recent immigrants to Central Texas to learn the Texas way of keeping African Americans in their place, socially and economically, by violence and intimidation. As William D. Carrigan phrased it, "In shaping the memories of those who committed certain acts of violence as community heroes and defenders of justice, [white] central Texans created, justified, and long preserved a robust culture of violence."[2]

Perhaps the most odious example of antiblack violence in Central Texas occurred in Waco in 1916, a violent occurrence known as the "Waco Horror." Jesse Washington, an illiterate seventeen-year-old black laborer was accused of raping and murdering his employer's wife. He was brutally forced to confess, though a few thought Washington's white employer the person responsible. After Washington was found guilty in a trial, a huge mob took his body, mutilated it, burned it, and souvenirs from his body were sold to those who wished to memorialize their presence at the gruesome spectacle. Thousands witnessed the lynching, many coming from outside the area surrounding Waco. Although a few white Wacoans spoke out against the violence, more seemed pleased with the turn of events, and none appeared willing to say that

Washington was not guilty. Nor was dissension tolerated in the black community. A. T. Smith, the black managing editor of the *Paul Quinn College Weekly* newsletter denounced the incident and was arrested and convicted for writing that Washington was not guilty. He was defended, although unsuccessfully, by local African American attorney, Richard D. Evans. The NAACP sent an investigator to determine what happened; based on her report, that civil rights organization subsequently published an eight-page article on the "Waco Horror," which offered graphic support for the antilynching movement.[3]

Central Texans in the early twentieth century not only resorted to violence against black lawbreakers for crimes, real or fabricated; violence and intimidation were adopted as methods of preventing black (and some white) efforts at organizing and protesting their subordinate status in the Jim Crow society. In August 1919, John R. Shillady, the white executive secretary of the NAACP, arrived in Austin to meet with state and local officials concerning Texas' harassment of Texas NAACP members and branches, particularly the branch in Austin. After meeting with the interim attorney general, he was taken before a special court of inquiry where he was verbally attacked with racist comments and threats. By this time, the Texas NAACP included thirty-five branches and a membership nearing eight thousand, a movement large enough to be perceived as a threat by whites. The next day, while Shillady walked in the street, a group of white men, including local Texas politicians, attacked and severely beat him. Texas governor W. P. Hobby blamed Shillady and the NAACP for the attack and ordered them to leave the state. The brutally battered Shillady resigned his position because of the beating.[4] Whites in Central Texas feared the growth of protest organizations such as the NAACP that challenged the antiblack culture that continued in Texas. However, within a few years, the white strategies together with the efforts of the Ku Klux Klan proved successful, and membership numbers in the Texas NAACP declined precipitously.

Yet blacks in Central Texas were undeterred by white efforts to maintain their social and economic subordination; they turned to the courts to ensure their right to vote. Before efforts to disenfranchise the black vote became successful, some politicians courted the black vote. A black-German alliance throughout Washington County can be seen in the Republican hold until 1884, and in nearby Colorado County, the Townsend family depended on the black vote to dominate the political scene until, with encouragement from Townsend opposition, the county enacted the white primary in 1902. The same year (1919) as the Shillady attack, whites in Waco, who had enacted a white primary law designed to keep blacks from voting in local primary elections, were challenged in court by black Wacoans. In Waco, as in other cities in Texas, blacks previously voted in local nonpartisan elections although not in statewide primary elections. A black civic and political organization, the Forum, challenged the white primary feature in Waco elections. Richard D. Evans, a black attorney in Waco, successfully fought the white primary, and in *Sublett v. Duke*, a Texas district court judge ruled that the Waco white primary violated the fifteenth amendment; regrettably, the *Sublett* decision was overruled by another judge in 1922.[5]

Born in Brenham, Texas, Richard Evans received his law degree from the Howard University School of Law in 1912 and in 1913 set up practice in Waco. In 1924, Evans represented a Houston black man who had been denied the right to vote in the primary by the Houston Democratic Party. The subsequent case, *Love v. Griffith*, was the first white primary case to be argued before the US Supreme Court; however, the court ruled against Love. Evans, a member of the NAACP, worked to rejuvenate the Texas NAACP, and after black Texans formed the Texas State Conference of NAACP branches in 1936, Evans became its first president in 1937. The following year, Evans was killed in a train accident. There is still some feeling that, newly elected to a leadership post in the state's only civil rights organization of any strength, Evans was killed purposely.[6] No matter what occurred, in Central Texas, African Americans showed that they would and could organize and challenge the injustices of the white majority. The right to vote was vitally important; unfortunately, that ability to vote in the Texas Democratic primary would not occur until 1944, as the state established and maintained the white primary as the sole avenue to elective offices.

While *Sublett* was being overturned in 1922, in Freestone County on the edge of Central Texas, a series of brutal acts of racial violence occurred in May. A mob in Kirven burned alive three black men who were accused of the murder of a young white woman; local authorities concealed the identities of the likely white murderers. White mobs then went on a monthlong binge of racial intimidation, terrorism, and murder in the county. To discover what in fact transpired during this rampant violence, the NAACP hired Dan Kezer Kelly, a white man from Waco, to investigate the violence occurring in Kirven and Freestone County. Acting as a newspaper reporter, and carrying a revolver, Kelly compiled a very different account from the official white position. Kelly's thorough report was delivered at the Thirteenth Annual Conference of the NAACP in 1922. Nonetheless, the power and influence of the antiblack efforts in Freestone County that continued to muffle dissent carried over into Limestone County; as late as 1939, a history of blacks in Limestone County, *History of Negroes of Limestone County: From 1860 to 1939*, written by African American author and resident Walter F. Cotton, made no mention of the 1922 antiblack rampage.[7]

While the black population of Central Texas in the early years of the twentieth century did not reach the level of numbers found in the slaveholding states of the Deep South, Central Texas blacks frequently found themselves beset by old, established antiblack white behavior and attitudes while at the same time receiving some support and encouragement from a few white citizens and from brave black contemporaries. These disparities can be noticed in other aspects of African American life in Central Texas. More blacks resided in Central Texas than West Texas, but the largest number of Afro-Texans resided in East Texas. This is a direct result of white settlement patterns before the Civil War: East Texas had a larger slave society, whereas fewer slaves existed in Central Texas, and fewer still were present in West Texas. In terms of their respective racial attitudes and behaviors, more violent anti-black antipathy was displayed against blacks in East Texas than in Central Texas, and fewer yet occurred in West Texas.

One may well ask, What is this region that has such repellent incidents as a part of its history, and what has shaped its cultural patterns? In general, of course, Central Texas is the portion of the Lone Star State between East Texas and West Texas and north of South Texas. But that is too simple; to a certain extent, Central Texas is determined by whom one asks or what book one reads. William D. Carrigan, in his important work *The Making of a Lynching Culture: Violence and Vigilantism in Central Texas, 1836–1916* defined Central Texas as the upper Brazos River valley and included seven counties in his study: Hill, Bosque, Coryell, Falls, Bell, McLennan, and Limestone. Cynthia Skove Nevels, in *Lynching to Belong: Claiming Whiteness through Racial Violence*, focused on Brazos County. Neil Foley, in *The White Scourge: Mexicans, Blacks, and Poor Whites in Texas Cotton Culture*, asserted that "central Texas forms a diamond shape from Dallas in the north to Corpus Christi in the south, bounded by San Antonio in the west and Houston in the east." Foley went on to iterate that "this region is the site of the cultural core, not because it occupies the geographical center of the state but because, more than any other region, it displays . . . the 'full range of intercultural tensions' that exist between east Texas, west Texas, and south Texas." According to Clyde McQueen, in his *Black Churches in Texas*, "The Central Texas Region included twenty-nine counties," and he noted that the "Brazos, Colorado, Leon, Navasota, and Trinity rivers flow through the area."[8]

The recently formed Central Texas Historical Association (CTHA), as do most other regional history associations, takes a broader view of its regional interests and includes the cities of Houston, San Antonio, Waco, Fort Worth, and Dallas. As the CTHA puts it, "If you think you are part of the Central Texas region, then you are."[9] For our purposes, we define Central Texas as those fifty-four counties south of the Red River; east of a line following from the western border of Wichita County, including Mason and Kerr; and west of a line beginning with Cooke County and including Limestone, Brazos, and Washington. The southernmost counties include Fayette, Guadalupe, Comal, and Kerr (see map). Essentially, as we mentioned earlier, Central Texas is the region between East Texas and West Texas and north of South Texas.

One of the reasons for publishing this book is that little has been written about the Afro-Texan experience in Central Texas, although a solid number of theses, dissertations, and journal articles have been written about varied aspects of African American history in this region, as well as some monographs. One additional reason for producing a book on Central Texas history is to fill a void in the works of coeditor Bruce Glasrud's studies of Texas' black community. Glasrud previously published, with James M. Smallwood, *The African American Experience in Texas*, as well as three regional works—*Blacks in East Texas History*, with Archie P. McDonald; *Slavery to Integration: Black Americans in West Texas*, with Paul H. Carlson; and *African Americans in South Texas History*.[10] To this date, the best place to begin the exploration of black history in Central Texas is with the books previously mentioned in our introduction—one gains considerable insight about the black experience in Central Texas from the works of Neil Foley, William D. Carrigan, and Cynthia Skove Nevels.

That is only a beginning, however. Central Texas comprises a few important urban centers whose racial pasts have been covered by numerous historians. The black American community of Waco can be explored in Garry H. Radford Sr.'s *African American Heritage in Waco, Texas*. On Fort Worth, African American author Reby Cary has produced a number of works, but see especially *Princes Shall Come out of Egypt, Texas, and Fort Worth* and *How We Got Over! Update on a Backward Look: A History of Blacks in Fort Worth*. Recently, author Richard F. Selcer published an informative work entitled *A History of Fort Worth in Black & White: 165 Years of African-American Life*. In *Black Community Control: A Study of Transition in a Texas Ghetto*, Joyce E. Williams depicted the effort of blacks in Fort Worth to wrest control of the black community from whites, a policy of liberation that they referred to as "Black Power for the Black Community." The African American community in Wichita Falls is well featured in C. Emerson "Prof" and Gwendolyn McDonald Jackson's *The History of the Negro, Wichita Falls, Texas, 1880–1892*. One book-length study of black Austin, the capital city of Texas, is Jason McDonald's *Racial Dynamics in Early Twentieth-Century Austin*. McDonald discussed not only the black community but also Austin's Mexican American community. Oswell Person, in *African American Bryan, Texas: Celebrating the Past*, briefly told the history of that community and its emergence through the present.[11]

Following the Civil War and the freedom that black slaves received, some black Texans grouped together and formed freedom colonies in Central Texas as well as the rest of the state. For the overall picture, turn to Thad Sitton and James H. Conrad's *Freedom Colonies: Independent Black Texans in the Time of Jim Crow*. Toward the end of their book, Sitton and Conrad included a remarkable list of freedom colonies by county; and they located at least one such colony in virtually all Central Texas counties. Two studies focus on freedom colonies in Central Texas: Drew Sanders's *The Garden of Eden: The Story of a Freedmen's Community in Texas* and Michelle M. Mears's *And Grace Will Lead Me Home: African American Freedmen Communities of Austin, Texas, 1865–1928*.[12]

Integration and civil rights in Central Texas have been discussed by Almetrius M. Duren and Louise Iscoe in *Overcoming: A History of Black Integration of the University of Texas at Austin*, Dwonna Goldstone in *Integrating the 40 Acres: The 50 Year Struggle for Racial Equality at the University of Texas*, and Robyn Duff Ladino in *Desegregating Texas Schools: Eisenhower, Shivers, and the Crisis at Mansfield High*. Adding to these is a recent study about Doris Miller, a hero of Pearl Harbor, by Thomas W. Cutrer and T. Michael Parrish, which argues that Miller was "directly

responsible for helping to roll back the navy's unrelenting policy of racial segregation and prejudice and, in the process, helped to launch the civil rights movement
of the 1960s that brought a legal end to the worst of America's racial intolerance."
Carolyn L. Jones probed the life and actions of a civil rights activist in *Volma: My
Journey—One Man's Impact on the Civil Rights Movement in Austin, Texas*. Black
teachers were affected by integration, as reported by Anna Victoria Wilson and William E. Segall in *Oh, Do I Remember! Experiences of Teachers during the Desegregation
of Austin's Schools, 1964–1971*.[13]

Additional books that cover facets of the African American experience in Cen-
tral Texas include James C. Kearney's *Nassau Plantation: The Evolution of a Texas
German Slave Plantation*, Robert Uzzel's *Blind Lemon Jefferson: His Life, His Death,
and His Legacy*, Augusta Gooch's *Life of Lenora Rolla: A Citizen Shapes Her World*,
James Smallwood's *A Century of Achievement: Blacks in Cooke County Texas*. Patri-
cia Bernstein's *The First Waco Horror: The Lynching of Jesse Washington and the
Rise of the NAACP*. William Oliver Bundy's *Life of William Madison McDonald*.
Suzanne J. Terrell's *This Other Kind of Doctors: Traditional Medical Systems in
Black Neighborhoods in Austin, Texas*, Karen Kossie-Chernyshev's *Recovering Five
Generations Hence: The Life and Writings of Lillian Jones Horace*, and Bob Ray
Sanders's *Calvin Littlejohn: Portrait of a Community in Black and White*. George-
town, a small community near Austin in Central Texas, included blacks in its
population; information on Georgetown blacks can be located in *Histories of Pride:
Thirteen Pioneers Who Shaped Georgetown's African American Community*. Two
exceptionally prominent black men were among the most celebrated black cowboys of the late nineteenth and early twentieth centuries—Emanuel Organ and
Bill Pickett. A black Austinite and native Texan, Shannon Dorsey Johnson published *Found in Black Texiana: Contemporary Poetry, Stories and Notes for Women
with Texas and Louisiana Roots*. Chris Tomlinson provided a historical look at the
emergence of two sides of the Tomlinson family, one black and one white, in a
well-researched study, *Tomlinson Hill: The Remarkable Story of Two Families Who
Share the Tomlinson Name—One White, One Black*. The foreword to his book was
written by an African American NFL star, LaDainian Tomlinson.[14]

African Americans first entered Central Texas with Spanish explorers, but few
if any remained in the center of Texas. It was nineteenth-century white slave owners, settling in what became Central Texas, who first brought black residents—as
slaves—to Central Texas. By 1860, 26 percent of the state's slaves were in Central
Texas, with six of the fifty-four counties—Austin, Bastrop, Fayette, Travis, and
Washington—declaring 24,584 slaves, or roughly half of the total number of
enslaved men, women, and children in the region.[15]

Circumstances varied for black slaves in Central Texas. A large number, although
fewer than in East Texas, worked on cotton plantations and smaller farms, especially in the aforementioned counties. Bob Maynard grew up on a large cotton plantation of two thousand acres in Falls County where the slave population was 47

percent of the county's population; it took three hundred slaves to operate that plantation. Although most Germans were antislavery proponents, in Fayette County, where the slave population was 33 percent of the county's population, German-Texans established Nassau Plantation as a slave-operated plantation. Other black slaves raised and tended cattle on Central Texas ranches and farms, contributing to their owners' success as they built the foundations for what would soon become the era of the great cattle barons. Trained from their youth, many became proficient horsemen and herdsmen and went up the cattle trails in the postwar drives. The black cowboys of Wichita County "were ingenious and skilled men and had no fears." However, they never "rightfully received their place solely because they were black." US military officers brought the first black slaves to Fort Worth and Tarrant County; 756 slaves were recorded in the county by 1860. Slaves in Fort Worth, Austin, and other urban centers, as Paul D. Lack reminded us, "forged a way of life that differed measurably from that of their rural counterparts." This can be seen in Guadalupe County, where some slaves were used to make pottery for commercial production. They often could locate their own employment, enjoy dances, attend religious gatherings, and in many ways act as free men and women, to the chagrin of many white inhabitants. A thorough consideration of slavery in Guadalupe County can be located in Mark Gretchen's *Slave Transactions of Guadalupe County, Texas.*[16]

Central Texas, as in the remainder of the state, was also home to a few free blacks. But as the situation of Rachel Hamilton illustrates, free blacks led a precarious existence. Born into slavery in Alabama, Hamilton arrived in Travis County in 1847. Her master, Andrew Jackson Hamilton, subsequently freed her, and Rachel Hamilton secured work as a hired servant in Austin. However, state law stipulated that freed blacks could not remain in Texas without legislative approval. Hamilton was arrested; she then re-enslaved herself and acted as a caretaker nurse for her new owner's daughter. She, as did other Texas slaves, achieved freedom on June 19, 1865.[17]

One other issue of import arose in Central Texas for blacks in the Texas slave society. How was it determined who was black or white; in other words, who was a slave? In a case originating from Limestone County, a woman, Ann, was claimed to be a slave by a slave owner. Ann's mother and grandmother had been slaves, but Ann appeared white and contended she was free. Two physicians examined her and declared they could discover no African blood. An 1856 jury found Ann to be white, but the judge determined that the jury's decision did not fit the evidence. At a retrial later in McLennan County, a jury once more set Ann free. Again, the justices ruled that the evidence was not followed. As scholar Linda S. Hudson pointed out, these decisions showed "clearly that local liberal attitudes were in conflict with the conservative statute law upheld by the conservative Texas Supreme Court."[18]

One pivotal aspect of slavery in Central Texas and its geography was the black slaves' efforts to escape. A significant number did in fact escape slavery and crossed the border into Mexico, while others ran toward their families in the East or the wide-open West—most returned within a short period of time. Even without the lure of

nearby Mexico and its offer of freedom from slavery, blacks sought to escape the con-
finement of slavery. Hundreds, possibly thousands, ran away from Central Texas
before the Civil War. They had resources: friendship with Native Americans, help
from Mexican settlers, a relatively unfettered path from their homes to crossing
the Rio Grande, and an antislavery society and view in Mexico. In 1844, a group
of twenty-five slaves fled Bastrop—while whites captured seventeen, the others
likely made it across the border into Mexico. The next year, six slaves escaped from
McLennan County and took twenty-five horses with them. Moreover, whites were
apprehensive about slave rebellions; in 1856, a possible rebellion was feared near
Austin, and in 1860, a massive slave rebellion was predicted. None occurred, and
the rebellion likely was more in white imagination than an actual plot. The Civil
War served as a confounding four years for Texas slave owners, as they faced escalating numbers of runaways and threats of slave uprisings by dissenting enslaved
men and women. These years challenged and changed owners' perceptions of their
bondsmen's loyalty and "provided their masters ample evidence of the desires for
freedom among Texas slaves."[19]

With the defeat of the Confederacy and end of the Civil War (what many blacks
referred to as the Freedom War), blacks in Texas acquired their freedom beginning
on June 19, 1865. The end of hostilities produced varied reactions from slave owners
as well as former slaves. Some owners did not notify their slaves they were legally
freed until several months after Juneteenth. Slaves on other plantations, upon learning of their freedom, immediately left to seek their livelihoods and their families
elsewhere. In other situations, owners and freedmen worked out a basis of paid
labor. Gov. E. M. Pease gave land to his ex-slaves who formed the Clarksville black
enclave, a freedom colony, in Austin; others sold land to their former slaves where
they created communities, such as J. K. and T. W. Mosier in Tarrant County. The
eight succeeding years, known as Reconstruction, provided blacks with voting rights,
office-holding, sharecropping, urban jobs, a reduction of illiteracy, and an opportunity to develop their own social and religious organizations. For many the rights
were illusory.[20]

Much of the progress was hindered by the harsh, militant treatment of the
recently freed black men and women by Central Texas whites. Examples abound.
For an overview of white antipathy toward recently freed black men and women,
turn to Barry A. Crouch in "Reconstructing Brazos County: Race Relations and
the Freedmen's Bureau, 1865–1868." In July 1868, armed blacks in Millican in Brazos County formed a black militia to investigate the possibility that a black man
had been lynched. The white sheriff formed a larger posse; the posse twice attacked
the black group and, in the forays, killed at least twenty-five black militiamen. A
similar incident happened at Cedar Creek in Bastrop County. In 1874, Sol Bragg,
a Fort Worth black man, was convicted of killing a white person—there were no
witnesses, no proof, no lawyer for the defendant, and a white judge and jury. This
conviction so pleased Fort Worth whites that a crowd of four thousand witnessed

his subsequent hanging. A recent digital project by Jeffrey Littlejohn, Charles H. Ford, Jami Horne, and Briana Weaver plots lynchings throughout Texas as well as provides narratives about those who were hanged. This important study speaks volumes about the racial violence and lack of justice for people of color in the state.[21]

African Americans did participate in the electoral process after the Civil War and were elected to the legislature. Two prominent Central Texas black politicians were Matt Gaines and Robert L. Smith. Gaines, born a slave in Louisiana, was brought to Texas by a slave owner and resided in Fredericksburg until the Civil War ended. He then moved to Washington County, where he served as a preacher. He was elected to the Texas Senate and diligently strove for educational and economic rights of blacks as well as to protect and enhance their political responsibilities. Robert L. Smith arrived in Oakland, Colorado County, in 1885. Four years later, he established the Village Improvement Society to encourage black Oaklanders to improve their lives, homes, and community. By 1894, the black section of Oakland had been transformed, and Smith successfully ran for the Texas legislature. He served in the legislature until 1899, the last of the nineteenth-century black legislators. Smith later moved to Waco, formed the Farmer's Improvement Society, and pushed his views for self-help to ensure the betterment of Central Texas Afro-Texans. By 1915, Smith, still active, vehemently opposed the racist movie *Birth of a Nation*.[22]

Some black leaders in Central Texas began their lives and careers in other states. In the latter part of the nineteenth century, John B. Rayner moved from North Carolina to Texas and settled in Robertson County by 1881. Rayner was born into slavery in 1850, and after the Civil War, supported by his former owner-father, he acquired a college education. In Texas, he soon taught school, gave talks, and joined the Populist Party. A great orator, Rayner toured the state encouraging the black community to support the Populist Party. With the decline of the Populists, he joined the Republican Party in 1898. By the First World War, Rayner's efforts included pushing for black entrance into the US military. He died in 1918.[23]

During these years, as John Rayner's background suggests, a college education was important to aspiring black success. For that aspect of the Afro-Texan experience, a few colleges, mostly private, emerged in postwar Central Texas. In 1872, Paul Quinn College started in Austin but soon moved to Waco, where it endured as an important institution in that city into the twentieth century. Guadalupe College, began by black Baptists in Seguin in 1884, successfully continued until ravaged by fire in 1936. Samuel Huston College, founded by the Freedmen's Aid Society in 1900, provided black leadership and educational opportunity in Austin until it merged with Tillotson College to become Huston-Tillotson College in 1952. Tillotson College had been chartered by the American Missionary Association in 1877. For blacks, however, Texas public schools were not available. Unlike its white counterpart, Tillotson was not located in Central Texas. Since the Texas Constitution included a provision for a public-supported university for black Texans, provisions and funding eventually were provided for an African American institution to be part of the state's agricultural and mechanical system. What is now Prairie View A&M University began in 1878, although in no way was it equal in funding and support to the white-only institutions. The paucity of opportunities for aspiring black students led a few to leave the state; Ollie Mae Jeffrey earned her college degree at Tuskegee, then taught at the Booker T. Washington school in Wichita Falls, and eventually published *Mrs. Jeffrey's Southern Cooking and Other Delights* in 1982.[24]

By the beginning of the twentieth century, African Americans in Central Texas could see some changes in their position relative to 1865, but full citizenship as well as economic equality was still to be sought. Strong leaders such as Robert L. Smith, John B. Rayner, and Fort Worth's William M. McDonald provided ideas, support, and energy. However, Central Texas African Americans lived in a Jim Crow society, and their position was prescribed by biased regulations, laws, white controls, and informal patterns of behavior. As Bruce Glasrud pointed out, "Separation of the races prevailed in public transportation, residences, public institutions, privately-owned establishments, courts, wherever" black Central Texans went.[25] These controls continued into the civil rights movement of the fifties and sixties, and to a certain extent, even today, they regulate black behavior in Central Texas. As a result, black Texans turned for help and support to institutions such as the church, education, and self-help organizations.

Religious institutions played a vital role in the development of the African American community, particularly after their emancipation from slavery. The church buildings were utilized not only for religious services but also for community gatherings and served as schools. Most black Central Texans preferred to attend independent churches; that is, those attended and controlled by Afro-Texans. On the other hand, most whites in Central Texas preferred that blacks become members of biracial churches to better control black social and religious behavior. In his *Black Churches in Texas*, Clyde McQueen discovered that 128 independent congregations in Central Texas survived more than one hundred years. Most were Baptist churches, with Methodist groups following next in number of congregations. One Catholic and one Church of Christ also lasted more than a century. Blessed Virgin Mary Catholic Church was in Washington County and began in 1849. Established in 1865, the Antioch Church of Christ was in Midway, Texas. Mount Zion United Methodist Church, the oldest black Methodist church in Texas, was established in Belton in 1893. Members and pastors of the churches also provided important leadership in and for the communities.[26]

One important religious leader in Central Texas was Lee Lewis Campbell, frequently referred to with his initials as L. L. Campbell. A black Baptist pastor, Campbell attended Bishop College in Marshall and then went on to the University of Chicago. Campbell was ordained into the Baptist ministry and in 1892 became pastor of Ebenezer Baptist Church in Austin. He had a record of accomplishments in Austin. He founded St. John's Institute and Orphanage and served as president of the

General Baptist State Convention and vice president of the National General Baptist Convention. He was president of St. John's Encampment Colored Association, a group that considered Central Texas race relations, and he also founded a newspaper, the Austin *Herald* in 1889. However, when it came to the civil and social rights of black Austin, Campbell was known as a conservative and frequently clashed with the NAACP. His situation in Central Texas was not abnormal; African American pastors often found themselves on the conservative side of race relations, although some also led campaigns for more equitable treatment in the Lone Star State.[27]

Afro-Texan women were valuable members of the congregations as well as providing leadership for the black churches and to their communities. One such, Algerene Craig, born and educated in Austin, earned BS and MS degrees from Prairie View College as well as teacher and library certification from the University of Southern California and the University of Texas. She became the first African American elementary-school librarian in Texas and served the Austin schools for forty-three years as a classroom teacher, librarian, and administrator. She was a member of the Ebenezer Baptist Church for more than seventy years, where she organized programs to help those in need. Craig worked with one other important female black Baptist leader, Maud A. B. Fuller. Fuller, born in Lockhart, attended Guadalupe College and Tillotson College and taught for twenty-five years in Austin schools. An active church member and lay leader in Ebenezer Baptist Church as well as national Baptist committees and meetings, she received an honorary doctorate from Union Baptist Theological Seminary in Houston among other awards and recognitions.[28]

One other black woman in Central Texas deserves especial recognition; that leader was Tillotson College Pres. Mary E. Branch. Born in Virginia, Branch earned a master's degree in English from the University of Chicago, studied toward a doctorate in education, and taught at Virginia State College for twenty years. She later received honorary doctoral degrees from Virginia State College as well as Howard University. She served as president of Tillotson College from 1930 until her death in 1944, the first black woman in Texas to become a college president. By that time, due in large measure to the effort and ability of Branch, Tillotson had earned an *A* rating from the Southern Association of Colleges and Secondary Schools. As well, Tillotson College leaders had begun working with the other black college in Austin, Samuel Huston, and that soon led to a merger of the institutions.[29]

As in the lives of Algerene Craig, Maud Fuller, and Mary Branch, the roles of the church and education frequently overlapped. Education became exceedingly important for blacks since they were not allowed to read or write prior to 1865. Even afterward, however, white barriers and actions precluded African Americans from receiving an equitable education. Private organizations, such as churches, frequently met the challenge by establishing schools and by providing teachers. But monies spent for the states' black population were much less than for whites, even after the 1954 Supreme Court decision *Brown v. Board of Education of Topeka*. Desegregation of the schools was not helpful to all African Americans in the state; black teachers sometimes found themselves receiving a lesser salary, forced to move, or with the loss of their jobs. But as most African American educators remarked about their experiences in Austin, in *Oh, Do I Remember!*, they supported the desegregation of the schools. On the other hand, white resistance to the desegregation of the schools was overwhelming and was readily apparent in Fort Worth; when integration began at Mansfield High, white opposition and rage even brought support from Gov. Alan Shivers and the Texas Rangers to keep black students from enrolling.[30]

Segregation impacted nationally known scholars, such as folklorist John Mason Brewer, known to friends as Mason. Though born in South Texas, Brewer taught at a Fort Worth high school during the twenties, where he also published two books of poetry. He soon taught at Samuel Huston College, where he and his students published works on the history and lore of Austin and Travis County. To obtain a graduate degree, he left the state to attend Indiana University. His next position was at Booker T. Washington High School in Dallas. Unable to acquire the type of Texas employment that he desired, he taught for a year at a black college in South Carolina before obtaining a position at Huston-Tillotson College in Austin. He next moved to Livingstone College in North Carolina. Not until 1969 was Brewer able to secure a faculty position at a previously white university in the Lone Star State when East Texas State University employed him. At all of these locations, he was known as an excellent teacher and was a nationally recognized folklorist.[31] Brewer was not the only African American author of import in Central Texas. In 1916, Fort Worth resident Lillian B. Jones (Horace) published a return-to-Africa novel titled *Five Generations Hence*; the work was the first published by a black woman in Texas and the broader Southwest. Jones later completed a second novel, but it was not published until scholar Karen Kossie-Chernyshev enabled its publication in 2008.[32]

The life and career of another Central Texas Afro-Texan—Azie Taylor Morton—clearly and devastatingly pointed out the talent and contributions that were lost over the years to the state and nation by the Texas policy of segregation and blacks' subordination. Born Azie Taylor at St. Johns Colony in northeastern Caldwell County in 1936, Taylor attended and graduated from Huston-Tillotson College in 1956. The University of Texas at Austin (UT) denied her admission to UT graduate school because African Americans were not allowed into that white, Southern institution. Nevertheless, she underwent a remarkable career—beginning as administrative assistant to the president of Huston-Tillotson and as administrative assistant for the AFL-CIO in Austin. In 1961, she moved to Washington, DC, where she served as community relations specialist for the Committee on Equal Employment Opportunity and soon became a complaint investigator for the US Equal Employment Opportunity Commission. She then worked from 1971 to 1977 as special assistant to the chair of the Democratic National Committee. As a result of her stellar record and service, Pres. Jimmy Carter appointed her as the US Treasurer, the first black person to be appointed to such a lofty position; she served in that capacity from 1977 to 1981. She worked for an investment firm in Washington after that appointment before returning to Austin. During the 1990s, among other tasks, she managed a bookstore for Huston-Tillotson students. She died in Austin in December 2003, a few months after her husband.[33]

Black women found strength and purpose in working together to improve social and moral issues throughout Texas. In 1905, Mrs. M. E. Y. Moore organized the Texas Association of Colored Women's Clubs (TACWC), as black women were excluded from white clubs. Joining the National Association of Colored Women's Clubs (NACWC) one year later, their motto was "Lifting as We Climb." Among other projects: "beginning in 1918, the ladies began campaigning for a state-supported home for delinquent girls. . . . In 1920, [they] purchased land in San Antonio for the home by putting $5500 down on a mortgage with $700 monthly payments." Construction for the home was authorized by the Texas legislature in 1927, but they waited until 1945 to finally appropriate $60,000 for the Brady State School for Negro Girls. Along with fighting for voting rights and against lynching, the TACWC worked for improved railroad accommodations, raised money for student loans, and provided scholarships. Out of the twenty-seven presidents to serve the organization, fourteen have been from the Central Texas region, with one, Ada Bell Dement, becoming the first woman from Texas elected as the president of the NACWC in 1941. Central Texas was well represented within the organization when Mary Alphin from Waco was elected president from 1910 to 1916, Ethel Ransom from Fort Worth from 1920 to 1922, A. Elsenia Soder Johnson from Marlin from 1926 to 1930, Ada Bell Dement from Mineral Wells from 1930 to 1934 and 1941, Urissa Chrisian from Austin from 1934 to 1938, and Faustina Bush Brackeen from Fort Worth from 1938 to 1942. In 1937, Fort Worth hosted the NACWC, with more than three hundred in attendance to discuss the threat of war and the need to band together to fight for peace.[34]

Life for African Americans in Central Texas did not revolve solely around work, church, and struggles against white racism; they also relaxed and sought entertainment, attended and participated in sports leagues, and listened to, danced, and played music. Archie "Tank" Stewart pitched baseball for the Houston Black Buffaloes in 1912. An article in the Houston *Post* reported before a June game that "the local battery will be composed of Black Tank and Baby Webb. . . . Black Tank is bigger and blacker than Jack Johnson [the current reigning heavyweight boxing champion] and he is a right hander with the stuff. With worlds of smoke and everything in the curve line, Tank is expected to show the Black Giants up today." The reporter was correct, as the Buffaloes won with a score of 2:1. Tank later signed with the Austin Black Senators, a member of the Texas Negro League, which was formed by Rebe Foster, an African American baseball pitcher who was born in Calvert, Robertson County, and who played for teams in both Waco and Fort Worth. Other black teams in Central Texas included the Fort Worth Wonders (1905), the Fort Worth Black Panthers (who won the inaugural league championship in 1920), and the Cleburne Yellow Jackets.[35]

The Texas Interscholastic League of Colored Schools formed in 1920 to govern extracurricular activities such as sports, art, literature, and music and in response to black students not being permitted to participate in the University Interscholastic League (UIL). By 1923, the organization's name was changed to the Prairie View Interscholastic League (PVIL), as it operated from Prairie View College under the guidance of Pat Patterson and Jack Yates. This effort gradually helped form a black middle class in Texas, as it created an option for black athletes in both education and job opportunities by recruiting black players into black colleges. Since no black players were admitted into the National Football League until the 1940s, black players became coaches or teachers and mentored black men who were destined to do the same until other opportunities became available. At one point, there were five hundred black Texas schools in the PVIL; many were in Central Texas. Integration brought the end of the PVIL, as black athletes began to enter the former all-white teams as well as athletic programs at the Central Texas universities, such as Texas Christian University, Baylor University, Texas A&M University, College Station, and the University of Texas at Austin.[36]

Central Texas music provided relief and entertainment. McMurry University scholar Joe W. Specht searched extensively for materials on black musicians in Central Texas; in his as yet unpublished article "Ain't No More Cane on the Brazos: African American Musicians of Central Texas," he discovered at least one well-known black musician and performer in twenty-three Central Texas counties.[37] As author Alan Govenar phrased it, there was a "long history of blues in Central Texas." Black Central Texas musicians were pioneers. The introduction of the electric guitar into jazz bands occurred first in regional bands pioneered by Eddie Durham of San Marcos and Charlie Christian of Fort Worth. Well-known songs appeared from Central Texas musicians; Fort Worth–born Euday L. Bowman's ragtime composition "Twelfth Street Rag" achieved outstanding success—he also penned the "Fort Worth Blues." Among the greatest 1920s performers, Blind Lemon Jefferson, the "King of the Country Blues," grew up in Central Texas; as historian Alwyn Barr stated, "Jefferson took his Central Texas style" on the road to new venues. Ben Christian, born in Rockdale, Milam County, performed country and western music as a fiddler and bandleader; among his well-known compositions was the "Rockdale Rag." Herschel Evans, a great tenor saxophonist born in Denton, wrote the influential hit the "Texas Shuffle." During the 1960s, the "Austin Sound" resonated around the state as well as spreading beyond its border. San Marcos–born Eddie Durham, a cousin of Herschel Evans, became a prominent swing-era composer-arranger. He began playing when he was ten and continued to record in impressive style at age seventy-five. The city of San Marcos recognized his especial contributions by naming a day of musical tribute and festivities for Eddie Durham.[38]

By the twenty-first century, African Americans in Central Texas were able to make their own decisions about their welfare and that of their families. In 2010, Central Texas contained 22 percent of the state's black population but dropped from 28 percent of the region's population to 10 percent, indicating a notable change between slave labor and free opportunity. From the years of slavery until the present, black Central Texans established institutions for education and religion, used fraternal lodges and self-help organizations to aid in the improvement of their lives, and organized to challenge white encroachment. The struggle for freedom did not come easily, but they pressed forward. During the twentieth century, blacks faced a segregated, Jim Crow existence, but years of organized and individual protest, with occasional white help, brought about significant changes. Enlightened black leaders were noteworthy in this forward direction. Organizations, such as the NAACP, provided vital support, resources, political skills, and knowledge in their quest to eliminate segregation and to acquire the rights of citizens due to all members of Central Texas. Today, African Americans continue to combat antiblack violence, voting restrictions, and economic discrimination; Texas racial antipathy remains present in Central Texas. As Texas Southern University scholar Cary D. Wintz wrote, in Texas, "equality for African Americans remains a goal, not a reality."[39] Afro-Texans go forward with the knowledge that they have overcome greater perils in the Central Texas of the past.

NOTES

1. Cynthia Skove Nevels, *Lynching to Belong: Claiming Whiteness through Racial Violence* (College Station: Texas A&M University Press, 2007), 1–2.

2. William D. Carrigan, *The Making of a Lynching Culture: Violence and Vigilantism in Central Texas, 1836–1916* (Urbana: University of Illinois Press, 2004), 8.

3. Patricia Bernstein, *The First Waco Horror: The Lynching of Jesse Washington and the Rise of the NAACP* (College Station: Texas A&M University Press, 2005); James M. SoRelle, "The Waco Horror: The Lynching of Jesse Washington," *Southwestern Historical Quarterly* 86, no. 4 (April 1983): 517–37; NAACP, *The Waco Horror*, supplement to *The Crisis* 12 (July 1916): 1–8.

4. NAACP, *Mobbing of John R. Shillady, Secretary of the NAACP* (New York: NAACP, 1919); Bruce A. Glasrud, "Anti-black Violence in Twentieth Century East Texas," *East Texas Historical Journal* 52, no. 1 (2014): 87–99; Bruce A. Glasrud, "Early NAACP Struggles in Texas, 1914–1932," *Journal of South Texas* 29, no. 2 (Spring 2016): 24–33.

5. Bruce A. Glasrud and Gregg Andrews, "Confronting White Supremacy: The African American Left in Texas, 1874–1974," in *The Texas Left: The Radical Roots of Lone Star Liberalism,* ed. David O'Donald Cullen and Kyle G. Wilkison (College Station: Texas A&M University Press, 2010), 157–90; James C. Kearney, Bill Stein, and James Smallwood, *No Hope for Heaven, No Fear of Hell: The Stafford-Townsend Feud of Colorado County, Texas, 1871–1911* (Denton: University of North Texas Press, 2016), 155; Katherine K. K. Walters, "The Great War in Waco, Texas: African Americans, Race Relations, and the White Primary, 1916–1922" (master's

thesis, Southwest Texas State
University, 2000), chaps. 2–3.

6. Ida Carey and R. Matt Abigail, "Evans,
Richard D.," *Handbook of Texas Online*,
accessed June 5, 2017, http://www
.tshaonline.org/handbook/online/
articles/fev26; *Love v. Griffith*, 266 US
32 (924).

7. Monte Akers, *Flames after Midnight:
Murder, Vengeance, and the Desolation
of a Texas Community* (Austin:
University of Texas Press, 1999);
Carrigan, *Lynching Culture*, 192;
Walter F. Cotton, *History of Negroes
of Limestone County from 1860 to 1939*
(Mexia, TX: J. A. Chatman and S. M.
Merriwether, 1939).

8. Carrigan, *Lynching Culture*; Nevels,
Lynching to Belong; Neil Foley, *The
White Scourge: Mexicans, Blacks, and
Poor Whites in Texas Cotton Culture*
(Berkeley: University of California
Press, 1997), 15; Clyde McQueen,
*Black Churches in Texas: A Guide to
Historic Congregations* (College Station:
Texas A&M University Press, 2000),
quotations on 116 and 123.

9. Central Texas Historical Association,
online title page, accessed June 26, 2017,
http://www.centexhistassn.org/.

10. Bruce A. Glasrud and James M.
Smallwood, eds., *The African American
Experience in Texas* (Lubbock: Texas
Tech University Press, 2007); Bruce A.
Glasrud and Paul H. Carlson, eds.,
*Slavery to Integration: Black Americans
in West Texas* (Abilene, TX: State
House Press, 2007); Bruce A. Glasrud
and Archie P. McDonald, eds.,
Blacks in East Texas History (College
Station: Texas A&M University
Press, 2008); Bruce A. Glasrud, ed.,
*African Americans in South Texas
History* (College Station: Texas A&M
University Press, 2011).

11. Garry H. Radford Sr., *African
American Heritage in Waco, Texas*
(Austin: Eakin Press, 2000); Reby
Cary, *Princes Shall Come out of Egypt,
Texas, and Fort Worth* (Pittsburgh,
PA: Dorrance, 2002); Reby Cary, *How
We Got Over! Update on a Backward
Look: A History of Blacks in Fort Worth*
(Fort Worth: privately printed, 2005);
Richard F. Selcer, *A History of Fort
Worth in Black and White: 165 Years
of African-American Life* (Denton:
University of North Texas Press, 2015);
Joyce E. Williams, *Black Community
Control: A Study of Transition in a
Texas Ghetto* (New York: Praeger,
1973); C. Emerson and Gwendolyn
McDonald Jackson, *The History of the
Negro, Wichita Falls, Texas, 1880–1982*
(Wichita Falls, TX: Humphrey, 1988);
Jason McDonald, *Racial Dynamics
in Early Twentieth-Century Austin*
(Lanham, MD: Lexington, 2012);
Oswell Person, *African American
Bryan, Texas: Celebrating the Past*
(Charleston, SC: History Press, 2012).

12. Thad Sitton and James H. Conrad,
*Freedom Colonies: Independent Black
Texans in the Time of Jim Crow* (Austin:
University of Texas Press, 2005);
Drew Sanders, *The Garden of Eden:
The Story of a Freedmen's Community
in Texas* (Fort Worth: Texas Christian
University Press, 2013); Michelle M.
Mears, *And Grace Will Lead Me
Home: African American Freedmen
Communities of Austin, Texas 1865–1928*
(Lubbock: Texas Tech University Press,
2009).

13. Almetrius M. Duren and Louise
Iscoe, *Overcoming: A History of Black
Integration of the University of Texas at
Austin* (Austin: University of Texas
Press, 1979); Dwonna Goldstone,
Integrating the 40 Acres: The 50 Year

Struggle for Racial Equality at the University of Texas (Athens: University of Georgia Press, 2006); Robyn Duff Ladino, *Desegregating Texas Schools: Eisenhower, Shivers, and the Crisis at Mansfield High* (Austin: University of Texas Press, 1996); Thomas W. Cutrer and T. Michael Parrish, *Doris Miller, Pearl Harbor, and the Birth of the Civil Rights Movement* (College Station: Texas A&M University Press, 2018), quotation from xiv; Carolyn L. Jones, *Volma: My Journey—One Man's Impact on the Civil Rights Movement in Austin, Texas* (Austin: Eakin Press, 1998); Anna Victoria Wilson and William E. Segall, *Oh, Do I Remember! Experiences of Teachers during the Desegregation of Austin's Schools, 1964–1971* (Albany: State University of New York Press, 2001).

14. James C. Kearney, *Nassau Plantation: The Evolution of a Texas-German Slave Plantation* (Denton: University of North Texas Press, 2010); Robert L. Uzzel, *Blind Lemon Jefferson: His Life, His Death, and His Legacy* (Fort Worth: Eakin Press, 2002); Augusta Gooch, *Life of Lenora Rolla: A Citizen Shapes Her World* (Lexington, KY: privately printed, 2013); James M. Smallwood, *A Century of Achievement: Blacks in Cooke County, Texas* (Gainesville, TX: Gainesville Printing, 1975); Bernstein, *First Waco Horror*; William Oliver Bundy, *Life of William Madison McDonald* (Fort Worth: Bunker, 1925); Suzanne J. Terrell, *This Other Kind of Doctors: Traditional Medical Systems in Black Neighborhoods in Austin, Texas* (New York: AMS Press, 1990); Karen Kossie-Chernyshev, *Recovering Five Generations Hence: The Life and Writings of Lillian Jones Horace* (College Station: Texas A&M University Press, 2013); Bob Ray Sanders, *Calvin Littlejohn: Portrait of a Community in Black and White* (Fort Worth: Texas Christian University Press, 2009); *Histories of Pride: Thirteen Pioneers Who Shaped Georgetown's African American Community* (Georgetown, TX: City of Georgetown, 1993); Shannon Dorsey Johnson, *Found in Black Texiana: Contemporary Poetry, Stories and Notes for Women with Texas and Louisiana Roots* (San Bernardino, CA: privately published, 2013); Chris Tomlinson, *Tomlinson Hill: The Remarkable Story of Two Families Who Share the Tomlinson Name—One White, One Black* (New York: St. Martin's Press, 2014).

15. T. Lindsay Baker and Julie Baker, eds., *Till Freedom Cried Out: Memories of Texas Slave Life* (College Station: Texas A&M University Press, 1997), 60–63; Eighth Census of the United States. The counties included in the Central Texas region are Archer, Austin, Bastrop, Bell, Blanco, Bosque, Brazos, Brown, Burleson, Burnet, Caldwell, Colorado, Comal, Comanche, Cooke, Coryell, Denton, Eastland, Erath, Falls, Fayette, Gillespie, Guadalupe, Hamilton, Hays, Hill, Hood, Jack, Johnson, Kendall, Kerr, Lampasas, Lee, Limestone, Llano, Mason, McLennan, Milam, Mills, Montague, Palo Pinto, Parker, Robertson, San Saba, Somervell, Stephens, Tarrant, Travis, Washington, Wichita, Williamson, Wise, and Young Counties.

16. Jackson, *History of the Negro, Wichita Falls*, quotation on 4; Kearney, *Nassau Plantation*; Deborah M. Liles, "Southern Roots, Western Foundations: The Peculiar Institution and the Livestock Industry on the Northwestern Frontier of Texas,

1846–1864" (PhD diss., University of North Texas, 2013); Paul D. Lack, "Urban Slavery in the Southwest," *Red River Valley Historical Review* 6 (Spring 1981): 8–27, quotation on 23. A study of slave transactions in Guadalupe County can be found in Mark Gretchen, *Slave Transactions of Guadalupe County, Texas* (Santa Maria, CA: Janaway, 2000).

17. Bruce A. Glasrud, "Black Texas Women and the Freedom War," in *Women in Civil War Texas: Diversity and Dissidence in the Trans-Mississippi,* ed. Deborah M. Liles and Angela Boswell (Denton: University of North Texas Press, 2016), 99–100.

18. Linda S. Hudson, "Black Women and Supreme Court Decisions during the Civil War Era," in ibid, 119–48.

19. Carrigan, *Lynching Culture,* 48–80; Andrew J. Torget, "The Problem of Slave Flight in Civil War Texas," in *Lone Star Unionism, Dissent, and Resistance: Other Sides of Civil War Texas,* ed. Jesús F. de la Teja (Norman: University of Oklahoma Press, 2016), 37–59, quotation from 56.

20. Barry A. Crouch, *Freedmen's Bureau and Black Texans* (Austin: University of Texas Press, 1992); James M. Smallwood, *Time of Hope, Time of Despair: Black Texans during Reconstruction* (Port Washington, NY: Kennikat Press, 1981).

21. Crouch, *Freedmen's Bureau,* 102–27; Selcer, *History of Fort Worth,* 53. Information for the digital site is not yet available. Jeffery Littlejohn with Charles H. Ford, Jami Horne, and Briana Weaver recently published "The Cabiness Family Lynching: Race, War, and Memory in Walker County, Texas," *Southwestern Historical Quarterly* 122, no. 1 (July 2018): 1–30. This article challenges contemporary accounts of the Cabiness lynching, which occurred just outside of the Central Texas region in Walker County in 1918. Originally explained as a preemptive attack on a dangerous black family, this article argues that the lynching was carried out by a racist white mob with national and international implications.

22. Merline Pitre, "Matthew Gaines: The Militant," in *Through Many Dangers, Toils and Snares: Black Leadership in Texas, 1868–1898* (College Station: Texas A&M University Press, 2016), 169–79; Merline Pitre, "Robert Lloyd Smith: The Accommodationist," in *Through Many Dangers, Toils and Snares: Black Leadership in Texas, 1868–1898* (College Station: Texas A&M University Press, 2016), 195–205. See also J. Mason Brewer, *Negro Legislators of Texas* (Austin: Jenkins, 1970).

23. Gregg Cantrell, *Feeding the Wolf: John B. Rayner and the Politics of Race, 1850–1918* (Wheeling, IL: Harlan Davidson, 2001); Jack Abramowitz, "John B. Rayner: A Grass Roots Leader," *Journal of Negro History* 36 (1951): 160–93.

24. Michael R. Heintze, *Private Black Colleges in Texas, 1865–1954* (College Station: Texas A&M University Press, 1985); Jackson, *History of the Negro,* 367; George Ruble Woolfolk, *Prairie View: A Study in Public Conscience, 1878–1946* (New York: Pageant Press, 1947).

25. Bruce A. Glasrud, "Jim Crow's Emergence in Texas," *American Studies* 15 (1947): 47–60, quotation on 56.

26. McQueen, *Black Churches,* 23–84.

27. Ibid.; McDonald, *Racial Dynamics,* 243–44, 256–60; Kharen Monsho, "Campbell, Lee Lewis," *Handbook of*

Texas Online, accessed June 1, 2017, https://tshaonline.org/handbook/online/articles/fcadz.

28. McQueen, *Black Churches*, 66–67; Algerene Akins Craig, "Fuller, Mud Anna Berry," *Handbook of Texas Online*, accessed June 1, 2017, https://tshaonline.org/handbook/online/articles/ffu17.

29. Olive D. Brown and Michael R. Heintze, "Mary Branch: Private College Educator," in *Black Leaders: Texans for Their Times*, ed. Alwyn Barr and Robert A. Calvert (Austin: Texas State Historical Association, 1981), 112–27; Olive D. Brown and Michael R. Heintze, "Branch, Mary Elizabeth," *Handbook of Texas Online*, accessed June 1, 2017, https://tshaonline.org/handbook/online/articles/fbray.

30. Wilson and Segall, *Oh, Do I Remember!*; Ladino, *Desegregating Texas Schools*.

31. Bruce A. Glasrud and Milton S. Jordan, eds., "J. Mason Brewer: Folklorist, Historian, Poet," in *J. Mason Brewer Folklorist and Scholar: His Early Texas Writings* (Nacogdoches, TX: Stephen F. Austin State University Press, 2016), 11–26.

32. Lillian B. Jones, *Five Generations Hence* (Fort Worth: Dotson-Jones, 1916); Lillian B. Horace, *Angie Brown*, ed. Karen Kossie-Chernysheve (Acton, MA: Copley Custom Textbooks, 2008). See also Karen Kossie-Chernyshev, ed., *Recovering Five Generations Hence: The Life and Writing of Lillian Jones Horace* (College Station: Texas A&M University Press, 2013).

33. Barbara A. Langham, "Azie Taylor Morton," *Handbook of Texas Online*, accessed June 3, 2017, https://tshaonline.org/handbook/online/articles/fmoag.

34. Ruthe Winegarten, "Texas Association of Women's Clubs," *Handbook of Texas Online*, accessed August 4, 2017, http://www.tshaonline.org/handbook/online/articles/veto1; Texas Woman's University, "TAWC History," accessed August 4, 2017, http://www.twu.edu/library/tawc_history.asp.

35. Robert C. Fink, "Semi-professional African American Baseball in Texas before the Great Depression," in *The African American Experience in Texas: An Anthology*, ed. Bruce A. Glasrud and James M. Smallwood (Lubbock: Texas Tech University Press, 2007), 218–30; Stephen V. Rice, "Archie Stewart," *Society for American Baseball Research*, accessed March 28, 2018, https://sabr.org/node/34917; Mark Presswood, "Black Professional Baseball in Texas," *Texas Almanac*, accessed March 28, 2018, https://texasalmanac.com/topics/history/black-professional-baseball-texas.

36. See Michael Hurd, *Thursday Night Lights: The Story of Black High School Football in Texas* (Austin: University of Texas Press, 2017).

37. Joe W. Specht, "Ain't No More Cane on the Brazos: African American Musicians of Central Texas" (copy in hands of editors, Bruce A. Glasrud and Deborah M. Liles).

38. Alan Govenar, "Blues," in *The Handbook of Texas Music*, ed. by Roy Barkley et al. (Austin: Texas State Historical Association, 2003), 24–28, quotation on 27; Alwyn Barr, *The African Texans* (College Station: Texas A&M University Press, 2004), 76–81, quotation on 77; Dave Oliphant, "Durham, Eddie," *Handbook of Texas Online*, accessed June 4, 2017, https://tshaonline.org/handbook/online/articles/fduqk; Dave

Oliphant, "Eddie Durham and the Texas Contribution to Jazz History," *Southwestern Historical Quarterly* 96 (April 1993): 491–525; Dave Oliphant, *Texan Jazz* (Austin: University of Texas Press, 1996).

39. US Census Bureau, *American Fact Finder*, accessed July 22, 2017, https://factfinder.census.gov/; Cary D. Wintz, "The Struggle for Dignity: African Americans in Twentieth-Century Texas," in *Twentieth-Century Texas: A Social and Cultural History*, ed. John W. Storey and Mary L. Kelley (Denton: University of North Texas Press, 2008), 100.

PART 1
Slavery and Its Aftermath

1

Livestock and Slavery in North Central Texas

A View from Stephens County

Deborah M. Liles

In this informative and challenging article, author Deborah Liles points out that cash-crop agriculture was not the only effective means for a slave owner to acquire profits in Texas. In Stephens County, slave owners raised and sold livestock more profitably than those in their communities who did not own slaves. Deborah Liles holds the W. K. Gordon Endowed Chair of Texas History at Tarleton State University. Her publications include Women in Civil War Texas: Diversity and Dissidence in the Trans-Mississippi, *coedited with Angela Boswell; winner of the 2016 Liz Carpenter Award,* Texas Women and Ranching: On the Range, at the Rodeo, in their Community, *coedited with Cecilia Gutierrez Venable; and the forthcoming* Southern Roots, Western Foundations: The Livestock Industry and Slavery on the Northwestern Frontier of Texas, *which examines the connections between successful slave owners and the livestock industry.*

★

The consensus regarding slavery in regions where low numbers of slaves were reported is that the institution served little to no importance in the communities' economic development. Only thirty-three slaves were listed in Stephens County by 1864, reputedly "brought there by slaveholders who moved to the area during the conflict."[1] A study of Stephens County, however, reveals that those who owned slaves prospered considerably more than those who did not and that the slaves were brought by a mostly related group of cattlemen who moved to the area before and during the Civil War years.

Located directly west of Palo Pinto County and south of both Young and Throckmorton Counties, Stephens County's center point is 32°45′ north latitude and 98°50′ west longitude. Historian Charles W. Ramsdell argued that slavery would not have been profitable and therefore would have died out naturally once it moved west of the Cross Timbers. Stephens County's location is significant to this argument as it is approximately 150 miles west of the Eastern Cross Timbers boundary and one hundred miles west of the Western Cross Timbers.[2] Ramsdell's focus on a plantation economy omitted slave owners who used chattel labor in industries other than cash-crop agriculture and negated the multiple uses of slave labor in environments other than one suited to crop cultivation. Livestock was located throughout Texas but primarily in counties along the western frontier, where settlements were thinner and labor sources were scarce. In these counties, most residents were engaged in the livestock industry.

Stephens County is also located outside of the area of study in Randolph B. Campbell and Richard G. Lowe's *Wealth and Power in Antebellum Texas.* Campbell and Lowe noted that several the westernmost counties "were engaged primarily in cattle raising," but that "antebellum Texas was by no means a ranching area." They did not believe that the sparsely populated counties past the ninety-eighth meridian should be included in their study as "calculations would have distorted statistical measurements and concealed more than it revealed about the Lone Star state in the 1850s." This builds on the idea that regions with few slaves were of minor significance to the institution and that the most profitable use of slaves in agriculture was in the production of a cash crop. This historical interpretation overlooks the versatility of slavery in frontier regions; it also dismisses the wealth of small slave owners and removes cattlemen from the general discussion. Additionally, this approach divorces the institution of slavery from the nascent years of the cattle industry throughout the South and Texas.[3]

Before it was Stephens County, it was known as Buchanan County, established in 1858 and named after the fifteenth president of the United States, James Buchanan. The name changed to Stephens County in 1861 to honor the vice president of the Confederate States of America, Alexander H. Stephens. Like many of the other frontier counties in this region, there are no records in the courthouse from 1858 to 1864; those that do exist begin in 1879.[4] Property tax records are missing from 1858 through 1860, and there are no records that describe slaves' activities in the county, which also presents a challenge.[5] With no court records, such as deeds or bills of sale pertaining to the institution of slavery, and no tax records for those initial years, reconstructing the history rests upon the words of early settlers, the 1860 census, and property tax records from 1861 through 1864. This challenge is one that is typical in many frontier regions, which also contributes to the lack of studies examining the value of slaves in these communities.

Buchanan/Stephens County is a prime example, a microcosm, of successful ranchers and the foundations of the cattle-trailing history in a time generally discarded by historians. There were 202 men, women, and children living in Buchanan County in 1860—thirty-two of them, approximately 15 percent of the population, were enslaved blacks and mulattos. There were thirty-six occupied households that year; six of those (17 percent) owned slaves. Out of the fifty-two people who declared a profession, twenty-six (50 percent) were stock raisers, five were stock drivers (10 percent), and three were stock traders (6 percent), making at least 66 percent of the professions listed related to the livestock industry. The remaining 34 percent comprised a blacksmith, three farm and six-day laborers, and eight farmers whose work could also have been related to the livestock industry. Suffice to say that livestock was the driving economy in the county.[6]

There were seven slave owners in 1860: William Browning, John Snyder (Snider), Thomas H. Dawson, John B. Dawson, Joel W. Curtis, Francis A. Sloane, and W. H. Stockton. Between them they listed $55,070 (approximately $1.5 million in 2017 when adjusted for inflation) in real estate and personal property, which included thirty-two slaves. Fifteen of the slaves were male: eleven were younger than fourteen years old, and four were older. Seventeen of the slaves were female: nine were younger than fourteen, and eight were older. This composition is very much in line with the other frontier counties, where females were preferred to help with household chores and children, to work outside tending crops and livestock, and for reproduction purposes. Women were the better investment for the future of slavery on the frontier, not men. Younger slaves were cheaper than those in their prime and often began chores associated with the livestock trade by the time they were three years old. With twenty (nearly two-thirds) of the slaves under the age of fourteen, and the average and median ages considered, there was a very young slave population in the county. Except for one sixty-year-old woman, it appears that a concerted effort was made by owners to retain younger and healthier slaves (table 1.1).[7]

It is difficult to tell how many slaves there were in the county from 1860 to 1865, but there were somewhere between thirty and thirty-five each year (see table 1.2). The difference in the number of holdings in 1860, 1861, and 1862 is in line with other counties where cattlemen did not report to pay taxes as they were often on the trail to markets, cow hunting, or gathering stock from people in multiple locations. Most counties include supplemental declarations for years taxpayers missed. There was only one taken during the period of study in this county, but it was not itemized; it did, however, include five of the missing slave owners in 1862.[9]

TABLE I.I. AGE BREAKDOWN OF BUCHANAN/STEPHENS COUNTY SLAVES IN 1860[8]

Age breakdown	Newborn to 13	14 and older	Oldest	Average age	Median age
Males	11	4	35	11	7
Females	9	8	30 (60)	17	12

TABLE I.2. NUMBER OF SLAVES OWNED WITHIN SPECIFIED GROUPS[11]

Year	Slaves owned in groups of 1–4	Slaves owned in groups of 5–9	Slaves owned in groups of 10–14	Slaves owned in groups of 15–19	Slaves owned in groups of 20+	Largest number of slaves by one owner	Total slaves in county
1860	9	13	10	0	0	10	32
1861	2	0	0	0	0	1	2
1862	9	0	0	0	0	3	9
1863	14	21	0	0	0	8	35
1864	13	20	0	0	0	8	33

During the five-year period, none of the owners reported more than ten slaves (see table 1.2). The drop in the number of slaves in 1861 and 1862 totals reflects the absent owners. In 1863 and 1864, the largest numbers of slaves were owned in groups of five to nine slaves. What is notable is that Joel W. Curtis reported ten slaves in 1860 but seven in 1864, suggesting that he sold three of them.[10]

No one can possibly understand slavery from the inside except a slave, but it is possible to recreate at least one scenario that many bondsmen faced daily. Without bills of sale from Stephens County, it cannot be said with certainty that slaves were sold there. It can be said, however, that they were sold in neighboring Young County. The slaves themselves were undoubtedly aware that they could and would be sold at their owner's whim. Slave auction houses such as those found in big cities throughout the South were not needed for transactions, as owners frequently sold to each other or others in the community. It is approximately thirty-three miles from Breckenridge to Graham, the current county seats of Stephens and Young Counties, respectively. This means that slaves were being sold within a little more than a day's ride away—and possibly closer. This afforded owners the ability to obtain cash, credit, or trade for the sale of their human chattel and was an advantage that should never be overlooked when considering the benefits of slave owning.

Bills of sale from Young County record several transactions: Eliza A. Hamner sold fifteen-year-old Mary to Mary Ann Miller on Christmas Day, 1858; Isaac Manly sold thirty-three-year-old Rufus to Philip S. George for $1,700 on March 19, 1859; H. K. Vollintine sold twenty-six-year-old Malina to Z. I. Harmerson for $1,000 on July 22, 1859; George W. Fisher sold twenty-six-year-old Evaline and her unnamed eighteen-month-old daughter for $1,500 to Solomon Miller on August 17, 1859, the same day that Miller sold a twenty-four-year-old man named Green and a sixteen-year-old young woman named Mary to Fisher for a combined $2,500.[12] The high prices of these slaves are noteworthy in the westernmost county on the

North-Central Texas frontier, as are the age at which they were sold. Returning to the aforementioned Joel W. Curtis, whose slave holdings decreased from 1860 to 1864, it is not known which of his slaves were sold or given away, or if they might have died or run away, only that there was a market for them. Slaves in Stephens County would not be oblivious to their value or their owners' ability to sell them away on any given day or that their owners seldom kept slaves after a certain age.

Slave owners' professions say much about why they needed slave labor. Throughout the country, people were identified in census records with different professions and, although many leave the door open for interpretation, the terms *stock raiser, stock herder,* or *trader* are very specific and leave no doubt that their primary income derived from participation in the livestock industry. In Stephens County, William Browning was a fifty-seven-year-old stock raiser from Georgia, John Snyder (Snider) was a thirty-nine-year-old stock raiser from Virginia, Thomas H. Dawson was a fifty-year-old farmer from Kentucky, John B. Dawson was a twenty-nine-year-old trader from Kentucky, Joel W. Curtis was a thirty-seven-year-old trader from Ohio, Francis A. Sloane was a forty-three-year-old trader from Virginia, and W. H. Stockton was a fifty-year-old farmer from Kentucky. Using property tax records, it can be surmised that while listed as a farmer, Thomas Dawson declared no land and seventy-five head of cattle in 1864 (the only year he reported and without the two slaves that were listed in the 1860 census), suggesting his primary source of income came from livestock—two horses, four milch cows, and seventy swine—not crops. Additionally, he reported that no crops were cultivated on the twenty improved acres he claimed (but did not pay taxes on). The other "farmer," W. H. Stockton, listed thirty acres of improved land (also not included in his property taxes) that produced no crops but had two horses, one hundred milch cows, two oxen, and one hundred head of other cattle. Stockton did not report property taxes in 1861 or 1862, but in 1863, he declared four hundred head of cattle, and in 1864, he listed 450 head of cattle and forty-two sheep. The general term of *farmer* in the census records is often substituted for *stock raiser,* which seems to be the case with Dawson and Stockton. This negates the economic importance of livestock by inferring that crops were the main source of income for many and contributes to the fallacy that slavery was not important or needed by ranchers. With the combined information from the census and the tax records, it can safely be said that all these slave owners were engaged in the livestock trade and that their slaves' labor and lives revolved around that business.[13]

Along with low numbers of slaves, slave owners reported relatively small land-holdings in Stephens County, but that acreage can be deceiving. Small landowners are often overlooked in slavery studies as their economic output is considered minimal when compared to those with large landholdings. The assessment of how much product an acre of land could produce is a guide to slaveholding success, but land ownership was not needed for grazing cattle due to open range laws that allowed free grazing in all areas—including unfenced cotton plantations. It is notable that land ownership among slave owners is disproportionately higher than among non–slave owners in Stephens County in three of the four years—the outlier being 1861. It should also be noted that these slave owners declared more land outside of the county than their contemporaries, even though it was not needed to practice their trade. In 1862, slave owners were 7 percent of the tax-paying population but owned 21 percent of the land in the county and 100 percent of the land declared in other counties. In 1863, they were 11 percent of the tax-paying population, owned 31 percent of land within the county, and owned 94 percent (a slight drop) outside of the county. In 1864, they represented 12 percent of the tax-paying population and claimed 23 percent of the county land. Land outside of the county was not declared by slave or non–slave owners in this year.[14] As most of the stock raisers with slaves owned disproportionately larger amounts of land than those without slaves, and as this pattern of land ownership was duplicated throughout the state, it stands to reason that they were generating enough profits to invest in acreage when others were not.

These disproportionate totals in land ownership say much about the slave owners. Frank Owsley's influential study of the plain folk—small slave and non-slaveholders who were generally farmers or stock raisers—stated that they purchased land they preempted as a means of transitioning from stock raising to farming or to farm smaller plots of land to provide for their herds and families.[15] Any improved land with crops grown to feed the stock raisers' families and herds would involve slave labor; however, Stephens County's slave owners' actions before and after they arrived in Texas show that they had no intention of becoming full-time farmers or raising cash crops.[16] It is more likely that their extra land purchases were speculative investments or a way to secure grazing lands, rather than transitional attempts. What these disproportionate landholdings indicate is that slave owners had the means to obtain, purchase, or retain land. Initially, land owned outside Stephens County was generally in counties where they once lived, suggesting that they did not need to sell this land before they moved west, that they used that land for grazing purposes, or that they chose to retain it for investment purposes. As the years progressed, land declared in other counties was more often located west, or adjacent, to the county of residence, probably to secure additional grazing lands and invest in regions that would soon open up. Whatever the reasons, those who owned and used slave labor in their Stephens County cattle businesses owned more land than those who did not own slaves. Much like cash-crop agriculture, this suggests that those who had slaves to fulfill labor needs had the ability to generate higher profits than those who did not.[17]

The county also exhibited another common trend that can be found throughout the state. At first glance, it appears that most tax-paying residents of Stephens County were non–slave owners. A closer examination reveals that several people listed on the county's property taxes owned bondsmen in neighboring counties. These men and women did not declare land in Stephens

County, only livestock. Isabella Ikard from Parker County and J. J. Cureton and John Pollard from Palo Pinto County were a few of those people; among them they owned an additional 3,350 head of Stephens County's cattle, worth $20,100 in 1864. The addition of just these three people raises the percentage of slave owners with cattle holdings from 16 to 23 percent for 1864 (the percentage of cattle owned is covered later in this chapter). Other taxpayers listed may also have been slave owners from surrounding counties: L. Steel, W. Stockton, Phillip Burrow, and John and James Prewitt could easily be Lawrence Steel from Tarrant County, William Stockton and P. Burrow from Parker County, and J. J. Prewitt from Johnson County; and James Drue, whose declaration of 1,100 head of cattle was the second largest by a supposed non–slave owner, was assuredly the same James Drew in Erath County who declared eighty-eight slaves.[18] All these people are significant in multiple ways, not least of all that the wealth of ranchers—slave owners with specified numbers of livestock—was and continues to be underestimated.[19] The wealth of planters is based on the land and number of slaves they owned, not livestock. Ranchers, however, did not need large numbers of slaves to raise their stock or large landholdings in a time of open-range grazing. With their cattle, horses, and sheep often grazing in neighboring counties, which is missed if a researcher does not look in other county declarations, their wealth has been underassessed and overlooked, as has the contribution of slaves to their overall wealth.[20]

There are also many residents whose surnames suggest a kinship to larger families that owned slaves, both inside and out of Stephens County. Some of those were the Stocktons and Millers, whose families owned slaves in Stephens County, and the Sloans, who were also listed in Stephens and Young Counties. It cannot be said with certainty that some of the slaves owned by other cattlemen were benefitting other family members by working herds that were undoubtedly mixed together on the open range, tending crops to feed humans and livestock, or serving in any other number of ways, but conversely, it cannot be said that they were not.[21] Then there was Jane Williams who declared 450 head of cattle, worth $2,700, in Stephens County. Undoubtedly the same Jane who was married to slave owner W. W. Williams in the adjacent Bosque County, her participation falls into the blurred lines of property ownership and women's participation in the livestock industry. Other connections not to be overlooked are the Lindseys, Matthews, Lynches, Smiths, Terrys, and Veals, as neighboring counties' tax rolls record slave owners by those same names. As Owsley observed, not only did families and friends migrate in groups, in part to work together in the new location, but often "herdsmen settled as farmers on land which they had purchased; and they sent their livestock out on the frontier in charge of some member of the family, or allowed it to graze, along with that of neighboring farms, on the unfenced farm and government lands of the community."[22] The possibility that slaves belonged to other family members in neighboring counties but were used to help tend the cattle in Stephens County is high. When one considers these extra probabilities along with the number of ranchers who owned slaves in other counties but grazed their herds in this county, the perceived value of slave labor in the cattle industry on the northern frontier of Central Texas increases exponentially.

As noted, one of the names listed in a neighboring county was Isabella Ikard (table 1.3). Ikard was the wife of Dr. Milton Ikard, from Parker County. From 1856 to 1860, she owned slaves, horses, and cattle. The following year, she reported slaves and horses but no cattle; in 1862, the slaves were no longer recorded under her name (her husband declared them from 1862 to 1864, a common incidence with women who owned livestock),[23] and the remaining livestock were declared on the tax records in Stephens County. Why remains a mystery, but the number of other settlers who were raising livestock in that area suggests that it might have been a business decision to locate her herd where the industry was thriving despite the oft-told threat of Indians.[24]

When the Ikards moved to Texas in 1852, they first went to Lamar County and then, in 1856, to Parker County. Among the slaves they owned was one of the northwestern region's most famous black cowboys, Bose Ikard. Bose was born in 1843 to a mulatto slave woman named King. Milton Ikard, who owned King, was reputedly Bose's biological father (see aforementioned reasons for owning a female slave). Bose learned to handle cattle in his youth, was entrusted with the Ikards's cattle, and by the time Isabella listed the large herd in Stephens County, he may have periodically helped with tending, rounding-up, or preparing the Stephens County herd for market, as this was his acknowledged task in Parker County. As stated, the Ikards were only one of several families who owned cattle in Stephens County but declared slave-holdings elsewhere; so while there were low numbers of slaves listed in the census and property tax returns, slaves from other counties could easily have been tending livestock alongside those that lived there, changing both the number of slaves in the county as well as the economic value of cattle to slave owners in the region.[26]

It was not unusual for slave owners to use their bondsmen in more than one location, as slaves were often taken to other locations to tend livestock during the practice of transhumance. Joseph H. Polley from Sutherland Springs took full advantage of the open-range conditions while he searched for markets to sell his stock. By 1859, Polley's herds were estimated at 150,000 head (possibly the largest holdings in the state), and by 1860, he owned over 13,500 acres throughout Texas—bought with the profits from cattle sales. The nineteen slaves he declared in 1859 numbered one short of planter status despite the obvious ability to attain it, another common practice among ranchers, removing him from previous studies that have examined the correlation between livestock and slave ownership.[27] Like Ikard and other slaves, some of Polley's slaves worked and drove his cattle from different locations in the state. Polley was not in Stephens County, but the Central Texas frontier was not unique and was a part of the overall story of cattle, slaves, and settlement throughout the Old South.[28]

TABLE I.3. IKARD PROPERTY IN PARKER AND STEPHENS COUNTIES[25]

Year	Owner / location (county)	Slaves / value (in dollars)	Horses / value (in dollars)	Cattle / value (in dollars)	Sheep / value (in dollars)
1856	Isabella/Parker	3/3,350	5/190	50/350	0
1857	Isabella/Parker	8/3,350	6/300	45/270	0
1858	Isabella/Parker	9/3,350	2/120	42/345	0
1859	Isabella/Parker	9/3,350	1/120	42/345	0
1860	Isabella/Parker	9/6,000	9/600	60/390	0
1861	Isabella/Parker	5/3,000	2/125	0	180/540
1861	Isabella/Stephens	0	0	0	0
1862	Milton/Parker	7/3,500	15/850	24/290	200/600
1862	Isabella/Stephens	0	0	0	0
1863	Milton/Parker	7/4,800	22/1,760	41/390	145/580
1863	Isabella/Stephens	0	0	519/4,072	
1864*	Milton/Parker	8/$3,800	Total	Livestock	1,480
1864	Isabella/Stephens			600/3,600	

* Livestock was not itemized this year, so the value in the sheep column includes horses, cattle, and sheep.

Polley's widowed daughter, Mary, married Walter K. Baylor, "a fledgling cattleman," in 1852. Baylor's brother was John Robert Baylor, who fought in different Indian campaigns, was elected to the state legislature in 1851 and by 1855 was the Indian agent for the Comanche Indians on the Brazos Reserve in the aforementioned Young County. In 1857, Baylor set up the first cattle ranch in the future Stephens County. Credited with agitating settlers to the point of demanding the removal of the reservation Indians, Baylor is an example of the influence wielded by many of the small slave and livestock owners in the North-Central region of Texas.[29]

Baylor sold some of his cattle to George Thomas Reynolds.[30] His father, B. W. Reynolds, moved his family to the Cantrell ranch in Stephens County, then around 1862 to the Dawson ranch, where large cattle herds were often traded and where Thomas Dawson and his son, John, had anywhere from four to seven slaves.[31] Reynolds was absent at the time, as he was in the Confederate Army. Medically discharged with a "wounded soldier's bonus of $300 in Confederate money . . . the sum total of his worldly possessions,"[32] he purchased an unspecified number of cattle from Baylor, and he used a "negro girl" valued at $1,000 as part of the payment. In various accounts, Reynolds is credited with driving the first herd to Mexico from the Stephens County area in early 1865, from which he made a good profit. This was an option many Texas cattlemen chose toward the end of the war, despite laws that required a signed pass to cross the Rio Grande. Once there, cattlemen simply paid a bribe of a dollar or two per head and continued to various markets, where they sold to anyone they could.[33]

While this may appear to be a seemingly insignificant story in the history of slavery and cattle in Stephens County, it is an example of the value of both, as well as one that shows the value of livestock from one end of the state to the other and an additional use of slaves in the livestock industry. Between 1863 and 1865, after the Emancipation Proclamation and depletion of much of the South's livestock,[34] Reynolds traded a female slave for $1,000 in cattle to a man who played no small part in the removal of the Indians from the two northwestern Texas reservations and for the capture of the Confederate Territory of Arizona. Reynolds knew the value of cattle as, by 1863, his father, Stephens County's Barber Watkins Reynolds, declared 950 head of cattle worth $6,000. From this exchange of a young girl or woman for cattle, George Reynolds went on to be a highly successful rancher and, after the Civil War, owned extensive land in Texas and North Dakota. Along with his landholdings, he was also involved in the banking business in Texas and Oklahoma.[35]

When discussing the use of slaves by those who raised livestock instead of cash crops, the questions of profits and benefits to the slave owner are always raised. The success and popularity of slavery can be seen in the growth of Stephens County's declared livestock from 1861 to 1864—from $44,395 to $307,985 in just four years. Slave owners were not the only residents who were stock raisers, herders, and traders, as livestock was the county's primary economy, and many non–slave owners were extremely successful in the industry. At first glance, it appears that non–slave owners were the most successful due to the total number of cattle they declared, but a breakdown shows the irrefutable difference and the advantage of slave ownership in just this one county (table 1.4). As slaves participated in all phases of the rancher's businesses—raising crops for humans and animals, milking cows, hunting and tending livestock, household chores, and other tasks—much like slaves involved in plantation economy, it can be stated that their owners benefitted from the labor and value of their bondsmen; this included profits from sales of products raised (livestock and crops), additional help with daily and scheduled chores, and the monetary value of a slave that could be exchanged for other property, mortgaged, or rented.[36]

Most of the slave owners had relationships of some kind with each other. Out of the ten in the county, seven had been neighbors in Arkansas, before they moved to Texas—Joel Curtis, Thomas and John B. Dawson, J. A. DeGraftenried, R. D. Miller, and Tom L. and W. H. Stockton—and they settled close to each other again in New Mexico Territory after the Civil War. All these men were heavily invested in the cattle trade.[38]

Curtis and John B. Dawson (who were brothers-in-law) were among a group of men, women, and children who, in 1853, left Franklin County, Arkansas, and

TABLE I.4. AVERAGE CATTLE PER TAXPAYER[37]

Year	Slave-owner cattle (head)	Non-slave-owner cattle (head)	Average number owned per slave owner (head)	Average number owned per non–slave owner (head)	Difference absolute numbers (head) / percentage more
1861	1,655	5,852	828	125	703 / 562
1862	2,555	20,105	511	247	264 / 107
1863	5,698	31,201	570	371	199 / 54
1864	6,997	37,439	700	493	207 / 42

traveled through Colorado, up to Salt Lake City, and on to California. For two years, they lived in a camp known as "Rough and Ready" (named after Zachary Taylor, under whom the town's founder had served) in Nevada County, California, and then they returned to Arkansas in 1855. Tom Stockton, who soon became Dawson's brother-in-law and another Stephens County resident, traveled the same route. The familiarity with the route to and from California via Colorado soon proved to be a worthy asset.[39]

Dawson wrote, "I returned to California in the fall of 1855. I drove a herd of cattle from Arkansas to California and located at the Butte Mountains near Marysville [in California]." Dawson saw that it was better to sell to the prospectors than to be one; because he had lived in gold-mining country for a couple of years, he gained first-hand knowledge of the markets there. Curtis, Stockton, and his cousins Jasper DeGraftenried and Tom Miller all accompanied Dawson on the return trip. These men were all future Stephens County residents who owned cattle and slaves. All were from Franklin County, Arkansas, located in the northwestern upcountry, where livestock was the primary economy, corn and subsistence crops were grown, approximately 15 percent of the population owned low numbers of slaves, and out of those slaves, women and children were the majority—all commonalities with Stephens County after they arrived.[40]

When the Colorado Gold Rush began in 1858, Curtis, Dawson (the namesake of the trail), and other cattlemen in the region saw the opportunity to profit selling beef. As they had all lived through the lucrative cattle-driving years of the California Gold Rush, it did not take them long to head north to the new mines. Curtis, a cattle trader, drove four hundred head of cattle up the Dawson Trail to Pikes Peak in 1859, where he sold them to Col. Francisco Chavez. Within less than a year, on May 19, 1860, Curtis arrived in St. Louis with approximately $7,000 (approximately $194,000 when adjusted for inflation) of Denver's gold dust. These proceeds came from the sale of another drive from Fort Belknap, Young County, which consisted of seven hundred cattle led by Curtis and assisted by six hands. Although the distance as the bird flies was only 600 miles, the drive was closer to 1,200 miles, as they took a longer route to avoid problems with Comanche and Kiowa Indians. Despite the added mileage and dangers, the high profits generated by the sale of livestock were worth the risk.[41]

In August 1860, shortly after Curtis returned home, Palo Pinto cattleman, slave owner, and trader Oliver Loving drove one thousand steers up the trail to Colorado with Curtis. This was Loving's second trip, as his first had been in the spring of 1859; Curtis, however, was now very familiar with the route. They went up to the Red River (most probably through the area that became Red River Station in Montague County, as the ground was flat and easy for cattle to cross) and into Indian Territory; then they followed the Arkansas River from below the Great Bend, up to the north of Pueblo. Once in Pueblo, they set up winter camp. When the snow melted and the cattle fattened back up, they continued to Denver, where they sold out.[42]

It is not known how long Dawson, Curtis, and others trailed cattle to Denver, but Curtis witnessed the wrath of Union soldiers on a trip in the summer of 1862. Arriving not long after the Battle of Glorieta Pass, which occurred on March 26–28, Curtis reported that "rations and rewards for Texas scalps" were being offered. To make his way home, "Mr. Curtis wrote himself a passport and commission to buy mules for the Federal Government."[43]

Dawson, like other cattlemen in the county and throughout the state, did not only limit himself to trading cattle with gold miners. Historian Thomas Smith listed a James Dawson as the supplier for Fort Belknap in 1856, 1857, and 1860, but that is most probably John, not James. John B. Dawson was reputedly informed about the opportunities with Fort Belknap by Kit Carson, and this served as the impetus to move from Arkansas. There is no taxpayer with the last name of Dawson listed in the Young County tax records from 1857 through 1861; nor is there a Dawson in the 1860 census for Young County. However, as stated earlier, John B. Dawson was listed as a "Trader" one county south, in the future Stephens County. Additionally, his lack of trade with Fort Belknap in 1858 and 1859 is explained by drives to Colorado, where mining towns were a far more lucrative market than the fort.[44]

During the war, people in Stephens County, like others in the region, forted up to protect themselves from Indians, but despite all this, cattlemen—both slave owning and non–slave owning—kept moving westward. They risked the lives of themselves and their families not only in daily ranching activities but also on long drives to market. Dawson, like other cattlemen in the region, profited by supplying cattle to the Union posts of Fort Sumner, Fort Union, Fort Marcy, and Fort Bascom. Money was the determining factor for many cattle traders during the war, not loyalty to one side or the other.[45] The only acceptable answer for living in conditions that were described by many of the early residents as treacherous is financial gain.

Ramsdell's argument that slavery would not be profitable west of the Cross Timbers, coupled with the lack of attention to small slaveholders with livestock, misrepresents the diversity of slavery. Additionally, the concept that the most lucrative use of slaves was to maximize profits per acre, as in plantation-style agriculture, negates the use of open-range grazing options that were practiced before the use of barbed wire and overlooks the wealth of stock raisers during that period. Stock raisers earned huge profits before the post–Civil War drives, and many lived in the North-Central Texas region in counties where low numbers of slaves were recorded. These slaves participated in varied aspects of the business, from daily activities to serving as legal tender in livestock acquisitions, to maximize their owners' ability to generate profits.

NOTES

1. Randolph B. Campbell, *An Empire for Slavery: The Peculiar Institution in Texas, 1821–1865* (Baton Rouge: Louisiana State University Press, 1989); Randolph B. Campbell and Richard G. Lowe, *Wealth and Power in Antebellum Texas* (College Station: Texas A&M University Press, 1977). Quotation from John Leffler, "Stephens County," *Handbook of Texas Online*, accessed February 6, 2013, http://www.tshaonline.org/handbook/online/articles/hcs14.

2. Leffler, "Stephens County"; "Cross Timbers," *Handbook of Texas Online*, accessed February 9, 2013, http://www.tshaonline.org/handbook/online/articles/ryc04; Charles W. Ramsdell, "The Natural Limits of Slavery Expansion," *Mississippi Valley Historical Review*, September 16, 1929, 151–71.

3. Campbell and Lowe, *Wealth and Power*, first and second quotation from 75, third quotation 15.

4. From phone interview with Stephens County Clerk's Office, January 15, 2013, and an onsite survey; Leffler, "Stephens County." Despite its outward reverence for the Confederacy, the county did not return a vote for or against secession. *Stephens* and *Buchanan* will be used to refer to what is now Stephens County. *Buchanan* will be used for the time period before 1861; *Stephens* will be used for afterward.

5. For more about slaves in the livestock industry, see Deborah M. Liles, "Before Emancipation: Black Cowboys and the Livestock Industry," in *Black Cowboys and Their Imprint in the West*, ed. Bruce Glasrud and Michael N. Searles (Norman: University of Oklahoma Press, 2016), 19–30.

6. I have not yet found a definite percentage of the population that definitively shows the county was engaged in livestock instead of cash crops; however, the range of 12–17 percent is consistent.

7. Eighth Census of the United States, schedule 2 (Slave Inhabitants), 1860, Buchanan County, Texas; See Cecil Earl Harper Jr., "Slavery without Cotton: Hunt County, Texas, 1846–1864," *Southwestern Historical Quarterly* 88 (April 1985): 387–405, for an excellent study of an interior county with low numbers of slaves

and no cotton economy. Harper found
that 14 percent of the community
owned slaves, slave owners had the
most property, slave owners were
involved in politics, low numbers of
slaves were the norm, and livestock was
the most valuable commodity. He did
not, however, connect slavery to the
livestock industry.

8. Eighth Census, Buchanan County,
schedule 2.

9. Ibid.; Stephens County tax records,
1861–64 (microfilm, Willis Library,
University of North Texas, Denton,
Texas).

10. Stephens County tax records, 1861–64.
This argument is the basis for the
author's dissertation, "Southern Roots,
Western Foundations: The Peculiar
Institution and the Livestock Industry
on the Northwestern Frontier of
Texas, 1849–1864" (PhD dissertation,
University of North Texas, 2013).

11. Eighth Census, Buchanan County,
schedule 2; Stephens County tax
records, 1861–64.

12. Bill of sale from E. A. Hamner to
Mary Anne Miller, December 25,
1858, Deed Records, book 1, 264,
Young County Clerk's Office, Graham,
Texas; bill of slave from I. N. Manly to
Philip S. George, March 19, 1859, Deed
Records, book 1, 338, Young County
Clerk's Office; bill of slave from H. K.
Vollintine to Mary Ann Miller, July 22,
1859, Deed Records, book 1, 443, Young
County Clerk's Office; bill of sale from
George W. Fisher to Solomon Miller,
August 17, 1859, Deed Records, book 1,
460, Young County Clerk's Office; bill
of sale from Solomon Miller to G. W.
Fisher, August 17, 1859, Deed Records,
book 1, 461.

13. Eighth Census of the United States,
schedule 1 (White Inhabitants),
Buchanan County, Texas; Eighth
Census of the United States, schedule
4 (Agriculture), Buchanan County,
Texas; Stephens County property
tax records, 1861–64. Slave owners
that were listed in the following
years' property tax records but not
on the schedule 2 were Mrs. F. A.
Dotson (Dobson; a widow without
property), J. A. Degrafferied, Taylor T.
Maulding, G. Matthews, R. D. Miller,
J. W. Price, Thomas L. Stockton, and
J. Westbrooks. Out of those, only
Thomas Stockton, a twenty-seven-
year-old stock raiser from Tennessee,
and Taylor Maulden (Maudling), a
twenty-six-year-old stock raiser from
Tennessee, were listed in the Buchanan
(Stephens) County census. Combined
information from the census and tax
records shows that these slaves were
used in conjunction with their owners'
livestock professions.

14. Stephens County tax records,
1861–1864.

15. Frank Lawrence Owsley, *Plain Folk of
the Old South* (Baton Rouge: Louisiana
State University Press, 1949), 7–25
(quotation from 25).

16. The only slave owner who did report
crops was Francis Sloane. He raised
twenty bushels of wheat on his land in
1860. To the north in Young County,
northwest in Shackleford County, east
in Palo Pinto County, and south in
Eastland County, Indian corn was the
majority crop. Indian corn was used
to feed livestock; thus, crops grown
by the slave owners, and tended by
the slaves, was raised to benefit their
livestock business. See Eighth Census,
schedule 4, census returns for Young,
Shackleford, Palo Pinto, and Eastland
Counties for more specifics.

17. Stephens County tax records, 1861–64.

18. James Drew declared eighty-eight slaves, worth $61,600 (approximately $1 million when adjusted for inflation to 2017), in Erath County in 1864. These slave declarations were only present that year, and it is unknown where Drew (or Drue) came from. He could possibly be James C. Drew from Carroll Parrish, Louisiana, who declared forty-five slaves in the 1860 census, but that is pure speculation. See Erath County property tax records, 1864; and Eighth Census of the United States, Carroll Parrish, Louisiana, schedule 2 (Slave Population).

19. *Rancher* is a term used to describe slave owners who engage in the livestock industry (raising horses, cattle, and sheep). Much like planters, their economic statuses, success, and livelihoods were dependent to some measure on slaves. See Liles, "Southern Roots, Western Foundations," 15–16.

20. Stephens County tax records, 1861–64; Palo Pinto County tax records, 1857–64 (microfilm, Willis Library, University of North Texas, Denton, Texas); Parker County tax records, 1856–64 (microfilm, Willis Library, University of North Texas, Denton, Texas); Johnson County tax records, 1854–64 (microfilm, Willis Library, University of North Texas, Denton, Texas).

21. Stephens County tax records, 1861–64; Palo Pinto County tax records, 1857–64; Parker County tax records, 1856–64; Johnson County tax records, 1854–64.

22. Stephens County tax records, 1862; Eighth Census of the United States, schedule 1 (Free Population), Bosque County, Texas. See also endnote 23; Owsley, *Plain Folk*, quotation from 35.

23. See Deborah M. Liles, "Martha Alice Loring: An Unlikely Woman on the Texas Frontier," *Central Texas Studies 2* (December 2017): 9–24; Deborah M. Liles, "In Search of Lucinda: Women in the Cattle Industry in Early Texas," in *Texas Women and Ranching: On the Range, at the Rodeo, in their Community*, ed. Deborah M. Liles and Cecilia Venable-Gutierrez (College Station: Texas A&M University Press, 2019): 40–58.

24. Stephens County tax records, 1861–64; Parker County tax records, 1856–64.

25. Stephens County tax records, 1861–64; Parker County tax records, 1856–64.

26. Joseph Andrew Blackman, "Ikard, Bose," *Handbook of Texas Online*, accessed February 20, 2013, http://www.tshaonline.org/handbook/online/articles/fik03; Ikards's sons, William "Sude" and E. F., became successful cattlemen after the war and drove cattle north with J. C. Loving, Oliver's son. Sude is credited with bringing the first Hereford cattle to Texas. Bose Ikard also worked with the Ikard brothers on their drives. For more information, see Rupert N. Richardson, "William S. Ikard and Hereford Raising in Texas," *West Texas Historical Association Year Book* 25 (October 1949): 39–49. Bose Ikard is buried in the white section of Greenwood Cemetery in Weatherford, Parker County. His grave marker, written by Goodnight, speaks volumes to the respect he garnished in the industry: "Bose Ikard served with me four years on the Goodnight-Loving Trail, never shirked a duty or disobeyed an order, rode with me in many stampedes, participated in three engagements with Comanches, splendid behavior."

27. Terry Jordan wrote that "no positive or negative correlations existed between slave ownership and cattle ownership," but he, like others, focused on planters, not small slave owners. See Terry G. Jordan, *Trails to Texas: Southern Roots of Western Cattle Ranching* (Lincoln: University of Nebraska Press, 1981), quotation from 98.

28. Richard B. McCaslin, "On the Road to Sutherland Springs" (unpublished manuscript, in possession of author, n.d.), 61–70. This manuscript was published as Richard B. McCaslin, *Sutherland Springs, Texas: Saratoga on the Cibolo* (Denton: University of North Texas Press, 2017).

29. Jerry Thompson, "Baylor, John Robert," *Handbook of Texas Online*, accessed February 1, 2013, http://www.tshaonline.org/handbook/online/articles/fbaat; quotation from McCaslin, "On the Road to Southerland Springs," 63; Baylor sold his herd of 150 head to Emily, his wife, for $1,200 on April 16, 1857. It is unclear why this sale took place, but it may well have been to transfer his assets out of his name after he was dismissed as an Indian agent so that they could not be confiscated. See bill of sale from J. R. Baylor to E. Y. Baylor, April 16, 1857, Deed Records, book 1, 14, Young County Clerk's Office.

30. Reynolds brother, William D. Reynolds, was a member of the party who returned Oliver Loving's body from Fort Sumner, New Mexico, to Weatherford, Texas. For more information, see "Reynolds, William D.," *Handbook of Texas Online*, accessed January 30, 2013, http://www.tshaonline.org/handbook/online/articles/fre33.

31. Frances Mayhugh Holden, "Reynolds, George Thomas," *Handbook of Texas Online*, accessed January 30, 2013, http://www.tshaonline.org/handbook/online/articles/fre31; J. Marvin Hunter, comp., *The Trail Drivers of Texas* (Austin: University of Texas Press, 1985), 671; For more information, see Sallie Reynolds Matthews, *Interwoven: A Pioneer Chronicle* (Austin: University of Texas Press, 1958).

32. Holden, "Reynolds"; Matthews, *Interwoven*, 11.

33. Hunter, *Trail Drivers of Texas*, 671. It was not uncommon to trade livestock for slave property. A May 5, 1855, advertisement in the *Texas State Gazette* read, "Low for cash or likely young negro property, 400 head of gentle stock cattle; 600 head of sheep, a cross of the [S]axon and merino; 25 head of Spanish and [A]merican mares." See Glen Sample Ely, "Gone from Texas and Trading with the Enemy: New Perspectives on Civil War West Texas," *Southwestern Historical Quarterly* 110 (April 2007): 438–63.

34. For an outstanding study of the effects on livestock and the Confederate Army, see R. Douglas Hurt, *Agriculture and the Confederacy: Policy, Productivity, and Power in the Civil War South* (Chapel Hill: University of North Carolina Press, 2015).

35. Stephens County tax records, 1861–64; Hunter, *Trail Drivers of Texas*, 671–72.

36. Stephens County tax records, 1861–64.

37. Ibid.

38. Deloris Kay Curtis-Ward, *Pioneer Settlers of New Mexico Territory: The Journeys of a Tough and Resilient People* (Bloomington, IN: AuthorHouse, 2008). Curtis-Ward used cattle records, diaries, and memoirs that primarily

belonged to Joel Curtis and John B. Dawson, to whom she is related, to recount the early days of many Stephens County cattlemen. While there were a few observations of slaves who belonged to Curtis, those were scant. The other men listed in the book were not mentioned as slave owners. The connection of the slave owners to Curtis-Ward's family members and the cattlemen she mentioned in her book were made using the Stephens County tax records, 1861–64. As already noted, Curtis and Dawson were listed on the 1860 census but did not declare slaves in their property taxes until 1863. This author believes that both men owned the same slaves throughout all five years.

39. The general mood of Rough and Ready can be gauged in the fact that it seceded from the Union in 1850, when residents objected to a mining tax. See "Nevada Gold Country," *Nevada County Gold*, accessed February 10, 2013, http://www .nevadacountygold.com/about/ history-western-nevco/rough-a -ready; Curtis-Ward, *Pioneer Settlers*, 5–29 (quotation from 29). The 1860 census for Buchanan County lists four children for Joel W. and Henrietta Curtis. The oldest were ten and eleven years old and born in Arkansas; the second-youngest child was eight and born in California; the youngest was three and born in Texas. As the date on the census was July 27, this places the Curtis family in California at the end of 1852 or the beginning of 1853 and in Texas by the end of 1857 or the beginning of 1858.

40. Curtis-Ward, *Pioneer Settlers*, 5–29 (quotation from 29); "Dawson Family Papers," *Online Archive of California*, accessed February 20, 2013, http://www .oac.cdlib.org/findaid/ ark:/13030/tf3k4006bd/; "Cattle Trails from Wyoming Tales and Trails," *Wyoming Tales and Trails*, accessed February 10, 2013, http:// www.wyomingtalesandtrails.com/ cattleaus.html; "Dawson, Goodnight and the Great American Cattle Drives," accessed January 24, 2013, http://www .cimarronnm.com/uploads/ 2/3/9/7/23975243/dawson -goodnight-loving_history.pdf. For studies of the Arkansas up-country, see John Solomon Otto, "Slavery in the Mountains: Yell County, Arkansas, 1840–1860," *Arkansas Historical Quarterly* 39, no. 1 (Spring 1980): 35–52; and Gary Battershell, "The Socioeconomic Role of Slavery in the Arkansas Upcountry," *Arkansas Historical Quarterly* 58, no. 1 (Spring 1999): 45–60.

41. "Historic Trails of Arizona: Chávez Trail," Azstateparks.com, accessed February 5, 2013, http://azstateparks .com/trails/historic/trail_06.html. Chavez established a 125-mile trail in 1864, from Winslow, Arizona, to Prescott, home of Fort Whipple. See also Curtis-Ward, *Pioneer Settlers*, 22; "Texas Beef in the Far West," San Antonio *Ledger and Texan*, June 16, 1860; St. Louis *Democrat*, June 5, 1860. The offer for the gold was less than what Curtis wanted ($15.75 an ounce), so he shipped it to the mint in Philadelphia.

42. Curtis-Ward, *Pioneer Settlers*, 32; Red River Station was settled in 1860 and later became the crossing for cattle as they went north up the Chisholm Trail. For more information, see Brian Hart,

"Red River Station, Texas," *Handbook of Texas Online*, accessed February 23, 2013, http://www.tshaonline.org/handbook/online/articles/hvr24.

43. "Texan Scalps," *Henkel Square Herald* (Round Top, TX), July 1862, transcribed by Vicki Betts, accessed February 23, 2013, http://www.txcwcivilian.org/sitebuildercontent/sitebuilderfiles/july62format.pdf.

44. Curtis-Ward, *Pioneer Settlers*, 22, 30; Young County tax records, 1857–61; Eighth Census, Buchanan County, schedule 1; Eighth Census, Young County, schedule 1 (Free Population).

45. Curtis-Ward, *Pioneer Settlers*, 20.

Slavery on the Frontier

The Peculiar Institution in Central Texas

William Dean Carrigan

"Slavery on the Frontier" challenged aspects of the slave system in the United States by evaluating the use of slaves in a region not assumed by some early historians to be profitable for the continuance of slavery. In Central Texas, however, slavery was used not only on plantations for the growing of cotton but for numerous other aspects of the Texas economy. The author, William Dean Carrigan, currently is history department chair and professor of history at Rowan College in New Jersey. Among his publications is the first-rate monograph, The Making of a Lynching Culture: Violence and Vigilantism in Central Texas. *He has expanded his challenging research and currently researches the lynching of Mexican Americans.*

★

Elsewhere at the South, slavery had seemed to be accepted generally, as a natural, hereditary, established state of things. . . . But in Texas, the state of war in which slavery arises, seems to continue in undertone to the present.

FREDERICK LAW OLMSTED, 1857[1]

"One thing is certain," wrote a Texas newspaperman in the 1850s, "unless something be done to arrest the escape of slaves, this class of property will become valueless in Western Texas. . . . As yet, but few of those escaping have been caught."[2] Another observer remarked, "Texans were more or less used to losing their slaves, who would often run away."[3] Such comments cannot be dismissed as the opinions of naturally exaggerating Texans or as the panic-stricken cries of paranoid slaveholders. The southwestern frontier of the antebellum United States did indeed witness an exodus of African slaves. Despite an upsurge of resistance on the Texas frontier, few historians have chosen to investigate slave resistance in Texas during the antebellum period.[4]

One reason that scholars have shied away from research on slavery in Texas lies in the 1989 publication of Randolph B. Campbell's *Empire for Slavery: The Peculiar Institution in Texas*. Campbell's thorough research and balanced conclusions justly earned his study recognition as the definitive work on slavery in Texas. Prior to Campbell's work, popular attention on Texas had focused on such Western images as ranching, outlaws, and cowboys. By exploring slavery in Texas, Campbell sought to remind scholars that they could not continue to ignore Texas' Southern past. In reorienting the study of antebellum Texas, Campbell made an invaluable historiographic contribution. Campbell's revisionist mission, however, may have led him to overstate his case. Although he was undoubtedly correct when he asserted that "slavery played a vital role in shaping antebellum Texas and determining its future," he went too far when he argued that slavery "in Texas did not differ in any fundamental way from the institution as it existed elsewhere in the United States."[5] It is my contention that the development of slavery in Texas between 1836 and 1861 was quite different from the simultaneous history of slavery in any other contemporary slave state. Although Campbell is certainly correct to point out that by 1860, slavery had assumed a dominant role in Texas' economy and society, the *process* of creating a slave society diverged in important ways in Texas. It is precisely those differences that make Texas a revealing location for an exploration of slavery and slave resistance.

Historians of Texas have not been alone in ignoring the struggle over slavery and the issue of slave resistance in the Lone Star State. Historians of slavery in the United States have rarely sought to understand how the peculiar institution was transformed by its frontier experience. Eugene D. Genovese noted that in "Texas, Arkansas, and Louisiana, slaveholders had to exercise vigilance, for many slaves went over the Mexican border or escaped to friendly Indians."[6] But Genovese did not pursue his insight. Like many of his fellow Southern historians, he saw the frontier as an exception to the mainline story of Southern history. Although occasionally interesting, the story of the Southern frontier did not appear to be a reliable window into the character of the Old South.[7] Yet times of cultural conflict, argue Western historians, often bring to light the deepest values of a society. David J. Weber suggests that it is the very strangeness of the frontier that can make it so illuminating. "Along frontiers, new opportunities," remarked Weber, "often intensify . . . internal struggles for power."[8] The powerful property of frontiers is to defy expectation and bring to the surface struggles not easily seen in settled society.

How and why did Texas emerge as a deeply contested western frontier of slavery? The answer has much to do with antebellum Texas' recent settlement and position on the southwestern borderlands. When white and black Southerners entered Central Texas in the mid-nineteenth century, they encountered a world torn in three directions by four different cultures.[9] From the east came Anglo settlers and enslaved Africans of the young and expanding United States. To the north and to the west,

Native Americans roamed throughout the Texas plains and prairies. And in the south, outposts and settlements of Mexico continued to dot the landscape. To be sure, the success of the Texas Revolution limited the reach of Mexico in Central Texas. And the continuing struggle against the Indians of the Texas prairies had reduced their power in the region as well. Nevertheless, these four Texas cultures remained embroiled in a host of bloody conflicts throughout the nineteenth century. The struggle for hegemony not only revealed what each of these cultures thought of each other but exposed what each society thought about itself.

This essay uses a case study of antebellum Central Texas to argue that the frontier highlighted the ongoing contest for power between masters and slaves. As the farthest region west where plantation agriculture was profitable in the antebellum US South, Central Texas offers an intriguing laboratory for such an investigation.[10] Indeed, an analysis of the Central Texas frontier during the middle of the nineteenth century alters our understanding of runaway slaves in the United States and challenges narratives of Southern history that assume a decline of slave resistance in the antebellum South.[11] In the conflicts that ensued on the Texas frontier, thousands of slaves took the opportunity to escape to freedom. In the process, they tested the master-slave relationship and revealed something of the depth of slave resistance. Although masters had successfully contained the scope of the power struggle between masters and slaves in the earlier-settled regions of the South, the new opportunities of the frontier raised their battle to a new level. As slaves sought to escape the authority of their masters and slaveholders strove to reestablish control over their servants, both combatants revealed much about the peculiar nature of their society.

During the quarter-century between Texas' independence and the American Civil War, a massive wave of Anglo-American migrants flocked to Central Texas and the Upper Brazos River Valley. Over 90 percent of these migrants came from Southern states, and the vast majority engaged in agriculture—primarily cotton production and subsistence farming. Although the Upper Brazos became home to a substantial number of yeomen farmers and cattle ranchers with no slaves, by 1860, approximately one of every three of the incoming families to the growing region held perpetual servants. On the eve of the Civil War, slaves accounted for a third of the valley's population.[12] Spurred on by friends and relatives or pushed by circumstances beyond their control, white settlers came west, following the Southern promise of a new start in a new land and hoping to build a prosperous society on the edge of the South. If they were to succeed, they first had to overcome the hardships and the dangers of their new environment.

Although hostile Indians and rough living conditions had been common problems for generations of Americans pioneers, settlers found the dangers of antebellum Texas especially menacing. Even after the Texans won independence from Mexico in 1836, their southern neighbor continued to pose problems. In addition to repeated denials of Texan independence, Mexico's refusal to return fugitive slaves boiled the blood of many Texans. Mexico, however, was not the most pressing danger facing Texas settlers. Hostile Native Americans, led by the Comanche, violently defended their homeland by raiding white settlements throughout Texas. While the settlers may have believed in their right to claim the "wilderness" of Central Texas from its occupants, most migrants knew that the Indians had other ideas and would resist. Hostile Indians and a recalcitrant Mexico, however, did not catch Texas migrants off guard. Many of the new Texans had been warned of these twin dangers before coming to the Lone Star State. What the Texas pioneers understood less well was that they had brought one of their largest problems with them—rebellious slaves.

Mexico's stance on slavery had long proven to be a thorn in the side of Texas slaveholders. Indeed, fears over the security of slavery played an important role in the coming of the Texas Revolution. Yet as many historians have pointed out, Mexican actions before 1836 had not unduly disrupted the development of the peculiar institution in Texas. Ironically, a revolution fought to secure slavery from Mexican interference provided far more opportunities for slave resistance than had ever existed under Mexican rule.[13]

As the army of Mexican leader Santa Anna marched northward, Anglos feared that the army might liberate their slaves or, worse, entice them to rebel against their masters. In the summer of 1835, a report emerged that the commander of a Mexican schooner of war had sailed into Galveston Bay, intending to "take all the negro slaves in the country that he could get in his possession, and offer them their liberty after one year's service."[14] An open letter to the Texas public warned that one of the goals of the impending Mexican invasion of Texas was the "emancipation of her slaves."[15] In separate letters, Benjamin Milam and Horatio Allsberry declared that the official policy of the Mexican army was far worse—they intended to "get the slaves to revolt" and "let them loose upon their families."[16] According to William Parker, Sam Houston ordered the retreat of the colonists and the Texas army across Texas "to prevent the negroes from joining the enemy in small parties."[17]

In reality, the policy of the Mexican army to African slaves was far from coordinated. On 16 February 1836, the commander-in-chief of the Mexican army queried the secretary of war on their policy toward Texan slaves. "There is a considerable number of slaves in Texas," observed Santa Anna, "who according to our laws should be free." Although he offered no concrete plan for their liberation, he asked, "[Shall] we permit these wretches to moan in chains any longer in a country whose kind laws protect the liberty of man without distinction of cast or color?"[18] Despite their enlightened concern for the enslaved, no evidence exists that the Mexican army actively pursued a policy of liberating Africans during the Texas Revolution.

While the actions of the Mexican army toward slavery did not live up to the fears voiced by anxious Anglos, Texas slaves raised concern by taking matters into their own hands. As Mexican soldiers attempted to cross the Colorado River on 10 April 1836, "several natives, a mulatto woman, two Negro women and several Negro men" appeared to help them cross the river.[19] Another fugitive slave volunteered to serve General Filisola as his coachman.[20] By joining the Mexican army and making themselves useful, these fugitive slaves sought to win their freedom. A slaveholder's wife recalled that four of her husband's slaves ran away to the Mexican army.[21] Slaves belonging to John F. C. Henderson and Thomas Jamison found refuge in the Mexican army.[22] Even after the Mexican army was defeated, at least thirteen fugitive slaves joined the retreating body on its way to Matagorda.[23]

Flight to the Mexican army, however, was not the most powerful form of slave resistance to emerge during the Texas Revolution. Although details are few, the most radical act of the Texas Revolution may have been an attempted slave uprising. In a 17 October 1835 letter to Stephen F. Austin, B. J. White wrote that he had "found much confusion" and now possessed "unpleasant news to communicate." White's bad news was that "the negroes on Brazos [River] made an attempt to rise." The rebels had decided exactly what parts of the property they gained in the rebellion would belong to each former slave. They planned to continue to raise cotton and ship it through New Orleans, but they intended to reverse positions with their masters and have the white men serve them. This radical plan was no spontaneous revolt of a few discontented slaves, but "near 100" had participated in the rebellion. Fortunately for Anglo leaders, the revolt was quickly put down. Slaveholders forfeited some of their valuable property in order to issue a warning to potential enslaved insurgents. They had "many [of the rebels] whipd [sic] nearly to death some hung etc."[24]

This dramatic revolt occurred in the Lower Brazos River Valley, a region south of Central Texas that in 1835 had more than a decade of experience with plantation slavery. Slavery in the interior could not yet boast such a history, but that did not stop the slaves in Central Texas from attempting to profit from the confusion caused by the Texas Revolution. "The Negroes high upon the Trinity have manifested a disposition to become troublesome and in some instances daring," wrote Col. Thomas Morgan on 24 March 1836. Although they had not yet taken any direct action, he believed that they were seeking an alliance with the Coushatta Indians and were preparing to come south and "murder the inhabitants and join the Mexicans."[25] Although too few slaves lived in Central Texas during the Texas Revolution to make it a hotbed of resistance, these "daring" slaves on the Trinity gave ample warning that the reach of antislavery Mexico, combined with the region's frontier conditions and proximity to hostile Indians, would continue to play havoc with the development of slavery in the region.

In many ways, the upsurge of black activism in 1835 and 1836 was not that surprising to Texas slaveholders. Increased resistance from their slaves, they knew, was not an uncommon consequence of civil war. It was perhaps more frustrating that, even after the Anglo-Texans had thrown off Mexican rule and expelled its army of slave liberation, the new republic's southern neighbor continued to pose a danger to the institution of slavery. "The proximity of Texas to the Mexican border," noted a Texas historian, "made the escape of slaves a rather frequent occurrence."[26] Fugitive slaves who escaped to Mexico entered a free nation, freer than the American North, which was burdened with the Fugitive Slave Act. Because diplomatic relations between

Mexico and Texas remained strained, the two countries had no extradition treaty. As a result, Mexico became a haven for runaway slaves. One San Antonio newspaper reported that the land across the Rio Grande "has long been regarded by the Texas slave as his El Dorado for accumulation, his utopia for political rights, and his Paradise for happiness."[27]

"Seen anything of a runaway nigger over there, anywhar?" a Texan asked in 1854. According to a conversation recorded by Frederick Law Olmsted, a fugitive slave had fled his master for the border of Mexico. The Texan claimed that the slave had been out "nigh two weeks." He "liked to have killed the judge" who owned him, and he cut his young master "right bad." After trailing the fugitive for days, they said, "We caught him once, but he got away from us again.... We shot at him three times with rifles, but he'd got too far off, but we must have shaved him close." They eventually lost the slave, however: "We run him close, though, I tell you. Run him out of his coat, and his boots, and a pistol he'd got. But 'twas getting dark, and he got in them bayous, and kept swimming from one side to the other." We stayed after him for ten days, said the Texan, but "if he's got across that river, he'd get to the Mexicans in two days, and there he'd be safe. The Mexicans'd take care of him."[28]

Despite such concerted efforts on the parts of slaveholders to recapture their fleeing slaves, the escape of fugitives into Mexico became a recurring theme for Texans in the 1850s. "Something should be done," one newspaper roared in 1855, "to put a stop to the escape of Negroes into Mexico. If the General Government cannot protect us, we should protect ourselves."[29] Although no precise figures for the numbers of runaways can be given, it surely was in the thousands. One source claimed in 1851 that Texans estimated there to be three thousand escaped slaves living in Mexico. Olmsted noted three years later that "runaways were constantly arriving" at Piedras Negras on the Mexican side of the Rio Grande. A Texas Ranger claimed that four thousand fugitive slaves lived in northern Mexico in 1855.[30]

Although slaves in southern Texas had a shorter distance to reach the Mexican border, runaways came from as far away as Arkansas and Louisiana for a chance at freedom. The sheriff of McLennan County reported the capture of a runaway slave in January 1861. A. A. Blankenship had captured Jim a month earlier, on 18 December 1860. The sheriff of McLennan County described Jim as being twenty-nine or thirty years old, 5'10", and 160 pounds. This "very intelligent" slave of "copper complexion" had stolen four horses in his escape attempt. Although Jim belonged to Robert Grant of Mississippi, the slave had been hired to Jeff Galloway of Shreveport, Louisiana. For his part, Jim had traveled several hundred miles, a long way in search of freedom. He was not simply hiding out in the woods. He could have been searching for a family member who had been removed to Texas, but he could have been heading for the Mexican border.[31]

Like Grant and Galloway, Central Texas slaveholders had their own problems with rebellious and runaway slaves. According to one historian, six runaway slaves "headed for Mexico from near Waco in 1845 with a herd of twenty-five horses."[32]

In that same year, a number of Cherokee Indians received a "sum of three hundred dollars ... for the apprehension and delivery of the runaway negroes, the property of R. H. Porter, viz., Isaac, Rheuben and Charles." The Central Texas merchant noted that they were "taken up about 15 miles west of the head of the Guadalupe river, making their way to the Spanish country."[33] Former Texas slaves themselves recalled slave flight to Mexico. "My grandfather run 'way an' went down to Mexico," recalled one ex-slave.[34] "De Mexicans," recalled a former slave in Falls County, "would try to git dem [rebellious slaves] ter run away an' stay across de border wid dem an' some ob dem did."[35] George Glasker, an ex-slave who lived on the Brazos River in McLennan County, remembered that "de Mexicans down on de border would git de slaves to run away befo' the Civil War cum."[36]

Texas slaveholders often found it difficult to accept that their supposedly devoted servants had taken advantage of the Texas frontier to escape bondage. According to Kenneth Porter, many slaveholders even selected their most loyal slaves to accompany them to Texas.[37] How could these most-trusted bondsmen and women turn their backs on their masters? Were these Texas slaves not the same slaves who had seemed so loyal back in Georgia, Mississippi, and Alabama? While some owners may have realized that the master-slave relationship was far more tenuous than they had believed, most chose to blame "outside agitators" for their troubles. Mexicans, in particular, drew the blame for the increased rebelliousness of Texas slaves. One historian reported that Anglos charged Mexicans in Texas with "exercising a mischievous influence among the slaves."[38] Another historian noted that Anglo-Texans held public meetings in Austin, Gonzales, and other places advising their fellow planters not to employ Mexican laborers because they "thought a portion of the Mexican population in Western Texas aided their escape."[39] In 1854, noted observer Frederick Law Olmsted remarked that Mexicans in Texas "are regarded by slaveholders with great contempt and suspicion, for their intimacy with slaves."[40] In 1856 and 1857, due to the alleged connection between Mexicans and slave resistance, three Texas counties—Colorado, Matagorda, and Bastrop—took the extreme action of expelling all Mexicans.[41] Even in Central Texas, where few Mexicans resided, slaveholders worried about alliances between transient Mexican workers and slaves. In September 1857, in Limestone County, authorities uncovered a plot between a group of Mexican laborers and ten to twelve slaves. Allegedly, the Mexicans had promised the slaves their freedom if they ran away with them to Mexico. When the plot was discovered, authorities punished the slaves immediately and jailed the Mexicans. Before the case could come to trial, however, the Mexicans escaped.[42] Such plots—some no doubt real, most no doubt imagined—continued to surface throughout the antebellum period. As late as 1858, the San Antonio *Herald* announced that Anglos had uncovered and thwarted a Mexican plot to help runaway slaves in Gonzales.[43]

While Anglo warnings of Mexican-slave alliances far exceeded the actual existence of such combinations, the two groups did unite just often enough to maintain white apprehensions. In 1838, two years after Thomas Morgan cautioned that black slaves were pursuing an alliance with Indians and Mexicans, "a motley gang" of Mexicans, fugitive slaves, Coushatta Indians, and others attacked an armed force of Anglos under General Rusk near Kickapoo Town. Rusk's force suffered eleven men wounded, but the Anglos killed eleven of the insurgents.[44] A few months later, in March 1839, fugitive slaves, mulattos, and free blacks fought with the Mexican rebel Vicente Cordova in his attempt to topple the Texas Republic.[45] In November 1856, citizens in Rio Grande city reported that three Mexicans and five armed Negroes, riding what appeared to be stolen horses, passed through their town on the way to Mexico.[46]

Although some slaves united with their Mexican neighbors in armed rebellion against the Texas slaveholders, most slaves—especially after 1840—considered flight across the Rio Grande to be their best avenue of escape from bondage. Exactly how many slaves escaped to Mexico will never be known, but Texas slaveholders and their allies spent considerable time and energy attempting to recapture fugitive slaves. A former McLennan County slave reported that "lots of slaves run away, but dey'd most always ketch 'em and bring 'em back."[47] On occasion, the problem of the fugitive slaves became so great that slaveholders employed professional slave catchers and "blood hounds to track the run-a-way slaves." According to Burke Simpson, an ex-slave from Central Texas, "I kin 'member dey names as well as if hit wuz today, dey wuz Milo, Jenny Lane, Rock an' Red. I kin hear in my memory how dey would go thro' de country a yelpin' as dey chase de niggers thro' de bottom an' den w'en dey had him up a tree yer could tell by de way dey would bark. W'en dey ketch de nigger dey bring him back an' turn him over to de overseer, an' sometimes dey would lock him up or give him a whippin' an' send him to de field."[48] Another important way that slaveholders sought to catch runaway slaves was to offer large rewards to Indians for their return. Barnard's Trading Post in the Upper Brazos River Valley gladly exchanged goods and materials for runaway slaves brought in by local Indians.[49]

One should not suppose, however, that slave catchers had an easy time recapturing fugitives in Texas. Not only did these runaways have the benefits of a sparsely settled landscape; they often took advantage of the relatively plentiful number of horses and guns present along the Texas borderlands to aid in their escape. Noah Smithwick observed firsthand the dangers of confronting fugitive slaves in Texas. One night, Smithwick noticed a strange campfire near his home on the Colorado River. After discovering the trespassers to be runaways, he decided to perform his duty as a citizen and attempt to recapture the escaped slaves. With six friends and a pack of bloodhounds, he descended upon the two black men at dawn the following morning. However, Smithwick and his friends were in for a shock because the runaways possessed a gun. After one of the slaves shot a hound, Smithwick recalled that this "put a serious aspect upon the affair; we had not counted on armed resistance." Showing the determination of a true Texan (and realizing that his party had several guns and a half-dozen dogs to the single rifle of the slave), Smithwick did not give up. "We intercepted them and demanded an unconditional surrender," remembered Smithwick, but the only reply given was "the presentation of a rifle in the hands of a powerful black fellow." After a bloody exchange of fire, "the negroes had gotten the best of the fight and were off." Smithwick and his party now wisely retired. What happened to these brave escaped slaves? "Several days later the fugitives were heard from over on Sandy," recalled Smithwick, "where they held up Jim Hamilton and made him give them directions for reaching Mexico." Smithwick went on to note that "one or two" other parties attempted to capture the two runaways but had also failed. Reflecting on the humbling experience, Smithwick noted of his opponent that morning, "Single-handed—his companion being unarmed—he had whipped six white men, all armed, and as many fierce dogs."[50] Although such an example was surely unusual, slaveholders certainly believed they were all too common.

While fugitive slaves heading for the free border of Mexico angered Texas slave-holders, hostile Native Americans posed a deadlier threat. Many of the Indians of Texas refused to peacefully acquiesce to the cultural annihilation (if not outright genocide) that white and black settlement entailed. Taking to the warpath, these Indians routinely raided and harassed white and black settlers. Many of the families to settle in the Upper Brazos River Valley in the antebellum period suffered a fatality at the hands of Indian raiders.[51]

In their attacks on Southern society, Native Americans often failed to distinguish white from black. For the Indians, it was easy to associate the coming of the black with the coming of the white. Anglos and Africans lived and worked together. They often fought the Indians together. According to historian Kenneth Porter, the Comanche Indians "regarded white and Negro settler alike with ferocious antipathy and even contempt."[52] In time, fugitive slaves might convince the Indians that they were not the willing allies of the whites. But runaway slaves did not always get such time. In 1845, soon after the Indian trader George Barnard arrived in the Upper Bra-zos River Valley, a number of free white traders and their Indian employees returned runaway slaves to Barnard in exchange for financial rewards.[53]

Similarly, for black slaves, it was easy to see the Indians, as their white masters did, as a threat to their well-being. Ex-slave Green Sims recalled, "In dem days de Indians, wuz roaming every-whar, an' hit made us feel uneasy."[54] Porter remarked that the rela-tionship most likely to develop in initial encounters between blacks and Indians was one of "unalloyed mutual hostility."[55] Henry Caufield's report of the two blacks killed at the hands of the Comanche in 1858 was not unique. In 1839, hostile Indians murdered an enslaved servant of Hamilton White while he was hauling lumber from Bastrop to Austin.[56] At the same time, in Central Texas, Indians killed an enslaved member of a surveying crew.[57] In 1843, a group of Indians murdered a slave in Milam County. In Bosque County, Texas Ranger Buck Barry recalled that in 1857, the Indians "killed a man named Bean and his negro man."[58] When assailed by Native Americans, Afri-can slaves showed no hesitancy in responding in kind. In 1839, an armed Fannin County slave named Smith successfully defended himself when three Indians attacked him in a cornfield. In 1842, an enslaved woman died fighting Indians at Caney Creek.[59]

Other former slaves, however, remembered positive relations with friendly Native Americans. Ex-slave Amos Clark hunted with Indians in Central Texas.[60] Not all the Indians in Texas proved hostile to the Southern settlers or blacks. Anderson Jones remembered that "dey wuz de East Texas Indians mostly, an' most of dem wuz friendly Indians. . . . My gran-mammy being a Choctaw Indian could talk to some of dem."[61] Slaves learned to distinguish between the various types of Native Americans in Texas. Although they rightly feared and avoided the more hostile Indians, African Americans culled relationships with their more amicable neighbors on the frontier.

Occasionally, slaves did more than establish a friendly relationship with the Indians. A number of fugitive slaves, in fact, became accepted members of Native American societies. As one former slave recalled, "De Brazos bottom wuz a good place for de run-a-way slaves to hide an' sometimes dey would cum from way down in Texas an' live up in de Tehuacana an' de Brazos bottom wid de Indians."[62] Why was Central Texas such a "good place" for blacks and Indians? One reason was that, by the mid-nineteenth century, there was already a long history of interaction between fugitive slaves and the Indians of the Texas prairies. During the eighteenth century, slaves from French and Spanish Louisiana escaped westward and sought refuge among the Indians.[63] In 1770, the Louisiana government demanded that the Indian chiefs of East Texas arrest and bring back any and all blacks found in their territory or that of their neighbors, the Indians of the Texas prairies.[64] While Plains Indians, such as the Comanche, may not have understood that blacks and whites were far from willing allies, many of the Indians of East and Central Texas knew from decades of experience about the peculiar relationship between Anglos and Africans.

Evidence of blacks peacefully acclimated to Indian life can be found at least as early as 1834. Two years before the Texas revolt against Mexican rule, a party of whites encountered an escaped slave living with the Tawehash Indians in Northeast Texas. He had been initially captured by the Comanche, but perhaps because they had little experience with Africans, they gave him to their Tawehash allies. The fugitive servant told the whites that the Indians "had treated him well [and] had given him corn mellons, Buffaloe meat etc. to eat." The Anglos themselves noticed that "he appeared very well satisfied with his situation" because the Indians required "of him nothing but to graze their horses."[65] After some interrogation, the slave admitted that "he had his own horse & Indian equipment & was much better contented there than at home."[66] Although the Anglo party probably restored this slave to his master, more enduring examples of black adoption into Indian societies can be found. For example, four years later, Anglos encountered a black man acting as a translator for a party of Cherokee Indians, who were then living on the east bank of the Brazos River in Central Texas.[67] In 1840, an Anglo in Red River County reported that "negros have been seen with the Hostile Indians and Mexicans on our frontier."[68] In August 1848, the Annual Report of the Commissioner of Indian Affairs noted that "a fine looking gentleman of color, somewhat inclined to be bowlegged, also very dark . . . says his name is Abraham, and belongs to John Ecleson on the Brazos, near Nashville" was in camp with a band of Wacoans and other Indians of the Texas prairies.[69]

So successful were some of these fugitive slaves in adapting to Indian society, they were able to establish families and attain positions of leadership in their new culture. Sophia Bereall's father was an Indian chief and her mother an escaped slave. Had she been born in white society, her mother's status would have meant her enslavement. But Bereall was born in Indian society. She married an Indian and did not enter white society until after the Civil War.[70] In 1837, a group of Indians and a black man—"a large Negro who was looked upon with great respect by the tribe and seemed to hold undisputed dominion with the chief himself"—appeared in Houston and shocked the racial sensibilities of resident Anglos.[71] In 1852, Anglos discovered a black woman who had been so thoroughly adopted by the Comanche that she had given birth to four children of Indian and African ancestry.[72] Despite a common current of hostility between Indians and blacks, a number of fugitive slaves managed to cross the cultural divide and start a new life among the Native Americans.[73]

In some instances, fugitive slaves did more than merely trade white society for Indian society. On rare occasions, rebellious slaves used their connections with Native Americans to wreak havoc on Anglo society. Individual slaves sometimes committed acts of violence before fleeing to the Texas interior and their (hopeful) Indian allies. Edward Jenkins was reportedly killed by "a half-Negro, half-Indian slave of Moses Rousseau" who "was never again heard from in civilized circles, it was supposed that he joined the Indians or was killed by them."[74] While the inability to bring such criminals to justice angered slaveholders, more fearsome combinations of Indians and blacks haunted the Anglo-Texans. For example, fugitive slaves, Coushatta, Caddos, and Keechies all fought against General Burleson at Kickapoo Town in 1838. A year later, blacks and Biloxi Indians joined forces with Cordova in his attempted insurrection.[75] On 1 August 1841, a party of blacks and Indians attacked a family of white settlers in Fannin County. The settlers repulsed their assailants, killing "a big burly negro."[76] Although such attacks remained infrequent at best, the threat of black and Indian unions prompted concern among Anglo-Texans.

While such alliances were indeed uncommon, it would be difficult to dispute that relations between blacks and Indians on the Texas frontier differed considerably from both black-white and white-Indian interactions. George Woolfolk argued long ago that "the Indian in the western borderlands was to afford the Negro, slave or free, a fruitful alternative to personal discrimination and spiritual emasculation."[77] Although Woolfolk may have overstated his case, the Indians did undoubtedly provide such an alternative for a small number of blacks. Nevertheless, Kenneth Porter probably provided a more balanced assessment of contact between blacks and Indians on the Texas frontier when he noted "a general pattern of mutual hostility."

Even Porter, however, reasoned that the few "examples of cooperation" proved that black-Indian hostility was based more on cultural conflict than on racial prejudice.[78]

Cooperation between blacks and Indians had deep repercussions for Central Texas slave society. Although most blacks and most Indians did not join together in some romantic uprising on the Central Texas frontier, Native Americans—by providing an alternative toward which slaves could flee, by occasionally welcoming blacks into their community, and by inhibiting the development of the controls necessary for any slave society—disrupted the most important domestic institution of Central Texas. The evidence for increased slave resistance, at least as presented in this article so far, has come largely from Central Texas. Subsequent research may reveal that other parts of Texas also played host to high levels of slave flight, but it is certain that several characteristics of late antebellum Central Texas greatly enhanced the ability of that region's enslaved men and women to resist their bondage.

The physical environment of the Upper Brazos River Valley itself was one important factor in encouraging slave flight in the area. Before undertaking the long trip to Mexico or allying with Texas' nomadic Indians, Central Texas slaves had to first elude the determined pursuit of local slave catchers. In this early stage of slave flight, Central Texas' wooded hills, forested river bottoms, plentiful game, and abundant wild plants proved to be key advantages. Indeed, George Barnard's records concerning the recapture of runaways indicate that fugitive slaves had already recognized the environmental benefits of Central Texas before white settlers even reached the area. Willis Easter recalled that the river bottoms of the Upper Brazos River Valley "wuz good hidin' places on er count ob de caves an' woods in de hills."[79] As important as the environment of the Upper Brazos River Valley may have been, it was not the sole reason for Central Texas' high rate of slave resistance. Many other areas in Texas and in the US South possessed such environmental advantages but had lower rates of slave flight. In fact, the geography of some of these areas was no doubt superior to Central Texas for eluding pursuit. Conducive terrain may have been necessary, but it was not, by itself, sufficient to bring about high levels of slave flight.

Low population density was one factor that set Central Texas apart from other regions in the slaveholding South. Central Texas, located on the ninety-eighth meridian, was the farthest region west where plantation agriculture proved profitable during the antebellum period. Although settlers had known for a long time that the fertile Upper Brazos River Valley could produce large amounts of cotton, readily available lands closer to the Atlantic and Gulf Coasts and difficulties with hostile Indians limited growth in the region. As late as 1850, the entire region above the falls of the Brazos River—an area of some three hundred thousand square miles— held less than nine thousand people.[80] At a time when the population density of the entire slaveholding South was more than ten residents per square mile, the prairies of Central Texas held less than one person for every three square miles.[81] During the next ten years, thousands of Anglo immigrants with thousands of slaves arrived in Central Texas. Nevertheless, the population density of the Upper Brazos River Valley in 1860 reached only 4.11 residents per square mile and still lagged far behind that found in other slaveholding states. Even when compared to other slaveholding areas in Texas, Central Texas maintains a significantly lower density of population (see tables 2.1 and 2.2).

Low population densities in Central Texas significantly benefited fugitive slaves. In places like antebellum Central Texas, where there were immense distances between the farms of the few free citizens, a fugitive slave's chances of eluding white

TABLE 2.1. POPULATION DENSITIES OF SELECTED SLAVEHOLDING STATES, 1860[82]

State	Number of residents per square mile
Alabama	18.65
Arkansas	8.19
Florida	2.40
Georgia	17.95
Kentucky	28.60
Louisiana	14.92
Mississippi	16.59
Missouri	16.96
North Carolina	18.85
South Carolina	22.62
Tennessee	26.33
Texas	2.26 (includes unsettled western Texas)
Virginia	24.56
Totals	12.92

TABLE 2.2. POPULATION DENSITIES OF SELECTED SLAVEHOLDING REGIONS IN TEXAS, 1860[83]

Region of Texas	Number of residents per square mile
Upper Brazos River Valley	4.11
South-Central Texas	5.48
Middle Brazos River Valley	7.39
Lower Brazos River Valley	9.08
Northeast Texas	10.47

patrols greatly increased. All slave owners depend on the use of power and violence to maintain appropriate discipline, prevent rebellions, and deter flight. Outside of his or her plantation, the reach of a Central Texas slaveholder's power was greatly limited. Unlike their fellow slave owners in the older settled slave states, Central Texas slaveholders could not rely, at least initially, on the vigilance of organized white patrols, the institutions of local government, or even an abundance of neighbors in their quest to recapture escaped slaves.

In detailing the advantages for slave resistance in Central Texas, however, there is an even more important one than low population density. The most important advantage that Central Texas possessed over other slaveholding areas in the American South was its borderlands position between Mexico, the US South, and the multiple nations of Indians living in the American West. I am not the first to single out the borderlands characteristics of Central Texas. In 1929, Walter Prescott Webb described Central Texas, particularly the area around Waco, as the meeting ground for "all the elements of the two forces which were contending for the soil of Texas."[84] Webb meant that the Upper Brazos River Valley was a focus for Texas' Anglo-Indian conflicts, but Neil Foley has recently broadened this understanding of Central Texas as a cultural crossroads. In *The White Scourge: Mexicans, Blacks and Poor Whites in Texas Cotton Culture*, Foley describes Central Texas as the region where the "cultural elements of the South, West and Mexico have come to form a unique borderlands culture."[85] Although Foley and Webb were not concerned with the conflict between masters and slaves, their observations about the region are important. Although it was not the region of the state closest to the Mexican border, and it was not even the region of the state closest to the Indian Territory that is now present-day Oklahoma, it was the region in the best position to take advantage of both such borders. When combined with the fact that Central Texas was nearer to the Plains Indians than any other slaveholding region in the American South, one begins to appreciate the opportunities that slaves possessed in the region.

Slaveholders did not readily accept the enhanced power of their slaves in Central Texas. They never believed that the advantages held by fugitive slaves in the region were insurmountable, and they took steps from the beginning to protect their investments in slave labor. First, they turned to the power of their state government to help them corral their rebellious slaves. In the very first Congress of the Republic of Texas in 1837, lawmakers assigned the most severe penalty to the crime of aiding and abetting fugitive slaves: "Every person who shall steal or entice away any slave, out of or from the possession of the owner or owners of such slave, shall be deemed guilty of felony, and on conviction thereof, shall suffer death."[86] Over the next twenty years, the Texas legislature continued to pass regulations designed to limit the ability of slaves to escape their bondage. In 1840, the legislature declared that slaves could not carry deadly weapons with the written permission of their master, mistress, or overseer. In 1841, lawmakers authorized the sale of any free blacks caught aiding runaway slaves. The Seventh Legislature of the State of Texas passed "An Act To Encourage the

Reclamation of Slaves Escaping Beyond the Slave Territories of the United States."
This law provided that slave hunters would be given one-third the value of any slave
they could bring to Travis County who had escaped beyond the slave territories
of the United States.[87]

Although these slave codes undoubtedly hindered runaways, they did not immediately lead to a significant decline in the number of successful escapes. Not until
the middle of the 1850s did slaveholders finally succeed in ending Texas' heightened
opportunities for slave flight. One of the reasons that it became more difficult to
flee bondage in Texas was the addition of covert military action to the other strategies pursued by the Anglo-Texans. For example, in May 1850, a Central Texas man
named McIntere, growing tired of the problem and the inability of the governments
to control the escape of fugitive slaves, crossed the border with some accomplices
and, after a violent encounter with local residents, forcibly recovered a fugitive slave.[88]

While these individual actions reminded escaped slaves that their freedom was
never certain, even in Mexico, it took more organized action to turn the tide of
runaways from the border. By 1855, the Anglo-Texans had decided that, despite
the illegality of crossing the border, a direct attack on the fugitive slave colonies
in Mexico was needed. One settlement in particular aroused the hatred of the
Anglos, the black Seminole colony led by John Horse and under the protection
of Wild Cat's Seminole Indians. In the early 1850s, these Mexican colonies lured
runaway slaves from their plantations in Texas, Arkansas, and Louisiana. In 1855,
after several years of diplomatic and political failure to halt the migration, Anglo-
Texans planned a covert strike across the Mexican border to recapture their human
property. Using the excuse that they were trailing marauding Indians, an expedition
led by Texas Ranger Capt. James Callahan crossed the Mexican border in hopes
of capturing runaway slaves. After a clash with the Seminoles, both black and Indian,
Callahan retreated to Piedras Negras. Eventually, he fled after plundering the village. According to a report issued by the Mexican government nearly twenty years
after the invasion, "The pretext was the pursuit of the tribe of Lipan Indians of
whom the Texans complained . . . [but it] is probable, nevertheless, that one of the
incentives was the capture of fugitive slaves."[89] Historian Ronnie C. Tyler demonstrated persuasively in 1967 that the capture of escaped slaves was the primary
mission of Callahan's foray. Although the expedition recaptured no fugitive slaves,
Callahan sent a message to Mexican officials and to potential fugitives that the Texans would respond with force to recover their property.[90] Mexican officials, cognizant
of the Callahan raid, became less interested in harboring fugitives and irritating
militant Texans. Perhaps more important, the United States, wary of embarrassing
border problems, stationed more troops on the border and made it more difficult
for slave flight.

While the Anglos attempted to seal off Mexico, the so-called frontier defense
harassed the Indians living in Central Texas. Native Americans, engaged in this losing war with whites, retreated farther and farther west. The removal of the Indians

both eliminated a potential ally for runaway slaves and made patrolling the Central Texas frontier easier for white slaveholders.

The most important factor in diminishing opportunities for slave runaways, however, may have been the growth of the white population in Central Texas. In 1844, George Barnard, an Indian trader, had been one of the first whites to settle in the Upper Brazos River Valley. In the five years following the 1845 annexation, Texas' population increased by 40 percent, from approximately 120,000 whites and 30,000 slaves to 154,431 free people and 58,161 slaves. In the 1850s, the population continued to explode. By 1860, the Upper Brazos River Valley had grown from one permanent Anglo settler (George Barnard) and a handful of runaway slaves to 10,409 whites and 5,054 blacks. Although the population density of Central Texas still trailed other slaveholding regions, the flood of white and black settlers had greatly changed the character of the valley. Not only were there more and more white people available to pursue runaways, but the increase in population had eliminated the large game that made life on the run easier.[91]

The changing fate of George Barnard and the city of Waco epitomized the shifting conditions of the Central Texas frontier. First, in 1849, Barnard decided to move his Indian trading post farther northwest, to a location more convenient to his Native American customers. Second, seeing that he could profit from the incoming white and black population, Barnard set up a second trading post in the just-established city of Waco.[92] First established in 1849, the city of Waco became one of the symbols of the growing stability of Central Texas. Although Waco's population remained small in the decade preceding the Civil War, the Brazos city was the political and religious center of the Upper Brazos River Valley. Waco became a meeting ground for local whites. On the steps of the courthouse, in their houses of worship, and along the aisles of the trade stores, local planters and farmers learned of the Indians, heard of runaway slaves, and debated ways to solve these problems. Within a few years, the talk began to take the form of action.[93]

During the 1850s, Central Texas slaveholders consciously began to limit the slaves' routes to freedom.[94] In East Waco, Anglos constructed a whipping post and an auction block to loom as physical symbols of their desire to crack down on slave resistance.[95] In June 1855, Waco began construction of the city's first jail, in part so that they would have a place to deposit recaptured slaves.[96] Prior to the arrival of the Waco jail, Central Texas facilities for detaining fugitives had been barely adequate. James Barry, sheriff of Bosque County, recorded numerous difficulties with runaway slaves in Central Texas. On 24 June 1855, Barry imprisoned a fugitive slave named Peter. The wooden jail, in truth, probably held more resemblance to a barn. Peter soon escaped from this less-than-secure prison. A local man named William Lockhart, however, recaptured the runaway. Peter's misfortune, however, did not deter him from continuing to test the strength of his jail. Late one night, Barry awoke "alarmed about 12 or 1 oclock of a Negro named Peter set fire to the jail and was about to burn up in it." Barry doused the fire and had the rebellious arsonist "whipped severely."[97] The resistance of fugitives such as Peter convinced Central Texas slaveholders that their tax dollars were well spent on a more reliable jail in Waco.

Two years later, Central Texas slaveholders took an even more important step. In early 1857, the planters of the Upper Brazos River Valley had become strong enough to institute formal restraints on slave resistance. In January, the city council of Waco approved measures to check the runaway slave problem. No doubt based on their previous experiences in slaveholding communities, Wacoans authorized funding for two patrols of four persons, one for each side of the city. The men, who patrolled from nine in the evening until daylight, received five dollars every week. The council instructed them to "suffer any negro to pass unmolested who shall have a special pass" but to jail all others about. Before imprisoning the escaped slaves, however, the patrols frequently subjected the fugitive to "a penalty of thirty-nine stripes."[98] The master of each slave confined to jail would be fined one dollar.[99]

As the power of slaveholders expanded in Central Texas, their influence grew on the state level as well. Between 1850 and 1860, the number of slaveholders in the Texas legislature rose from 38.8 percent to 54.3 percent. At the same time, the number of seats held by the richest slaveholders—planters who owned at least twenty slaves—jumped from a mere five in 1850 to twenty-five ten years later.[100]

Frederick Law Olmsted wrote that "the proximity of the frontier, suggesting and making easy the escape of slaves" had hindered the settlement of the Texas interior. By the mid-1850s, white immigration had finally checked this problem by giving rise to state and local governments with enough institutional coercive power to discipline Texas' rebellious slaves. This growing power collapsed virtually all the opportunities for slave flight once provided by the Texas frontier. As in the rest of the South, however, little opportunity to escape slavery did not mean the end of slave resistance. For African Americans, the growing strength of slave society did not lead to submission but rather led to a change in strategy.

Few Texas slaves have left behind written documents that allow us to know what they were thinking in the mid-1850s about the attempts of their Anglo masters to limit their ability to escape slavery. Whites, however, did record the actions of some Texas slaves in this critical period. By carefully considering how slaves reacted to the changing character of the frontier, the ethnohistorian can gain some insight into what they thought about their transforming world.

In 1856, slave resistance in Texas departed from a two-decade-old pattern. For the twenty years following the conclusion of the Texas Revolution, the most common form of slave resistance had been slave flight. Not since 1835 had Texas played host to even an aborted slave insurrection.[101] All that changed in 1856.

On 9 September 1856, John H. Robson, H. A. Tatum, and J. H. Hicks of Colorado County in South-Central Texas sent a letter to a variety of newspapers in Texas with the heading "Contemplated Servile Rising in Texas." The letter of the Vigilance Committee does not say how they learned of the plot, but their "suspicions were aroused" in the last week of August. The slaveholders of this mid-Brazos county formed a Vigilance Committee "to ferret out the whole matter." They uncovered "a well-organized and systematized plan for the murder of our white population, with the exception of the young ladies, who were to be taken captives, and made the wives of the diabolical murderers of their parents and friends." The rebellion was set to begin late at night on 6 September. The slaves, in groups ranging from two to ten, were to go to nearly every house in the county, kill the white men, plunder their homes, take "their horses and arms" and fight their way to a "free state," believed to be Mexico by the Vigilance Committee. The Vigilance Committee believed that two hundred slaves were involved in the conspiracy, and they punished all these rebels with whippings so severe that two died from the lash. Three of the insurrection's leaders were hung. According to the Vigilance Committee, the entire Mexican popu- lation of Colorado County "was implicated," and "they were arrested, and ordered to leave the county within five days, and never again to return, under the penalty of death."[102] The LaGrange *True Issue* reported on 5 September that the Colorado County slaves "had organized into companies of various sizes, had adopted secret signs and passwords, sworn never to divulge the plot under penalty of death, and had elected captains and subordinate officers to command the respective companies."[103]

Although the 1835 slave revolt during the Texas Revolution may have come closer to fruition, the aborted Colorado County rebellion was probably the most extensive plot ever concocted on Texas soil. Yet it may not have stood alone in 1856. Over the last three months of 1856, three additional slave plots were uncovered in Texas. In October, in Lavaca County, a white man was given one hundred lashes after confess- ing to his role in a plot set for 31 October in which local slaves would rebel, kill their masters if necessary, and flee to Mexico. A month later, a slave betrayed the plans of his enslaved comrades in DeWitt, Lavaca, and Victoria Counties. Apparently, the slaves had already taken the first step in their plot—killing all the dogs in the neighborhood—before their revolt was ended. Later in November, both a Texas and a Louisiana newspaper reported on a vague slave plot between the slaves of East Texas and Louisiana.[104]

The evidence for these later plots is quite limited, and escalating white fear— more than increased black rebelliousness—may have had more to do with the reports of these slave insurrections.[105] Such a panic was certainly behind the alleged slave uprisings that occurred in Texas in 1860. The plots of late 1856, however, may have indeed occurred. On 17 January, the Galveston *News* admitted that some of the evidence for the recent plots was "very unsatisfactory" but argued nonetheless that never "has there been a time in our recollection when so many insurrections, or attempts at insurrection, have transpired in rapid succession as during the past six months." The Cherokee County *Texas Enquirer* proclaimed that "servile insurrections seem to be the order of the day in this State."[106] Although we may never be able to say for sure whether or not these additional plots did in fact occur, it seems obvious that whites in late 1856 perceived a growing spirit of resistance among their slaves.

Why would 1856 emerge as the year for slave rebellion in Texas? The power of Texas slaveholders had never been stronger. After Callahan's raid, the welcoming arms of Mexico were not then stretched so widely. Growing numbers of whites made the planning of revolts more difficult. Rather than check insurrections, however, these changes prompted rebellion. Until the mid-1850s, the best chance to escape slavery for discontented Texas bondsmen and women had been flight, either to Mexico or to the Indians. Although escape was never easy, before the mid-1850s, it stood a better chance of success than did a violent assault on the slave owners. Callahan's raid, the continued success of the federal army in fighting the Indians, and white population growth in Central Texas, however, dramatically shifted things. Slave flight became a less realistic option. In 1856, despairing of their dwindling chances for escape from bondage, enslaved men and women began to consider rebellion. A more radical assault on slavery, insurrection was also considerably more dangerous than attempted flight. In the end, Afro-Texans had waited too long to revolt. By the 1850s, Texas slaveholders were too powerful to be toppled. The execution of five slaves in Colorado County reinforced this lesson.

In the early settlement in the Upper Brazos River Valley, slaves sought freedom in Mexico or among the Indians. In the late 1850s, as it became less and less likely that one could escape the reach of their masters, slaves adopted different strategies of resistance. Central Texas slaves increasingly sought refuge in the Upper Brazos River Valley itself. In wooded hills and forested river bottoms, slaves could live off game and wild food and find temporary respite from their bondage. "De Brazos bottom wuz a good place for de run-a-way slaves" concurred George Glasker, and "mos every one of de plantations had some who wuz always runnin' away."[107] The river bottoms were such good hiding places and the Texas frontier so full of game that one slave recalled that fugitives could hide out for as long as a year before returning to their plantation.[108] More commonly, "Some of the negroes would run off an' stay in de woods for weeks at a time," said one ex-slave. "I 'member de furst time my ole mistress got atter me to whup me, I runned off an' stayed four or five days."[109]

Slaves quickly discovered that their ability to flee into the woods of Central Texas was a powerful bargaining chip with their masters. Former slaves often recalled fleeing their plantation in order to protest cruel treatment or overwork. One slave remembered that "we had an overseer so mean de nigger a runned off in de woods."[110] After a violent encounter with their owner, a mother and child fled into the woods for "two or three months."[111] According to ex-slave Caroline Wright, "One slave who ran away . . . he came back when he got ready. He wasn't punished, cause he wasn't mean, jes' lazy." Running away might have even proved a factor in the ability of a master to sell his slaves. One former slave recalled that "I was just makin' up my mind to run off de first chance I got if he did sells me."[112]

Similar patterns of resistance developed throughout the Old South.[113] In Central Texas, however, slaves held more leverage by the virtue of their enhanced ability to resist slavery. During the summer months, Central Texas jails seemed frequent stops for fugitives and their masters.[114] Although comparisons of slave resistance are always difficult, Central Texas slave narratives suggest resistance occurred more frequently in the Upper Brazos River Valley than in the South in general. Thirty out of fifty ex-slaves in Central Texas reported some incidents of resistance (60 percent), considerably more than the rate that Paul Escott found in his study of ex-slaves throughout the South—826 acts of resistance in 2,358 narratives (35.03 percent). Central Texas bondspeople, it appears, resisted more often than slaves across the entire South.[115]

The continued resistance displayed by Central Texas slaves did not please their masters. Slaveholders, after all, had presided over the proliferation of slave patrols, the growth of white settlement, and the rise of institutional controls in the city of Waco. Those masters who attempted to crack down on slave escapes by increasing punishments discovered that they actually encouraged the flight of their slaves. In short, although they had undercut the ability of their slaves to escape slavery permanently, the Upper Brazos River Valley continued to provide a safe haven for rebellious slaves. Realizing that a successful plantation depended on a stable workforce, the wisest slaveholders realized that they could not rely on coercion alone.

In the Upper Brazos River Valley, planters were forced to confront the fact that, even with the growth of white settlement in the 1850s, slaves in Central Texas possessed more power to resist bondage than elsewhere. Although there were a great many more whites in Central Texas in 1860 than ten years earlier, the population density of Central Texas was still far lower than any other slaveholding state. Although some owners sought to curb slave resistance through harsher and more frequent punishments, increasingly, many slaveholders came to realize that they would have to make concessions to their slaves. Planters learned and the slave narratives confirm that punishment often led to slave flight. Many Central Texas masters sought a more effective means of personally controlling their slave populations. They found that they could better reduce slave resistance by giving into certain demands made by their slaves than by increasing their punishment. After ex-slave Allen V. Manning arrived in Central Texas, he remembered that his master "seem like he changed a lot since we left Mississippi, and seem like he paid more attention to us and looked after us better."[116] Former slave Henry Childers remarked that his master had fewer problems than others in Central Texas because he "wuz a good Master an' [therefore] his slaves wuz not always a runnin' away like [s]ome did."[117]

Travelers who visited Texas remarked that the slaves in the state possessed intolerable levels of rights and freedoms. One white woman reported that she had heard that in Texas "the [N]egroes are as much respected as the whites and go on their fines horses."[118] In Central Texas, many masters employed their slaves to handle stock. One ex-slave from Central Texas recalled that "some ob de slaves wuz trained ter be good cowboys as dey call de ones dat ter cattle on de range." Giles Cotton, an enslaved servant of Central Texan Logan Stroud, "was allowed to own a wagon and a team of mules, and did haul supplies from the port of Galveston to" Central

Texas.[119] Jasper McMullins, a slave in Hill County, traveled on several occasions to New Orleans with herds of cattle. After selling the cattle, he returned to his master with the profits. McMullins's owner allowed his trusted slave to own "several head of cattle and to retain any profits that came from their sale."[120]

The ability to ride horses, however, was limited neither to work duties nor to an elite group of slaves on each plantation. Henry Masters allowed some of his slaves to ride horses for recreational purposes. After being apprised that two of his slaves had been out riding horses all night long, "he jes' laff and laff," saying "Sam an' Moor allus git time to git ter de fiel." Even though their owner furnished them with passes, Sam and Moore enjoyed outrunning the slave patrols. One of the Masters family's ex-slaves recalled that such antics led "our neighbors" to "all call dem Marster's free niggers."[121]

With twenty-three slaves in 1860, E. C. Zollicoffer was the fourth largest slave owner in Hill County. None of the Zollicoffer slaves worked as field hands, instead tending to stock on horseback.[122] Former slave Tobe Zollicoffer had been trained to herd cattle. Riding Jim—his favorite "cutting horse"—and roaming throughout the Texas hills, Tobe possessed rights and privileges not dreamed of by slaves in the Deep South. Tobe recalled that "the Zollicofer slaves were only whipped when they didn't obey orders and then not very hard like some white owners did."[123] Although we may not think of someone who beat his workers as benevolent, E. C. Zollicoffer's slaves seemingly accepted his compromise. Zollicoffer may have realized that the intense control necessary for gang labor would have meant constant battle with his bondsmen and women. In allowing his slaves more independence and freedom than found on most plantations, Zollicoffer succeeded in minimizing such conflict by getting his slaves to accept their improved positions.

A less common but more surprising facet of slave life on the Texas frontier was the preponderance of slaves allowed to carry firearms daily. Slave-owner Moses Johnson "had allowed [his slave, Brit Johnson] the *enlarged liberty which belongs to the frontier*, often relying upon his strong arm to help defend the family and neighborhood from the raids of hostile Indians [my italics]."[124] In 1838, a slave named Tom—wielding a gun and an ax—protected his mistress from the threatened attack of Tonkawa Indians.[125] In 1839, a Fannin County slave named Smith successfully defended himself from attack by Indians because his master had armed him with a gun and a knife.[126] Armistead, the enslaved servant of Wacoan Shapley Ross, drove off an Indian attack with a rifle given to him by his master.[127] On one level, the threat of Indian attacks made arming one's slaves in Texas quite logical. Yet Texas lawmakers passed codes limiting such behavior because of the difficulties of dealing with armed fugitive slaves. In the final analysis, only the dangers of the most remote parts of the Indian frontier were able to overcome the slaveholders' common fear of arming their slaves.

The existence of greater privileges for Texas slaves does not, however, necessarily indicate that paternalism was a stronger or a more important part of slave life on the frontier. By the time that Central Texas slave owners reasserted control over their African bondsmen and bondswomen, the slaves of the Upper Brazos River Valley had already revealed the tenuous nature of the master-slave relationship. The most important lesson we learn from the slaves of Central Texas may be one about the slaves of Mississippi, Alabama, and Georgia. The rebellious slaves of the Upper Brazos River Valley came from every Southern state. Yet these newly arrived Texans reported nearly twice as much resistance to slavery as did their brethren in the earlier-settled states. What the slaves of the Upper Brazos River Valley had that the slaves of Georgia, Alabama, and Mississippi did not was opportunity—the opportunity to successfully resist their enslavement. The history of slavery in Central Texas does not suggest that paternalism did not exist in the older settled states of the South. What the history of bondage in Central Texas reveals is that paternalism in these states was, for a large number of slaves, contingent on the particular conditions of their enslavement. Simply put, paternalism was directly linked to the paucity of opportunities for successful resistance throughout the Deep South. If the slaves of the Old South failed to rise up in a large-scale rebellion, the story of slave flight in Texas assures us that it had nothing to do with the character of the African American slave and everything to do with the power of white Southerners.

This article was originally published as Carrigan, William Dean. "Slavery on the Frontier: The Peculiar Institution in Central Texas." Slavery and Abolition 20 (August 1999): 63–86. Reprinted by permission of the author and the publisher Taylor and Francis Ltd., http://www.tandfonline.com.

NOTES

1. Frederick Law Olmsted, *A Journey through Texas: Or, a Saddle-Trip on the Southwestern Frontier* (New York: Dix, Edwards, 1857), 123.
2. The editor of the *San Antonio Ledger*, quoted in Olmsted, *Journey through Texas*, 332.
3. Paul Adams, "Amelia Barr in Texas, 1856–1868," *Southwestern Historical Quarterly* 49 (1946): 367.
4. Of the notable exceptions to this statement, all were published over twenty years ago. See Kenneth Wiggins Porter, *The Negro on the American Frontier* (New York: Arno Press, 1971); Ronnie C. Tyler, "Slave Owners and Runaway Slaves in Texas" (MA thesis, Texas Christian University, 1966); Ronnie C. Tyler, "Fugitive Slaves in Mexico," *Journal of Negro History* 57 (January 1972): 1–12; Wendell G. Addington, "Slave Insurrections in Texas," *Journal of Negro History* 35 (1950): 414–18; and George Ruble Woolfolk, *The Free Negro in Texas, 1800–1860: A Study in Cultural Compromise* (published for the *Journal of Mexican American History* by University Microfilms International, 1976).
5. Randolph B. Campbell, *An Empire for Slavery: The Peculiar Institution in Texas* (Baton Rouge: Louisiana State University Press, 1989), 258, 257.

6. Eugene D. Genovese, *Roll, Jordan, Roll: The World the Slaves Made* (New York: Vintage, 1974), 648.

7. Among the most important recent scholars to buck this trend and focus on the southern frontier are Joan Cashin, *Family Venture: Men and Women on the Southern Frontier* (New York: Oxford University Press, 1991); James Oakes, *Slavery and Freedom: An Interpretation of the Old South* (New York: Vintage, 1990); and James Miller, "South by Southwest: Planter Emigration and Elite Ideology in the Deep South, 1815–1861" (PhD dissertation, Emory University, 1996).

8. David J. Weber, *The Spanish Frontier in North America* (New Haven: Yale University Press, 1992), 13.

9. I take my definition of the frontier from Weber, *Spanish Frontier*. Weber defines the frontier as a zone of cultural interaction. It should be noted that this definition differs significantly from a conception of the frontier as a new, "open" wilderness awaiting the next generation of immigrants to tame it, the view held by many of the white and black settlers coming to Central Texas.

10. Central Texas, as defined by historical geographer D. W. Meinig, extends south of the present-day city of Dallas to a southwestern corner at San Antonio and a southeastern corner in Houston. Its western border extends along the line where the Texas prairies meet the Great Plains, and the eastern border corresponds roughly to the Trinity River. The heart of the region lies along the banks of the Brazos River, but it is important to point out that the long-settled plantation counties of the Lower Brazos River Valley are not included in Central Texas.

Although I believe that my findings will prove valid for this entire region, I have not attempted a rigorous analysis of such a sprawling region. Instead, I have focused upon the heart of Central Texas, the region as it extends above the falls of the Brazos River to the edge of the Plains. In particular, I have focused my research on the counties of McLennan, Falls, Bosque, and Hill. I believe that these four counties embrace as best as possible the characteristics of greater Central Texas. D. W. Meinig, *Imperial Texas: An Interpretive Essay in Cultural Geography* (Austin: University of Texas at Austin Press, 1969), 93, 108–9.

11. The recent overview of United States slavery by Peter Kolchin, *American Slavery, 1619–1877* (New York: Hill and Wang, 1993), mentions the increased likelihood of successful slave flight from the border states but does not mention the western frontier in regards to slave resistance. John Blassingame's path-breaking work, *The Slave Community: Plantation Life in the Antebellum South* (New York: Oxford University Press, 1972), revealed that resistance was commonplace in the Old South, but he largely failed to consider change over time or within the subregions of the Old South. The same can also be said of the work of Genovese, *Roll, Jordan, Roll*; and Robert Fogel, *Without Consent or Contract: The Rise and Fall of American Slavery* (New York: W. W. Norton, 1989). With regard to the chronology of slave resistance, most Southern historians either ignore the subject altogether or suggest a decline in resistance after Nat Turner's rebellion. The notable exception is Herbert Aptheker, *American Negro Slave Revolts*

(New York: International Publishers, 1943).

12. In 1860, the four Central Texas counties of Falls, McLennan, Bosque, and Hill held 10,409 whites, 5,054 slaves and 11 free blacks. In 1860, those same four counties totaled 597 slaveholders. A sample of the manuscript returns of McLennan County found that one of every three heads of household were slave owners. United States Bureau of the Census, *Population of the United States in 1860: Compiled from the Original Returns of the Eighth Census* (Washington, DC: Government Printing Office, 1864), 472–81; United States Bureau of the Census, *Agriculture of the United States in 1860: Compiled from the Original Returns of the Eighth Census* (Washington, DC: Government Printing Office, 1864), 240–41; Manuscript Returns of the Bureau of the Census, Eighth Census of the United States, 1860, schedule 1 (Free Population) and schedule 2 (Slaveholdings), McLennan County, Texas.

13. Campbell, *Empire for Slavery*; David J. Weber, *The Mexican Frontier, 1821–1846: The American Southwest under Mexico* (Albuquerque: University of New Mexico Press, 1982); Weber, *Spanish Frontier*; and Paul D. Lack, *The Texas Revolutionary Experience: A Political and Social History, 1835–1836* (College Station: Texas A&M University Press, 1835–1836).

14. Sworn statement of A. J. Yates, I. N. Moreland, and A. C. Allen, August 29, 1835, in John H. Jenkins, ed., *The Papers of the Texas Revolution*, vol. 1 (Austin: Presidial Press, 1973), 376–78.

15. James H. C. Miller to the Public, September, 1835, in Jenkins, *Papers of the Texas Revolution*, vol. 6, 517.

16. Benjamin R. Milam to Francis W. Johnson, Punto Lampasos, July 5, 1835, in Eugene C. Barker, ed., *The Austin Papers*, Vol.III (Austin: University of Texas Press, 1927), 82–83; Horatio Allsberry to the Public, Columbia, 28 August 1835, in Barker, *Austin Papers*, 107–8.

17. William Parker to Editor of the Free Trader, Natchez, 29 April 1836, in Jenkins, *Papers of the Texas Revolution*, vol. 6, 123.

18. Antonio Lopez de Santa Anna to Jose Maria Tomel, 16 February 1836, in Carlos Castafieda, trans., *The Mexican Side of the Texas Revolution* (Washington, DC: Documentary Publications, 1971), 65.

19. Jose Enrique de la Pella, *With Santa Anna in Texas: A Personal Narrative of the Revolution* (College Station: Texas A&M University Press, 1975), 104.

20. Ibid., 179.

21. "Reminiscences of Ann Raney Thomas Coleman," Ann Raney Thomas Coleman Papers, Center for American History, University of Texas at Austin.

22. Henderson and Jamison to Editor, *Colorado Gazette and Advertiser*, January 8, 1840, cited in John Milton Nance, *After San Jacinto: The Texas-Mexican Frontier, 1836–1841* (Austin: University of Texas Press, 1963).

23. Lack, *Texas Revolutionary Experience*, 245.

24. B. J. White to Stephen F. Austin, October 17, 1835, in Barker, *Austin Papers*, 190. No evidence exists, to my knowledge, that any state government ever compensated the slave owners whose servants were executed for their roles in the 1835 slave revolt.

25. Porter, *American Frontier*, 381.

26. Frank W. Johnson, *A History of Texas and Texans*, vol. 1 (Chicago: American Historical Society, 1914), 515.

27. Quoted in Campbell, *Empire for Slavery*, 180.

28. Olmsted, *Journey through Texas*, 256–57.

29. Quoted in Campbell, *Empire for Slavery*, 63.

30. For the above estimates, see Tyler, "Runaway Slaves in Texas," 22; Campbell, *Empire for Slavery*, 180, and Olmsted, *Journey through Texas*, 324.

31. *The Southwest* (Waco, TX), 16 January 1861.

32. Alwyn Barr, *Black Texans: A History of African Americans in Texas, 1528–1995* (Norman: University of Oklahoma Press, 1996), 28–29.

33. George Barnard Papers, Manuscript Division, Texas Collection, Baylor University, Texas; also see John K. Strecker, "Chronicles of George Barnard," *Baylor University Bulletin* 5 (September 1928): 14–15. This points to one of the most unusual aspects of slave flight in Texas—the fact that groups of fugitive slaves, not just individuals, attempted and succeeded in reaching Mexico. Other examples of this phenomenon include: in 1837, a group of runaways reached Mexico after a violent encounter with the sheriff of Gonzales. The runaways killed the sheriff and left his body so well concealed that it was not found for five years. See Tyler, "Runaway Slaves in Texas," 7–8. Also, in 1845, an even-larger group of fugitives attempted to reach Mexico. On 27 December 1844, a group of twenty-five slaves fled Bastrop for the border. A little over a week later, Anglos near Gonzales caught seventeen of the rebels. Authorities believed that the remaining eight had made good their escape. See Addington, "Slave Insurrections," 414.

34. Wesley Burrell in George P. Rawick, ed., *The American Slave, Supplement,* series 2 (Westport, CT: Greenwood Press, 1979), 534.

35. Nelson Taylor Densen in ibid., 1,172.

36. George Glasker in ibid., 1,505; Although these interviewers indicate that the Mexicans attempted to lure rebellious slaves away, the evidence does not support this statement. More likely, during the reign of Jim Crow, these black interviewees, when questioned by a white about slave resistance, sought to place the responsibility with the Mexicans in order that they would not arouse white suspicions about black rebelliousness.

37. Porter, *American Frontier*, 463.

38. George P. Garrison, *Texas: A Contest of Civilizations* (Boston: Houghton Mifflin, 1903), 273–74.

39. H. S. Thrall, *A History of Texas: From the Earliest Settlements to the Year 1876* (New York: University Publishing, 1876), 146.

40. Olmsted, *Journey through Texas*, 163. For a discussion of Olmsted's reliability as a witness, see Arthur M. Schlesinger, "Was Olmsted an Unbiased Critic of the South?," *Journal of Negro History* 37 (April 1952): 173–87.

41. Tyler, "Runaway Slaves in Texas," 68–69; Addington, "Slave Insurrections," 414–18.

42. Frank H. Smyrl, "Unionism, Abolitionism, and Vigilantism in Texas, 1856–1865" (MA thesis, University of Texas at Austin, 1961), 34.

43. *San Antonio Herald*, February 6, 1858, cited in Arnoldo de León, *Apuntes Tejanos: An Index of Items Related to Mexican Americans in Nineteenth-Century Texas Extracted from the San Antonio Express (1869–1900) and the San Antonio Herald (1855–1878)*, vol. 1 (Ann Arbor: University Microfilms International, 1978).

44. H. McLeod to M. B. Lamar, October
22, 1838, in Harriet Smither, ed., *The
Papers of Mirabeau Buonaparte Lamar*,
vol. 2 (Austin: Von Boeckmann-Jones,
1922), 412–13.

45. J. W. Wilbarger, *Indian Depredations in
Texas* (Austin: Hutchins, 1889), 151–57.

46. Smyrl, "Unionism, Abolitionism, and
Vigilantism," 32.

47. President Wilson in Rawick, *American
Slave*, 4,206.

48. Burke Simpson in ibid., 3,562.

49. George Barnard Papers; also in John
Willingham, "George Barnard: Trader
and Merchant on the Texas Frontier,"
Texana Quarterly 12 (1974): 311; and
Strecker, "Chronicles of George
Barnard," 14.

50. Noah Smithwick, *The Evolution of a
State: Recollections of Old Texas Days*
(Austin: Gammel, 1900), 325–27.

51. Nelson Taylor Densen, a former slave
from Falls County, recalled a host of
violent encounters between the whites
of Central Texas and the Indians.
Densen claimed that in one "fight wid
de Indians," two prominent Central
Texans were killed. In another incident,
Densen remembered that "de house of
Mr. Morgan six miles above de falls ob
de Brazos being attacked by dem, an five
people being killed." In a battle at Brushy
Creek between whites and Indians,
Densen recalls that four prominent
Central Texans died. See Nelson Taylor
Densen in Rawick, *American Slave*, 1,
172–73. Former slave Henry Childers
said that the family that owned him
had to leave their home on three
different occasions because they feared
an Indian raid. See Henry Childers in
Rawick, *American Slave*, 698. Henry
Canfield wrote to his brother in 1858
that "the Indians have been committing
depredations up [near the western end

of the North Bosque River, in the Upper
Brazos River Valley], recently there have
been four white men and two [N]egroes
murdered by them." See Henry Caufield
to Watt Canfield, January 30, 1858,
Caufield Papers, Manuscript Division,
Texas Collection, Baylor University,
Texas.

52. Kenneth Wiggins Porter, "Negroes
and Indians on the Texas Frontier,
1831–1876," *Journal of Negro History* 41,
no. 4 (October 1956): 208–9.

53. George Barnard Papers. Also in
Willingham, "George Barnard," 311;
and Strecker, "Chronicles of George
Barnard," 14.

54. Green Sims in Rawick, *American Slave*,
3,591.

55. Porter, "Negroes and Indians," 208.

56. Wilbarger, *Indian Depredations*,
266–67.

57. Porter, "Negroes and Indians," 210.

58. James K. Greer, ed., *Buck Barry: Texas
Ranger and Frontiersman* (Waco, TX:
Friends of the Moody Texas Ranger
Library, 1978), 96.

59. Porter, "Negroes and Indians," 197–201.

60. Amos Clark in Rawick, *American Slave*,
726–27.

61. Anderson Jones in ibid., 2,068.

62. George Glasker in ibid., 1,505.

63. Runaway slaves in eighteenth-
century Louisiana are discussed in
Gwendolyn Midlo Hall, *Africans in
Colonial Louisiana: The Development
of Afro-Creole Culture in the Eighteenth
Century* (Baton Rouge: Louisiana State
University Press, 1992); and Daniel H.
Unser Jr. *Indians, Settlers, and Slaves
in a Frontier Exchange Economy: The
Lower Mississippi Valley Before 1783*
(Chapel Hill: University of North
Carolina Press, 1992).

64. Unser. *Indians, Settlers, and Slaves*,
58–59, 133.

65. Fred S. Perrine, ed., "The Journal of Hugh Evans," *Chronicles of Oklahoma* 3, no. 3 (September 1925): 194.

66. Porter, "Negroes and Indians," 194.

67. Ibid., 198.

68. W. M. Williams to M. B. Lamar, April 1, 1840, in Harriet Smither, ed., *The Papers of Mirabeau Buonaparte Lamar*, vol. 3 (Austin: Von Boeckmann-Jones, 1921), 361.

69. "Annual Report of the Commissioner of Indian Affairs, 1848," *House Executive Documents*, 30th Congress, 2nd session, I (537), no. 1, 215.

70. Sophia Bereall in "Ex-Slaves in Waco" (unpublished manuscript, Texas Collection, Baylor University [1920?]), 14–15.

71. Andrew Forest Muir, *Texas in 1837: An Anonymous Contemporary Narrative* (Austin: University of Texas Press, 1958).

72. Porter, "Negroes and Indians," 213–14.

73. According to an estimate by the *Houston Telegraph*, 1,500 former slaves were said to have joined the Comanche Indians on the warpath against the Texans. See Aptheker, *Slave Revolts*, 343; as in the *Pennsylvania Freeman*, October 30, 1851.

74. John Holmes Jenkins III, ed., *Recollections of Early Texas* (Austin: University of Texas Press, 1958).

75. H. McLeod to M. B. Lamar, October 22, 1838, in Smither, *Mirabeau Buonaparte Lamar*, vol. 2 (Austin: Von Boeckmann-Jones, 1922), 412–13; Wilbarger, *Indian Depredations*, 151–57.

76. Wilbarger, *Indian Depredations*, 405–11.

77. Woolfolk, *Free Negro in Texas: 1800–1860*, 132.

78. Porter, "Negroes and Indians," 308.

79. Willis Easter in Rawick, *American Slave*, 1,252.

80. An approximate population density of 0.29 for Central Texas in 1850 is found by dividing a total population of 8,629 (the number of residents estimated by the US census for the counties of Robertson, Limestone, Navarro, and Milam in 1850) and dividing it by a square mileage of 300,000, estimated from the map in William Thorndale and William Dollarhide, eds., *Map Guide to the US Federal Census, 1790–1920* (Blaine, WA: Dollarhide Systems, 1987), 329; see J. D. B. DeBow, *The Seventh Census of the United States: 1850, An Appendix* (Washington, DC: Robert Armstrong, Public Printer, 1853).

81. Detailed population-density data for the American South in 1850 can be found in the appendix.

82. See the appendix for expanded statistics concerning population density in the United States South. Statistics for square mileage have been compiled from *The World Almanac and Book of Facts* (New York: Pharos, 1992). Virginia's total includes the square miles listed for Virginia and West Virginia. Population statistics from the US Bureau of the Census, *Population of the United States in 1860*.

83. See the appendix for expanded statistics concerning population density in Texas. Statistics for square mileage have been compiled from the list of county measurements found in Mary G. Ramos, ed., *1996–97 Texas Almanac and State Industrial Guide* (Dallas: Dallas Morning News, 1995). Population statistics from the US Bureau of the Census, *United States in 1860*.

84. Walter Prescott Webb, "The Last Treaty of the Republic of Texas," *Southwestern Historical Quarterly* 25 (January 1922): 151–71.

85. Neil Foley, *The White Scourge: Mexicans, Blacks and Poor Whites*

in Texas Cotton Culture (Berkeley: University of California Press, 1997), 2.

86. W. E. Lockhart, "The Slave Code of Texas" (MA thesis, Baylor University, 1929), 22.

87. Ibid., 49–50.

88. Quoted in Tyler, "Runaway Slaves in Texas," 19; citation from John M. Clayton to Luis de la Rosa, in William R. Manning, ed., *Diplomatic Correspondence of the United States*, vol. 9 (Concord, NH: Rumford Press, 1937), 50, 57.

89. *Report of the Committee of Investigation Sent in 1873 by the Mexican Government to the Frontier of Texas* (New York: Baker and Godwin, 1875), 178.

90. Ronnie C. Tyler, "The Callahan Expedition of 1855: Indians or Negroes?," *Southwestern Historical Quarterly* 70 (1967): 574–86.

91. Population statistics for the Republic of Texas are sketchy, but an excellent account that pays close attention to the number of slaves is Randolph B. Campbell, *Empire for Slavery*; US Bureau of the Census, *Population of the United States in 1850.*

92. George Barnard Papers.

93. For the early political development of Waco, see Walter Baker, "Political History of McLennan County" (MA thesis, Baylor University, 1936).

94. The Callahan expedition served to warn Mexican authorities that the Texans would no longer tolerate the harboring of fugitive slaves. Ronnie Tyler suggests that the warning in fact worked. Mexicans, he argues, returned slaves more often after 1855. Tyler, "Runaway Slaves in Texas." The establishment of Fort Belknap on the Texas frontier and the destruction of the Brazos Indian reservation served

to push the Native Americans of Central Texas to the north and west. On Belknap, see Roger N. Conger et al., *Frontier Forts of Texas* (Waco, TX: Texian Press, 1966), 5–19. On the Brazos Reservation, see Kenneth S. Neighbors, "Robert S. Neighbors and the Founding of the Texas Indian Reservations," *West Texas Historical Association* 31 (October 1955): 65–74; and Kenneth S. Neighbors, "The Assassination of Robert S. Neighbors," *West Texas Historical Association* 34 (October 1958): 38–49.

95. Waco's whipping post and auction block are remembered by a number of ex-slaves, including Aaron Ray in Rawick, *American Slave*, 3,257; and Andy Williams in Rawick, *American Slave*, 4,070.

96. See Baker, "Political History," 75.

97. James Buck Barry, "Diary," June 24–July 20, 1855, James Buck Barry Papers, 1847–1917, Center for American History, University of Texas at Austin, Austin, Texas.

98. "The Early Days of Waco," *Waco Tribune*, June 16, 1895.

99. *Brazos Statesman* (Waco), January 3, 1857.

100. Ralph A. Wooster, "Membership in Early Texas Legislatures, 1850–1860," *Southwestern Historical Quarterly* 69 (October 1965): 163–73.

101. One newspaper reported that whites in Nacogdoches feared a slave insurrection in 1841. See Addington, "Slave Insurrections," 413.

102. *Galveston News* (Galveston, TX), September 11, 1856, quoted in Olmsted, *Journey through Texas*, 503.

103. Quoted in Olmsted, *Journey through Texas*, 504.

104. Addington, "Slave Insurrections," 417–18.

105. Randolph Campbell describes them as "more imaginary than real." Campbell, *Empire for Slavery*, 184.

106. Addington, "Slave Insurrections," 418.

107. George Glasker in Rawick, *American Slave*, 1,505.

108. President Wilson in ibid., 4,205.

109. Calvin Kennard in ibid., 2,179.

110. Wesley Burrell in ibid., 535.

111. William Moore in ibid., 2,768–769.

112. Calvin Moye in ibid., 2,836.

113. A number of scholars have suggested that slaves used resistance to protest the abuse of power by masters, including Genovese, *Roll, Jordan, Roll*; Peter Kolchin, *Unfree Labor: American Slavery and Russian Serfdom* (Cambridge, MA: Harvard University Press, 1987); and Charles Joyner, *Down by the Riverside: A South Carolina Slave Community* (Urbana: University of Illinois Press, 1984), 232.

114. In less than three months in 1855, one of several Central Texas sheriffs recorded the capture of three runaways. Barry, "Diary," May 21–August 14, 1855.

115. For the statistical comparison of slave resistance, I adopted the coding system found in Paul Escott, *Slavery Remembered: A Record of Twentieth-Century Slave Narratives* (Chapel Hill: University of North Carolina Press, 1979), and applied it to fifty ex-slave narratives that discuss enslaved life in Central Texas. The resulting data indicated that resistance was indeed more frequent in Central Texas. Yet this information does not mean that Texas slaves were somehow less content than those slaves living in the earlier-settled regions of the South. After all, the majority of Central Texas slaves had just recently arrived from those states. Most slave communities throughout the South exhibited the same signs of rebelliousness displayed by the Central Texas slaves, but those communities did not have the opportunities provided by the Texas frontier.

116. T. Linday Baker and Julie Baker, eds., *The WPA Oklahoma Slave Narratives* (Norman: University of Oklahoma Press, 1996), 284.

117. Henry Childers in Rawick, *American Slave*, 697.

118. Mary Ann Carter to Laura Perry, October 5, 1851, Laura L. Perry Papers, Manuscript Division, Texas Collection, Baylor University, Texas.

119. Walter Cotton, *History of Negroes of Limestone County from 1860–1939* (Mexia, TX: J. A. Chatman and S. M. Merriwether, 1944), v, 5.

120. Jeffrey Kent Lucas, "Hill County History: Early Settlement through Congressional Reconstruction" (MA thesis, Baylor University, 1993), 94–95.

121. Lou Austin in Rawick, *American Slave*, 121–32.

122. Lucas, "Hill County History," 44.

123. Tobe Zollicoffer in Rawick, *American Slave*.

124. Wilbarger, *Indian Depredations*, 580.

125. Rena Maverick Green, ed., *Samuel Maverick, Texan: 1803–1870* (San Antonio: Private Printing, 1952), 73.

126. Wilbarger, *Indian Depredations*, 431.

127. L. W. Kemp, ed., "Early Days in Milam County: Reminiscences of Susan Tumham McCown," *Southwestern Historical Quarterly* 50 (January 1947): 366–76.

The Transition from Slave Potter to Free Potter

The Wilson Potteries of Guadalupe County

E. Joe Brackner Jr.

As has been pointed out in the two previous chapters, black slaves engaged in various labors on behalf of their owners, from working in the fields or kitchens to herding and controlling cattle. Joe Brackner adds one other intriguing story to this broad spectrum—in Guadalupe County, black slaves were taught to be potters and, after freedom arrived, continued in that role. Folklorist Elmer Joe Brackner resides in Alabama, where he also published a book titled Alabama Folk Pottery. *Brackner earlier completed a master's thesis in 1981 at the University of Texas entitled "The Wilson Potteries."*

★

The remains of several nineteenth-century potteries exist near Capote, a small community just east of Seguin in Guadalupe County, Central Texas. The present article summarizes what has been learned about two of these archeological sites—the John M. Wilson and Hiram Wilson potteries. The study was done mainly from an examination of waster shards and a study of local history. Also treated, briefly, is the economic life of local black potters during Reconstruction.

The history of the Capote pottery works begins in 1856, when the Rev. John M. Wilson, a Presbyterian minister, arrived in the neighborhood of Seguin with his family and some twenty black slaves. Wilson soon realized the potential for pottery manufacturing, as there was an enormous need in the area for vessels that could be used in the preparation and preservation of food. Land records reveal that he leased acreage in 1857 for the purpose of making ceramics. Wilson's effort is one of the earliest recorded for Anglo American settlers in Texas, although earthenware was produced much earlier at Spanish settlements and at the Indian missions.

Limited excavations were carried out at the sites of the potteries by the writer in 1981. At the pottery established by the Reverend Wilson (site 41GU6), a stone-lined well, the remains of a groundhog-type kiln, and a very large waster pile of stoneware shards survive. The groundhog kiln was a standard feature of southeastern potteries and ordinarily consisted of a long, burrow-like chamber (whence came the name "groundhog") with a chimney at the elevated end. The one at the John Wilson pottery appears to be considerably longer than many kilns used in the East. Its great length (about forty feet) was not determined by excavation, however, but was estimated with a proton magnetometer that measured the site's magnetic field. Features such as tombs, ditches, kilns, and other disturbances produce a distinct image on magnetometer maps, as did the Wilson kiln.

Since real-estate deeds indicate that the John Wilson pottery ceased operations after only twelve years, a fairly large workforce must have run the establishment if one is to account for the enormous waster pile that survives. In 1869, the Rev. John Wilson sold his interest in the pottery to a white potter already working there. M. J. Durham, the new owner, promptly moved the business to a nearby location (site 41GU4). Durham's establishment continued operations until 1903.

The US Census for the year 1870 lists six potters in the county: M. J. Durham (white) and John Chandler (black) from South Carolina; Isaac Suttles (white) from Ohio; and Hiram, James, and Wallace Wilson (black) from North Carolina—the freed slaves of the Rev. John Wilson. Since Rev. Wilson admits in his article for the Texas Almanac of 1870 that he knew nothing about ceramics when he moved to the Capote area, the first three potters—Durham, Chandler, and Suttles—probably had a hand in training the Wilson men when they were slaves. The records of the Freedmen's Bureau indicate that Durham was present in the area in 1866, and it was likely that Durham, Chandler, and Suttles were all there before emancipation.

Isaac Suttles is probably responsible for the introduction of salt glazing at the John Wilson pottery, since that glaze was dominant in his home state of Ohio. Alongside the traditional alkaline-glazed shards from the John Wilson waster heap, which are typical of the southeastern United States, are others with the distinctive texture caused by salt glazing, which was not a common glaze in the antebellum South, especially the Carolinas. Also, large salt drops on shards from alkaline-glazed vessels reveal that they were fired in a kiln that was sometimes used for salt glazing. In the test pit dug at the Wilson site, levels with shards of alkaline-glazed vessels were found below levels containing both alkaline- and salt-glazed pottery. This strongly suggests that the South Carolinians, with their alkaline glaze, were the initial potters.

Except for the salt glazing, the John Wilson ceramics are comparable in formal attributes to those of Edgefield County, South Carolina, which was perhaps the single most influential manufacturing region for southeastern stoneware. Indeed, the Durham and Chandler families are well associated with pottery making in

Edgefield County, and M. J. Durham was present in Edgefield when the US Census of 1850 was taken. The most convincing material link to Edgefield is the evidence of slip-trailed decoration at the John Wilson pottery, as this technique is a trademark of some of the finest Edgefield products, including those made at the Trapp-Chandler site in South Carolina. Other traits also found in Edgefield County include the attachment of jug handles from shoulder to body (instead of neck to body), the use of wheel-thrown lug handles on large storage jars, and the production of flat-topped, "tie-down" rims. The rim of a lidded vessel often has a lid ledge within the mouth, while a "tie-down" rim is simply thickened and can be covered by a cloth tied below the thick area.

Physical and documentary evidence casts doubt on Wilson's assertions in the Texas Almanac of 1870 that he arrived by experimentation at a method to produce stoneware. By this he may only have meant that he discovered the best mixture of sand and clay for this area, for he certainly did not introduce or develop the ground-hog kiln or the style of ceramics made at his pottery. This ceramic tradition was at least fifty years old by the middle of the nineteenth century.

The position of black freedmen in Guadalupe County society is a revealing topic of study. The conflict between whites and blacks after emancipation affected the pottery industry and practically every other aspect of the local economy. The progress made by blacks during the early days of Reconstruction was quickly undone by the effects of racism and also because of insufficient power and interest on the part of the Freedmen's Bureau. Yet after emancipation, there were several physical manifestations of the resilience and cohesion (as well as isolation) of the black community at Capote. The most notable were Capote Baptist Church (1872) and H. Wilson and Co. pottery (1870), both founded by Hiram Wilson. It seems that Hiram, James, and Wallace Wilson struck out on their own when Durham took over the John Wilson pottery. Interestingly, the site of H. Wilson and Co. pottery (41GU5) is noticeably farther from the main road than the others. At the site today, there are surface indications of a groundhog kiln of modest proportions and two small waster piles of salt-glazed shards. The association of a groundhog kiln with salt-glazed ceramics is unusual, since the beehive kiln is usually used with that glaze.

The men at H. Wilson and Co. produced a line of high-quality stoneware vessels much like those made at the original John Wilson pottery. Three departures from the earlier ware, however, are striking. These are the predominance of salt glazing, the use of lids on vessels instead of "tie-down" rims, and the presence of an unusual horseshoe-shaped handle. While the salt glazing may have been a response to market preferences or the need for economy, the subtle formal variations in handles, lids (rare at the earlier John Wilson pottery), and rims are almost certainly creative innovations or borrowings by the three black potters.

The precise reason the Wilsons split away from the original white-owned pottery is not known, but it happened at a time when tension between the whites and the freedmen was high. Records of the Freedmen's Bureau indicate that the white population harassed the ex-slaves of the county both physically and politically. Trumped-up charges and actual physical assaults against members of the Wilson community are documented. The allowed economic outlet for freedmen was sharecropping, with all its attendant evils and poverty, not private business. Freedmen complained to Bureau agents that their material well-being had deteriorated since slavery, and they sometimes blamed the Freedmen's Bureau for raising false hopes. In fact, the Wilson potters and John Chandler may have been the only blacks in the vicinity to find gainful employment outside of working for shares on a crop. Although the end of the H. Wilson pottery apparently came with the death of Hiram Wilson, its founder, James Wilson's son claimed that the pottery ceased in 1884 because they ran out of good clay. The remaining potters then lost their independence and went to work for the son of M. J. Durham.

It is unclear to what extent the difficulties experienced by Hiram Wilson's pottery reflect general trends in Southern society during Reconstruction. Undoubtedly, in other parts of the southeastern United States, freedmen were rudely and violently treated as they attempted to start a new way of life beyond the cotton field. It is not known whether the Wilsons were manufacturing for a black clientele and perhaps participating in a barter stem or whether they produced mainly for a white market. Regardless, vessels from Hiram Wilson's pottery still exist and can be found throughout Central Texas in barns, homes, and antique shops. They are tributes to gifted craftsmen using skills learned in slavery and amplified by creativity to establish a viable business, however short-lived.

This article was originally published as Brackner, Elmer Joe, Jr. "The Transition from Slave Potter to Free Potter: The Wilson Potteries of Guadalupe County, Texas." In Texana II: Cultural Heritage of the Plantation South, edited by Candace Volz, 39–53. Austin: Texas Historical Commission, 1982. Reprinted by permission of the Texas Historical Commission.

BIBLIOGRAPHY

Brackner, Elmer Joe, Jr., "The Wilson Potteries." MA thesis, University of Texas at Austin, 1981.

Burrison, John A. "Georgia Jug Makers: A History of Southern Folk Pottery." PhD dissertation, University of Pennsylvania, 1973.

———. "Alkaline-Glazed Stoneware: A Deep-South Pottery Tradition." *Southern Folklore Quarterly* 39, no. 4 (1975): 377–403.

———. *Brothers in Clay: The Story of Georgia Folk Pottery.* Athens: University of Georgia Press, 1983.

Greer, Georgeanna H. *American Stonewares: The Art and Craft of Utilitarian Potters.* Exton, PA: Schiffer, 1981.

———. "Groundhog Kilns: Rectangular American Kilns of the Nineteenth and Early Twentieth Centuries." *Northeast Historical Archaeology* 6, nos. 1, 2 (1977): 42–54.

————. "Preliminary Information on the Use of the Alkaline Glaze for Stoneware in the South: 1800–1970." *Conference on Historic Site Archaeology, Papers*, 5, no. 2 (1970): 155–70.

Greer, Georgeanna H., and Harding Black. *The Meyer Family: Master Potters of Texas.* San Antonio, TX: Trinity University Press, 1971.

Litwack, Leon F. *Been in the Storm So Long: The Aftermath of Slavery.* New York: Knopf, 1979.

Malone, James M., Georgeanna H. Greer, and Helen Simons. *Kirbee Kiln: A Mid-19th Century Texas Stoneware Pottery.* Report 31, Office of the State Archeologist, Texas Historical Commission, Austin, 1979.

Smith, Samuel D., and Stephen T. Rogers. *A Survey of Historic Pottery-making in Tennessee.* Research Series, No. 3, Division of Archaeology, Tennessee Department of Conservation, Nashville, 1979.

Texas Almanac, 1870. Galveston: Richardson and Company.

Vlach, John M. *The Afro-American Tradition in the Decorative Arts.* Cleveland, OH: Cleveland Museum of Art, 1978.

Willett, E. Henry, and Joey Brackner. *The Traditional Pottery of Alabama.* Montgomery, AL: Montgomery Museum of Fine Arts, 1983.

DOCUMENTS

Freedmen's Bureau. Records of the Assistant Commissioner for the State of Texas, Bureau of Refugees, Freedmen, and Abandoned Lands, 1865–1869 (microfilm, Federal Archives and Records Center, Fort Worth, Texas).

Seventh Census of the United States, 1850: Schedule 1—Free Inhabitants; South Carolina (microfilm, National Archives, Washington, DC).

Eighth Census of the United States, 1860: Schedule 1—Free Inhabitants; Texas (microfilm, National Archives, Washington, DC).

Ninth Census of the United States, 1870: Population Schedules; Texas (microfilm, National Archives, Washington, DC).

Black Political Power and Criminal Justice

Washington County, 1868–1884

Donald G. Nieman

Following the Civil War, African Americans in Texas engaged in the political sphere, quite naturally supporting and working with the Republican Party—the party of their continued liberation. Not only did they vote; they campaigned and were elected to office. Since whites used the criminal justice system to control black behavior, blacks also fought to be included on juries as well as in other aspects of that system. In the following essay, author Donald G. Nieman depicts well the involvement of blacks in the political process in Texas' Washington County. Nieman is the provost and executive vice president of academic affairs at Binghamton University. He has authored/edited at least six books, including the well-received Promises to Keep: African-Americans and the Constitutional Order, 1776 to the Present.

★

Black participation in the political process was perhaps the most remarkable phenomenon in the postemancipation South. Less than two years after the defeat of the Confederacy assured the destruction of slavery, Congress guaranteed universal suffrage for black males in the unreconstructed states. During the months and years that followed, black men eagerly grasped the opportunity to wield political power by registering, joining political clubs, attending political meetings, and voting in the face of their former owners' use of suasion, economic coercion, and physical violence to deter them. Among slave societies, only the United States experienced such widespread political participation by freedmen in the aftermath of emancipation. Yet most American historians have minimized the importance of the ballot,

arguing that political rights afforded impoverished, economically dependent freedmen inadequate means to defend their freedom.[1] Having dismissed the ballot, it is
not surprising that scholars have neglected a systematic study of how blacks used
political power. Only recently have historians begun to explore the political world
of the freedmen.[2]

The current reassessment of the postemancipation black experience is generating
a large and exciting body of literature, but it will not be complete until we understand
this world. We must examine blacks' efforts to use political power to improve their
lives and to expand their freedom. And we must explore the ways in which enfranchisement affected the outcome of the postemancipation struggle between blacks
and their former owners—the former demanding freedom from white control, the
latter determined to preserve white domination. Certainly, black political power was
short lived, and blacks ultimately lost their bid for influence over public policy. But
as Fernand Braudel has suggested, we must give such efforts their due if we are
to understand the past fully "because the losing movements have at every moment
affected the final outcome."[3]

This essay addresses these issues by examining the impact of black political
power on the administration of criminal justice. Throughout the postemancipation
era, whites attempted to use criminal law to restrict black freedom and to reinforce
white dominance. They demanded that white men continue to determine which
acts the community would define as crimes and the punishments to be meted out to
those marked as criminals. Their experiences during slavery and presidential Reconstruction made former slaves painfully aware of the consequences of white control
of criminal justice. Blacks, therefore, demanded color-blind justice and, in order to
ensure this end, a voice in the legal system. The battle for control of criminal justice
was thus at the center of postemancipation conflict. Because those who operated the
criminal justice system were popularly elected local officials whose actions were subject to scrutiny by their constituents, moreover, blacks' ability to use political power
was crucial to the outcome. In order to explore the politics of criminal justice systematically, this article will focus on the experience of a single county—Washington
County, Texas—from 1868 through 1884.[4]

At the end of the Civil War, Washington County was one of the oldest and
wealthiest counties in Texas. Originally settled in the early 1820s by families who
came to Texas with Stephen F. Austin, the county grew steadily in population
and by 1860 was the second-most populous county in the state.[5] Located in the
Brazos River Valley midway between Houston and Austin, it offered rich lands well
suited to cotton cultivation. On the eve of the Civil War, it was among the half dozen
leading cotton-producing counties in the state, a position it retained in the postbel-
lum decades.[6] Blacks provided much of the labor for the cotton crop and accounted
for approximately 52 percent of Washington County's population from 1860 through
1890.[7] This small black majority, which was concentrated on the rich loamy soils
of the eastern half of the county, persisted in the face of heavy German immigration.

The German-born population, which settled mainly on prairie lands in the western part of the county, grew from slightly more than 1,000 in 1860 to almost 3,500 in 1890, when one in four residents of Washington County was of German extraction.[8] Although the county was predominantly rural and agricultural, Brenham, the county seat, enjoyed sustained growth during the postwar decades. Shortly after the war, the Houston and Texas Central Railroad served Brenham, and ten years later, the town became an important inland rail center when Gulf, Colorado, and Santa Fe Railroad construction crews arrived. The town flourished as a cotton entrepôt and center for a number of small manufacturers, and its population grew from fewer than 1,000 in 1860 to more than 2,200 in 1870 and 5,200 by 1890.[9]

Between 1867 and 1869, as US Army personnel implemented the Reconstruction Act of 1867, a powerful Republican Party emerged in Washington County. Local black leaders and a small number of white Unionists joined recent migrants from the North and a few former Whigs who had supported the Confederacy to organize the party in 1867 and 1868. Former slaves, mobilized by the Union League, eagerly joined the party and constituted the vast majority of its rank and file.[10] Strong German support augmented the party's strength. By appealing to Germans' unionism and their hostility to the planter elite that had dominated local politics before the war, Republican leaders brought several hundred—perhaps half—of the county's German voters into the party in the early 1870s.[11] This combination of blacks and Germans created a formidable, if unstable, political alliance. It enabled Republicans to dominate county government in an area with a slim black majority from 1870, when civil government was restored, until 1884, more than a decade after Democrats redeemed state government from Republican control.[12]

During fifteen years of Republican control, Washington County blacks possessed significant political power. Freedmen did not win a share of county offices equal to their percentage of the population, and no black man received the party's nomination for the powerful positions of sheriff, district judge, or county judge. Nevertheless, they were not excluded from the spoils. They won most of the Republican nominations for the state legislature during the 1870s and 1880s and, increasingly, secured the party's nomination for such countywide offices as clerk of court and treasurer. After 1876, when a new state constitution created a county commission with broad administrative and fiscal authority, black Republicans consistently won two of the four seats on the commission.[13]

Growing black influence within the party was the result of Republican office seekers' dependence on black support. Initially, Republican candidates needed the support of the county's Union Leagues, in which black leaders had a powerful voice. The Union Leagues disbanded in the early 1870s but were replaced by Republican precinct caucuses, meetings local Democrats derisively referred to as "owl meetings." (They met at night when black workers who formed the party rank and file could attend.) Particularly in the Republican strongholds of eastern Washington County, the caucuses were chaired by black precinct leaders and attended almost exclusively by freedmen. In these meetings, which convened frequently during election years, candidates sought support, and the party faithful selected delegates to the county convention. When the convention met to choose nominees, a solid majority of delegates were freedmen who had been chosen at these meetings, and a black man was generally in the chair. This process gave blacks a powerful voice in party affairs and accounted for the steady growth in the number of black candidates and officers during the 1870s and 1880s. Moreover, it encouraged white Republican officials to cultivate a good reputation among blacks. Black support was crucial to politicos' intent upon expanding their influence in party councils or preventing rivals within the party from unseating them.[14]

Consider the case of Stephen Hackworth, a native white Republican of modest means. Hackworth was an early member of the Brenham Union League and a political ally of the freedmen. As an investor, he helped numerous Washington County blacks obtain land on credit in nearby Fort Bend County. At a meeting in 1879 called to discuss black emigration to Kansas, Texas black leaders were so impressed with Hackworth's efforts to encourage black landownership that they passed a resolution thanking him. The only other person so honored was William Lloyd Garrison. A fellow Republican noted that Hackworth had "great influence with the colored people" and "was looked on as the leader of the colored Republicans" in Washington County because "he is a man who has always proved to be true and faithful" to them. A political enemy confirmed this. He suggested that Hackworth enjoyed good relations with blacks and noted that his association with them went beyond electioneering: "I very seldom saw him on the street without he spoke to a nigger. I never saw him except in company with a nigger. . . . He has niggers around him the whole year, from the commencement to the end." Hackworth's popularity in the black community paid off. Throughout the 1870s and early 1880s, he was the most important Republican leader in the county and achieved substantial influence with state and national Republican leaders.[15]

Republican political success had a direct effect on Washington County's criminal justice system. During the 1870s and early 1880s, the judges who presided over the district court—the tribunal with jurisdiction over felonies—were all Republicans. Prior to 1876, these men were appointees of the Republican governor, but with implementation of the 1876 constitution, they were nominated in Republican conventions and popularly elected. All but one of the district and county attorneys—the officials who worked with grand juries to determine which criminal complaints should result in indictments and then prosecuted the cases—were popularly elected Republicans. Between 1870 and 1884, four Republicans served as sheriff and thus played an important role in selecting jurors as well as in making arrests, pressing charges against those accused of crimes, and making decisions concerning the release of prisoners on bond. Although all four were white, they brought blacks into the sheriff's office in significant numbers. Approximately one-fourth of the deputies they appointed were freedmen. Finally, most of the county's justices of the peace, who had the authority to hold preliminary hearings in felony cases as well as to try petty cases, were Republicans. Like other criminal justice officials, they were subject to popular election and depended on the support of black leaders to gain and to retain their positions.[16]

The most noticeable change in the criminal justice system wrought by Republican officials was black participation on juries. Determining the racial composition of juries—as well as identifying the race of defendants and other parties involved in the district court's proceedings—is problematical. Because court records fail to identify persons by race, one must rely on the federal manuscript censuses of population for 1870 and 1880 to find the race of jurors. Grand juries, which had between fifteen and twenty members until 1876 and a dozen members thereafter, decided whether there was sufficient evidence to indict persons accused of crimes. The censuses and the Brenham *Banner* permit identification of the race of 428 (92 percent) of the 463 grand jurors who sat between October 1870 and December 1884. Petit juries were twelve-member panels that heard cases that went to trial, decided whether defendants were guilty, and determined their sentences. The district court minutes give the names of jurors who sat on 159 petit juries impaneled between 1870 and 1884. Of these 1,908 jurors, the censuses identified 1,312 (69 percent) by race.

Freedmen clearly played a prominent role on the county's juries—especially between October 1870 and July 1876, a period when a popularly elected Republican county court and sheriff selected jurors from voter registration lists. On most (eleven of eighteen) of the grand juries impaneled during this period, blacks constituted at least 40 percent of the jurors whose races are known (see table 4.1). Because indictments required the assent of twelve jurors, black grand jurors could not be ignored. Whites never possessed enough votes to return a true bill; indeed, on half of the grand juries (nine of eighteen), whites needed at least three black votes to indict. Black strength on the grand jury was important, although it did have limitations. Given the dramatic changes in race relations that followed emancipation and black enfranchisement, criminal cases frequently became politically and ideologically charged. If white jurors feared that growing black assertiveness was responsible for a rise in crime and supported indictment of freedmen even though the evidence was weak, blacks had the votes to block passage of true bills. However, black jurors' ability to win indictments in the face of white opposition—in controversial cases involving white violence against freedmen, for example—was more circumscribed. They needed the support of two to seven white jurors, and that support could be difficult to obtain. While some white grand jurors were Republicans and thus potential allies of black jurors in these cases, most were not. Consequently, black jurors found it more difficult to initiate indictments against whites than to block indictments that they felt were unjustified.[17]

A significant number of freedmen also sat on petit juries between October 1870 and July 1876. The district court minutes provide the names of the jurors on 107 petit juries that sat during these years. Among the members of these juries whose races have

TABLE 4.1. RACE OF GRAND JURORS, 1870–1884

1870–76				1877–84			
Term	Black	White	Unknown	Term	Black	White	Unknown
Oct. 1870	2	11	2	Feb. 1877	4	8	0
Feb. 1871	4	10	1	July 1877	3	9	0
June 1871	5	6	4	Jan. 1878	2	9	1
Oct. 1871	6	8	1	Jan. 1879	5	7	0
Feb. 1872	6	9	4	Mar. 1881	3	9	0
June 1872	10	10	0	Sept. 1881	3	8	1
Oct. 1872	6	11	0	Mar. 1882	4	8	0
Feb. 1873	4	11	1	Sept. 1882	2	9	1
June 1873	5	10	2	Mar. 1883	3	9	0
Sept. 1873	8	9	1	Sept. 1883	4	8	0
Feb. 1874	6	9	0	Mar. 1884	1	9	2
June 1874	4	10	1	Sept. 1884	3	7	2
Sept. 1874	7	11	0				
Feb. 1875	6	8	2				
June 1875	9	8	1				
Oct. 1875	7	10	1				
Feb. 1876	7	9	1				
July 1876	5	7	0				

Source: Washington County District Court, Minutes; US Census of Population, 1870, 1880 (Washington County, TX).

been identified, 36 percent were black. If this accurately reflects the proportion of jurors who were black, it means that the average number of freedmen on each petit jury was 4.3.[18] The black presence on trial juries prior to 1877 is more clearly suggested if one considers only juries on which the race of nine or more jurors is known.[19] Among the 107 juries under consideration, there are 52 such juries (see table 4.2). On 20 of these, at least half of the jurors whose races are known were blacks, while on another 16, 25 to 49 percent of the jurors whose races are known were blacks. If these proportions held true for the entire membership of each of these 52 juries, there were between six and twelve blacks on 39 percent of these juries and between three and five blacks on 31 percent of the juries. Only 5 percent contained no blacks, and 25 percent included one or two blacks. This suggests that freedmen served in more than token numbers, something that undoubtedly reduced their sense of isolation and vulnerability to the blandishments of white jurors. Because guilty verdicts required the assent of all

TABLE 4.2. PERCENTAGE OF BLACKS ON SELECTED PETIT JURIES, 1870–1884*

	0	1–24%	25–49%	50–74%	75–100%	Total
Juries 1870–76	3 (5%)	13 (25%)	16 (31%)	14 (27%)	6 (12%)	52 (100%)
Juries 1877–84	3 (15%)	8 (40%)	7 (35%)	2 (10%)	0	20 (100%)

Source: Washington County District Court, Minutes; US Manuscript Census of Population, 1870 and 1880; Washington County Voter Registration List, 1868.
* This is the percentage of those jurors whose races are known who are black. On all of

twelve petit jurors, black jurors were therefore well positioned to play a crucial role in deciding the fate of defendants.

In 1876, the Texas legislature, firmly under Democratic control, enacted a new jury law. It not only placed the selection of grand and petit jurors in the hands of three jury commissioners appointed by the district judge but also stipulated that all jurors must be literate. Given the high rate of illiteracy among Washington County blacks (three-fourths of the black grand jurors who served between 1870 and 1876 were illiterate), this drastically limited the pool of potential black jurors and led to a decline in their numbers. However, it by no means eliminated freedmen from juries. Popularly elected Republican district judges invariably appointed one freedman as well as a white Republican to serve on the three-member jury commission. And this guaranteed that freedmen maintained a significant, albeit smaller, presence on juries.[20]

The names of grand jurors are available for twelve of the sixteen grand juries that served between 1877 and 1884.[21] Under the new jury law, grand juries were reduced to twelve members and the number of votes required for indictment to nine. During the years from 1877 through 1884, these panels usually included at least three or four freedmen, enough to give black grand jurors real influence. To be sure, on half of the grand juries (six of twelve) there were at least nine white jurors—under the new law, enough to return an indictment even if all the black jurors voted in the negative. However, some of these white jurors were Republicans, and when cases affecting freedmen came before the jury, they were probably responsive to the arguments of their black colleagues.[22]

Blacks also continued to serve as petit jurors in more than token numbers. The district court minutes give the names of jurors on fifty-two petit juries that sat between 1877 and 1884. Of the 624 jurors on these panels, the censuses permit identification of the races of 416 jurors (67 percent), almost one-fourth of whom were freedmen. This suggests that during the late 1870s and early 1880s, the average petit jury contained three blacks. The continued prominence of blacks on petit juries is also suggested by the composition of the twenty juries (1877–84) on which the races of at least nine jurors are known (see table 4.2). On two of these juries, at least half of the jurors whose races are known were freedmen, while on another seven, blacks constituted from 25 to

49 percent of the jurors whose races are known. If these proportions held true for the entire composition of these juries, 10 percent included six or more blacks; 35 percent, from three to five blacks; 40 percent, one or two blacks (in fact, there were two blacks on seven of the eight juries in this category); and 15 percent, no blacks. Thus black jurors were numerous after 1877, and blacks were rarely isolated from other members of their race when they served on petit juries.

Even after implementation of the 1876 jury law, then, enough blacks sat on juries to give them the opportunity to influence the criminal justice system. But did black jurors exercise independent judgment? Or were they unduly influenced by pressure from white colleagues once the jury retired for deliberations? Given whites' propensity for violence against blacks and blacks' economic dependence on white employers, one might expect that black jurors feared retribution if they took issue with white jurors. And after 1876, when blacks were usually distinct minorities on juries, it seems likely that black jurors would have been especially vulnerable to white influence. Not surprisingly, there is very little information about what transpired in the jury room during deliberations. Nevertheless, numerous comments on cases that ended in mistrials suggest that black jurors could be fiercely independent. In 1880, for example, the county attorney complained to the governor that the scion of "a rich and influential family" had been tried for the murder of an English immigrant but had escaped conviction. Although the attack had been unprovoked and the evidence of guilt substantial, the prosecutor noted that ten jurors had voted to acquit and only two—"one a poor colored man and the other a poor American"—held out for conviction and hung the jury. A year later, the *Banner* noted that in the trial of a black woman charged with burglary, "the jury stood one strong-minded colored man for acquittal and the other eleven jurors, nearly all white, in favor of conviction." As a result, the judge declared a mistrial, and the district attorney dismissed the case. Reports in the *Banner* of other hung juries offer further evidence that black jurors were not ciphers controlled by their white colleagues.[23]

Despite the presence of blacks on grand juries, there was a great disparity between the numbers of blacks and whites indicted for property crimes. While there were 1.13 times as many blacks as whites in the county, grand juries indicted 3.2 times as many blacks as whites for property crimes (see table 4.3).[24] One should not assume that this disparity was the result of white majorities on grand juries or the decline of black participation after 1876. Whites, even if united, rarely had sufficiently large majorities to win indictments without black support, and some white jurors were political allies of the freedmen. Moreover, there is no direct relationship between white strength on the grand jury and the ratio of blacks to whites indicted for offenses against property. During 1874 and 1875, for example, one of the six grand juries had a black majority, and four of the others were at least 40 percent black. Nevertheless, these grand juries indicted eighty-four blacks for property crimes. This was eight times the number of whites indicted for property offenses during these two years and 27 percent of all blacks indicted for such offenses between 1870 and

TABLE 4.3. INDICTMENTS, 1870–1884

	Property crimes			Crimes vs. person		
Year	Black	White	Unknown	Black	White	Unknown
1870	18	7	30	12	7	22
1871	17	9	32	9	15	17
1872	15	11	38	9	17	28
1873	24	9	17	12	7	14
1874	49	7	30	13	29	26
1875	35	3	29	21	23	17
1876	20	9	25	7	7	8
1877	21	7	17	10	8	21
1878	20	5	15	20	7	4
1879	14	1	13	14	8	4
1880	9	5	15	4	8	4
1881	30	4	11	16	11	4
1882	20	3	4	23	5	11
1883	9	2	6	22	11	4
1884	12	14	5	22	1	7
Totals	313	96	287	214	164	191

Source: Washington County District Court, Minutes and Dockets.

1884. Nor did the disparity between the numbers of blacks and whites indicted for property crimes increase after 1876 when black strength on the grand jury declined. Consequently, the conclusion that white majorities on grand juries were primarily responsible for the disproportionate number of freedmen indicted is invalid.[25]

Perhaps class was more important than race in determining the behavior of black grand jurors. If most black grand jurors were preachers, teachers, and artisans who owned modest amounts of property, they might have been unsympathetic to property-less black laborers accused of theft and predisposed to indict them.[26] Clearly, this was not the case. Prior to implementation of the 1876 jury law, the great majority of black grand jurors were laborers who owned little property, as table 4.4 suggests. Of those who appeared in the 1870 census, 60 percent were common laborers. Another 28 percent that the census listed as "farmers" were, for the most part, tenants, since few of them owned real property. Most black grand jurors, not surprisingly, were very poor. Eighty-five percent owned no real property, and 60 percent owned less than $100 worth of personal property. Even those who owned personal property valued at $100 or more were

TABLE 4.4. BLACK GRAND JURORS, 1870–1884

	1870–1876[*] (N = 82)	1877–1884[**] (N = 21)
Occupation		
Farm laborer	46 (56%)	2 (10%)
Laborer	3 (4%)	0
Farmer	23 (28%)	9 (43%)
Drayman	2 (8%)	0
Artisan	8 (10%)	3 (14%)
Professional	0	7 (33%)
Literacy		
Literate	17 (21%)	17 (81%)
Illiterate	61 (74%)	3 (14%)
Partially literate	4 (5%)	1 (5%)
Color		
Black	77 (94%)	14 (67%)
Mulatto	5 (6%)	7 (33%)
Real property		
Yes	11 (13%)	
No	71 (87%)	
Personal property		
$0–99	49 (60%)	
$100	8 (10%)	
$200	3 (4%)	
$300	5 (6%)	
$400	7 (9%)	
$500 and over	10 (12%)	

[*] Information drawn from US Census of Population, Washington County, Texas, 1870. Only 82 of the 107 black grand jurors who sat during these years could be identified in the census.
[**] Information drawn from the US Census of Population, Washington County, Texas, 1880. Only twenty-one of the thirty-seven black grand jurors who sat during these years could be identified in the census. Information concerning ownership of property was not included in the 1880 census.

not particularly well-off; more than two-thirds of these men owned property worth no more than $400. Given the poverty of most of these men, the number of blacks indicted for property offenses cannot be attributed to the class status of black grand jurors.

The 1876 jury law, which stipulated that jurors must be literate, dramatically changed the socioeconomic profile of black grand jurors. The 1880 census, which is the source for data on black grand jurors who sat between 1877 and 1884, gives no information on property holdings but does give an indication of the socioeconomic statuses of individuals. As table 4.4 shows, black grand jurors who served after 1876 included a substantial number of artisans and professionals and very few laborers. Moreover, unlike the jurors who sat before 1877, a substantial number of these men were mulattoes. Nevertheless, this did not result in more draconian treatment of freedmen. Neither the number of blacks indicted for offenses against property nor the ratio of blacks to whites charged with such crimes increased. Thus it appears that the socioeconomic statuses of black grand jurors do not account for the large number of freedmen indicted for property offenses.

The most likely reason for the disparity is that blacks actually committed more property crimes than did whites. The vast majority of whites in Washington County, including German immigrants, were landowners. As studies of crime in rural areas of the antebellum North and South suggest, landowners committed few property crimes. Most freedmen, however, were hard-pressed agricultural laborers whose poverty encouraged theft. Black sharecroppers and farm laborers lived hard lives during the best of times, and the temptation to steal a pig or a steer or to break into a storehouse to steal food or clothing must have been powerful. During years in which too much or too little rain ravaged their crops and slashed their incomes, it could become overpowering. Indeed, if the three years in which Washington County sharecroppers and agricultural laborers suffered most—1874, 1875, and 1881—are excluded, blacks were indicted 2.3 times (as opposed to 3.3 times if the three years are included) as often as whites for offenses against property.[27] There were other, related reasons for blacks to steal. Horse theft constituted one-fifth of all property-crime indictments in Washington County, and over 80 percent of those charged with horse theft were freedmen. This suggests that some blacks viewed theft as one route to economic advancement in a society in which economic opportunity for them was severely limited; stolen horses could be—and frequently were—converted into cash.[28]

It is likely that black grand jurors simply did their duty under the law and supported indictments when the evidence suggested that blacks had stolen. Perhaps selection as a grand juror—a position that carried substantial responsibility and prestige in nineteenth-century rural America—led blacks to take seriously their obligations, as prescribed by the law and the district judge.[29] Moreover, blacks were frequently complainants in larceny prosecutions against other blacks. In 20 percent of the property-crime prosecutions against blacks, the victim's race is known, and in 35 percent of these cases, the victims were black. Thus black grand jurors probably viewed theft as a threat to the black community and did not hesitate to indict blacks against whom there was sufficient evidence.[30]

This is not to suggest, however, that the presence of blacks on the grand jury served only to protect property rights. It appears that they also kept the disparity between indictments against blacks and indictments against whites significantly lower than it otherwise might have been. The data that Edward Ayers has presented on Greene County, Georgia, are suggestive on this point. In Greene County, black political influence was short-lived, and freedmen did not serve on juries. There, the disparity between the numbers of whites and blacks indicted was much greater than in Washington County, a phenomenon that cannot be accounted for by the larger percentage of blacks in Greene County. Between 1866 and 1879, almost seventeen times as many blacks as whites were indicted for property offenses, a far larger disparity than in Washington County. This suggests that black grand jurors in Washington County were unwilling to deal leniently with black theft but did use their influence to prevent the indictment of blacks against whom the evidence was weak. Consequently, the presence of black grand jurors limited the capricious impulses of whites to indict those whom they merely suspected of theft.[31]

Although the gap between the number of blacks and whites indicted was not as great as for property crimes, more blacks than whites were charged with crimes against the person in Washington County (see table 4.3). This disparity did not exist throughout the period from 1870 through 1884 but developed after 1876. Between 1870 and 1876, 1.4 times as many whites as blacks were charged with violent crimes, while after 1876, 2.6 times as many blacks as whites were indicted for these offenses. A dramatic decline in indictments against whites was more responsible for this than the rise in indictments against blacks. While the average number of indictments against freedmen for crimes against the person rose from 11.9 per year (1870–76) to 16.3 per year (1877–84), the average number of indictments for such offenses against whites dropped from 16.2 per year (1870–76) to 6.4 per year (1877–84). Perhaps there was a decline in the number of violent crimes committed by whites, but this is an unlikely explanation for such an acute decline. Rather, it probably reflected declining black strength on grand juries. White jurors probably used their growing power to block indictments against whites charged with violence against freedmen. Perhaps given whites' willingness to accept violence as a legitimate means to settle personal difficulties or to defend one's honor, white grand jurors also used their growing strength to block indictments in cases involving white violence against whites.[32]

The larger white majorities on grand juries after 1877, however, probably do not account for the growing number of indictments against blacks, since it took a greater number of jurors to indict than to block an indictment. Almost 80 percent of the blacks charged with crimes against the person after 1876 had allegedly attacked members of their own race.[33] Given Southern whites' lack of concern about crime in the black community, white grand jurors were probably not eager to use county revenues to prosecute these cases—especially at a time when the local newspaper frequently complained that the expense of criminal prosecutions was bankrupting the county.[34]

Rather, black grand jurors probably demanded that black victims have redress and pressed for these indictments. Indeed, on the three grand juries responsible for returning the largest number of indictments against blacks for violent crimes, blacks were well represented. Two of the panels included four blacks, and the other contained at least three.[35] Members of the black elite were perhaps more concerned than other freedmen about violence, and their increased strength on grand juries after 1876 might have been responsible for the growing number of indictments. It is easy to overemphasize this, however. The increase in the number of blacks indicted for crimes against the person, while significant, was not a radical departure from pre-1877 patterns. At most, it represents an intensification of a concern that already existed in the black community. Of course, it may also have indicated a greater incidence of violent crime among blacks.

There is yet another reason to doubt that the growing number of indictments against freedmen after 1876 for crimes against the person was the result of white control of the grand jury. Whites were much more concerned about black theft than about violence among blacks. If they had controlled the indictment process after 1876, there would probably have been an increase in the number of blacks charged with property crimes and in the gap between the number of whites and blacks indicted for such offenses. Yet as table 4.3 shows, neither occurred.

Once indicted and taken into custody, the accused were committed to jail unless they were able to post bond. This was also the case when justices of the peace held preliminary hearings and decided that there was sufficient evidence to detain persons charged with crimes. Since the district court held only two or three brief terms each year, criminally accused blacks might spend weeks or even months in jail awaiting trial, much to the detriment of their economic prospects and the well-being of their families. Consequently, the decisions of local officials to set bail and to accept the sureties that blacks offered (defendants generally used the property of sureties rather than cash to guarantee their appearance in court) were extremely important. Washington County officials did not set bond so high that it was beyond the reach of blacks; the average bond set for black defendants accused of property crimes ranged from $138 for theft of hogs, mules, oxen, and sheep to $289 for burglary. Indeed, the average amount of bond set for freedmen was substantially lower than that set for whites (as table 4.5 shows), and there are indications that Republican officials, aware of blacks' poverty, did this consciously.[36]

A substantial proportion of blacks arrested for serious crimes were released on bond, although it is impossible to say precisely how many. In slightly fewer than half of the cases of crimes against persons and property, the district court minutes and dockets contain information indicating the amount of bond and whether defendants posted bond.[37] In these cases, 71 percent of the blacks posted bond, a figure that compares favorably with the 77 percent of whites who did so (see table 4.6). The cases in which there is no information concerning bond pose serious problems for interpretation. It is, of course, possible that in these cases the defendant was unable to post bond, and the clerk, therefore, simply failed to enter information concerning

TABLE 4.5. AVERAGE AMOUNT OF BOND SET FOR SELECTED
OFFENSES, 1870–1884

	Black defendants	White defendants
Theft	$201 (N = 61)	$294 (N = 18)
Horse theft	$268 (N = 79)	$329 (N = 16)
Cattle theft	$207 (N = 30)	$320 (N = 11)
Theft of other livestock	$138 (N = 51)	$167 (N = 5)
Burglary	$289 (N = 42)	$200 (N = 2)
Theft from house	$206 (N = 43)	$220 (N = 8)
Swindling	$233 (N = 25)	$815 (N = 27)
Murder	$675 (N = 84)	$1,846 (N = 36)
Assault with intent to kill	$293 (N = 107)	$423 (N = 73)

Source: Washington County District Court, Minutes and Criminal Dockets; US Census of
Population, Washington County, Texas, 1870, 1880; Brenham *Banner.*

TABLE 4.6. SUCCESS IN POSTING BOND, 1870–1884

	Black	White
Number of cases*	225	128
Number and percentage of defendants posting bond	159 (71%)	98 (77%)

Source: Washington County District Court, Minutes and Dockets; US Census of
Population, Washington County, Texas, 1870, 1880; Brenham *Banner.*
* These cases are those for which information concerning bond is available. They are derived
from a total of 527 cases involving black defendants and 260 involving whites charged with
offenses against both persons and property.

bond. If this were true, then only 30 percent of all black defendants and 38 percent
of all white defendants escaped incarceration while they awaited trial. This would
mean that many defendants languished in jail while awaiting trial but nevertheless
suggests that Republican officials did not discriminate against black defendants.

These figures, however, substantially overstate the number of defendants who
went to jail because they were not able to post bond. Many persons under indictment successfully evaded arrest. Indictments against them remained on the record for
years until the district attorney entered a nolle prosequi or transferred their cases to
the retired docket. The absence of information concerning bond obviously does not

mean that these persons spent time in jail awaiting trial. In yet other cases, persons were indicted for misdemeanors that fell within the jurisdiction of inferior courts. The district court minutes and dockets are silent about bond in these cases because they were routinely transferred to justices of the peace, who made decisions on bond.[38] Moreover, in many cases, the district clerk probably failed to enter information concerning bond, regardless of whether bond was set or posted. Entries in the minutes and dockets are not legal records that indicate that defendants or others had pledged money or property to guarantee defendants' appearance in court. Consequently, recording this information in the minute or docket books was not vital. The fact that the clerks entered the names of petit jurors in some cases that went to trial but not in others suggests that they were not meticulous and consistent record keepers. This is underscored by the fact that they sometimes recorded information concerning bond in the dockets but omitted it from the minutes, and vice versa. While it is therefore not certain that 71 percent of blacks and 77 percent of whites held for trial posted bond, the figures were substantially higher than 30 percent for blacks and 38 percent for whites.

Even though many black defendants succeeded in posting bond, they might have been forced to rely on employers or other whites to stand as sureties. Indeed, the Brenham *Banner*, the Democratic newspaper, repeatedly asserted that "it has long been a notorious fact that whenever a freedman gets into trouble . . . he invariably goes to a Democrat." If this were true, whites had an opportunity, as the *Banner* suggested, to project the image of white paternalism and to foster a sense of dependency among blacks. It would also offer labor-starved planters an opportunity to obtain cheap labor, since incarcerated freedmen were in a poor position to reject terms proposed by those who offered to obtain their release. The *Banner's* claim, however, was an exaggeration. There are twenty-eight cases with black defendants in which the names and races of sureties are known. In thirteen, all sureties were black; in ten, all were white; and in five, sureties included blacks and whites. Thus while blacks sometimes turned to whites, it is significant that Republican officials proved willing to accept black sureties even when they did not own sufficient property to secure the bond. This liberality weakened one of the props of white dominance.[39]

When black defendants finally appeared for trial, they depended upon effective counsel in order to escape the penitentiary or the gallows. An experienced lawyer could keep hostile jurors out of the jury box, obtain a continuance if necessary to guarantee the presence of defense witnesses, demonstrate that the prosecutor's case was flawed, subject prosecution witnesses to vigorous cross examination, and perhaps even convince the prosecutor to drop a weak case. While virtually all black defendants were represented by lawyers, most, being poor, were probably represented by court-appointed counsel. Nevertheless, many criminally accused blacks chose not to rely on appointed counsel. For two terms of the district court—September 1879 and March 1880—the docket entries specify the names of defense counsel and indicate which were appointed by the court. In fourteen cases with black defendants, six were argued by court-appointed counsel and eight by privately retained attorneys. This small sample, of course, does not prove that most black defendants hired attorneys, but it suggests that many did so.[40]

The mere presence of counsel did not guarantee that blacks were effectively represented. As one might expect, attorneys who received a fee from their clients appear to have been more effective than court-appointed attorneys. In the fourteen cases with black defendants that were initiated in September 1879 and March 1880, all six blacks with appointed attorneys were found guilty; but four of the eight who hired lawyers escaped conviction, and one of the four found guilty was convicted of a reduced offense. In this small sample, none of the defendants with court-appointed counsel fared well, but such was not always the case. Newspaper reports of trials suggest that appointed attorneys sometimes aggressively defended their clients.[41] What appears to have been crucial was the appointment of counsel sufficiently in advance of trial to permit thorough preparation. In sixty-two cases with black defendants tried between 1870 and 1884, the court dockets reveal both the dates of appointment of counsel and the dates of trial. Although lawyers were appointed well before trial in a majority of these cases, court officials allowed one case in four to go to trial on the same day that counsel was appointed and thus minimized defendants' chances for effective representation. In only two of these fifteen cases did the defendants escape conviction. Nevertheless, in the forty-seven cases in which attorneys were appointed in advance, freedmen fared much better, winning acquittals or dismissals in seventeen (36 percent). Appointed counsel could be effective.

The behavior of the prosecutor was also very important to black defendants. Although all but one of the Washington County prosecutors who served during the 1870s and early 1880s were Republicans, they did not necessarily display favoritism toward black defendants. Undoubtedly, Republican prosecutors took their roles seriously, sought to enhance their professional reputations, and prosecuted cases aggressively by pressing every advantage. This could easily result in injustice for black defendants, particularly those who received only token representation. In the 1874 prosecution of Andrew Davis for the rape of a ten-year-old black girl, for example, the evidence was clearly insufficient, since two physicians who examined the girl did not believe that penetration—an essential element of the crime under Texas law— had occurred. In addition, the testimony suggested that the door of the room where the alleged rape took place was open, that several persons were in the adjoining room, and that the defendant made no effort to prevent the victim from calling for help. Despite what appears from the record to have been a weak case, Thomas Davidson, the district attorney, pressed for a conviction. He put the alleged victim on the stand and asked questions that the Texas Supreme Court later noted were "as leading as it was possible to make them" and "suggested to a person of the lowest capacity the answers desired." Not only did Davidson win a guilty verdict, but the jury decided that the defendant should hang. Only an appeal and a reversal by the Texas Supreme Court saved Davis from the gallows. When retried in 1875, he won acquittal.[42]

Although this case demonstrates that Republican prosecutors could be overzealous, they often used their discretionary authority on behalf of black defendants. Prosecutors dismissed 33 percent of the felony prosecutions against black defendants, frequently explaining that there was insufficient evidence to proceed. This was almost identical to the dismissal rate for whites, which stood at 36 percent. Thus Republican county attorneys were remarkably evenhanded in using their discretionary authority to keep many black, as well as white, defendants out of jeopardy.[43]

Examination of conviction rates and sentencing also suggests that Republican criminal justice was remarkably objective. As table 4.7 shows, for the period from 1870 to 1884, blacks were convicted at a slightly higher rate than whites (61 percent to 51 percent) when tried for property crimes and at about the same rate as whites when charged with crimes against the person (57 percent for blacks, 54 percent for whites). Given that whites were, on the whole, better able than blacks to hire counsel, these data suggest that juries, too, were remarkably evenhanded in deciding cases. Patterns of sentencing reinforce this view (see table 4.8). In each of the major categories of property crime, the average sentence imposed on blacks was slightly shorter than the average sentence white convicts received. The facts that Texas juries were responsible for sentencing and that blacks sat on juries in significant numbers undoubtedly help explain this.[44]

TABLE 4.7. CONVICTION RATES, 1870–1884

	Black	White
Offenses against property		
Cases tried	191	74
Guilty	116 (61%)	38 (51%)
Not guilty	75 (39%)	36 (49%)
Offenses against the person		
Cases tried	121	63
Guilty	69 (57%)	34 (54%)
Not guilty	53 (43%)	29 (46%)
Offenses against persons and property		
Cases tried	312	137
Guilty	185 (59%)	72 (52%)
Not guilty	127 (41%)	65 (48%)

Source: Washington County District Court, Minutes and Dockets; US Census of Population, Washington County, Texas, 1870, 1880; Brenham *Banner*.

TABLE 4.8. SENTENCING IN PROPERTY OFFENSES, 1870–1884

	Mean sentence blacks (years)	Mean sentence whites (years)
Theft	1.8 (N = 11)	2.0 (N = 7)
Horse theft	6.3 (N =32)	6.7 (N = 3)
Burglary	3.1 (N = 14)	
Theft from house	2.7 (N = 20)	3.7 (N = 4)
Swindling	2.0 (N = 5)	2.0 (N = 1)

Source: Washington County District Court, Minutes and Dockets; US Census of Population, Washington County, Texas, 1870, 1880; Brenham *Banner*.

A deeper analysis of the data on prosecutions of violent crime might at first glance suggest the need to qualify this conclusion. In murder cases, for example, blacks were not only convicted at a significantly higher rate than whites (59 percent to 35 percent), but they received more severe sentences. While the most common sentence imposed upon persons charged with murder was five years, half of the black convicts but only 17 percent of the whites received more severe sentences. In prosecutions for assault with intent to kill, whites were more likely than blacks to be convicted of a reduced offense (83 percent for whites to 56 percent for blacks) and to receive a fine rather than a prison sentence. But even if they were convicted on the original charge, whites typically received a less severe sentence than blacks.[45]

Beneath the surface of these statistics lie some predictable and some not-so-predictable conclusions. One of the reasons that murder-conviction rates were lower for whites than for blacks was the difficulty of winning convictions of whites charged with the murder of freedmen. Although local officials did prosecute whites who killed blacks, there is no evidence that a white person was ever convicted of murder or manslaughter for the homicide of a black person between 1868 and 1885.[46] When whites were charged with assault with intent to kill blacks, prosecutors won convictions in 60 percent of the cases that went to trial, but juries found the defendants guilty only of aggravated assault or simple assault and imposed fines rather than prison terms on the defendants.[47]

Failure to deal firmly with whites who committed acts of violence against blacks reflected the mores of the white community. Whites believed that they had to have a great deal of freedom to discipline blacks, that disrespect or "insolence" on the part of blacks justified whites resorting to violence, and that authorities had to be circumspect in punishing whites for acts of violence against blacks lest they remove the keystone in the arch of white dominance. This meant, for example, that whites were reluctant to testify against neighbors who murdered or assaulted blacks, while black witnesses might feel that giving public testimony against whites in such cases was dangerous. Thus when Hiram Craig, "a [white] stock dealer, who is well known in this county," was tried for the murder of John Foster, a black agricultural laborer, the testimony of the prosecution witnesses, once they took the stand, was equivocal. As a result, it was "apparent that the state had no case," and the judge, at the request of the county attorney, instructed the jury to return a verdict of not guilty.[48] Even if cases went to the jury for deliberation and a verdict, the prosecutor had little chance of success. Juries hearing these cases always included some whites, and since jury verdicts required unanimity, they could easily block conviction. Or they might refuse to vote for conviction unless other jurors agreed to a reduction of the offense. This was especially likely in prosecutions for assault with intent to kill, in which it was particularly difficult for prosecutors to meet the evidentiary standards necessary to establish intent. Given the mores of whites and the nature of the jury system then, Republicans were singularly unsuccessful in affording redress to black victims of white violence.

There is yet another reason for the disparity in conviction rates and sentences in murder cases. Blacks charged with the murder of blacks were convicted at a significantly higher rate than were whites indicted for murdering whites (67 percent to 40 percent).[49] In cases of assault with intent to kill, 75 percent of blacks who attacked other blacks were convicted, while 67 percent of whites who assaulted whites were convicted.[50] Sentencing followed a similar pattern. While only one of the four whites convicted of killing white persons received more than a five-year sentence, fifteen of the twenty-two blacks convicted of slaying blacks received more than five years. And of these fifteen, juries imposed life terms on five and sentenced two to hang. Of the two whites convicted of assault with intent to murder whites, one received a one-year jail sentence; the other was sentenced to two years in prison. In comparison, of the seven blacks found guilty of assault with intent to murder members of their own race, four received two years and the other three were each sentenced to more than two years in prison.

These data are very revealing. Freedmen were particularly well represented on juries that tried black-against-black murder and assault cases, while whites predominated on juries that tried cases involving white intraracial violence. And Texas law gave jurors the authority to impose sentences. It appears that black jurors were more likely than white jurors to be intolerant of violence, to believe that the grounds for justifying homicide were narrow, and to deal firmly with those guilty of murder or assault. This suggests that black jurors did not adhere to white norms that sanctioned the use of violence to avenge personal insults and defend one's honor. Instead, they used their authority to deter intraracial violence and to preserve order and stability within the black community. Thus the harsher treatment of blacks charged with crimes of violence was not a manifestation of racism but an indication of the responsiveness of the Republican criminal justice system to black demands for justice and respect.[51] As John Dollard pointed out many years ago, it was contempt for blacks that led white officials in the years after disfranchisement to ignore black-against-black violence. ("If a nigger kills another nigger, that's one less nigger," was a saying common among early twentieth-century Southern police.) And this malign neglect, as Dollard and others have pointed out, played an important role in fostering the widespread black-against-black violence that threatened the black community.[52]

Cases in which blacks were indicted for acts of violence against whites are also suggestive. Consider that of Alexander Mason, a black drayman who in December 1880 killed Ferdinand Bohnenstengel, a German bar and grocery keeper who had lived in Brenham for eight years. When Mason entered Bohnenstengel's shop, Bohnenstengel demanded that Mason retract statements he had made about him. Mason refused, left the store cursing, and remained outside the shop, daring Bohnenstengel to come after him. When the enraged merchant approached Mason with a buggy whip, the black man first warned him to stop, then picked up "a piece of scantling or board about six feet long and weighing eight or ten pounds," and struck Bohnenstengel. The next day, the shopkeeper died. Because whites were outraged by the killing—the Brenham *Banner* carried a lengthy story on the altercation under the headline "A WHITE MAN KILLED BY A NEGRO"—Mason promptly fled. Two months later, however, he sent a messenger to local officials and explained that he was ready to surrender. Mason was then taken into custody by a black deputy sheriff and brought before Republican justice of the peace Stephen Hackworth for a preliminary examination. The county attorney agreed that it was not a case of first-degree murder, and Hackworth set bail at $1,250, which Mason promptly posted. One month later, a jury of seven blacks and five whites acquitted Mason. Bohnenstengel was not a prominent citizen, but he was a white man, and as the *Banner* headline suggested, the white community viewed Mason's action as an outrage. Nevertheless, the system afforded the black drayman justice.[53]

Mason's case was not an isolated example. Freedmen were convicted in only three of six black-against-white murder cases that went to trial (four other cases were not prosecuted), a lower conviction rate than in black-against-black murder cases. And blacks were convicted in only two of the four black-against-white assault-with-intent-to-murder cases that went to trial—again, a lower conviction rate than in black-against-black cases. Thus with freedmen present in the jury box, blacks who used force against whites in self-defense escaped retribution. While this might seem insignificant in light of the small number of cases involved, it was undoubtedly important to the black community. Large numbers of black men and women attended court and spoke with their friends about what went on there. Cases like that of Mason unquestionably attracted attention and suggested that whites' assumption that it was never justifiable for blacks to use force against whites no longer had the imprimatur of law. This encouraged blacks to be more aggressive in defending their rights and, in the process, further eroded the foundations of white dominance.[54]

The foregoing analysis of the impact of black political power on criminal justice is limited to one Texas county. A great deal of work remains to be done in order to know if there were similar developments in other parts of the South. Nevertheless, it clearly demonstrates the importance of the ballot to the freedmen. Of course, political power did not end many of the injustices that blacks suffered. It did not afford blacks adequate redress against white violence, although it did encourage them to use force in resisting whites who menaced them. It did not guarantee that impoverished blacks would have adequate legal representation when tried for felonies, and obviously, it did not free blacks from the poverty that encouraged some of them to commit the property crimes that led them into the arms of the law. Nevertheless, black political influence did make the criminal justice system more responsive to the freed people in numerous important ways. When grand juries were not lily white, blacks were less likely to be subject to capricious indictment. If indicted, they were not likely to spend weeks or months in jail awaiting trial. They did not need to resign themselves to conviction once indicted, given the number of cases that were dismissed by prosecutors or that ended in acquittals. Blacks also gained because officials took crime within the black community seriously, thereby stemming the corrosive effect of intraracial violence.[55]

Black influence on the criminal justice system challenged white dominance in other less tangible but no less significant ways. Participation on grand and petit juries not only gave blacks a voice in institutions that directly affected their lives but also destroyed a powerful symbol of white supremacy. White authority was also eroded when black testimony was taken seriously by mixed juries and when black men were considered worthy of serving as sureties on bail bonds. Moreover, when juries returned verdicts acquitting blacks who had resorted to violence against whites, they challenged a central assumption of white supremacy. Together with other changes made possible by political power—casting ballots in the face of white opposition, electing blacks to office, having legal forums in which to assert rights against their employers—these advances weakened the institutional props of white dominance and fostered black assertiveness, both prerequisites for meaningful black freedom. This growing black confidence and assertiveness precluded realization of postemancipation race relations whites sought to impose through the black codes of 1865 and 1866. Redemption and the reassertion of white dominance undoubtedly weakened black militance, but to recall Braudel's remark, losing movements are not without consequence. The confidence and assertiveness among blacks that the process of politicization encouraged altered the terms on which blacks and whites confronted one another and left a legacy that Redemption did not completely destroy.

This study of the politics of justice in Washington County, Texas, also lends support to a substantial body of work suggesting that Southern race relations remained flexible during the years following Reconstruction. As C. Vann Woodward, J. Morgan Kousser, and Lawrence C. Goodwyn, among others, have suggested, the years preceding the wave of legal disfranchisement and segregation that swept the South between 1890 and 1910 were a period of "forgotten alternatives," to use Woodward's phrase. Blacks had important options that vanished when they lost the vote and whites created a rigid, legally sanctioned caste system. The Washington County experience demonstrates that black political activism—not merely the white paternalism or the threat of federal intervention emphasized by Woodward—was crucial to the possibilities that existed during the post-Reconstruction years.[56]

Black political activism may also help to explain whites' powerful reaction in the 1890s against black rights. Howard N. Rabinowitz has argued that the assertiveness of urban blacks who were born after emancipation and who reached maturity in the 1880s frightened whites and encouraged them to demand legal segregation as a means of keeping blacks in their place.[57] It was not merely the "new Negroes," however, who alarmed whites. Black political participation and success in places like Washington County fostered self-confidence and assertiveness among former slaves as well as their children, something that was weakened but not destroyed by Redemption. This probably deepened white concern and encouraged the dramatic increase in lynching that began in the 1880s and the disfranchisement and segregation movement of the 1890s. A great deal of work must be done to test this hypothesis, but such research promises to deepen our understanding of the crucial and complex developments in Southern race relations that occurred in the 1880s and 1890s.

Donald G. Nieman was an associate professor of history at Clemson University at the time he authored this article. It was originally published as Nieman, Donald G. "Black Political Power and Criminal Justice: Washington County, Texas, 1868–1884." Journal of Southern History *55 (August 1989): 391–420. Copyright 1989 by the Southern Historical Association. It is reprinted by permission of the editor of the* Journal of Southern History *and the author.*

NOTES

1. For a comparison of emancipation in the United States and other slave societies, see Eric Foner, *Nothing but Freedom: Emancipation and Its Legacy* (Baton Rouge: Louisiana State University Press, 1983). Criticisms of this neglect of black political activity include Herman Belz, "The New Orthodoxy in Reconstruction Historiography," *Reviews in American History* 1 (1973): 106–12; LaWanda Cox, *Lincoln and Black Freedom: A Study in Presidential Leadership* (Columbia: University of South Carolina Press, 1981), 142–84; and Eric Foner, "Reconstruction Revisited," *Reviews in American History* 10 (1982): 82–100.

I wish to thank LaWanda Cox, Linda Nieman, Eric Foner, Leslie Rowland, Harold Hyman, William Nelson, Albert Hamscher, John McCulloh, Allen Trelease, Samuel Walker, and members of the New York University School of Law's Legal History Colloquium for valuable comments and criticism. Paul Scott has provided invaluable assistance in using the large collection of Washington County records housed in the Texas A&M University Archives, helping me locate materials in the Washington County Courthouse, and placing his deep knowledge of the region's history at my disposal. Gertrude Lehrmann, the Washington County (Texas) clerk;

Blondean Kuecker, the clerk of the Washington County District Court; and the late Otto Beckendorf of Brenham, Texas, graciously assisted my research. Grants from the American Bar Foundation, the New York University School of Law, and the American Association for State and Local History have supported the research on which this article is based.

2. Eric Foner's magisterial *Reconstruction: America's Unfinished Revolution, 1863–1877* (New York: 1988), which appeared after this article was completed, emphasizes the importance of black political participation. Other prominent examples of recent work on black politics include Thomas Holt, *Black over White: Negro Political Leadership in South Carolina during Reconstruction* (Urbana: University of Illinois Press, 1977); Eric Anderson, *Race and Politics in North Carolina, 1872–1901: The Black Second* (Baton Rouge: 1980); Foner, *Nothing but Freedom*; LaWanda Cox, "From Emancipation to Segregation: National Policy and Southern Blacks," in *Interpreting Southern History: Historiographical Essays in Honor of Sanford W. Higginbotham*, ed. John B. Boles and Evelyn T. Nolen (Baton Rouge: Louisiana State University Press, 1987).

3. Braudel, as quoted in Herbert G. Gutman, *Work, Culture, and Society in Industrializing America: Essays in American Working-Class and Social History* (New York: 1976), 67.

4. On the relationship between criminal law and the postemancipation conflict between blacks and whites, see Donald G. Nieman, *To Set the Law in Motion: The Freedmen's Bureau and the Legal Rights of Blacks, 1865–1868* (Millwood, NY: KTO Press, 1979), passim; Edward L. Ayers, *Vengeance and Justice: Crime and Punishment in the 19th-Century American South* (New York: Oxford University Press, 1984), 141–276; William Cohen, "Negro Involuntary Servitude in the South, 1865–1940: A Preliminary Analysis," *Journal of Southern History* 42 (February 1976): 31–60. The relationship between black political power and criminal justice has been almost wholly neglected. Ayers's important study deals primarily with the political economy of Southern criminal justice and does not assess the impact of black political power on justice. It relies heavily on case studies of criminal justice in Chatham, Greene, and Whitfield Counties, Georgia. However, all three were counties in which Republicans either never controlled local government or their dominance was extremely short lived and thus did not bear on the impact of black political power on justice. Albert Colbey Smith's impressive doctoral dissertation examined the relationship between property crime and economic structure, race, and class in Baldwin, McIntosh, and Terrell Counties, Georgia. While he was concerned with the relationship between black property holding and black political power, he did not explore the operation of the criminal justice system or the impact of black political power on criminal justice. Smith, "Down Freedom's Road: The Contours of Race, Class, and Property Crime in Black-Belt Georgia, 1866–1910" (PhD dissertation, University of Georgia, 1982). Mark Allen Reed, "Thieving Times: Criminals, Victims, and the Criminal Justice System in

Richmond, Virginia, 1868–1872" (MA
thesis, University of Virginia, 1985),
analyzes both crime and criminal
justice in Richmond, Virginia, over a
five-year period. During two of those
years (1868–70), city government was
under the control of a Republican
administration appointed by federal
military officials. However, this short
lived regime, which did not owe its
existence to black votes and showed
its contempt for blacks by keeping
the police force and juries lily-white,
speaks only indirectly to the impact
of black political power on justice. It
provides a case study that—like Ayers's
county studies—suggests the way that
criminal justice operated in areas in
which blacks did not effectively exercise
political power.

5. Charles R. Schmidt, *History of
Washington County* (San Antonio:
Naylor, 1949), 1–20; US Census Office,
*Compendium of the Tenth Census, Part
I* (Washington, DC: Government
Printing Office, 1883), 5, 255.

6. US Census Office, *Report on Cotton
Production in the United States*
(Washington, DC: 1884), 101–2.

7. US Census Office, *The Statistics of
the Population of the United States:
Compiled from the Original Returns
of the Ninth Census* (Washington, DC:
1872), I, 372–73; US Census Office,
*Compendium of the Eleventh Census:
1890* (Washington, DC: 1892–97), I,
511. According to the 1860 census, only
three free blacks resided in Washington
County in that year. Because the
number of free blacks present in the
antebellum period was so small and
because there is no evidence that other
blacks who had been free before the
Civil War migrated to the county
after the war, the term *freedmen* has

been applied generally to black men in
postwar Washington County. See US
Census Office, *Population of the United
States in 1860* (Washington, DC: 1864),
478–79.

8. US Census Office, *Statistics of the
Population*, I, 322; US Census Office,
Compendium of the Eleventh Census, I,
511, 654–55; II, 672. The German-born
population is calculated by combining
those listed in the 1890 census figures
as having been born in Germany
(3,217) and in Austria (204). Census
office tabulations referring to the 1890
population do not give the number
of persons who were the children of
German-born parents but give only the
numbers of persons who
were the children of foreign-born
parents (4,573). On the assumption
that the percentage of persons of
German descent among the children of
the foreign-born reported in the 1890
census is equal to the percentage of
Germans among the foreign-born (85
percent), 3,887 residents of Washington
County were children of German-born
parents in 1890. Thus the number of
Washington County residents who
were German born (3,421) or the
children of German-born parents
(3,887) was 7,308, or 25 percent of the
county's 1890 population of 29,157.

9. US Census Office, *Statistics of the
Population*, I, 274; US Census Office,
Compendium of the Eleventh Census, I,
401.

10. Louis Edward to Gen. Charles Griffin,
July 15, 1867; Capt. Edward Collins
to Lt. Col. E. Morse, January 15, 1868;
and A. E. Thomas to Gen. Charles
Griffin, July 16, 1867, Correspondence
of the Office of Civil Affairs, District
of Texas and Fifth Military District,
1865–70, Records of the US Army

Continental Commands, 1821–1920, RG 393 (National Archives and Records Service, Washington, DC), microfilm publication M1188, reels 5, 8; B. O. Watrous to Gen. J. J. Reynolds, March 21, 1868, Letters Received and Registers of Letters Received, District of Texas and Fifth Military District, 1865–70, RG 393 (National Archives and Records Service, Washington, DC), microfilm publication, M-1193, reel 9; Thomas J. Lockett to E. M. Pease, September 18, 1867; F. P. Wood to E. M. Pease, August 25, 1868, and May 28, 1869; Stephen Hackworth to E. M. Pease, September 22 and November 1, 1868, and May 28, 1869; Jay S. to Dear Brother, June 28, 1870; B. Arnold to E. J. Davis, June 29, 1870; Lyd Smith to E. J. Davis, July 21, 1870; J. S. Bachelder to E. J. Davis, August 31, 1870; Matt Gaines to E. J. Davis, June 16, 1871; A. E. Thomas to E. J. Davis, December 16, 1871, Governors' Papers (Texas State Archives, Texas State Library, Austin [hereinafter cited as GP]); Stephen Hackworth to J. S. Tracy, n.d., James Pearson Newcomb Papers (Barker Texas History Center, University of Texas at Austin [hereinafter referred to as BTHC]); Brenham Banner, February 28, 1871, n.d. [probably July or August 1871], August 11, 15 and September 15, 1871; May 31, 1873.

11. William Schlottman to E. J. Davis, n.d. [probably January 1871], GP; Senate Miscellaneous Documents, 50 Cong., 2 sess., no. 62: Testimony on the Alleged Election Outrages in Texas (Serial 2616, Washington, DC: 1889), 156–69, 486–89, 591, 619.

12. The county was redeemed through a combination of shrewd political strategy and violence. Democrats assiduously wooed Germans and sought to exploit their hostility to blacks during the 1870s and early 1880s, thus winning increased German support. In 1884, they virtually eliminated German support for local Republican candidates. They intensified charges of Republican corruption when the county treasurer (ironically, a German) defaulted. And they spearheaded the formation of a People's Party (not to be confused with the Populist Party of the 1890s), which claimed to unite public-spirited men in restoring honesty and intelligence to local government. In the 1884 elections, all but one of the People's Party candidates won narrow victories. See Brenham Banner, December 11, 1873; February 25 and March 3, 1876; August 22, 1882; August 31, September 4, October 26, 29, and November 4, 8, 11, 1884; Testimony on Alleged Election Outrages in Texas (Washington, DC: US Government Printing Office, 1889), 6, 13, 169, 216, 242, 380–91, 401–5, 455, 468. The large-scale defection of Germans was critical. Because the black majority was slim and the black population very young, the number of black and white males of voting age was roughly equal. Indeed, the 1890 census would show that among males over twenty-one years old, the number of whites exceeded blacks by 250. See US Census Office, Compendium of the Eleventh Census, I, 805. With diminishing German support, Republicans, who had few other white supporters, found their hold on power tenuous. During the 1884 campaign, there were several attacks on black Republicans that culminated in a raid on a polling station in a heavily black precinct in which three black election judges were seriously wounded.

This lowered the black turnout and contributed to the narrow Republican defeat. Two years later, Democrats retained their grip on power in another extremely close election by stealing ballot boxes in three heavily Republican precincts. Moreover, they permanently crippled the party by lynching three black Republicans and running three prominent white Republican leaders, including Stephen Hackworth, out of the county. Brenham *Banner*, November 6, 1884; *Testimony on Alleged Election Outrages*, passim; Rudolph Kleberg to A. H. Garland, March 4 and December 21, 1887; Anonymous, Brenham, Washington County, Texas, to the Attorney General of the United States, September 3, 1889, file #87–1293, box 305, Central Files, Department of Justice, RG 60 (National Archives, Washington, DC); Brenham *Banner*, November 4, 5, 6, 7, 9, 14 and December 3, 7, 8, 19, 1886.

13. The ratio of black Republican nominees to offices elected on a countywide basis is as follows: 1870 (1:4), 1873 (3:7), 1876 (5:16), 1878 (6:16), 1880 (5:16), 1882 (5:16), 1884 (6:17), and 1886 (6:15). Election Returns, 1860–92 (County Clerk's Office, Washington County Courthouse, Brenham, TX [hereinafter referred to as WCC]).

14. B. Arnold to E. J. Davis, June 29, 1870, GP; Stephen Hackworth to James Newcomb, June 24, 1871, James Person Newcomb Papers, Dolph Briscoe Center for American History, University of Texas at Austin; Brenham *Banner*, May 24, 1873; February 18, 1876; July 5, 12, 19 and August 16, 1878; July 22 and August 1, 5, 19, 1880; August 6, 17, 1882; August 19, 27, 1884.

15. Hackworth to E. M. Pease, September 22, 1868, and May 28, 1869,

GP; Hackworth to E. M. Pease, November 11, 1880, Niles-Graham-Pease Papers, Austin-Travis County Collection, Austin Public Library, Austin, TX; Hackworth to Gov. John St. John, July 5, 8, 1879, Governors' Papers (Kansas Historical Society, Topeka, KS); *Testimony on Alleged Election Outrages*, 159 (first and second quotations), 165 (third quotation), 463 (fourth quotation).

16. Information on elected officials is taken from Election Returns, 1860–92. Of the 135 deputy sheriffs named between 1870 and 1884 whose race can be determined, 31 (23 percent) were black. See Record of Official Bonds, 1868–75, and Record of Official Bonds, 1879–83, County Clerk's Office, WCC; Record of Official Bonds, 1876–81, Washington County Records (Texas A&M University Archives, College Station, Texas [hereinafter referred to as WCR]). The manuscript census returns of Washington County for 1870 and 1880 were consulted to determine the race of deputies.

17. For the statutory provisions governing selection of grand and petit juries during these years, see "General Laws of Texas, 1871," in *The Laws of Texas, 1822–1897*, vol. 7, comp. H. P. N. Gammel (Austin: 1898); George Washington Paschal, comp., *A Digest of the Laws of Texas*, 2nd ed. (Washington, DC: 1870), articles 2,806, 2,854.

18. These petit juries, which each contained twelve persons, were panels that heard and decided cases. Names of jurors are taken from the Criminal Minutes of the Washington County District Court, located in the District Clerk's Office, WCC. There were 1,284 jurors on the 107 juries that sat between

1870 and 1876. Out of these, 574 of the jurors were white, 322 were black, and the races of 388 jurors are not known because they could not be identified in the 1870 or 1880 census.

19. The present analysis of the racial composition of juries is limited to those juries on which the races of at least nine jurors could be determined. This provided seventy-two juries impaneled between 1870 and 1884, a number that is large enough to be representative. If the analysis had been limited to juries on which the races of ten jurors were known, that would have provided only thirty-seven juries, or slightly more than two juries per year. If juries with four or more members whose races are not known had been included, potentially distorted and unreliable figures would have resulted.

20. "General Laws of the State of Texas, 1876," in Gammel, *Laws of Texas*, vol. 8. For illiteracy among black jurors, see table 4.4. Names of jury commissioners are taken from the Criminal Minutes of the District Court.

21. The district court minutes, the source of grand jurors' names, are not extant for July 1878 through September 1880. Information on cases for this period is taken from the dockets, which, unfortunately, do not list the jurors. The names of persons who sat on one grand jury during this period, January 1879, were recorded in the Brenham *Banner*, January 7, 1879.

22. *The Code of Criminal Procedure of the State of Texas*, Galveston, Texas, 1879, articles 712, 723.

23. Carl Schutze to O. M. Roberts, March 4, 1880, GP (first quotation); Brenham *Banner*, September 20, 1881 (second quotation). For other indications of the independence of

black jurors, see Brenham *Banner*, April 1, 1880; October 11, 1883.

24. As table 4.3 shows, the races of 287 (41 percent) of the 696 persons indicted for offenses against property could not be determined. The analysis of the fates of defendants is limited to those identified by race, which was done by consulting the 1870 and 1880 manuscript censuses of population and the Brenham *Banner*. This study considers two categories of crimes: property crimes and crimes against the person. The former includes theft, receiving stolen property, burglary, swindling, forgery, embezzlement, malicious mischief, and arson. The category of crimes against the person includes first- and second-degree murder, manslaughter, assault with intent to kill, aggravated assault, assault, threatening the life of another, rape, and robbery.

25. For the numbers of black and white grand jurors during 1874 and 1875, see table 4.1. Beginning in 1870 through 1876, 178 blacks and 55 whites were indicted for offenses against property—3.2 times as many blacks as whites. Beginning in 1877 through 1884, 135 blacks and 41 whites were charged with these crimes—3.2 times as many blacks as whites.

26. For a recent work that argues the importance of class division within the black community, see Holt, *Black over White*.

27. On the small number of property-crime prosecutions in the antebellum years, see Ayers, *Vengeance and Justice*, 111, 311n28; Michael S. Hindus, *Prison and Plantation: Crime, Justice, and Authority in Massachusetts and South Carolina, 1767–1878* (Chapel Hill: University of North Carolina Press,

1980), 59–84; David J. Bodenhamer, "Law and Disorder on the Early Frontier: Marion County, Indiana, 1823–1850," *Western Historical Quarterly* 10 (July 1979): 323–36. The years excluded are 1874, 1875, and 1881, years that followed poor local harvests and caused severe hardship for sharecroppers and laborers. See Brenham *Banner*, March 19, 1874; March 24, 1876; December 7, 1881. With these three years excluded, 199 blacks and 82 whites were indicted for property crimes. On the relationship between poverty and black crime, see Smith, "Down Freedom's Road," 165–200.

28. Between 1870 and 1884, there were 145 indictments for horse theft in Washington County. The defendants' races have been identified in 82 of these; sixty-seven were black and fifteen white. On the commercial opportunities open to horse thieves, see Brenham *Banner*, December 24, 1874; March 25, 1877; March 6, 1878; April 3, 1881.

29. Typically, antebellum grand jurors were men of above-average wealth who met not only to decide whether persons accused of crimes should stand trial but to investigate and report on the performance of state and county government. See Ayers, *Vengeance and Justice*, 112–13; Jack Kenny Williams, *Vogues in Villainy: Crime and Retribution in Antebellum South Carolina* (Columbia: University of South Carolina Press, 1959), 31, 56–57, 69–70, 80, 113–14, 127–28; and Richard D. Younger, *The People's Panel: The Grand Jury in the United States, 1634–1941* (Providence, RI: Brown University Press, 1963), 79–84. Washington County grand jurors continued to supervise county affairs during the postwar years, investigating county finances, the county jail, and the maintenance of county roads.

30. In the 313 cases in which blacks were charged with property crimes, the victims in 67 cases have been identified. Forty-four of these were white, and twenty-three were black. The names of victims were found in reports of crimes in the Brenham *Banner* and in indictments returned by grand jurors. Unfortunately, the *Banner* failed to mention victims in most property-crime cases. Indictments frequently mentioned the names of the victims, but they are extant for only a few cases.

31. According to Ayers's data, 135 blacks and 8 whites were charged with offenses against property in the Greene County Superior Court. Ayers, *Vengeance and Justice*, 325n77. In 1870, Greene County's population was 66 percent black. US Census Office, *Compendium of the Tenth Census*, 342. Mark Allen Reed's examination of Richmond, Virginia, where blacks were excluded from grand and petit juries during the years under study, also supports the contention that black participation on grand juries resulted in greater fairness for accused blacks and reduced the disparity between the numbers of blacks and whites indicted. In the Richmond Hustings Court, 5.6 times as many blacks as whites (167 to 30) were charged with felonious property crimes. If both misdemeanor and felony property crimes before the Hustings Court are taken into account, 7.9 times as many blacks as whites were indicted. This disparity is far larger than that in the Washington County District Court. Moreover, one would

expect, other things being equal, the disparity in Richmond to be smaller because the percentage of blacks there was smaller, and propertyless whites made up a far larger proportion of the white population than in Washington County. The most likely explanation is that the absence of black jurors made Richmond grand juries more likely to indict blacks accused of crimes, even when the evidence against them was weak. Reed, "Thieving Times," table 4.6, 210.

32. On honor and Southerners' tolerance of violence, see Bertram Wyatt-Brown, *Southern Honor: Ethics and Behavior in the Old South* (Oxford: Oxford University Press, 1982); and Ayers, *Vengeance and Justice*. The editor of the Brenham *Banner* frequently noted the prevalence of these beliefs in articles criticizing Texas juries for being too lenient in dealing with killers. See, for example, Brenham *Banner*, March 23, 1878; July 2 and October 5, 1879; June 16, 1880. The editor also unwittingly demonstrated how widespread these beliefs were by frequently justifying individuals' resorting to violence to defend honor, avenge a family member, or settle a personal disagreement. See, for example, Brenham *Banner*, September 20, 1873; May 6, 1879; February 7 and April 13, 1880; August 30, 1883.

33. There were 131 indictments against freedmen for violent crimes between 1877 and 1884; in sixty-four (49 percent) of these, the races of the victims are known. In fifty-two of the sixty-four cases (81 percent), the victims were black.

34. On the concern about the heavy cost of criminal prosecutions, see Brenham *Banner*, January 22, 1875; July 12, 1877;

January 29 and March 5, 1879. For white Southerners' indifference to violence within the black community, see John Dollard, *Caste and Class in a Southern Town*, 3rd ed. (Madison: University of Wisconsin Press, 1957), 279–86; and Ayers, *Vengeance and Justice*, 231.

35. The grand juries were those that sat in September 1881 (twelve indictments), March 1882 (seventeen indictments), and September 1882 (twenty indictments).

36. See, for example, Brenham *Banner*, February 3, 1881.

37. Information was available for 225 of 527 (43 percent) cases with black defendants and 128 of 260 (49 percent) cases with white defendants.

38. Thirty-six indictments against blacks and eighteen against whites were transferred to the retired docket, an indication that no arrest had been made. The district attorney sometimes entered nolle prosequi in cases in which it was clear that the defendant had fled and would not be arrested. Nolle prosequi was entered in 148 cases with black defendants and eighty-six with white defendants. If one-third of these were in cases in which defendants had not been arrested (a conservative estimate), another forty-nine indictments against blacks and twenty-eight indictments against whites would have involved no arrest. Thus it is likely that eighty-five black defendants (16 percent) and forty-six white defendants (18 percent) were not arrested. In addition, the court transferred twenty-four cases involving blacks and twenty-six cases involving whites to inferior courts.

39. Brenham *Banner*, October 12, 1876. The names of sureties were taken from

district court minutes and dockets. The race of the sureties was determined by finding them in the 1870 and 1880 manuscript censuses of population. The law required that sureties have property, over and above the amount secured against seizure by the homestead exemption, equal to the amount of the bond. For indications that Republican officials accepted many black sureties who lacked sufficient property to back the bonds they made, see Brenham *Banner*, January 1, 1875; March 10, 1876; November 25, 1879.

40. Washington County District Court, Criminal Dockets, WCR. The district court minutes indicate that the district judge routinely appointed attorneys to represent poor defendants.

41. Brenham *Banner*, October 1, 2, 12, and 13, 1881; April 15, 1882; October 17, 1883.

42. *Cases Argued and Decided in the Supreme Court of the State of Texas during the Latter Part of the Galveston Term, the Entire Austin Term, and the First Part of the Tyler Term, 1875* (St. Louis, MO: Gilbert Book Company, 1883), quotations from 189–90; Washington County District Court, Minutes, June 25, 1875, WCC.

43. In cases involving offenses against persons and property, the district court disposed of 505 indictments against freedmen and 254 indictments against whites between 1870 and 1884. In 164 cases (33 percent) involving black defendants and 91 cases (36 percent) involving white defendants, the district attorney dismissed the charges. In tabulating dismissals, only those cases were included in which all charges against the defendants were dropped and they were no longer in jeopardy. Cases that were transferred to the retired docket were not included, since

these prosecutions could go forward if the defendants were apprehended. Also excluded were cases in which there was another indictment pending against the defendant, since she or he was still in jeopardy. This contrasts very favorably with the situation in the Richmond, Virginia, Hustings Court during the late 1860s and the early 1870s. There, officials were not popularly elected Republicans, and 35 percent of the white defendants but only 20 percent of the black defendants had their cases dismissed. Reed, "Thieving Times," 62.

44. There was much greater disparity in conviction rates and sentencing in Richmond, Virginia, where blacks did not serve as petit jurors, than in Washington County. This underscores the importance of black jurors. Reed, "Thieving Times," 72–73, 135–36.

45. Of seventy-seven blacks indicted for murder, fifty-six were tried for and thirty-three were found guilty of first- or second-degree murder or manslaughter. Of thirty-three whites indicted for murder, twenty were tried and seven convicted. Ninety freedmen were indicted for assault with intent to kill, sixty-five went to trial, and thirty-six were convicted—sixteen for assault with intent to murder and twenty for aggravated assault or simple assault. Sixty-four whites were indicted for this offense, thirty-five were tried, and twenty-four were found guilty— four for assault with intent to kill and twenty for aggravated or simple assault.

46. Four whites indicted for murder were charged with killing blacks. Because the races of the victims were determined in only nineteen of the thirty-three cases in which whites were charged with murder, however, it is possible that other whites were indicted for the

murder of blacks. In only four of the six cases in which whites were convicted of murder are the races of the victims known. Consequently, it is at least possible that in the other two cases, one or both of the victims was black.

47. Nine whites were indicted for assault with intent to kill blacks, five were tried, and three were convicted, all for aggravated assault. Again, this does not mean that only nine indictments for assault with intent to kill were found against whites who attacked blacks. The races of the victims are known in only twenty-six of sixty-four indictments against whites for assault with intent to kill. Undoubtedly, there are other indictments and probably convictions for attacks on blacks among the thirty-eight cases in which the victims' races are not known.

48. Brenham *Banner*, December 19, 1880 (first quotation); October 15, 1881 (second quotation).

49. Of the seventy-seven murder indictments against blacks, the races of the victims in sixty-two cases are known; in fifty-two of these, the victims were black, and in ten, the victims were white. In the fifty-two black-against-black cases, thirty-three went to trial, and twenty-two ended in convictions. There were thirty-three murder indictments against whites, but the victims in only nineteen cases have been identified; in fifteen, the victims were white, and in four, the victims were black. Of the fifteen white-against-white prosecutions, ten went to trial, and four resulted in convictions.

50. Following are the data on prosecutions for assault with intent to kill. Of ninety indictments against blacks, the races of the victims in thirty-one

cases are known: nine were whites, and twenty-two victims were blacks. Of the twenty-two cases with black victims, sixteen went to trial, and twelve of these ended in convictions. Of the sixty-four indictments against whites, the races of twenty-six victims have been determined—nine blacks and seventeen whites. Of the seventeen cases with white victims, only six went to trial, and four resulted in guilty verdicts.

51. Although the records of the Washington County District Court permit identification of the racial composition of few juries that tried black-against-black murder cases, what they reveal is suggestive. The records reveal the names of jurors who decided three black-against-black murder cases in the early 1870s: *The State v. Andrew Roberson, The State v. Henry Miller,* and *The State v. William Norris.* In each case, all the jurors whose races can be identified were black, the accused were found guilty, and the juries imposed stiff sentences. Two defendants were sentenced to hang, and one was sentenced to life in prison. Court records reveal the names of jurors in eight cases in which whites were tried for the murder of other whites. There were no blacks on three of the juries, one black on two juries, and from two to four black jurors on the other three panels. Washington County, Texas, District Court, Minutes; US Census of Population, Washington County, Texas, 1870, 1880.

52. Dollard, *Caste and Class,* 279–86. The quote is from Ayers, *Vengeance and Justice,* 231. The experience of Richmond, Virginia, between 1868 and 1872 also suggests whites' lack of concern about crime in the black community. The grand jury, which

contained no blacks during these years, refused to return true bills in only 8 percent of the cases involving white victims. It refused true bills in 15 percent of the cases with black victims. It did so even though the alleged perpetrators in the overwhelming majority of these cases were blacks. Reed, "Thieving Times," 158.

53. Brenham *Banner*, December 19, 1880; February 3, March 12, and April 3, 1881.

54. In ten cases in which blacks were charged with murdering whites, six went to trial, and three ended in convictions. On the presence of large numbers of blacks in the courtroom, see Brenham *Banner*, February 2 and August 2, 1878; March 27, 1883; April 9, 1884. It is not possible in an article of this nature and length to explore and demonstrate such a subtle phenomenon as the growth of black assertiveness. Examples of this are legion and include local blacks' repeated willingness to arm themselves to protect accused black criminals who were reputedly the targets of lynch mobs, a sustained campaign by blacks challenging segregation in local railroad waiting rooms and on trains departing from Brenham, black Republicans arming themselves to protect polling stations from white depredations, Brenham blacks' successful political campaign against a Redeemer city administration whose police systematically harassed blacks, and the frequent use of force by blacks against whites who threatened or insulted them. I shall deal with this phenomenon in detail in a book-length examination of the politics of justice in Washington County, Texas, 1865–1900.

55. The data for the period from 1885 to 1900 are still in the process of being prepared for computer analysis, and quantitatively, trends in criminal justice during this period cannot be discerned. However, an analysis of the sources relevant to this period clearly indicates that the criminal justice system became less responsive to blacks. Because Washington County Democrats faced an active Republican opposition during most of this period, they attempted to reduce black support for the Republicans by posing as friends of the freedman. To this end, they refrained from completely rooting out Republican innovations that had been popular with blacks. Thus blacks continued to serve on juries, albeit in token numbers. Despite such cosmetic efforts, Democrats systematically reduced black influence in the criminal justice process. In contrast to their Republican predecessors, Democratic sheriffs did not appoint black deputies, and law enforcement again became a prerogative of white men. Criminally accused blacks almost always turned to white landowners to sign surety bonds, a move suggesting that Democratic officials were reluctant to accept black sureties. Moreover, blacks convicted of misdemeanors and who had served short terms in the county jail during the 1870s and early 1880s were subject to far harsher punishment by the early 1890s. Democratic county commissioners created a county prison farm where petty criminals worked off their fines and court costs at the rate of fifty cents per day. Since fines and costs typically amounted to fifty dollars in convictions for such offenses as petty theft or carrying a pistol, those unable to pay spent long terms at hard labor on the county farm and on the county roads. Newspaper accounts from the 1890s suggest that inmates of

the county farm were almost exclusively freedmen. I shall treat developments in the years after 1885 in greater detail in my study of the politics of justice in Washington County, Texas, 1865–1900.

56. C. Vann Woodward, *The Strange Career of Jim Crow*, 3rd rev. ed. (New York: Oxford University Press, 1974), chaps. 2–3; J. Morgan Kousser, *The Shaping of Southern Politics: Suffrage Restriction and the Establishment of the One-Party South, 1880–1910* (New Haven: Yale University Press, 1974);

J. Morgan Kousser, "Progressivism— for Middle-Class Whites Only: North Carolina Education, 1880–1910," *Journal of Southern History* 46 (May 1980): 169–94, especially 192n35; Lawrence C. Goodwyn, "Populist Dreams and Negro Rights: East Texas as a Case Study," *American Historical Review* 76 (December 1971): 1,435–56.

57. Howard N. Rabinowitz, *Race Relations in the Urban South, 1865–1890* (New York: Oxford University Press, 1978), 333–39.

The African American Exodus from Comanche County

Billy Bob Lightfoot

Before, during, and after the Civil War in Texas, whites frequently blamed blacks for their difficulties, and in the process, too often blacks met their deaths by white mobs. In Coman-che County, as Billy Bob Lightfoot points out so well, whites took an even more officious step and removed blacks from the community. No African Americans were allowed in the county after 1886. It should be noted as one reads this poignant article that at times the author seems to assume that the black individual, although treated horribly, was guilty of some crime. Perhaps the word alleged *should have been utilized on a number of these instances. However, this is a powerful reminder of the vicious antiblack environment in Texas after the Civil War. Billy Bob Lightfoot earned his PhD at the University of Texas, his 1958 dissertation titled "The State Delegations in the Congress of the United States, 1789–1801."*

★

Comanche County, one of the last counties created from the Milam District, is on the extreme western edge of the Upper Cross Timbers; like most of the Cross Timbers counties, it is an exclusively agricultural region. Because it has no African American population, Comanche County is one of the few places in the South that has no apparent race problem. The 1940 census showed only one Mexican, no blacks, twenty-eight persons of foreign extraction, and 19,217 persons of Anglo American descent in a population of 19,246.[1]

The county, however, has been free of the tensions of racial strife only since four violent weeks in the summer of 1886, during which all persons of African descent were forced to leave because of a crime committed by one of their number.

The first settlers in Comanche County brought their slaves with them, and these blacks played an important role in the first days of the settlement of the county. One, Isham Hicks, supervised the construction of the first Methodist church in the county and later became one of the first victims of the raiding Comanche.

Comanche County became a separate unit in 1856; thus the first census recording the population for the county as a unit was the census of 1860. According to the tabulation of that year, the population was 709 persons, of whom sixty-one were black.[2] These slaves were an integral part of the community and a necessary laboring force. The men worked as field hands, farmers, teamsters, and artisans; their wives worked as domestic servants in the homes of their masters.

When the slaves were freed during the next decade, many of the blacks in Comanche County—one of the more exposed frontier settlements—took advantage of their new freedom to seek the comparative safety of the interior. The census of 1870, showing a total county population of 1,001, indicated a drop in the black population from sixty-one to twenty-four.[3] By the 1880s, the frontier had moved farther west, the Indian menace had passed, and the population had jumped from 1,001 to 8,608. Of this number, only seventy-nine were black.

The employment of mobs in a frontier environment was not unusual. Comanche County had had a long and successful experience in the use of mob violence for the protection of its citizens. Since the first settlement of the county, the townspeople had trailed raiding Indians, five hundred men had pursued John Wesley Hardin without success, and vigilantes had been active for a time. It is not surprising that the lack of efficient protection by the legally constituted authorities had induced the people to act for themselves; nor should it be expected that they would yield their customary practice overnight no matter how efficient the authorities became.

The emancipation of the slaves and their sometimes injudicious actions in that freedom had augmented the bitter aftermath of the Civil War throughout the South, and a wave of violent antiblack activities following the war had its effect upon the frontier. Many of the settlers in Comanche County had come to the new lands impelled by the necessity of beginning life again—a decision caused by the ruin of their former lives, a ruin for which many held the black race directly responsible.[4]

This race prejudice was a constant factor over the entire South, but it did not receive overt expression in Comanche County until 1875. On April 20 of that year, Mose Jones, a former slave of the Carnes family, ran amok and killed two young girls of his own race and the two young sons of his employer, T. J. Nabers. Mose had been employed by Nabers as a handyman for several years but had borne a grudge against the family that he revenged by splitting the skulls of Joe and Fleet Nabers after he had killed two black employees of the Nabers household. He then attempted to hide his crime and perhaps destroy the rest of the family by setting fire to the building after coating the kitchen walls with tallow and cutting the well rope to prevent ready access to water. Mrs. Nabers was awakened by the smoke, and the entire family was saved. J. B. Nabers, one of the older sons of the family, brought the bodies of his two young brothers out of the flames, but the bodies of the black girls could not be saved. A party was formed to search for the murderer, who had boasted of his crime to a crony. On the next afternoon, Mose was discovered and shot by Hode Games as he attempted to flee.[5] Mose had acted upon the impulses of a disordered brain and had, in the eyes of the community, received his just punishment; his actions, however, created a violent antipathy for the black race in some members of the Nabers family. In time, the tensions aroused by this deed became quiescent, and the blacks dwelt in comparatively undisturbed security for another decade.

The year 1886 was a hard one in Comanche County, a year of social and political upheaval, a year of hardship and drought. By the summer of 1886, the average citizen of Comanche was living on corn pone and blackstrap garnished with turnip greens if he were lucky. Meat was a thing of the past, cattle had to be driven from four to ten miles to water, and most of the herds had been sold before the cattle died of hunger. Farmers could not work, their crops died in the ground, and idle men turned to other things than labor that brought no profit.[6] The people of the county were further agitated by the appearance of a split in the county political organization, a split that soon developed into a full-fledged revolt and the formation of the Human Party, the first successful populist party in Texas. It did not succeed, however, without rousing some heat and flaring tempers still further, for the people took their politics seriously and fought bitterly and sometimes physically over their differing political opinions. Rash actions were the rule rather than the exception. The Indians had long ceased their raids on the moonlit nights in August, and John Wesley Hardin—the personal devil of Comanche County—had been behind bars for eight years, but night riding continued. Fierce tempers, made fiercer by the drought and the political disturbances, were making their points by threats of lawlessness. Mobs, in the nominal strength of the law, had paid several visits to the little village of Hazel Dell—a collection of saw and gin mills that rated its reputation as the toughest town in Texas—and had come away with prisoners to be left on the first stout limb. The Hazel Dellers, however, were not idle; a sample of their work is this anonymous letter that was reprinted in the newspaper *Town and Country* as an editorial inspiration.

Hazel Dell, June 13, 1886;

John Stone, you are notified to leave Comanche County by the First of July, if you are not gone by that time you are to abide the consequences. You take your sons Jim and Jay Stone, Red Pruitt, and Red Stone. Take Warning in time.

(signed)
Committy [sic] *of One Hundred*[7]

The editorial comment on this masterpiece, made by L. B. Russell, reflects the general atmosphere of the times: "Mob law is a fearful thing, but it becomes necessary sometimes to use it as a weapon of self-defense against such fiendish mobocracy as is indicated in the above letter."[8]

Comanche County was one watched pot that was beginning to boil.

The explosion came on Saturday, July 24, 1886. An eighteen-year-old black man killed Mrs. Ben Stephens, the wife of a farmer who lived about nine miles north of Comanche on the De Leon road, by shooting her in the back. Stephens had come into Comanche to buy supplies, and his first knowledge of the death of his wife came while he was in the J. R. Greene store buying parts for his plow. A man on a mule rode up and called to him, "Stephens, Tom just killed your wife a while ago."[9] Stephens immediately got the sheriff, Jim Cunningham, and posses were quickly organized to search for the killer.

Tom was on foot, and no one anticipated much trouble finding him, but there was a great deal of land to cover. The sheriff and his detachment searched the southern part of the county, and the rest of the men headed up the Leon Valley to pick up the trail at the Stephens' farm. Jim Nabers, who was a clerk in the Greene store and had overheard the announcement of Mrs. Stephens's death, and Frank Sherill, who had a rabid African American prejudice, were sent up the roads by the sheriff to warn the settlers of the upper Leon Valley of the chase and to try to cut off Tom in the north. The two foundered their horses outside De Leon and spent the night in the town. Meanwhile, the posse had assembled at the Stephens' farm and struck the trail in the late evening.

On the next morning, the posse continued its pursuit up the Leon Valley; Nabers and Sherrill borrowed horses and headed up the river to bypass the fugitive. They were working back down the Leon Valley with Tom between them and the rest of the posse when they heard that he had been caught by the trackers some miles below. Tom was taken to the farm of Green Saunders at De Leon. Because it was Sunday and late afternoon by the time Tom was caught, the hanging was postponed until Monday.

Monday morning, Tom was taken to the Stephens' farm, where a large crowd was gathering in anticipation of the hanging, which was scheduled for noon. Jim Nabers and Frank Sherrill suggested that Tom be burned alive, but Zack Hulsey, the father of the murdered woman, said, "Now, boys, the laws of our land say hanging, not burning; so we'll just hang him."[10] As the crowd was gathering, W. D. Cox, a deputy sheriff, rode in and made a token attempt to take the prisoner from the mob. Cox promised to guard Tom well and to see that he would get a legal trial if the men would surrender him into the custody of the law. Nothing happened. Green Saunders looked down at his shotgun and back at the deputy, who turned and rode away.

By this time, the mob had Tom standing in the back of the wagon that was to serve as a gallows platform. As the rope was being fitted on Tom's neck, Zack

Hulsey questioned him. After reminding Tom that he was about to die, Hulsey asked, "Tom, did Sally mistreat you?" Tom replied, "No, sir, she's the best kind to me." Hulsey asked, "Then why did you kill her?" Tom replied, "Just for meanness."[11]

Hulsey turned away, men in the wagon pushed Tom out, and men on the ground hauled on the rope. They hauled so hard that the limb over which the rope was thrown broke. A young man in the crowd, Alexander Ruff, climbed the tree and looped the rope over the stump of the limb.[12]

The blacks in De Leon were ordered to come out and bury the corpse. They dropped it into a shallow wash and caved in the bank on top of it. One of the more grisly aftermaths of this burial was a lucrative business in souvenirs carried on by an itinerant peddler who sold "authentic remains of the last Negro buried in Comanche County and pieces of the rope used to hang him with!" through the county as late as 1889.[13]

That same evening, before the crowd was completely dispersed, Green Saunders, who had been one of the leaders in the proceedings, mounted a stump and organized the remaining members of the mob into a mass meeting. After a philippic on the black character, he called for a vote on a proposition involving the expulsion of every African American from Comanche County. His argument was simple: twice in the last decade, blacks had committed outrageous crimes against the safety of the white citizens; blacks were by nature evil; and similar crimes might happen at any time unless some action was taken. Of the men who remained, not one voted against the proposal.

The people who had buried Tom were warned on the spot. It was arranged that the meeting would adjourn to reconvene that evening on the outskirts of the town of Comanche and to ride in a body to warn the blacks living there. Late in the evening, the mob rode into Comanche and visited every shack in the African American section with the warning to pack up and get out within ten days or be killed.[14] Take what they could, leave what could not be sold or carried, but be across the county line by sunset on August 6, 1886.

This action did not go unopposed. Persons who had not questioned the right or the justice in the hanging of "Nigger Tom" considered this deed a crime against society and called its protagonists "hotheaded, uncalled for citizens."[15] Editor L. B. Russell summed up the situation in these words: "Because one young scapegrace, who has been in this section of the country for less than two years, committed a diabolical murder, and at the hands of an infuriated people has suffered the full penalty of his crime, several hundred men have ordered the whole population of African descent to leave the country. What connection is there between him and the rest of the race in this community, and especially those who are known to be as harmless as the most inoffensive white man?"[16]

On Tuesday afternoon, July 27, a mass meeting of the citizens of Comanche was called to discuss "whether the action of a large body of men in entering the town of Comanche last night and ordering all of the negroes in the town to leave the country within the next ten days is approved or condemned by this community."[17]

After several extemporaneous speeches, a committee was appointed to draft resolutions condemning the action. These resolutions are an accurate gauge of the temper of the citizens of Comanche. The first resolution was a pledge to uphold the law. The second read, "Resolved, that we regard the demonstration in the town of Comanche last night as uncalled for, wrong, and lawless within itself, and we appeal to the good sense of those engaged therein to desist from their threatened violence."[18]

The third was a pledge to assist the sheriff in his efforts to maintain the law and "protect the law abiding citizens of the county." These resolutions were signed by fifty-five men and appeared in the Comanche newspapers. They had no effect on the situation, for the blacks, having been ordered to leave, went.

Individual efforts were made to retain those African Americans who wished to stay in defiance of the mob's command. C. W. Carnes, one of the more peppery citizens, found a member of the mob abusing one of Mart Fleming's black employees and interfered unsuccessfully by trying to provoke a fight with him. Fleming, a local butcher and a rugged soul in his own right, offered the services of his shotgun and himself to protect his two black employees, Horace Mercer and Dallas Dabness, if they wanted to stay. Both refused his offer, as Horace said, "To keep you from getting into trouble, Mr. Fleming." Dallas went to Waco and Horace to Cisco.[19]

One of the town's doctors refused to have his black maid driven from her home, but a visit from the mob made the girl insist that she be allowed to go to Dublin. The doctor finally gave in and drove the girl across the line himself. Some of the altercations growing out of this question were not so easily settled. Capt. J. F. Manning received an anonymous letter:

Sir,

you think you are very smart, try to play in with both sides, the other night you was standing in with the mob, we here [sic] that you are on the other side now, go slow or you may pull on the tight end of a rope.

"Comitty"[20]

Thinking that he knew the author of the letter, Captain Manning forthwith hunted up Tom Stewart and pistol-whipped him in spite of his denials of any knowledge of the incident.

The newspapers, on the day before the deadline, reached new heights of rhetoric with such statements as the following: "When midnight can command the sun at high noon to step aside and give place to Egyptian darkness, then, and not till then, will mobocracy reign instead of law."[21]

In spite of these words, the day of the deadline came, and the sun set long after the last African American had left Comanche County. Only a few had ventured to stay out the limit, and they only from necessity. Most went to Dublin, some went to Eastland County, and some few to Brownwood, but they all were evacuated quietly

in an almost preternatural order no doubt induced by the news that a company of
Texas Rangers was on its way to restore order in Comanche County.

Almost immediately, it seemed as though there had never been an African American in Comanche County, and within a month, the only reminder of the flaring
passions of the summer was a sign on the public well in De Leon: "Nigger, don't
let the sun go down on you in this town."[22] No further violence has been recorded
since this episode, but there are apocryphal tales of how cowboys in De Leon, the
only town with rail service in the county, roped the black porters off the trains and
dragged them through the streets. It is true that the black porters on the Houston
and Texas Central used to hide in the baggage cars during the time the train was in
Comanche County. There is also the more recent story of a black youth who made a
bet that he could cross from Dublin in Erath County to Blanket in Brown County
by way of Comanche County and was never seen again after he stopped at a farm
near De Leon for a drink of water.

As a consequence, African Americans are something of a curiosity to Comanche
people. The writer's uncles and aunts tell of the first time they saw a black person.
They had gone to Dublin to see a circus; on the lot, however, they saw a black woman
and followed her the rest of the day in hopes that they might catch her washing her
hands so they could see whether the black would rub off. Within the last few years,
this curiosity has been turned to financial account by the managers of the local ball
clubs in De Leon and Comanche who ensure themselves of sold-out crowds by hiring a black baseball team from Brownwood to play the home team.

Since the expulsion of the African Americans in 1886, the lack of a colored population has become one of the points upon which the citizens of Comanche pride
themselves. This attitude may be more readily understood when the average conception of the black character held in Comanche County is made clear. In 1907, there
was published a pamphlet extolling the virtues of Comanche County in hopes of
attracting new citizens, and one of the strongest selling points was this:

> The population of Comanche County, Texas, according to the census of 1900
> was 23,079. This population, it must be remembered, is entirely and absolutely
> all white; there is not a [N]egro in the county, and the chances are there will not
> be any for many years to come. There are many ways in which the [N]egro can be
> of service to the white race, but as a rule the community is better off without him.
> Wherever [N]egroes are numerous there crime abounds and all sorts of trouble.
> But in Comanche County he is an unknown quantity, and the court dockets are
> consequently light, there are no election frauds, and women are safe....Wherever
> the [N]egro herds, there crime has a breeding place. Comanche [C]ounty is free
> from this black curse, not by any written statute that she has enacted, but by an
> unwritten law which the [N]egroes throughout the length and breadth of the
> State understand.[23]

Perhaps the unfortunate fact is that since this pamphlet was written, nothing has happened that would cause a change in this opinion.

This article was originally published as Lightfoot, Billy Bob. "The Negro Exodus from Comanche County, Texas." Southwestern Historical Quarterly *56 (1953): 407–16. Reprinted by permission of the editor of the* Southwestern Historical Quarterly.

NOTES

1. *The Sixteenth Census of the United States*, vol. 2 (Population), Washington, DC, 1940, part 6, table 21.

2. J. C. G. Kennedy, *A Preliminary Report on the Eighth Census* (Washington, DC: US Census Office, 1864), 63.

3. *The Ninth Census of the United States* (Population of States by Counties), Washington, DC, 1870, table 2, 65.

4. *Statistics of the Population of the United States at the Tenth Census*, Washington, DC, 1883, table 23, 372.

5. J. B. Nabers to Billy Bob Lightfoot (B. L.), personal interview, January 28, 1949 (signed statement in Archives Collection, University of Texas Library).

6. Floy Cunningham to B. L., April 16, 1949 (signed statement in Archives Collection, University of Texas Library).

7. Comanche *Town and Country*, June 20, 1886.

8. Ibid.

9. Mrs. Tom Conaway to Mrs. Leona Allen, personal interview (signed statement in Archives Collection, University of Texas Library).

10. Nabers to B. L., personal interview.

11. Ibid.

12. Alexander Ruff to B. L., personal interview, November 26, 1948 (signed statement, Archives Collection, University of Texas Library).

13. E. H. Lightfoot and E. Lightfoot to B. L. (letters in possession of author).

14. Nabers to B. L., personal interview. Conaway and Ruff interviews all agree with this account.

15. L. F. Elkins to B. L., January 28, 1949 (signed statement in Archives Collection, University of Texas Library).

16. Comanche *Town and Country*, July 29, 1886.

17. Ibid.

18. Ibid.

19. Camille Fleming to B. L., personal interview, February 21, 1949 (signed statement in University of Texas Library).

20. Comanche *Town and Country*, August 5, 1886.

21. Ibid.

22. Ibid., September 9, 1886.

23. Mrs. F. L. Little in a special publication of the Comanche *Chief* edited by Sam Vernon and dated 1907 (clippings in scrapbook kept by Mrs. Dora Greene, Comanche, Texas).

PART 2
In Pursuit of Freedom

6

Black Trail Drivers of Caldwell County

Donaly E. Brice

In the latter nineteenth century, one of the occupations open to black men was that of working with cattle, and some were especially valued for their skills on the long trail rides. Central Texas provided some of these cowboys, as Donaly Brice points out in his article about Caldwell County. This is not a surprise, since we have already learned that black slaves sometimes grew up learning to work with cattle. Author Brice served as reference archivist at the Texas State Library and Archives for many years. He not only wrote about African American cattlemen; he also published The Great Comanche Raid *and a coedited work,* Texas Rangers: Lives, Legend, and Legacy.

★

Following the American Civil War in 1865, there was a great explosion of the cattle industry throughout the state of Texas. Wild longhorn cattle were destined to play a major role in the salvation of the state economy's struggle to regain some semblance of stability after enduring four long and bloody years of internecine War Between the States.[1]

Over the decades and throughout the years of an intersectional war that determined the country's future direction, the unbridled proliferation of literally millions of wild longhorn cattle throughout the southern half of Texas would prove to be a godsend to Texas. In the beginning, no one could imagine the scope and extent that the trail-driving era would play in the history of Texas and that of the entire United States.[2]

In 1924, Ike Pryor, a prominent cattleman and former trail driver, estimated the number of cattle driven up the trail between 1870 and 1890 as about ten million. He estimated that approximately half a million cattle were annually driven north to various points where they were placed on railroad cattle cars and shipped to meat-packing plants in the markets of the Northeast and East. It would take "an army" of men to handle such a task. Estimating five hundred thousand cattle a year divided into about two hundred different herds, Pryor calculated that it required about 2,400 drovers annually to accomplish this feat. It also required fourteen thousand saddle horses for such a massive undertaking.[3]

In 1925, George W. Saunders, president of the Texas Trail Drivers Association, estimated that thirty-five thousand cowboys had gone up the trail with herds during the height of the cattle drives between 1866 and 1895. Not all these cowboys had been white Anglo Americans. Saunders estimated that "about one third were negroes and Mexican." His calculations came from "the cattle owners, ranchers, and trail drivers who were on the drives of 1866–1895 and were members of the Texas Trail Drivers Association when he was president in the 1920s." Using Saunders's figures, Philip Durham and Everett L. Jones, in *The Negro Cowboy*, stated that about five thousand black cowboys had participated on cattle drives out of Texas. These figures indicate that during the period from 1866 to 1895, the makeup of the cowboys who drove cattle north out of Texas consisted of "slightly more than 63 percent whites, 25 percent Negroes, and slightly under 12 percent Mexicans."[4]

The occupation of being a cowboy was far from a glamorous line of work: "Cowboys were poorly fed, underpaid, overworked, deprived of sleep, and prone to boredom and loneliness." Although many of these young men, later in life, reminisced about the "good ole days" and the wonderful times they had out on the open range herding cattle to distant markets, the years seemed to cloud their true memories: "They choked in the dust, were cold at night, suffered broken bones in falls and spills from horses spooked by snakes or prairie dog holes. The cowboy work centered on the fall and spring roundups, when scattered cattle were collected and driven to a place for branding, sorting for marker [sic], castrating, and in later years, dipping in vats to prevent tick fever."[5] And then they had the wonderful three- to four-month trail drive to get an ornery herd of wild longhorn cattle to market, sometimes over a thousand miles away. But when it came to the black cowboys, there was much more to be expected. Regarding those young men who chose this tough occupation, Sara R. Massey, in her marvelous anthology *Black Cowboys of Texas*, may have said it best:

> Being African American cowboys though also meant surviving discrimination, bigotry, and prejudice, as well as escaping death. The lives of African American cowboys tell the story of skill and grit, as they did what was necessary to gain the trust and respect of those who controlled their destiny. For these men and women, it meant being the best—at roping, at bronc busting, at taming mustangs, at calling the brands, controlling the remuda, or topping off horses. They knew that if there were an outlaw horse to be broken, it was their job. If someone had to ride an extra night watch, it was their job to do. That's just the way it was. They were made the butt of jokes, went to the back room to eat, and tried not to

fight back. They made fun of themselves or did "the shamble," because they had to. Some say skill and the scarcity of labor counted more in the West, which may be true, but African American men and women earned respect the hard way—by becoming the very best at their work.[6]

Following the Civil War and the emancipation of Texas slaves in June 1865, the freedmen had few options in regard to pursuing an occupation. Extreme prejudice on the part of most Anglos limited black men. Uneducated and destitute, they could remain on the farms and plantations where they had resided and work as sharecroppers for their former masters, they could move on to other areas and look for similar work, they could move into the towns and cities and search for menial jobs that paid little and forced them to live in squalid conditions, or they now had an option to go into the cattle business. As can be seen by the figures quoted earlier, an estimated five thousand black men opted for this career that provided them with a way out of earlier unpleasant situations and an escape from some of the extreme prejudice and violence aimed at these newly freed people. It was hard and dangerous work, but most accounted well for their actions and actually earned and received praise and compliments from their Anglo counterparts who shared their hardships on the trail.[7]

Although early primary research on the trial drives from Caldwell County has focused on Anglo cowboys, many of whom became prominent citizens and leaders in the country, a meticulous search of the historical records and sources show quite a number of black cowboys from this county. These men served as cooks, horse wranglers, and drovers, performing most of the jobs that any of the other men were expected to perform. Following is a list of the names of the black cowboys from Caldwell County that have been identified: Jerry Thornton, Rowe McClain, Bill Davis, Uncle Guy Montgomery, Luther Merriweather, McStewart, Smith Whitis, Tom Hughes, Reuben Pollard, Louis Brooks, Russ Jones, Press Searcy, John Storey, and Jim Crayton.[8] If the readers of this article are aware of others, please let our society know so we can include them among those men who need to be recognized and remembered as a part of our history.

STEPHEN "ROWE" MCCLAIN

The first black trail driver from Caldwell County that this writer was aware of was Rowe McClain. Although his real name was Stephen, or Steve McClain, he was best known by his friends, family, and associates as Rowe, or Roe, McClain. Rowe was born about 1852 in Guadalupe County, Texas, just across the San Marcos River from the town of Prairie Lea. His father was Reuben McClain.[9]

As a youth, Rowe was said to have acquired the skills of riding and handling horses by participating in horse races. He rode in these races for Jeff Lilly, a "race horse man" during that time. As a teenager, Rowe was hired on by a number of the trail drivers from Caldwell County, and he made many trips up the Chisholm

Trail during his career as a trail driver. He worked for some of the more well-known cattlemen from Caldwell County: Col. John J. Myers, Marcus "Mark" Withers, J. W. "Black Bill" Montgomery, and John R. Blocker.[10] Although Blocker was associated primarily with the Blanco County area, he had many dealings with a number of Caldwell County cattlemen.

According to his obituary, Rowe McClain "went up the trails many times and no man, white or black, was more skilful [sic] in handling a herd." It was common knowledge that he could handle and ride any kind of horse used in the cattle business. Mark Withers stated that Rowe was adept at his trade. Withers said that some of the young men on the trail would act quite the daredevil and would sometimes rope wild buffalo and even elk for the sport of excitement. Mark, himself, was known to have roped wild buffalo and helped load the wild animals on railroad cars to ship them up north to advertise the cattle industry and to provide real buffalo for Wild West shows. However, he said that Rowe McClain was the only cowboy that he knew of who took this sport to a new level. He had actually roped a moose. He not only roped the beast, but it was well attested that Rowe then threw the animal down and tied his legs, as one would do in a bulldogging contest in a rodeo of today.[11]

Green W. Mills, who worked with Rowe McClain on several occasions, recalled an incident that exhibited the acumen, agility, and speed of this black cowboy. He said, "That one night on the trail a saddled horse shook himself and that meant a stampede of the herd." He and a number of other cowboys who were sleeping near the camp wagon "jumped up, mounted their horses and were prepared to follow when they noticed that the cattle were turned." It was soon determined that Rowe McClain, who had been sleeping some distance away, "was on his feet before the horse had finished shaking, was up and in barefeet and few clothes had run at the head of the herd and turned the leaders as the men would have done on horseback." This particular incident not only impressed the other white cowboys; it made a lasting impression on Rowe McClain. His friends said that for the rest of his life, "a saddled horse shaking as horses sometimes do would nearly always bring him to his feet." Rowe's family also said that "at night before he went to bed he would set all the chairs close to the wall." When asked why he would do this, Rowe would comment "in trail parlance, 'If anything happens, I want to have a clear run.'"[12]

Between 1868 and 1871, Rowe McClain made numerous drives up the Chisholm Trail. In 1871, on his last trail drive, he remained in Wyoming and worked for several years on the Shirley ranch, returning to Caldwell County in 1875.

Rowe finally decided to give up the life of a trail driver and settle down. On April 13, 1882, he and Viney Barksdale were married in Caldwell County by the Rev. Nick Greenwood. In 1888, Rowe and Viney purchased several tracts of land just east of what is now FM ("Farm to Market Road") 2001 (the Silent Valley Road), about four miles northwest of Lockhart. On this one-hundred-acre parcel of land, Rowe spent the remainder of his life farming and ranching. Over thirty-eight years of marriage, the couple raised six boys—Freddie, Oddie, Morris, Frank, Lonzo, and Norman—and three girls: Dessie, Lena, and Mattie.[13]

1. Dessie (April 20, n.d.–June 2, 1952) married Tom L. Jackson.
2. Fred (November 1885–n.d.) married Sudie Johnson.
3. Oddie (March 11, 1891–February 17, 1937) married Ima Sanders.
4. Morris (May 24, 1892–June 1, 1964) married Essie Braden.
5. Lena Lee (April 23, 1894–December 28, 1954) married Eldridge Farmer.
6. Frank (March 14, 1896–September 9, 1972) married (1) Mertis Holloway and (2) Mamie McMahan.
7. Lonzo (March 1898–n.d.) married Laura Broadenax.
8. Norman (May 17, 1900–June 11, 1934) married (1) Carrie Hysaw and (2) Alma Rees Franks.
9. Mattie M. C. (January 26, 1903–February 19, 1952) married Walter James.

Obviously, Rowe McClain held a special place in his heart for being a cattleman. Just several days before his death, it was said that he was seen assisting his neighbor James Cardwell in working among his stock. The Lockhart *Post-Register* of March 25, 1920, contained a lengthy article with the headline "Remarkable Negro Dead." Rowe had died and was buried the week before this article appeared. People who later knew this quiet, hardworking man would have been hard-pressed to imagine the same man "as the wild riding, bronco busting, dare devil roper of former times." All the men who rode with him during the exciting days of the trail drives counted Rowe McClain a friend until death. Mark Withers and Green W. Mills considered "his life as rather remarkable."[14]

The Western writer, Alfred Henry Lewis, probably provided the most appropriate eulogy for any former trail driver when he said, "He has struck in on the Long Trails where the hoof prints all point one way." Stephen "Rowe" McClain was survived by his wife, Viney, and all their children. After his death, Viney sold the country farm and moved into the eastern part of Lockhart, where she resided until her death on December 27, 1931, at the age of seventy-four years. She was buried in the Hooks Cemetery in Lockhart.[15]

JERRY THORNTON

Jerry Thornton was a trail driver from Caldwell County—a black trail driver from Caldwell County! And from all indications, he was a good one. Jerry "went up the trail" on two or three occasions. His first trip "up the trail" was in 1880, when he was hired on as a cook for the cattle-drive crew led by Dick Withers. According to another trail driver, Green W. Mills, Jerry made a good cook. When he had the supplies and the time, Thornton put together a fine meal. And it was not only the three meals a day that the men remembered about him. One of the things that the cowboys remembered most about him was that when one of them came into camp and was hungry, "at any time Jerry quickly prepared a snack and sent him on his way." A cook's job was obviously important to all the trail crew. He had to be proficient in handling and driving a chuck wagon. He had to prepare at least three meals a day, sometimes using the barest essentials to accomplish the job. The cook's job required that he be up as early as 3 a.m. to begin preparing breakfast for the other men when they awakened. He also served as an alarm clock for the trail crew, making sure everyone was "up and going" at the appropriate time. He usually had to move his work station (chuck wagon) at least twice a day, sometimes as far as ten to fifteen miles each time.[16]

On another trail drive, Jerry Thornton served as "a horse wrangler—one who saw to it that plenty of riding horses were at hand for the men." This was an important job on the trail crew, since the cowboys often had to change horses to prevent them from being overworked and fatigued. It was common for a trail-drive crew to have a remuda of between one hundred to three hundred horses. The horse wrangler was responsible for keeping this horse herd together and making sure they were getting an ample supply of grass and feed so they would be ready for the cowboys when they came in to change mounts. The horse wrangler also set up a rope corral several times a day and herded the remuda into this makeshift corral when the trail crew stopped along the trail. He also had to make sure that the other cowboys' saddle horses did not stray too far when not being used. As if this was not enough responsibility, it was the job of the horse wrangler sometimes to assist the cook in gathering wood for preparing meals and helping to harness the teams of horses.[17]

Little is known about the early life of Jerry Thornton. Although we do not know the names of his parents, we can discern that, according to his birth date, Jerry was born into slavery in about 1862, during the Civil War. There is one Jerry Thornton listed on the 1870 census for Fayette County that could conceivably be our trail driver. Unfortunately, no documentation has been found to verify that this was the correct person.

After making a number of trips "up the trail," Jerry decided to settle down in Caldwell County. On September 1, 1892, Jerry Thornton married Miss Ida Jackson, daughter of Burl and Martha Jackson. There are no records to indicate that this couple had any children. It appears that Ida must have died early, because on June 14, 1898, Jerry married for a second time, this time to Lou Ella Ellison, daughter of Sanderson "Sanders" and Elvira Hudspeth Ellison.[18]

Jerry and Lou Ella resided in Caldwell County for the remainder of their lives. They raised a family of six children: May "Mamie," Elijah "Lish," Liza, Myrtle, Eugene, and Fred D. For most of his life, Jerry Thornton worked as a farmer in various parts of the county. In 1910, he and his family were residing on land next to Alexander D. Mebane, a well-known and prominent farmer in Caldwell County. It is likely that he was a farm laborer for Mebane.[19]

In 1920, the Thornton family was situated in the northern section of Caldwell County, near the community of Mendoza. This was exceedingly good farmland, and it was reasonable for someone who was a farmer to be found in this section of the county. By 1930, Jerry's age and life of hard work had begun to take a toll on him. The census taker had him listed that year as sixty-five years of age, and for the first time, his occupation was shown as a laborer of odd jobs. By then, Jerry and his wife, Lou Ella, along with their youngest son, Fred, had moved into Lockhart, where they rented a modest house on South Commerce Street for the sum of $8 a month. It was here on Commerce Street that Jerry Thornton died on October 19, 1931.[20]

Jerry's wife survived her husband by seventeen years. Lou Ella had been born in Caldwell County in April 1874, lived in the county for her entire life, and died there on April 18, 1949, at the age of seventy-five years.[21]

This article was originally published as Brice, Donaly. "Black Trail Drivers of Caldwell County." Plum Creek Almanac 33 (Fall 2015): 111–18. Reprinted by permission of the author and the Publications Board of the Plum Creek Almanac.

NOTES

1. J. Marvin Hunter, comp., *The Trail Drivers of Texas* (Austin: University of Texas Press, 1985).

2. Sara R. Massey, ed., *Black Cowboys of Texas* (College Station: Texas A&M University Press, 2000), xv.

3. Philip Durham and Everett L. Jones, *The Negro Cowboys* (New York: Dodd, Mead, 1965; Lincoln: University of Nebraska Press, 1983), 3–12, 26, 44.

4. Massey, *Black Cowboys*, xiii.

5. Ibid., xvi.

6. Massey, *Black Cowboys*; Durham and Jones, *Negro Cowboys*.

7. Lockhart *Post-Register*, June 21, 1934; October 15, 1925.

8. Zona Withers, *Historical Lockhart: Then and Now*, vol. 2 (Lockhart, TX: Mark Withers Trail Drive Museum, 1981); "Crayton Cemetery, Guadalupe County," *Cemeteries of Texas*, accessed September 14, 2018, http://www .cemeteries-of-tx.com/etx/guadalupe/ cemetery/craytonB.htm.

9. Lockhart *Post-Register*, March 25, 1920.

10. Ibid.

11. Ibid.; Withers, *Historical Lockhart*.

12. Lockhart *Post-Register*, March 25, 1920.

13. Ibid.; Gregory A. Boyd, *Texas Land Survey Maps for Caldwell County* (Norman, OK: Arphax, 2008); Caldwell County Death Certificate #6897 for Odie McClain, Caldwell County Clerk's Office, Texas.

14. Lockhart *Post-Register*, March 25, 1920; Zona A. Withers, "Withers, Marcus A.," *Handbook of Texas Online*, accessed June 12, 2017, https://tshaonline.org/ handbook/online/articles/fwibc.

15. Alfred Henry Lewis, *The Sunset Trail* (New York: A. L. Burt, 1906); Lockhart *Post-Register*, May 8, 1980; Caldwell County Death Certificate #50282 for Vina McClain, Caldwell County Clerk's Office, Texas.

16. Withers, *Historical Lockhart*; Durham and Jones, *Negro Cowboys*, 52–56; Lockhart *Post-Register*, October 22, 1921.

17. Durham and Jones, *Negro Cowboys*, 47–49; Massey, *Black Cowboys*, x–xv; Lockhart *Post-Register*, October 22, 1921.

18. Caldwell County Marriage Records, book H, 103; Caldwell County Marriage Records, book I, 432.

19. Lockhart *Post-Register*, October 22, 1921; Caldwell County, Texas, Census, US Census Bureau, 1910.

20. Lockhart *Post-Register*, October 22, 1921; Caldwell County, Texas, Census, US Census Bureau, 1920, 1930; Caldwell County Death Certificate #45859 for Jerry Thornton, Caldwell County Clerk's Office, Texas.

21. Lockhart *Post-Register*, October 22, 1921; Caldwell County Death Certificate #16191 for Lou Thornton, Caldwell County Clerk's Office, Texas.

7

Lincolnville at Moccasin Bend

A Coryell County Freedom Colony

Rebecca Sharpless

For black Texans in the years after the Civil War, freedom meant seeking places to live as well as employment and physical survival in a state where they too frequently faced and endured racial violence. One alternative was to reside in what were referred to as "freedom colonies." These communities fostered a feeling of togetherness and protection and were scattered throughout Texas. In this article, Rebecca Sharpless describes the lives and labors of those who resided in a Coryell County freedom colony, Lincolnville at Moccasin Bend. Rebecca Sharpless is a professor of history and the director of graduate studies at Texas Christian University. A specialist in US women's history, Sharpless served as president of the Southern Association of Women's Historians, among numerous other achievements. Her publications include Fertile Ground, Narrow Choices: Women on Texas Cotton Farms, Cooking in Other Women's Kitchens: Domestic Workers in the South, *and with Elizabeth Turner and Stephanie Cole,* Texas Women: Their Histories, Their Lives, *which won the Liz Carpenter Award from the Texas State Historical Association.*

★

The journey from Tennessee grew long—at least three weeks, maybe much longer, on foot or by wagon. When "Black Jim" and his owners, John and Mahulda Mayberry, and the other ten or so slaves finally got to Coryell County in late 1860, what must he have thought? Jim was a grown man, brought to this wild new land, away from familiar surroundings. As Jane Bond contemplated the future in Texas, she surely grieved for her three children left behind in Tennessee, but perhaps she was comforted that at least she had her little son Gus with her. Uncertainty and fear must have ruled the enslaved people brought against their wills to the edges of Anglo settlement in Texas. Little could they have imagined that in less than ten years, they would have families and homes of their own—husbands, wives, children, houses, cows, chickens, and pigs—in the place they would name Lincolnville.

In the decades after emancipation, freedom colonies like Lincolnville were places of family, of autonomy, of independence. African Americans owned their own land, and no person, black or white, could tell them what to do with it. Their churches were their churches, and their schools were their schools. No one may ever know how many freedom colonies there were across the South. Near swamps, on arid land, and in areas far off main roads, freed African Americans bought land and formed communities. Lincolnville, at the ninety-first meridian, might have been the community that lay furthest to the west, the last gasp of the South as it lumbered up against the Great Plains.[1] In many ways, Lincolnville could have been anywhere in the South. But it was the land of the Leon River Valley, west of Gatesville, which became home to a community that made a dramatic difference to its inhabitants and whose impact remains today.

African Americans first arrived in Coryell County in the 1840s, and stories like that of Jim, who later took the surname Mayberry, were replicated across the South and across Texas before the Civil War. As older agricultural ways in Virginia and Maryland waned, and as the restless Anglo population chose to leave the eastern seaboard and spread across the South, slaves became an important part of the migration. With no choice in the matter, sometimes they came with their owners, and sometimes new owners bought them to bring along to fresh lands. In any event, by 1861, the number of slaves in Texas had reached almost 170,000.[2]

By the time Jim arrived, some of the slaves in Coryell County had been in Texas for a while. Green Brown may have come to Washington County, Texas, in the Brazos Valley before 1840 with the family of Frederick Grimes, and then moved again with them to Coryell County in the 1850s, as an adult.[3] Celie Ann Cook and her daughters, Frances, known as Fannie, and Louisa, belonged to Hiram W. Cook, who migrated to Texas from Tennessee in the early 1850s and arrived in Coryell County in 1855.[4] Celie Cook would have been in her early thirties when she and her two young girls first arrived in Texas, far from the land of her birth.

The number of slaves in Coryell doubled between 1855 and 1860—from 139 to 281 people, minuscule compared to places farther east but overwhelmingly important to the individuals involved. Another 140, including the Mayberry slaves, arrived by 1863.[5] The migrations had wrenching effects. Jane Bond Mayberry left three children in Hickman County, Tennessee: Charlie, who was sold to the Whiteside family; Ann; and a second little girl whose name went unremembered. Jane had recently been given as a wedding present to the daughter of her owner, who was accompanying her new husband to Texas. With Jane came her son Gus, born in 1848, the offspring of Jane and her owner. Gus, too, was a gift to the new bride—his half-sister.[6]

The land that the Tennesseans, black and white, found in Coryell County presented challenges, for sure. Only two decades before, the area had been the province of the Tonkawa, Waco, Comanche, and Lipan Apache Indians. In 1849, the US Army established Fort Gates to place a barrier between the growing Anglo population and the Indians being pushed steadily west. Although the army abandoned the fort in 1852, the Anglo population continued to increase, reaching a total of 2,360 free people and 306 slaves in 1860.[7] John Mayberry brought his family and his slaves to this land of promise, on a curve of the Leon River west of Gatesville named Moccasin Bend.[8]

Coryell County was never destined for lush agriculture. Most of the soil is chalky, underlain by limestone, and the rainfall is generally fewer than thirty inches a year. The short grasses of the Grand Prairie formed thick mats across the wide expanses, with trees kept in check by occasional fires. The bottomlands might foster row crops, but the upcountry was mostly suitable only for grazing livestock.[9] Cattle, hogs, sheep, and corn and wheat for home consumption, not cotton, dominated the antebellum agricultural activity.[10] The people from Tennessee, both enslaved and free, had to adjust to the landscape. Laborers who had perhaps attuned themselves to the rhythms of cotton farming had to reset their work habits. Jim Mayberry served as the foreman of the other Mayberry slaves, who numbered twelve in 1862.[11] As a small boy, Gus Weatherly herded sheep in his bare feet and a single piece of clothing that he called a shirt. He later told his daughter of suffering from the cold, his feet bleeding into the snow.[12]

Several enslaved women, including Jane Bond Mayberry, worked in the modest new homes of their owners, most likely cooking, cleaning, and providing childcare. Despite her long relationship with her owners, Celie Cook did not make things easy for them. Her grandson recalled, "She was the independent type. . . . They could not subjugate her. She never did bow to their will. She never would obey those people. She was independent and a fighter. . . . [laughing] They tried to use her in the house, and she wasn't too good at that because she didn't take orders from them. [Laughing] She didn't want to be a slave, and she resented it. They had to make— they had to force her to do most anything."[13] The daily conflict in the Cook household must have heightened tensions for all involved.

Living in small shacks behind their owners' homes, the slaves in Coryell County formed family units. Jim Mayberry and Louisa Cook, Celie's daughter, had a son, James Marion, and a daughter, Annie, before emancipation.[14] Simon and Milly Easley's daughters, Mary and Hannah, were both born enslaved. The female slaves also had families, willingly or not, with their owners. Louie Mayberry's grandmother Harriet Squyres bore six children with James Squyres, the oldest son of her owner, Wiley Squyres. The two sides of the family freely acknowledged one another. Mayberry's mother, Hannah Charlotte Squyres, was reared by her white aunt, Mittie Squyres Powell, near Lincolnville.[15]

When emancipation came, the former slaves were ready to embrace their new lives. A white Gatesville resident, R. L. "Uncle Bob" Saunders, recalled that the Coryell County sheriff, James C. Haynes, sent runners to the slave owners to inform them of General Order No. 3 after its announcement in Galveston. When the news of emancipation reached the Leon, the newly freed people organized a parade through the streets of Gatesville, with Gus Weatherly proudly carrying the US flag.[16]

According to R. L. Saunders, John Mayberry considered his options and decided to treat his former possessions well. He offered them land across the river from their old quarters so that they could build cabins of their own. They could work for him for "prevailing wages." Mayberry also permitted them to retain their tools and their personal property as well as oxen, horses, and milk cows.

Many of the former Mayberry and Easley slaves elected to take John Mayberry up on his offer. Other former slaves also gravitated toward Lincolnville. Gus Weatherly thought about returning to Tennessee, but he found that his roots had grown in Texas. His mother and little sisters, Harriet and Easter, were in Coryell County, and he no longer knew anyone back east. So he decided to remain in Texas and move across the river near Jim and Lou Mayberry. The newly freed people took family names including Barnes/Barrens, Bevel, Brown, David, Jefferson, Lothlen/Lothlin, Shavers/Chavers, Mack, and Woodall.[17] By 1870, Lincolnville boasted fifteen households and a total population of seventy-seven people. In the next ten years, the community expanded to include families named Dudley, Hudson, Hughes, Jones, Kimmons, Mack, McCowan, Sneed, and Terry, and the African American population of the area, numbered about 120.

Soon after emancipation, and well before the guarantees of the Fourteenth and Fifteenth Amendments to the Constitution, the men of Lincolnville eagerly claimed their rights as citizens. Tax records for 1866 show that at least thirty-two Coryell County residents designated as "freedmen" paid their one-dollar poll tax, including Lincolnville residents Willis Adams, Anderson Hughes, Thomas Jefferson, John Lothlen, James Mayberry, and Allen Shavers.[18] We know nothing about their actual voting, but they quickly identified themselves as people ready to participate in democracy.

The Lincolnville settlers soon began to acquire land. Berry and Simon Easley, along with Mariah David, bought the first 173 acres from H. L. Marshall in 1868, land abutting the property owned by John W. Mayberry. In 1871, Jim Mayberry purchased 120 acres, some of which belonged to John W. Mayberry and some that came from an estate for which the white Mayberry was executor. Through the first decades of freedom, at least four other African Americans bought more than five hundred acres of land.[19] Mahulda Easley Mayberry played an instrumental role in ensuring that Jim Mayberry had good titles to his land, according to Louie Mayberry, making sure that his purchases were recorded properly at the courthouse in Gatesville so that the white Mayberry heirs could not challenge his claim.[20] Mahulda Mayberry also encouraged Jim Mayberry to register his cattle brand. The white Mayberrys used a crow foot or turkey foot as their brand, and in 1867, Jim Mayberry added a bar beneath the foot as his brand and made it official. In the 1950s, Louie Mayberry adopted his grandfather's brand for his own cattle.[21]

The land around Lincolnville did not yield its residents an easy living. People worked, and they worked hard, in a combination of raising food for themselves and cotton for the market and laboring off the farm for wages. Most of the men farmed and raised stock, carrying out their tasks with horses and mules. Gus Weatherly oversaw a diversified farm, with cotton, wheat, hay, sugar cane, and peaches. His daughters, Ruth Manning and Rowena Keatts, remembered that as small girls, they herded and milked the family's small herd of Jersey cows, and Rowena bragged of her prowess as a cotton picker.[22] Deola Mayberry Adams, daughter of Gordon "Dee" Mayberry and Ivey Johnson Mayberry, recalled her family working in various ways. Her father raised cotton, and she and her brothers assisted in chopping and picking while her mother went to Gatesville to work as a laundress and house-keeper. Adams also worked with her mother washing windows: "I said I'd never wash nobody's windows no more. We used Bon Ami . . . hard, square-like soap. . . . And you had to take towels and scrub all that dirt. And those windows would really shining when you'd get through with them, but you'd be really tired, too."[23] After Jim Mayberry died in 1888, leaving her with eleven children still at home, Lou Mayberry began doing laundry in Gatesville as well. Their granddaughter, Ophelia Hall, whose family lived with her widowed grandmother, remembered, "And my father and them would take her and bring her to town with the bundles of clothes washed and they would deliver them to the white people here in Gatesville. She'd make a little money that way." Hall's family also worked for wages in the coun-tryside, hiring themselves out to other farm families to chop and pick cotton and pull corn. Her mother worked in the fields, cooked for people in town, and raised a garden and canned beans and beets. Hall summed up, "My mother has worked very hard, you know, to try to accomplish something."[24]

Despite the effort required, no one in Lincolnville went hungry. The families kept and killed hogs and chickens, and they grew corn to be turned into meal. Cows provided milk. Irish potatoes, sweet potatoes, and other vegetables rounded out the daily diet.[25] And there were treats. Her granddaughters fondly recalled Lou May-berry baking for their visits: biscuits, hoecake, and gingerbread, all cooked in a Dutch oven in the open fireplace. Rowena Keatts particularly loved the iced pound cakes that her grandmother made and decorated with cedar twigs for Christmas.[26]

Like many freedom colonies, Lincolnville was somewhat isolated, cut off from main roads by the Leon River and Dodd's Creek.[27] Before a bridge was built, people and animals forded the Leon at a spot called Mayberry's Crossing. About 1911, the Cotton Belt railway cut across the property belonging to the Easleys and the May-berrys. To the children of the family, the arrival of the train provided both enter-tainment and easier transportation. Pedestrians could use the trestle to cross the river, and the right-of-way provided a shortcut into Gatesville, four miles away.[28] And while fifteen cents bought a seat on a small train called a motorcar that came through twice a day, most Lincolnville residents saved their cash and used their feet instead. Lincolnville dwellers also traveled on horseback or by wagon, carriage, and occasionally mule until the 1920s. The Mayberrys prided themselves on their prowess with horses, but both Jim Mayberry and his oldest son, Marion, died from injuries sustained when they were thrown from their mounts.[29] Cars began arriving at Moccasin Bend before 1920—"old used cars," according to Rowena Keatts. Gus Weatherly waited until 1924, when he could afford a new Model T Ford. Weatherly never drove himself, relying on his oldest daughter, Ruth, or his brothers to drive, but he loved the pride of ownership.[30]

Most of the people of Lincolnville constructed their homes of local wood. Rowena Keatts recalled the house that Jim and Lou Mayberry built as a long structure of six rooms, separated into halves by a hall with a limestone rock fireplace at each end. A porch spanned the width of the front, and the kitchen with its wood-burning stove was attached to the back. Gus Weatherly's house sheltered many women: his mother, Jane Bond Mayberry; his first wife, Eliza Weatherly; and his second wife, Bettie Mayberry Weatherly, and their five daughters. When Gus and Bettie married, he added a second room and a kitchen to the original log cabin, all roofed with wood shingles. A "shed porch" on the front provided shelter from the elements and a place to relax or work. The original log room was open to the rafters, large enough to hold two full-size beds and still have ample seating in front of the limestone fireplace on one end. The single window opened near the fireplace. Kerosene lamps provided light, even during the day. Bettie cooked on an iron woodstove with a warming unit on top and an oven in the front. Water was relatively easy to obtain, as the Weatherly and Mayberry families had wells near their houses.[31]

Like many freedom communities, Lincolnville had only a few institutions that would identify it to an outsider.[32] The sole commercial establishment was a store operated briefly by Bonaparte Snow and Dave Shavers.[33] The church and the school occupied a single building, a structure that served as the focus of the community for upwards of seventy years.

Like many former slaves, the people of Lincolnville quickly identified themselves as Christians and, to be specific, Baptists. The Rev. G. C. Alexander established the Bethlehem Baptist Church in April 1872 on land given by Allen Shavers and his family.[34] Although sources vary on when the church moved to town, Eunice Brown Johnson distinctly remembered attending there, possibly as late as 1906: "And I can remember on Sunday mornings, we'd dress and go through the woods going to a little wood house—church-house, what they had church and school in. And we'd go there and go to church, which was a lot of fun, my cousins and all." She and her cousins, "the Barrens girls," made their professions of faith at the same time and were baptized in the Leon River.[35] After the church moved into Gatesville, Lincolnville residents regularly made the four-mile trip to worship, bringing lunch and "britches" quilts made of old pairs of pants for the children to rest on during the service.[36]

Family and children formed a huge part of life in Lincolnville. Before he married Louisa Cook, Jim Mayberry and Mariah Easley Mack had a daughter, Mollie. Mollie married William Snow, and they had eight children. Mollie and William bought two hundred acres of land in 1884 that remains in family hands in 2017.[37] Louisa and Jim Mayberry had nineteen children, including two sets of twins, between 1864 and

1889. Fifteen of them survived to adulthood, and most of them intermarried with other Lincolnville residents: Annie with Jake Barrens (with fourteen children), John with Hannah Squyres, Cliffie with Hannah's brother Zibe "Buddy" Squyres, Sarah with Jack Kimmons, Bettie with Gus Weatherly, Porter with Ella Lothlen, Emma with Dave "Bud" Easley, Lillie with Bud's brother Holmes Easley, Bev with Ollie Snow, and Hannah with Jake Terry. In the dialect attributed by the interviewer, Jake Barrens remembered that his wedding to Annie Mayberry, on February 13, 1881, was a modest affair: "I didn' have no fine close, I was workin' for small wages an' I jus' had what I could buy, a suit an' clean shirt, looked de best I could an' dat was all."[38]

One of the key features of Reconstruction was the organization of schools for freed slaves, sometimes by the US government through the Freedman's Bureau and sometimes by Northern churches. Jake Barrens noted the uneven reach of schools for African Americans, recalling his experience in adjacent Hamilton County: "No'm I can't read an' write 'cause I had no chance to go to school, since dere was no schools in de days of early youth an' my mother was a widder wid odder chillun dependent on me as I was de first born an' oldest chile my mother had." With its small, isolated African American population, Lincolnville evidently received no outside assistance. But the laws of the state of Texas did reach Coryell County, and when the state created a system of public schools in 1871, the Lincolnville school opened. Although the date of the opening remains unclear, Jim Mayberry paid school taxes of $2.49 in 1872, levied in accordance with the new state law authorizing the organization and maintenance of free public schools in the state of Texas.[39] Ophelia Hall, the granddaughter of an early teacher, recalled seeing a document noting that families paid seventy-five cents per month for younger children and $1.50 for older children, so it is possible that the school began with subscriptions. By 1883, the school carried the legal designation of Lincolnville, Public School Community No. 62 of Coryell County. On October 1, 1883, trustees James Mayberry, Gus Weatherly, and Silas Snow met to authorize the hiring of Thomas J. Lothlen as the teacher for the year. The school term was four months—November through February—and Lothlen was to receive a salary of forty dollars per month. Poignantly, none of the trustees could read or write, but each signed his mark on a document provided by the state. Lothlen was well known to the trustees, for he was the son of John and Pelvina Lothlen, who had come to Coryell County with their owner, Alfred Young Lothlen, from Tennessee, by way of Burleson County, Texas, and had six children before emancipation. Surely, Thomas Lothlen, a young man aged twenty-four, showed promise, for he had somehow attained enough education to qualify for a "2 Grade" teaching certificate.[40]

Rowena Keatts, the daughter of Gus Weatherly and Bettie Mayberry, was born in 1911, and she vividly remembered the Lincolnville school as both pupil and teacher. Her older sisters, Ruth and Lou Ann, started school at the required minimum age of seven, and Rowena, who was only six years old, kicked up such a fuss that her mother paid for her to attend. The Lincolnville school went through the seventh grade, and then students either ended their school careers or attended high school in Gatesville or even in Waco, forty miles to the east. Before World War I, the school was heavily populated with cousins—"a nice bunch of us," as Keatts recalled. The school was in a small wooden building, perhaps twenty feet by thirty feet in area, furnished with homemade wooden backless benches—"wash benches" like the ones that women did laundry on, according to Ophelia Mayberry Hall—with a chalkboard across the front and a wood-burning iron stove in the center. Curriculum materials consisted of used books from the city schools: blue-back spellers and arithmetic, geometry, and English books. Keeping teachers was difficult, said Ruth Weatherly Manning. They usually left after a year or so, tired of poor pay and living in the country.[41]

By the end of the nineteenth century, the slow exodus of the former slaves from the countryside was well under way. Among the older generation, Green and Fannie Brown moved to Gatesville by 1896, with Green making a living as a woodcutter. Many of the children of Lou and Jim Mayberry stayed in Lincolnville. Jake and Annie Barrens moved into Gatesville with their children before 1900, as did Zibe and Cliffie Squyres, building their community with other African Americans around Lutterloh Avenue. Hannah and Jake Terry soon followed. Between 1900 and 1910, John and Hannah Mayberry moved to various places around Texas, and Sarah and Jack Kimmons struck out for Muskogee, Oklahoma.[42] Bettie and Gus Weatherly and their daughters left the farm in 1929, when Gus became terminally ill.[43] The grandchildren of the founding generation scattered throughout the first third of the twentieth century.

Rowena Keatts was one of the last teachers at the Lincolnville school, beginning about 1936. The building remained unchanged since her days as a student, with the addition of some "old-fashioned desks." She fondly recalled Carl Snow, the youngest son of Mollie and William, arriving at the school on the coldest mornings to make the fire before she arrived on her walk from Gatesville. By then, the seven children of Carl and his wife, Tansy Murray Snow, were the only ones left, and the school closed in 1943.

The ties of family remained strong, however, even as its members dispersed. The relatives in town visited those still in Lincolnville, and those in the country were frequently in town for church, shopping, and the upper grades of school. Families from Lincolnville brought their Sunday dinners in boxes to Gatesville and gathered at Zibe and Cliffie Squyres's house for lunch each week.[44] The Mayberrys remained acutely aware of their kin. Rowena Keatts recalled a joyous gathering in the early 1920s:

> I never shall forget—we had a family—they didn't call it a reunion, but a family get-together. Aunt Sarah lived in Oklahoma. She came down and I think her daughter and two or three of her grandchildren came down. Aunt Annie and her bunch and Aunt Hannah and her bunch, Mama's bunch. Colvie Snow was in that bunch, too. Everybody brought lunch and everything and they just spread on the ground, and that was just the time of your life. . . . They didn't have any kind of tables at all, and everybody sat down on the ground and ate the food. But

they spent the day there and then the—Aunt Hannah and Aunt Annie and all lived in town and they had to leave early because it took a long time to get back, maybe a hour and a half to get back to town because they were all in buggies and surreys and wagons.[45]

In 1967, Ophelia Mayberry Hall decided to hold a Juneteenth celebration for her father, Porter "Big" Mayberry and his twin brother, Gordon "Dee" Mayberry, and the family gathered in Gatesville. Bettie Weatherly, by then ninety years old, loved seeing the relatives together again, and the event became annual. In the mid-1980s, the event titled the "Mayberry-Brown-Snow Reunion" drew hundreds of people from across the country. In July 1986, it began with a fish fry and included card and domino tournaments, a dance for the young people, a hayride through Lincolnville, a barbecue dinner, a stage play, and a worship service at Bethlehem Baptist Church. The reunion was a joint effort of the three families, with organizers in Gatesville, Waco, and the Dallas suburb of Carrollton.[46]

In March 2017, the family came together once again to dedicate a Texas State Historical Marker to Lincolnville. They brought photographs and artifacts. The marker, just off the Levita Road in Coryell County, notes the establishment and survival of the community. The stone house on the Snow family property is the only structure remaining from Lincolnville, but the elegant granite-framed marker stands to remind people in the new housing development nearby that their land was once the cherished prize of a people no longer enslaved.

NOTES

1. Thad Sitton and James H. Conrad, *Freedom Colonies: Independent Black Texans in the Time of Jim Crow* (Austin: University of Texas Press, 2005), 191–98.

2. Randolph B. Campbell, *An Empire for Slavery: The Peculiar Institution in Texas, 1821–1865* (Baton Rouge: Louisiana State University Press, 1989), 56; Clyde Bailey and Mabel Bailey, eds., *Vignettes of Coryell County* (Gatesville, TX: Gatesville Printing, 1976), 37.

3. 1860 US Census, Coryell County, Texas; Eunice Brown Johnson, *Oral Memoirs of Eunice Brown Johnson*, interviewed by Rebecca Sharpless on July 31, 1986 and April 14, 1986 in Gatesville, Texas, Baylor University Institute for Oral History, Waco, Texas, 26.

4. These three women are surely the slaves of Hiram Cook enumerated in the 1860 Slave Schedule of the US Census in the survey of the Raney's Creek area: black females ages forty, fourteen, and twelve. 1850 US Census, Slave Schedule, Coryell County, Texas. Texas Historical Commission (THC), "Lincolnville: A Texas Freedom Colony," narrative for Texas Historical Marker 15CV01. I gratefully acknowledge the research done by Wanda Waite in preparing the application and Bob Brinkman of the THC for making it available to me. "Hiram William Cooke," *Texas State Cemetery*, accessed June 26, 2017, http:// www.cemetery.state.tx.us/pub/user _form.asp?pers_id=135; Louie Edward

Mayberry, *Oral Memoirs of Louie Edward Mayberry*, interviewed by Rebecca Sharpless on March 19, 1987, in Goliad, Texas, Baylor University Institute for Oral History, Waco, Texas, 3.

5. Campbell, *Empire for Slavery*, 264.

6. Rowena Weatherly Keatts, *Oral Memoirs of Rowena Weatherly Keatts*, interviewed by Rebecca Sharpless between May 5, 1986, and April 15, 1987, in Waco, Texas, Baylor University Institute for Oral History, Waco Texas, 4–5. Perhaps Jane is the twenty-six-year-old female with three small children, owned by W. P. Weatherly in Hickman County, Tennessee, in 1850. See 1850 US Census, Slave Schedule, Hickman County, Tennessee.

7. Vivian Smyrl, "Coryell County," *Handbook of Texas Online*, accessed June 26, 2017, https://tshaonline.org/handbook/online/articles/hcc23; Zelma Scott, "Fort Gates," *Handbook of Texas Online*, accessed June 26, 2017, http://www.tshaonline.org/handbook/online/articles/qbf20.

8. Texas Historical Commission, "Lincolnville."

9. Texas A&M Forest Service, "Texas Ecoregions, Grand Prairie and Plains," *Trees of Texas*, accessed June 26, 2017, http://texastreeid.tamu.edu/content/texasEcoRegions/GrandPrairiePlains/.

10. Smyrl, "Coryell County."

11. Coryell County tax rolls, 1862. In 1862, owning twelve slaves made J. W. Mayberry the second-largest slaveholder in Coryell County, exceeded only by Lemuel Murrell, who owned thirteen.

12. Keatts, *Oral Memoirs*, 6–7.

13. Mayberry, *Oral Memoirs*, 5.

14. 1870 US Census, Coryell County, Texas, Precinct 1.

15. In the 1860 slave census, H. W. Squyres has only one slave, a thirty-three-year-old female. Might this be Harriet? In the 1862 tax rolls, he has four—maybe Harriet and her children. See 1860 US Census, Slave Schedule, Coryell County, Texas; Coryell County tax rolls, 1862.

16. Bailey, *Vignettes of Coryell County*, 34–36; Keatts, *Oral Memoirs*, 15.

17. Slaveholders with these names in Coryell County in 1860 included A. Y. Lothlen with ten slaves and James Barnes with twenty. In the 1862 tax rolls, Lothlen has seven, and Barnes is not listed. See 1860 US Census, Slave Schedule, Coryell County, Texas; Coryell County tax rolls, 1862.

18. Coryell County tax rolls, 1866.

19. Texas Historical Commission, "Lincolnville." The African American Easley family was almost surely somehow affiliated with the white family of Mahulda Easley Mayberry, but I have been unable to establish the connection. Many Easleys lived in Hickman County, and it is possible that the Easleys, like Gus Mayberry, took the name of their former owner rather than Mayberry. See W. Jerome D. Spence and David L. Spence, *A History of Hickman County, Tennessee* (Nashville, TN: Gospel Advocate, 1900), 316.

20. Mayberry, *Oral Memoirs*, 14.

21. Ibid., 16–17.

22. Keatts, *Oral Memoirs*, 31–33, 37–39; Ruth Weatherly Manning, *Oral Memoirs of Ruth Weatherly Manning*, interviewed by Rebecca Sharpless on April 25, 1987, in Gatesville, Texas, Baylor University Institute for Oral History, Waco, Texas, 8–9.

23. Deola Mayberry Adams, *Oral Memoirs of Deola Mayberry Adams,* interviewed by Rebecca Sharpless on August 4, 1987, Gatesville, Texas, Baylor University Institute for Oral History, Waco, Texas, 10–11. Chopping cotton is the process of thinning the sprouting plants with a sharp hoe, usually done in the late spring and early summer.

24. Ophelia Mae Mayberry Hall, *Oral Memoirs of Ophelia Mae Mayberry Hall,* interviewed by Rebecca Sharpless, May 26, 1986, and June 10, 1986, Gatesville, Texas, Baylor University Institute for Oral History, Waco, Texas, 12–13, 36–37.

25. Hall, *Oral Memoirs,* 25, 68–70; Keatts, *Oral Memoirs,* 8, 78, 135; Adams, *Oral Memoir,* 13–14.

26. Hall, *Oral Memoirs,* 71; Keatts, *Oral Memoirs,* 70–71.

27. Keatts, *Oral Memoirs,* 138; Hall, *Oral Memoirs,* 24.

28. Texas Historical Commission, "Lincolnville"; Jeanne F. Lively, "Stephenville North and South Texas Railway," *Handbook of Texas Online,* accessed July 05, 2017, http://www.tshaonline.org/handbook/online/articles/eqs33; Manning, *Oral Memoirs,* 6; Keatts, *Oral Memoirs,* 138, 143.

29. Manning, *Oral Memoirs,* 4–5, 6; Hall, *Oral Memoirs,* 19, 27; Mayberry, *Oral Memoirs,* 7.

30. Keatts, *Oral Memoirs,* 96–97.

31. Adams, *Oral Memoirs,* 6; Keatts, *Oral Memoirs,* 67–71; Manning, *Oral Memoirs,* 25.

32. Sitton and Conrad, *Freedom Colonies,* 2.

33. Geraldine Batty-Hoover and Ernestine Taylor, *They Stood the Test of Time* (n.p., n.d.), 8.

34. Rowena Weatherly Keatts, *The History of the Bethlehem Baptist Church,* 1978, typescript in author's possession. The 1870 and 1880 US censuses list an African American farmer named Granvill Alexander, born about 1844 in Texas, living in Gatesville. I have been unable to find other information about G. C. Alexander.

35. Johnson, *Oral Memoirs,* 19–20.

36. Ibid., 10–11, 20; Keatts, *Oral Memoirs,* 130.

37. Texas Historical Commission, "Lincolnville." Mollie Snow was born in Tennessee in 1858, so clearly, Jim and Mariah knew each other before they came to Texas. Jim would have met Louisa, who came with Hiram Cook, after his arrival in Coryell County.

38. "Texas Slave Narrative: Jake Barrens," *RootsWeb,* accessed July 3, 2017, http://freepages.genealogy.rootsweb.ancestry.com/~ewyatt/_borders/Texas%20Slave%20Narratives/TEXAS%20B/Barrens,%20Jake.html.

39. Tax receipt, December 21, 1872, copy in possession of author.

40. Hall, *Oral Memoirs,* 29–31; "Contract for Trustees of School Community No. 62, Coryell County, Texas," October 1, 1883, copy in possession of author; US Census, 1850; US Census, 1870. A. Y. Lothlen paid taxes for seven slaves in 1862. See 1862 tax rolls, Coryell County, Texas.

41. Hall, *Oral Memoirs*; Manning, *Oral Memoirs,* 13–14.

42. Mayberry, *Oral Memoirs,* 10.

43. Manning, *Oral Memoirs,* 10.

44. Keatts, *Oral Memoirs,* 130–31.

45. Ibid., 62–63.

46. Letter from R. E. Mayberry to "Family Member," May 6, 1987, copy in author's possession.

The African American Military Experience in Central Texas, 1863–1900

James T. Matthews

Among the occupations open to black men in the years after the Civil War was, as we have seen, serving as a cowhand, but also many black males were able to serve in the US Army. Blacks from Central Texas, as early as the last year of the Civil War and through the 1890s, indeed benefited from that experience. As author James T. Matthews noted, military service provided African American men with a "chance to improve their lives." In addition to writing history, Matthews works for the San Antonio Area Boy Scouts and, with his wife, Becky, edits The Cyclone, *the newsletter of the West Texas Historical Association. He is the author of* Fort Concho: History and Guide.

★

In May 1937, the Federal Writers' Project of the Works Progress Administration interviewed William Branch of San Antonio for the "folk history of slavery" they were preparing. Their interviews focused on early reminiscences of those born in slavery, but with Branch and many other African American men interviewed in Texas, military service played an important part in their lives and in their memories. Branch served ten years in the all-black Twenty-Fifth Infantry, mostly in Texas. When asked if he liked being a soldier, he replied, "Did I like de army? Yahsur, Id ruthuh be in de army dan a plantation slave." For many newly freed African American men in the Central Texas area or moving to Texas after the Civil War, the regular army provided a vital opportunity to make a new life in a profession that had little in common with domestic service or life on a plantation. The work experience, in a totally different environment than that to which most former slaves had been accustomed, gave them a chance to learn and excel in the post–Civil War society.[1]

Military service provided an escape for those born in slavery in Central Texas, beginning during the latter part of the Civil War. Henry Buttler, who later settled in Fort Worth, recalled that his chance to escape came when he was transported to Pine Bluff, Arkansas: "The general faithfulness of the slave was noticeable then, as they had a chance to desert and go to free states." He enlisted at Union headquarters at Fort Smith in 1863 and served in Arkansas for the remainder of the war. Many other young black men traveled to recruiting depots in Helena, Arkansas, or New Orleans, Louisiana, to enlist in the volunteer regiments of the US Colored Troops. New Orleans had long been a center for the recruitment of African American soldiers, starting with their own local militia known as the Native Guard. Frederick Sullivan of the Dallas area traveled there to join the First US Colored Infantry in December 1864, receiving a $100 enlistment bounty. Enlistment bounties appear to have been paid by the recruiting station in New Orleans as a regular incentive for the US Colored Troops. Other Central Texas men who took advantage of receiving cash payments included Robert Wright of Washington County and John Anderson who enlisted in the Fourth US Colored Cavalry just as the war was ending in April 1865.[2]

Those who did not go east to New Orleans could reach a Union recruiting station by traveling north into Arkansas. In Helena, the First Arkansas Infantry, African Descent, organized in May 1863. Harry Jones, a twenty-year-old farmer from North Texas enlisted as one of the original muster. Nelson Barton and Thomas Hall of Washington County also joined the regiment, crossing Texas and Arkansas to reach the headquarters in Helena. After his long journey to enlist, Hall died in camp of tuberculosis on October 3, 1864. The First Arkansas mustered into federal service in May 1864, becoming the Forty-Sixth US Colored Infantry. They were attached to the post at Milliken's Bend, Louisiana, through the latter part of 1864, but with the Confederate surrender, the regiment received orders to proceed to Brazos Santiago, Texas, in May 1865. The Texas soldiers had returned to their home state, manning stations from Fort Brown to Fort Clark along the Rio Grande. One of the primary missions assigned to the Forty-Sixth was to prevent Confederate forces from avoiding surrender by crossing the border into Mexico.[3]

Those Confederate forces that had served in the Trans-Mississippi Department also included black soldiers and support troops. Despite the fact that many black men did join the Union army to escape slavery, some served the Confederacy in Texas. Many of them accompanied their masters into battle or served as cooks, laborers, or drivers. One of those was Martin Jackson, who later described himself as a "black Texan" and a "lugger-in of men that got wounded." He claimed that his position was actually similar to that of a Red Cross worker. Jackson recalled mixed feelings about serving the Confederacy: "I knew the Yanks were going to win, from the beginning. I wanted them to win and lick us Southerners, but I hoped they was going to do it without wiping out our company." His "company" was the First Texas

Cavalry under Col. Augustus Buchel. Jackson remembered that he held Colonel Buchel as he died following the battle of Pleasant Hill, recounting that he was "as fine a man and a soldier as you ever saw."[4]

Although the war ended in the spring of 1865, US Colored Troops frequently remained on active duty for up to a year longer as the regular army was reorganized for frontier defense and enforcement of Reconstruction laws. The Forty-Sixth Colored Infantry mustered out of service on January 30, 1866. Some of the volunteer soldiers reenlisted in one of the six black regiments organized in 1866. Others returned to their home states. Many remained in Texas to start new lives. Nelson Barton, now a corporal, left the army, married, and became a minister. As the volunteer army began to disband, in early 1867, one of the newly formed black regiments in the regular army, the Forty-First Infantry, arrived in Texas and took over the posts along the Rio Grande River. Over the next thirty years, each of the regular black regiments would serve in Texas, stationed at all the active forts and participating in every campaign along the southwestern frontier.[5]

Vital to the strategic defense of the Texas frontier was Fort Richardson in Jack County. It was not only the most important post in Central Texas following the Civil War, but in 1872, it became the largest army installation in the United States, with over 650 soldiers. Established in November 1867 as the northern point on the line of defense for the Texas frontier, construction on the post progressed slowly, and most of the troops lived in buildings made of canvas-lined pickets throughout the first year. By June 1869, when the first African American troops arrived on post, Fort Richardson had become a major staging area for Indian campaigns in Texas and the surrounding territories. From that time until the post was abandoned in May 1878, companies of black soldiers served continually at the fort.[6]

On March 3, 1869, Congress enacted the Army Appropriations Act that reduced the number of infantry regiments from forty-five to twenty-five and consolidated the four black infantry regiments into two. The Thirty-Eighth and Forty-First Infantry became the Twenty-Fourth Infantry, and the Thirty-Ninth and Fortieth became the Twenty-Fifth. When the orders arrived, the Thirty-Eighth was stationed in New Mexico and Kansas, while the Forty-First remained at the posts along the Rio Grande. To affect the consolidation, a battalion of the Thirty-Eighth Infantry marched from New Mexico to Fort Richardson, arriving on June 22. From there, they were assigned to other posts along the Texas frontier, including Fort Griffin and Fort Concho. During the summer, Companies G and I of the Thirty-Eighth marched south from Kansas, where they had been patrolling the military roads and railways in the western part of the state. Arriving at Fort Richardson, they reorganized as Company I of the Twenty-Fourth Infantry in September 1869.[7]

Fort Richardson became the first regular duty station for Company I. Most of their time was spent in garrison duty or providing escorts for supply trains between the Texas forts. In June 1872, they did accompany Col. William R. Shafter on his expedition across the Llano Estacado. While they did not experience any casualties in the field, one soldier, Pvt. James Osborne, died of gunshot wounds in a fight outside the garrison shortly after they arrived in September 1869. The black soldiers shared the post with companies of the white Sixth Cavalry. During his visit in 1870, the Inspector General noted "no trouble or bad feeling between white and colored troops. They do not mix, neither do they quarrel." Sgt. Harry McConnell of the Sixth Cavalry did compliment the high spirits of Company I, recalling "their volatile, devil-may-care characters fitted them for the ups and downs of the army."[8]

After Company I left Fort Richardson, Companies E, I, and L of the black Tenth Cavalry served at the post until its closure in 1878. During a typical month in 1873, the Tenth scouted for Indians, escorted supply trains to Fort Griffin, investigated the death of a local citizen by Comanche, and pursued an escaped prisoner and a member of the guard who deserted with him. Desertion remained a constant problem in the army, appearing to be worst just before soldiers left the post on patrol or just after they returned from duty in the field. It was less of a problem in the black regiments throughout the nineteenth century, whether because they placed more value on the opportunities the army provided or simply because there was no attractive escape near most of the posts where they served. One black Texan, Randall Williams of Colorado County, did desert before his company even left the recruiting station, but overall desertion from the African American regiments in Texas remained relatively low. In one company of the Tenth Cavalry, twenty of the eighty-seven men recruited in 1867 deserted during their first enlistment, one of them on three separate occasions. While that might seem high, during the same period, the Seventh Cavalry experienced an average of seventy desertions per company or 3.5 each month. In 1877, the average number of desertions in an infantry regiment was thirty-one. Only seven men deserted from the Twenty-Fourth Infantry that year, while a total of only forty desertions were reported from all four black regiments.[9]

The growing town of Jacksboro did not prove a popular place for former soldiers of the Tenth Cavalry and Twenty-Fourth Infantry to settle when Fort Richardson closed in 1878. The 1870 census lists a total of 694 men in Jack County. Seventy-two were black, of whom almost fifty were members of Company I, the Twenty-Fourth Infantry. By 1880, after the post had been abandoned, the county had a population of 6,626, out of which 118 were black. In 1920, the population had grown to 9,863, yet there were only thirty-five African Americans in Jack County. Most former soldiers who stayed in the area probably moved to Fort Worth or Dallas. The black population of Dallas County remained constant from 1870 to 1920 at about 15 percent, while in Tarrant County, it continued to be about 12 percent. Madison Bruin of the Tenth Cavalry went to work for the railroad after several enlistments and eventually settled in Dallas. Civil War veteran Henry Buttler became an educator among the black community in Fort Worth.[10]

A similar trend can be seen in the South-Central Texas farming communities in Fayette and Colorado Counties. A significant number of young black men joined the army from that area, yet many did not return after their enlistments.

Farmer Joseph Brown of Fayette County settled in Houston after his army service, while his neighbor, Willie Polk, married and moved to San Antonio. The Fayette County census shows that in 1870, black settlers were 35 percent of the population. By 1920, they accounted for only 22.5 percent. Army experience and training may have given the black soldiers a chance to find better jobs in the growing Texas cities. Certainly, the army provided many with the opportunity to learn to read and write. Because officers objected to an illiterate enlisted force that left them to handle all the required army paperwork and documentation, they encouraged schools for the black soldiers on post. Many of those were established by army chaplains, such as George M. Mullins of the Twenty-Fifth Infantry. Mullins applauded the spirit of black soldiers at Fort Davis in 1877 when he stated, "The ambition to be all that soldiers should be is not confined to a few of these sons of an unfortunate race. They are possessed of the notion that the colored people of the whole country are more or less affected by their conduct in the Army."[11]

From their organization in 1866 until the defeat of the Apache under Victorio in 1880, the black regiments saw extensive service on the Texas frontier. Natives of Central Texas continued to travel to recruiting stations to enlist, only to return to Texas for active duty. Edmond Jones, a soap maker from Fairfield, enlisted in the Thirty-Ninth Infantry in Greenville, Louisiana, in May 1867. Thomas Holliman of Austin County enlisted in the Thirty-Eighth Infantry in Baltimore, Maryland, only to be dishonorably discharged at Fort Seldon, New Mexico, a year later. Thomas Maddox of Grayson County joined the Tenth Cavalry at Fort Sill in Indian Territory in 1878. He served honorably in Companies G and H, rising to the rank of sergeant. In the summer of 1880, Maddox accompanied a battalion under the command of Capt. Louis Carpenter in search of Victorio and the Apache who had escaped the Mescalero reservation. On August 6, Carpenter's troops caught the Apache at Rattlesnake Springs in the Sierra Diablo range, forcing Victorio to retreat south into Mexico. Although that proved to be the last major action against the Indians in Texas, the Tenth Cavalry continued to patrol the Trans-Pecos region for the next few years. Thomas Maddox died in the hospital at Fort Stockton, June 1, 1884, of an abscessed liver.[12]

George McCampbell of Gonzales enlisted in Company M of the Ninth Cavalry at New Orleans in 1866. Assigned to Fort McKavett when the Ninth moved to Texas, he took part in a campaign against the Comanche in September 1869 that tracked several raiding parties to the headwaters on the Salt Fork of the Brazos River, where they destroyed a camp of almost two hundred lodges. By 1876, his company was stationed at Fort Bayard, New Mexico. On one patrol into the Florida Mountains, they overtook a group of Mescalero fugitives, killing one and capturing eleven horses. His company continued to patrol against Apache until after the defeat of Victorio in 1880. In 1885, McCampbell, now a sergeant, received an assignment to Fort Washakie, near the Wind River Reservation in Wyoming. He died there of acute meningitis on February 2, 1888, after twenty years of exemplary service.[13]

Other African American soldiers stationed in Texas came from Virginia, Kentucky, and Tennessee but elected to remain in Central Texas after their enlistments ended. William Branch of Virginia settled in San Antonio, where he worked for Bell Jewelry and remained active with the Abraham Lincoln Lodge, National Indian Wars Veterans. Branch had enlisted in the Twenty-Fifth Infantry in 1870 at Baltimore and sailed to Galveston to reach his station in Texas. He later recalled, "Den we marches from Galveston to Fort Duncan. It was up, up de whole time. We ties our bedclothes and rolls dem in a bundle wid a strap. We walks wid our guns and bedclothes on our backs, and de wagons wid de rations follows us. . . . For rations we got canned beans, milk and hardtack. De hard tacks is 3 or 4 in a box, we wets 'em in water and cooks 'em in a skillet." Branch served at Fort Davis in the early 1870s. His company marched north to Fort Sill in 1874 to enroll the Cheyenne and Arapahoe on the reservation. He remembered that after the Cheyenne escape under Chief Red Food, Col. William Shafter addressed the troops in his shirt sleeves in the snow, saying, "Whut's dis order Gen. Davidson give? Don' kill de Cheyennes? You kill 'em all from de cradle to de Cross." Branch also recalled, "De Cheyennes got Winchesters and rifles and repeaters they used to shoot us from de government. Yahsur, de government give 'em de guns dey used to shoot us. We got de ole fashion muzzle loaders." After they captured some of the Cheyenne, Branch's company turned their repeating rifles over to the regiment.[14]

William Watkins also remembered that campaign in Indian Territory, claiming of the Cheyenne, "Dey's great big Indians 'bout seven feet tall." During one attack, he was wounded in the wrist by a Cheyenne arrow. Watkins originally came from Charlotte County, Virginia, to enlist at Jefferson Barracks in 1870. Assigned to the Twenty-Fifth Infantry in Texas, he later remembered that one of his first duties was to stand guard at the Alamo. From there, he proceeded to Fort Davis, where he served in the same company as William Branch. While Branch served two enlistments with distinction, Watkins did not end his military service as well. According to Watkins, his sergeant at Fort Clark decided to bring charges against him without justification, leading to his dishonorable discharge. He lamented, "I ain't had no court martial nor no trial and I cain't git no pension 'count of de dishonorable discharge." Watkins eventually settled in San Antonio. When William Branch's wife died in the 1930s and his eyesight began to fail, his old army friend William Watkins moved in.[15]

William Davis enlisted in the Twenty-Fourth Infantry in 1869 at Nashville, Tennessee, and was assigned to Fort Stockton. He later claimed that while there "all us do am build 'dobe houses." He also recalled, "Out dere I votes for de first time, for Gen'l Grant when Greeley and him run for president." At age seventeen, Madison Bruin decided he was tired of school in Indiana and left to join the Tenth Cavalry. After reporting for duty at Fort Sill, he soon came to Texas to serve at Fort Davis and Fort Quitman. In 1878, Bruin took part in a scouting expedition into the Guadalupe Mountains to establish a permanent outpost. He also participated in the campaign against Victorio's Apache in 1880. He remembered having three horses while serving with the Tenth Cavalry: "De fust one plays out, de next one shot down on campaign and one was condemned." When he settled in Dallas after working for the railroad, Bruin applied for and received an army pension.[16]

Even with the end of the Indian Wars, more African American men chose to enlist in the 1890s. The economic upheaval of the Panic of 1893 made jobs even harder to find for young black men, and a larger number than usual enlisted during 1893–97. Then, in 1898, the United States went to war with Spain. All four black regiments served in Cuba as part of the expeditionary force led by one of their former commanders, Maj. Gen. William Shafter. Volunteer regiments also served alongside the regulars. In Texas, the black militia known as the Battalion of Colored Infantry petitioned to be activated but could not receive authorization from the legislature. Many of the militia's soldiers joined the Ninth US Volunteer Infantry, also known as the Ninth Immunes because of the mistaken idea that black soldiers were immune to tropical diseases. Other volunteers, like former slave and Confederate Sam Kilgore of Johnson County, joined the commissary service.[17]

Black Texans continued to join the regular army regiments as they prepared to depart for Cuba. Marvin Bell, a chauffeur in Dallas, enlisted in the Ninth Cavalry, while Ben Littlejohn of Colorado County joined the Twenty-Fourth Infantry, Company B. They were with their regiments as part of the successful assault on San Juan Heights beside Theodore Roosevelt's Rough Riders. Johnson Ray of San Antonio joined the Twenty-Fifth Infantry and took part in the battle at El Caney. Phillip Treadwell enlisted in the Hospital Corps and served at a field hospital in Cuba. Many of the wartime enlistees returned from Cuba in 1899 and mustered out of service. Others reenlisted in the regular army units as they departed for the Philippines to fight insurgents in 1900.[18]

By the end of the nineteenth century, African American troops had earned an enviable reputation as efficient, dedicated soldiers. Capt. Louis Carpenter, who commanded black soldiers in Texas, commented, "My experience has been . . . that they are as reliable as white soldiers in action. I have seen them in a number of Indian fights, and they behaved unusually well." He went on to point out that in the Tenth Cavalry, there had been fewer desertions, fewer courts-martial, and "as good general discipline as can be found anywhere in the army." Despite the evidence, some officers still objected to working with black troops, and the enforcement of Jim Crow laws, beginning in the 1890s, meant that the opportunities many black men had earned since the end of the Civil War would be seriously limited in the opening years of the twentieth century. The successful use of black soldiers in combat was forgotten for a time, yet their service had made a real, positive difference during the last half of the nineteenth century. And military service had given many African American men from Central Texas as well as those who later settled in Central Texas a real chance to improve their lives and lasting experiences that became a vital part of those lives.[19]

NOTES

1. *Federal Writers' Project: Slave Narratives*, vol. 16 (Washington, DC, 1941), interview with William Branch, 143–46.

2. Compiled Military Service Records of Volunteer Union Soldiers, 1861–65, for John Anderson, Frederick Sullivan, and Robert Wright, National Archives, Washington, DC, RG94; *Slave Narratives*, vol. 16, interview with Henry H. Buttler, part 1, 179–81.

3. Compiled Military Service Records of Volunteer Union Soldiers, 1861–65, for Nelson Barton, Thomas Hall, and Harry Jones, National Archives, Washington, DC, RG94; *The War of the Rebellion: A Compilation of the Official Records of the Union and Confederate Armies*, vol. 48 (Washington, DC: Government Printing Office, 1880–1901), part 2, 842, 931.

4. *Slave Narratives*, vol. 16, interview with Martin Jackson, part 2, 187–92.

5. Compiled Military Service Records of Volunteer Union Soldiers, 1861–65, for Nelson Barton, RG94; Regimental Returns for the 41st Infantry for June and July 1867, National Archives, Washington, DC, RG98.

6. Donald W. Whisenhunt, "Fort Richardson, Frontier Post in Northwest Texas, 1867–78" (unpublished thesis, Texas Tech, 1962), 12–13, 20.

7. Report of the Secretary of War, Forty-First Congress (Washington, DC: Government Printing Office, 1869), 170–71; Regimental Returns for the 38th Infantry for June–September 1869, RG98.

8. Registers of Deaths in the Regular Army, 1860–89, for James Osborne, RG94; William A. Dobak and Thomas D. Phillips, *The Black Regulars 1866–1898* (Norman: University of Oklahoma Press, 2001), 147, 257.

9. Regimental Returns for the Tenth Cavalry, March 1873, RG98; Report of the Secretary of War, Forty-Fifth Congress (Washington, DC: Government Printing Office, 1877), 49; US Army Register of Enlistments, 1798–1914, for Randall Williams, RG94.

10. United States Ninth Census (1870), Population Schedules for Jack, Dallas, and Tarrant Counties, Texas; Tenth Census (1880), Population Schedules for Jack, Dallas, and Tarrant Counties, Texas; Fourteenth Census (1920), Population Schedules for Jack, Dallas, and Tarrant Counties, Texas; *Slave Narratives*, interviews with Henry H. Buttler and Madison Bruin, 169–73.

11. United States Ninth Census (1870), Population Schedules for Fayette County; Fourteenth Census (1920), Population Schedules for Fayette county; George M. Mullins, Chaplain's Report for Fort Davis, 1877, RG94.

12. US Army Register of Enlistments, 1798–1914, for Edmund Jones, Thomas Holliman, and Thomas Maddox, RG94; Registers of Deaths in the Regular Army, 1860–89, for Thomas Maddox, RG94.

13. Regimental Returns for the Ninth Cavalry for September–October 1869 and April 1876; S. Army Register of Enlistments, 1798–1914, for George McCampbell, RG94; Registers of Deaths in the Regular Army, 1860–89, for George McCampbell, RG94.

14. *Slave Narratives*, interview with William Branch, 143–46.

15. Ibid., vol. 16, interview with William Watkins, part 4, 141–43.

16. Ibid., vol. 16, interview with William Davis and Madison Bruin, part 1, 169–73.

17. Ibid., vol. 16, interview with Sam Kilgore, part 2, 255–59.

18. US Army Register of Enlistments, 1798–1914, for Marvin Bell, Ben Littlejohn, Johnson Ray, and Phillip Treadwell, RG94.

19. Omaha *Bee*, April 1, 1883.

William Madison McDonald

Business and Fraternal Leader

Bruce A. Glasrud

Unlike most Texas African American politicians mentioned previously in this Central Texas study, William McDonald's greatest achievements, although he was a staunch Republican politician who headed the Black and Tan portion of the Republican Party, arose due to his relationship to the fraternal orders and to his business acumen. Author Bruce Glasrud, a specialist in teaching and writing African American history for more than fifty years, examined the known information about McDonald. Glasrud also has published more than thirty books depicting the multicultural history of the United States.

★

"America has produced no greater man than William Madison McDonald," concluded McDonald's major biographer in 1925. That author, William Oliver Bundy, further declared that McDonald's integrity has never been questioned: "His honesty is above suspicion. His judgment is sought by all classes. His love of justice and fair play is recognized by all. He stands today as the leading Negro, in many respects, upon the Western Hemisphere." Not all observers agreed with this highly laudatory view of McDonald. One commentator asserted that "McDonald used his political prestige by exploiting the Negro for his economic gain." A recent writer called him "an educated but abrasive, quarrelsome Negro." Another, an acquaintance of McDonald's, more cautiously related that "many Negroes . . . felt that McDonald was an opportunist."[1]

Despite such comments, surprisingly little, either of a scholarly or of a popular nature, has been written about this black Texan, perhaps because of the dearth of personal papers and correspondence and because of the caution of potential writers. The existing studies lack a critical eye. The extremely eulogistic biography written by his friend and associate, William Oliver Bundy, twenty-five years before McDonald's death, portrays McDonald as he would wish to be remembered. And an article entitled "From Poverty to Banker," which borrowed heavily and favorably from Bundy, was published by *Negro Achievements* in 1951–52.[2] McDonald also was referred to as one of the "Ten Richest Negroes in America" in a 1949 article in *Ebony*; the following year, a posthumous article in the same magazine declared that "Death Comes to the World's Richest Negro."[3] For other sources, the prospective biographer of McDonald must search for descriptions and comments from secondary studies, which mention but do not linger on McDonald, and from newspapers, especially the black press of the state, although McDonald's activities were carried quite extensively in the white press as well. But this man who dominated black Texas for so many years was not included in even one of the seven editions of *Who's Who in Colored America*.[4] In retrospect, however, it seems clear that his contributions and influence were far greater than that of some of his Texas contemporaries who were included in one or more editions of *Who's Who*.

McDonald's voice and authority permeated most black activities in the Lone Star State. He was a powerful force in many black organizations, particularly the fraternal groups, which he used as a base for both political advancement and economic advantage. As grand secretary, he was the real voice of the Prince Hall Free and Accepted Masons of Texas, one of the oldest and most important black fraternal orders in the United States. McDonald commanded the Black and Tan faction of the Republican Party for more than thirty years and, at times during that period, the entire Republican Party in Texas. The personal objectives he sought were wealth and power, coequal branches of the same tree; but he also sought to advance the interests of the black race in Texas.

Undoubtedly, McDonald's physical attributes aided his rise to wealth and power. The adulatory Bundy described him as looking something like an Indian chieftain, "six feet tall, slender, wiry, and of brown complexion," with a prominent brow, a Roman nose, and sparkling eyes. Other writers noted that "McDonald was tall, robust . . . smoked cigars constantly . . . wore Texas-style hats and bow ties," and "was always immaculately, yet plainly, dressed." In a less favorable portrait, a contemporary described McDonald as a "tall, gaunt, colored man with thin hawk-like features, a tufted crop of jet-black hair, and a narrow head, mounted on a scrawny neck."[5] This thin neck was the source of McDonald's nickname, "Gooseneck Bill," which derived from a report from the Republican national convention of 1896 in the Dallas *Morning News* that a black at the convention "has an Irish name, but is a kind of goosenecked Negro."[6] McDonald also was a polished speaker. Contemporary writers extolled his oratorical skills: the Fort Worth *Star-Telegram* called him "a finished orator," the Dallas *Express* announced in 1924 that he had delivered a "burning message to businessmen" at Dallas, and perhaps Bundy only slightly exaggerated when he stated that "nature has blessed him with all the elements of the great orator."[7]

McDonald was born on June 22, 1866, in Kaufman County, Texas, to parents who had been slaves. His mother, Flora Scott, whose father was a Choctaw Indian, was born in Alabama and died when McDonald was only five years old. His father, George McDonald, who at one time had been purchased by the notorious slave trader, Nathan Bedford Forrest, was born in Tennessee. He eventually labored as a blacksmith, a farmer, and a teamster in order to support his family. McDonald's background gave him advantages, particularly educational, which were often not available to his black contemporaries. In 1872, McDonald began attending a small segregated school that ran for about three months a year. During his school years, he worked for Z. T. Adams, a white Kaufman County lawyer and cattleman, who gave McDonald additional tutoring and encouragement in law and business matters— help that was eventually to be of substantial commercial benefit to McDonald. He received his high school diploma from a Kaufman County school in 1884 at the age of eighteen. A good student, perhaps, as the Houston *Informer* suggested years later, "the most brilliant student, white or black, in the schools in Kaufman County," he graduated at the top of his high school class.[8]

Even though a few sources, including the author of this article when it was first published, argued that after graduation from high school McDonald attended college, either at Roger Williams University in Nashville, Tennessee, or Wilberforce University in Ohio, neither scenario seems likely. Except for a 1949 report in the Dallas *Morning News* that McDonald attended Wilberforce, no other evidence has been located. William Oliver Bundy, who published the only book-length monograph of McDonald's life, made no mention of McDonald's collegiate career, and his life during the years when he might have attended college was packed with Texas posts and responsibilities. Bundy also noted that "a young man with a high school education had an excellent chance to help his people."[9]

Following his graduation from high school in 1884 and during the years when he apparently attended the Tennessee college, McDonald engaged in various activities before finding his métier in black capitalism. He taught for a year at the Flat Rock Public School in Kaufman County, but the meager salary soon sent him to Fort Worth in search of more remunerative employment. He accepted a position as a clerk with D. Schwartz and Company, where he remained until the business concern went broke in 1887. The following year, his abilities as an organizer and promoter were called into play when he became president of the Texas Colored State Fair Association, which he had helped organize the previous year. The first fair was held in 1887 at Fort Worth; the following year, at Marshall. Both were well-attended ventures. Despite the crowds, the fairs apparently were financially unsuccessful. McDonald resigned his post in 1889, and losing its guiding hand, the fair shortly became more local in nature. After resigning, he accepted employment as a teacher and the principal at the black high school in Forney, where he remained for six years.[10]

The first of McDonald's several marriages was contracted during the time he was affiliated with the Colored State Fair Association. He and Alice Gibson married in

1888, but in about a year, his wife became ill and apparently died, since McDonald married again in 1896, this time to Helen Ezell. Two years later, McDonald's only child was born. The son, named for his father, died in 1918 while attending Howard University; that death was a cruel blow to McDonald.[11]

McDonald's second wife died in 1926 after thirty years of marriage. Although some years later, the lonely McDonald asserted that "I have no kinfolk," he reportedly married again three more times. In 1937, he married his fifth wife, a recent graduate of Wiley College, Mae Pearl Grayson, to whom he was married at his death in 1950. An intelligent, quiet person, she was described as "an olive brown beauty with thick, lovely hair and light hazel eyes, stately figure and quiet mannerisms." His last three wives were considerably younger than McDonald, prompting comments such as that of the Houston *Informer*, that he "is sixty or more, but likes young wives."[12]

Also, reported one observer, "wealth became an obsession to him," and McDonald eventually acquired considerable financial holdings.[13] He used the essential ingredients available to him to acquire and maintain wealth and power—a solid base of individual and organizational support from his extensive social and fraternal associations. McDonald received substantial financial backing and developed an understanding of how to use influence, perseverance, an image of prestige, and a willingness to develop diversified approaches and techniques. McDonald succinctly asserted in a 1925 speech at Houston that "successful men must hold three very essential qualities: financial, mental and physical ability." In terms of political power, his basic limitation was his inability to dominate whites, although he used them. As a result, he "lost his power [in the Republican Party] which he later spent a fortune trying to regain."[14]

His early emergence as an influential Texan arose from his use of and support from the secret societies of black fraternal and benevolent associations. These organizations furnished security, friendship, and unity to members. They helped develop a tradition of organized charity, self-help, and self-reliance. They provided a place for community gatherings and social intermingling and for political and economic advancement. They were responsible for training members for leadership roles in the black community and for enabling individual blacks to develop efficient technical and business skills. Help for the black community as a whole came in the form of effective and trained leaders, increased economic efficiency, active state and local political involvement, and struggles for civil rights. Specifically, the black community was aided by establishing insurance systems, charity funds, old-age and orphans' homes, credit unions, banks, printing presses, and scholarship funds. The failure of Texas whites to be concerned with black life, the relatively small size of the black middle class, and a dearth of other agencies for black involvement meant that fraternal and benevolent associations bore a much larger share of support for the black community than was the case in white society. As an editorial in the black Dallas *Express* pointed out, "Fraternities in Texas are the bed-rock of our success. . . . They represent our greatest accumulation of cooperative wealth. They have brought together in a compact organization more individuals of the virile sort than any other of our organizations, the church included."[15] Few other avenues for political, economic, and social activity, with the exception of churches, were open to blacks.

For McDonald, as for a few other black Texans, membership and, ultimately, leadership in the fraternities brought advantages. He developed his political and economic skills; he became well known as a black leader; and he gained the voting support of his fraternal brothers (and later, sisters) for the Black and Tan wing of the Republican Party (or for any independent political maneuvers for which McDonald needed backing). The fraternities gave financial aid when he decided to open a bank in Fort Worth, and as a leader in the societies, he was called upon to speak both in and out of the state, further enhancing his own prestige and gathering supporters for his own causes. At times, McDonald apparently used fraternal funds to pay poll taxes for blacks who could not afford to pay their own. As Arthur H. Lewis asserted, "Using every possible means, even if it meant depleting the treasury of some local lodge, he saw to it that poll taxes were paid and that members of his race voted." McDonald's active participation in the lodges of Texas led him to become "one of the leading fraternalists of the race."[16]

McDonald's first venture into the realm of the secret orders began in 1882, when he joined the Seven Stars of Consolidation of America, an order that had been formed in 1881 on the principles of wisdom, love, and truth. Leaders of the Seven Stars encouraged McDonald to be an active member because they needed "a clever bookkeeper and a man who could encourage others to join." McDonald apparently succeeded. By 1885, he was a delegate to the Grand Lodge meeting at Shreveport, Louisiana, and the same year, he became Lecturer for the state of Texas—no small achievement, since by 1889, the order claimed a national membership of ten thousand. That year, members of the Seven Stars elected McDonald to the position of Supreme Grand Chief.[17] Although his wife's illness later that year prevented his candidacy for reelection, he had enjoyed the prestige, money, and travel that came with leadership in a fraternal order. And among blacks he had gained statewide recognition.

Although McDonald's initial activities in the secret societies were with the Seven Stars, in 1886, he joined three older, larger, and more prominent bodies, fraternities with which he remained affiliated for the duration of his life: the Knights of Pythias, the Odd Fellows, and the Prince Hall Free and Accepted Masons. Even though McDonald apparently never held statewide office in the first two organizations, he was a leading member who frequently addressed local, state, and even national gatherings of those fraternities. These appearances enhanced both his reputation and his following in the two societies. More important, financial support from those organizations enabled him to start a Fort Worth bank, which provided a solid foundation for his financial empire.[18]

It was, however, McDonald's position of leadership in the Prince Hall Free and Accepted Masons upon which his support and influence were founded. The Texas Masons for blacks originally started in San Antonio in 1871, spread to six cities by 1875, and then moved rapidly throughout the entire state. By the early 1920s, membership numbered about thirty thousand.[19] The Masons, as did other fraternal orders, grew because it furnished its members with insurance and death benefits. In addition to being a social and benevolent organization, after 1907, when Texas blacks were essentially politically disfranchised, the Masons, as well as other lodges, offered limited political activities to its members through selection and election of local, state, and national officers. The lodge was also used as a civic gathering place. Eventually, the Masons moved their activities into other fields. In 1901 in Dallas, they launched the New Century Cotton Mills, which by 1903 produced three thousand pounds of yarn daily. In 1912, the Masons supported McDonald's efforts to erect a bank, and they later entered the publishing field. Their operation of a printing press was attacked by C. F. Richardson, editor of the Houston *Informer*, because its rates were so low that it took business from the established printing companies. The Texas Masons published *The Masonic Quarterly*, which helped spread the Masonic message to black Texans.[20]

McDonald's rise in the Masonic lodge was meteoric, and he remained the dominant force in that organization for most of his life. The Masons began paying him a small salary in 1890, probably for recruiting purposes. He helped organize the Heroines of Jericho in 1892 and, for about half a century, was the leader of the Heroines, with the official title of Hero. In 1899, after thirteen years of membership and nine years of travel and service, the Masons selected him as their Right Worshipful Grand Secretary, a position he retained for nearly fifty years. The job of secretary was vital to the organization; as Bundy remarked, "This office is the most important in the order." In 1929, the Grand Lodge of Texas held an elaborate celebration honoring McDonald's long tenure of thirty years as Grand Secretary of the Masons. The principal speaker, Roscoe Conkling Simmons of Chicago, declared that "no history of America is complete without Texas, and no history of Texas is complete without McDonald, who is known wherever Texas is known."[21]

McDonald's position as secretary of the Masonic lodge is illustrative of the way he wielded power. He was "not the titular head of the Texas Masons," the Grandmaster, but from his post as secretary, he exercised control over the entire organization. William A. Muraskin referred to him as the "kingpin," "the absolute ruler of Texas black Masonry." Because of his position, admirers and detractors called him the kingmaker, since others, commonly believed to be selected by McDonald, held the titled offices while he ruled the Masons and made the decisions. As Carter Wesley, the influential black editor of the Houston *Informer* and the Dallas *Express*, asserted, "He chose not to be Grandmaster but to select and to run the Grandmasters of the Masons over the years." McDonald recognized the extent of his power and in 1949, a year before his death, ruefully pointed out that "I don't run . . . The Texas Negro Masonic Grand Lodge like I used to."[22] Not only was McDonald able to dominate the Masons because of his controlling post, but he was physically proximate to the Grand Lodge, which enabled him to keep close tabs on its activities. In 1906, probably due to pressure from McDonald, the Masons agreed to hold all subsequent annual meetings in Fort Worth and to build a Masonic temple in the city in which McDonald's residence was located. The Masons built the temple, and a drug store and a bank, which McDonald eventually established, held space in the Masons' building.[23]

Running a well-established fraternal order such as the Masons was not always an easy task. From his position as secretary, McDonald controlled the finances of the organization. He needed to be careful to see that the order was financially secure and to prevent any potential mishandling of funds. He also strove to keep members satisfied, to enroll new ones, and to pay insurance benefits when necessary. McDonald received both direct and indirect financial aid from the Masons for his services. He was a paid official of the lodge; in a 1929 report, he contended that he had grossed only $21,700 during "the thirty years in which he had been secretary, an average of $723.33 per year."[24] He received financial aid, however, from the Masons to help finance his bank in 1912, and Masons were encouraged to use the bank as well as other McDonald enterprises.

The greatest difficulty McDonald faced while Grand Secretary of the order arose from the emergence of a plethora of other black Masonic groups in Texas. They challenged the McDonald order, especially over the question of which was the official, established fraternity and which the newcomer. These rival groups, such as the Free and Accepted Ancient York Masons, the Ancient Free and Accepted Scottish Rite Masons, and the United Most Worshipful King Solomon Grand Lodge, were also a threat to the financial and numerical security of the Free and Accepted Masons with which McDonald was associated. McDonald refuted the usurpers by pointing out the history of Texas Masonry among blacks, by tracing the roots of his order to Prince Hall (the founder of black Masonic orders in the United States), and by showing the wealthy status of the Free and Accepted Masons, particularly the value of their insurance and death benefits. He referred to the leaders of the other organizations as "the bootleg peddlers and grafters of these clandestine, so-called local, Masonic Lodges." On another occasion, McDonald noted a rival fraternalist's "colossal deception, cheek, ignorance, and effrontery."[25] Despite competition, criticism, and varying other difficulties, the Prince Hall Free and Accepted Masons grew numerically and financially, due in no little part to its secretary.

The Masons and other fraternal orders were not the only organizations that received McDonald's membership and encouragement. He realized that to grasp and retain power, he needed a wide-ranging base of influence. Although not a deeply religious man, he attended a Baptist church. Also, he served as chief justice of the Sanhedrin Court, a Fort Worth society that met on Saturdays to debate issues, listen to speeches, and review the behavior of members. Organized by McDonald, this court "controls the actions of the colored citizens in and about Fort Worth."[26] Among many other ventures, in 1931, he supported the Negro Civic and Economic League of Texas. He was one of a few black Texans who issued a call in 1934 for a meeting "which will result in a statewide movement for the civic betterment of the Race," and in 1936, he served on a committee to celebrate "a century of Negro progress at Fort Worth."[27]

"From fraternal activities . . . [McDonald] slid into politics"; it was as a politician that he achieved his greatest fame.[28] From his partisan involvement, McDonald secured power, national and local prestige, and a solid financial base. His successes stemmed in part from his background and training, his character strengths, and his personal skills. McDonald skillfully used the support and influence that he gained from his work with the fraternal orders, and—probably of even greater significance, as the Dallas *Morning News* reported years later—the "political sagacity and the friendship of Colonel E. H. R. Green . . . made him a dominating figure in Texas."[29]

McDonald launched his political career when he joined the Republican Party of Kaufman County in 1890. His initial advancement was rapid, and within two years, he became chairman of the Kaufman County Republicans. That same year, he was a delegate to the state Republican convention. He soon became the second most important black politician in the state, next in line to Norris Wright Cuney, the brilliant and influential leader of the Texas Republicans. The Texas Republican Party of the 1890s that McDonald entered had split into two factions: the Lily-Whites and the Black and Tans. The Black and Tan faction, composed mainly of black members of the party, held the majority. The leader of the Black and Tans, until his death in 1897, was Norris Wright Cuney.[30] The Lily-Whites, as the white Republicans became known, sought a solitary goal: the elimination of blacks from leadership ranks of the Republican Party and, ultimately, removal of blacks from the party.

After the death of Cuney in 1897, the leadership of the Black and Tans passed to McDonald and his white ally, E. H. R. Green. In 1896, McDonald had met and joined forces with Green, a New York millionaire who had moved to Texas to become president of the Texas Midland Railroad, which was owned by his mother, the very wealthy Hetty Green. McDonald and Green entered into a mutually agreeable and profitable alliance. Green wanted to enter state politics and needed the help of an astute politician, and McDonald needed financial support for his political and financial activities. Green gave McDonald a salary of $575 per month, ostensibly to act as secretary but in reality to help Green become the dominant political figure in Texas. The alliance of Green and McDonald lasted from 1896 to 1909, and as one writer claimed, for a few years "this pair, with Green as titular party chairman and McDonald as his chief advisor and dispenser of patronage, ran the Texas Republican party."[31]

Ironically, just when McDonald assumed command of the Black and Tans, they were dispossessed of the leadership of the Texas Republican Party, not necessarily through any fault of McDonald's and despite substantial effort on his part to prevent the Lily-White takeover. Actually, Cuney and the Black and Tans had been defeated in 1896, perhaps partially because of a split between McDonald and Cuney; and neither Cuney while he lived nor McDonald later was able to wrest control back to the Black and Tans. In comparing the qualities of Cuney and McDonald, newspaper editor Carter Wesley reported that "[Norris] Wright Cuney was the personification of individual, rugged leadership, and of dominance in politics as an individual, Gooseneck Bill was the personification of the Warwick or the Kingmaker, who was pushing Joe Green to the top in politics."[32]

As political kingmaker, McDonald operated within the party in a manner similar to the way in which he directed the fraternal orders. He never held, nor appeared to seek, either of the two major offices at his party's disposal in Texas. Instead he helped Green pursue office. Some writers have asserted that McDonald was offered a number of patronage positions but that he refused them because he did not desire to hold office. This would fit with his general demeanor, but none of the alleged offers are substantiated by the evidence. McDonald held the status he wanted—he was known as the most important black politician in the state. As Steve D. Gulley stated, albeit in an uncomplimentary tone, "To do anything in the political affairs of Texas one had to follow the formula laid down by McDonald."[33] One symbol of power that McDonald did seek was to be a delegate to the national conventions of the Republican Party. Although he attended all the Republican conventions from 1896 to 1928, he was officially seated as a delegate only in 1904, 1912, and 1916. At the other sessions, he and the Black and Tans unsuccessfully challenged the Lily-Whites for official recognition. Nonetheless, as a result of McDonald's political participation, particularly his role as kingmaker, he became "the political sage of Texas . . . one of the most astute and resourceful political leaders in America."[34]

McDonald's political promise was quickly proven as he and Green initially retained partial control of the state Republican Party. In 1896 and again in 1898, McDonald helped elect Green chairman of the state executive committee, one of the two most important state Republican posts. Perhaps the initial successes of McDonald and Green were due in part to the solid party organization developed by Cuney, but certainly, Green's money and McDonald's astuteness contributed. But continued political control rested on a large black voter turnout, patronage distribution, and national party support. Suffrage restrictions reduced the black vote in the early twentieth century, and with the reduction of the black vote went a lessening of the influence of the Black and Tans within the state Republican Party. And in 1900, the Lily-Whites, led by Cecil A. Lyon, a close friend of Theodore Roosevelt, wrested the post of state chairman from Green, and with that went control of the party from McDonald and the Black and Tans. Although continually challenged by the Black and Tans, led by the McDonald-Green coalition, Lyon and the Lily-Whites retained their dominance until the tumultuous election of 1912.[35] But McDonald and the Black and Tans could not be disregarded by the Lily-Whites; McDonald was an official delegate to the 1904 National Republican Convention, and he traveled to Washington, DC, to confer with Republican advisers about patronage distribution in Texas.[36]

The election of 1912 returned the Black and Tans to political prominence in the Republican Party of Texas for a few years. The national split between Theodore Roosevelt and William Howard Taft played a major role in the state party lineup. At the national convention, the Taft steamroller commanded the meeting and seated McDonald and other Taft delegates rather than Cecil Lyon and the Lily-Whites, who supported Roosevelt.[37] Thus after twelve years, the hegemony in Texas of Cecil Lyon and the Lily-Whites was broken, but McDonald's victory was short-lived. Leadership of the state party did not pass to blacks but passed to whites who previously had been Taft boosters. But for a few years, McDonald and the Black and Tans helped determine state party nominees and participated fully in the party processes. McDonald held considerable influence in the party and attended the 1916 national convention, where he served on the Committee on Permanent Organization, but the emergence of the Black and Tans brought little additional personal power since the national administration shifted to the Democrats, which meant that Texas Democrats, not Republicans, would be distributing patronage.[38]

The 1920s witnessed the final removal of the Black and Tans, and with them, McDonald, from a position of influence in Republican Party politics. Naturally, many potential candidates vied for the Republican presidential nomination in 1920, since that party was virtually assured of victory; McDonald and the Black and Tans threw their support to Gen. Leonard Wood, clearly the candidate most favorable to blacks. Rival Texas delegations were sent by the Lily-Whites and the Black and Tans to the national convention; the Lily-Whites were seated and retained control of the state party. Warren G. Harding captured the Republican nomination, leading McDonald to warn that "if Harding is elected President of the United States, Negroes in Texas will get no post offices, no internal revenue jobs, and no representatives in Washington." He declared that "he would probably go fishing on election day."[39]

Although McDonald dismissed his defeat in 1920 by asserting that "it's all in the great game of politics. . . . One cannot always be on the winning side," it was McDonald's misfortune to be on the wrong side—probably inevitable since he was a black in Texas. Failure in 1920 drastically altered McDonald and the Black and Tan's influence in Republican Party politics. No longer would his voice be heeded. As R. B. Creager, the white Republican leader, later announced, the Republicans stood "unquestionably for white leadership."[40]

McDonald's behavior in the election of 1920 clearly illustrated another key political trait of his—his independence, his willingness to forsake the Republican Party when he deemed it necessary and expedient. He had shown this political characteristic earlier in his career. When the Republicans and Populists adopted a policy of fusion in 1896, McDonald opposed them and actively campaigned for the Democratic gubernatorial candidate, Charles A. Culberson. In 1905, a thoroughly disillusioned McDonald declared that "I am not in politics any longer—not the kind of Republican politics we have in Texas. . . . I am looking to the Democrats of Texas."[41] But his choice for the Democratic Party's gubernatorial nomination lost, and McDonald returned to the Republican Party in 1906.

His independence was further accentuated during the 1920s. When the Lily-Whites ran a particularly racist nominee for the governorship in 1920, McDonald and the Black and Tans ran their own candidate, a tactic they had sometimes used in the early twentieth century. That McDonald and the Black and Tans had little other alternative is evidenced by comments of the white Republicans. In the 1920 campaign, the Lily-White gubernatorial nominee, John G. Culberson, referred to black political activists, such as McDonald, as "odorous beasts with charcoal complexions." In 1924, McDonald backed Democrat Miriam "Ma" Ferguson for governor, rather than the Republican candidate. McDonald's support of Ferguson led the Republican candidate, Dr. George C. Butte, a recipient of the Ku Klux Klan vote, to claim that "for every vote that Gooseneck Bill delivers to Ferguson I will get the vote of ten thousand of the finest and best democrats who ever cast a ballot in Texas."[42]

For McDonald, an even more drastic change took place during the presidential elections of 1924 and 1928, when for the first time on the national level, he switched allegiance from the Republicans, first to the Progressives and then to the Democrats. In 1924, McDonald refused to "support the [Republican] party as now led and managed" and decided to back the nominee of the Progressive Party, Robert M. La Follette.[43] As did many other prominent black leaders throughout the nation in 1928, McDonald actively campaigned for Democrat Al Smith rather than Republican Herbert Hoover. McDonald was "opposed to the way the Republican party has been led, used and directed for the past eight years." He further stated that he had "a right to enter my protest, as I am a Republican."[44] But the efforts of McDonald and other black leaders were largely futile: both the Republicans (with their Lily-White policy) and the Democrats (with their statewide white primary) actively discouraged black political participation on the state level.

By the middle 1920s, McDonald decided to leave the political arena. Bundy reported in 1925 that "he was retired from politics now." In the campaign of 1926, "he decided to let the younger men 'carry on' in the political arena." But by December 1927, he entered the fray once more and urged Republicans to "clean up house"; in 1928, he continued his involvement, in most respects for the last time, when he campaigned for Smith.[45] Generally, during the last twenty years of his life, McDonald was not actively engaged in politics. This was due partly to age (he was sixty-four in 1930), partly to the fact that he had grown tired of politics, but primarily because there really was not a place for him, or for other blacks, in the political structure of Texas.

Having switched to the Democratic presidential nominee in 1928, McDonald continued his allegiance in 1932 and again in 1936 by voting for Franklin D. Roosevelt. In fact, he boasted that he had been responsible for bringing blacks to the Democratic side. But he apparently tired of the New Deal, described New Deal measures as "cranky tomfoolery," and in 1940 delivered a speech in Houston urging black support for Republican Wendell Willkie, in order once more to create a viable two-party system in the state. In 1944 and 1948, McDonald apparently supported Republican Thomas E. Dewey for president.[46] However, with the exception of his speech in 1940, he took little part in the political process after 1928.

Political participation proved beneficial to McDonald. He acquired prestige, influence, and power from his partisan role. By dominating the Black and Tan faction of the Republican Party, he not only influenced Texas political decisions but had a national impact as well. As early as 1896, Matt Quay, the Pennsylvania Republican political boss, summoned McDonald to the national capital to enlist his support for Thomas B. Reed's bid for the presidency. During Theodore Roosevelt's administration, as previously mentioned, McDonald traveled to Washington to discuss patronage. In World War I, he was one of the "big guns" used by the government to enlist support among Texas blacks for the war effort. When black Republicans, finding themselves increasingly outside the national leadership ranks of the Republican Party, organized the Republican Lincoln League, McDonald acted as state chairman. In 1928, leading black politicians started the National Negro Voters League in Chicago, and McDonald was elected treasurer of the organization. National news publications, such as the white New York *Times* and the black Kansas City *Call*, covered his activities. Certainly, McDonald was "known wherever Texas is known."[47]

Participating in politics was also financially lucrative for McDonald. His association with Green brought him a salary of $575 per month for a number of years. Such a sum enabled him to establish his financial independence. Perhaps McDonald also received money from the sale of patronage. Critics charged him with such behavior, and in a 1936 tax trial, he reportedly announced that he had earned over $300,000 by selling patronage to the highest bidder.[48] But it is difficult to believe that he could have sold as much patronage as he supposedly claimed, given the circumstances of the years when he was a political power. According to one author, "His chief concern was to see how much he could make this position pay in dividends." On occasion he also was criticized by a few blacks who were unable to buy these offices because they could not outbid the whites. Nonetheless, the Fort Worth *Star-Telegram*, in a 1920 article, may have best explained his anomalous position: "His enemies charge that his participation in politics is mercenary at the base but his negro supporters believe him to be devoted to the best interest of his race."[49] As a political and fraternal leader, McDonald did seek rewards for his race as well as for himself.

In many respects, as Carter Wesley has pointed out, "the collapse of Negro dominance in politics generally coincided with the death of Wright Cuney. But for Gooseneck Bill it was the beginning of the fruition of his power and leadership in other fields of life." During the succeeding years, "he was accumulating property shrewdly, carefully, and quietly"—and successfully, since by the mid-1930s, McDonald's financial worth approached $500,000, and at his death in 1950, he retained a substantial estate.[50] Compared to his black contemporaries, and most of his white ones as well, McDonald amassed a large fortune. The substantial sums derived from political remuneration added to McDonald's wealth, but other factors played a part in his financial achievements. Two white leaders helped him: Z. T. Adams early drilled him in financial matters; and later, as Richard Bardolph remarked, "His tutelage under [E. H. R.] Green enabled him to dabble with great success in banking and real estate." McDonald also developed an almost single-minded drive for money; as one commentator declared, "Wealth was an obsession for him." There was a method to his obsession; he "saw that one of the best ways to overcome the Southern prejudice against his race was the power of money." As Carter Wesley and others depicted, he possessed other attributes of the successful businessman: he was shrewd, careful, and "cautiously conservative."[51] McDonald acquired money from salaries, from property investments, from farming, from business operations, and from controlling a bank. He also had access to large sums of money from the fraternal orders.

McDonald's early employment laid a basis for his later financial gains. Even before graduating from high school, he worked as a houseboy, on a cattle ranch, and in the law offices of Z. T. Adams. By 1895, he had taught school for seven years and had worked as a clerk in a Fort Worth business for an additional two years. Beginning in 1890, he also received a salary from the Masons, and in 1896, one from E. H. R. Green. This steady income permitted an independence and risk taking in financial affairs unusual for an aspiring black capitalist. While president of the Colored State Fair Association in 1888, he undoubtedly received financial compensation from it. McDonald astutely utilized more than one source of salary in his efforts to acquire money during the latter nineteenth century. During these years, "he conducted a lucrative loan shark business on the side," and he began to acquire property.[52]

Property meant land. To begin with, McDonald "farmed on shares and by skimping saved enough to buy a farm of his own" in Kaufman County.[53] He used sharecroppers to work it, and with the profits, he gradually bought more land. Early in the twentieth century, he acquired land in Fort Worth, which he developed into a substantial residential section for blacks. Still later, he bought real estate in Dallas, in Oklahoma, and as far away as Chicago. Not only did McDonald prosper as a landowner, receive salaries, obtain money from politics, and lend to other blacks at a high rate of interest; he also operated independent businesses. In Fort Worth, he ran a drug store, was a real estate agent, and according to Paul Lewinson, owned a newspaper.[54] Even more important, in 1912, McDonald became a banker.

In 1911, he convinced some black fraternal orders—the Knights of Pythias, the Heroines of Jericho, the Ancient Order of Pilgrims, the Odd Fellows, and the Masons—to help him establish a bank by purchasing shares in it. The shares sold for eleven dollars, and McDonald opened the Fraternal Bank and Trust Company in 1912. Although he was the controlling stockholder, McDonald's penchant for remaining out of titular positions is apparent in his role at the bank. From 1912 to 1924, the president was Tom Mason, not McDonald. Instead, McDonald ran the bank from the post of cashier. However, with Mason's death in 1924, McDonald became president, a title he held until 1948, when he was named president emeritus.[55] McDonald's guidance kept the bank afloat during the years when many other banks established for blacks were going bankrupt. It was not always an easy task. Shortly after the bank opened, McDonald was besieged with requests from officers of some of the shareholding lodges for preferential treatment. They "demanded unreasonable personal loans," and when McDonald refused to grant these special favors, the officers convinced their orders to withdraw support from McDonald's bank. But the bank was solidly established. Eventually, only the Masons and the Heroines continued to support the bank, and it became essentially "a clearing house for funds of Negro Masons in Texas, New Mexico, Arizona, Utah, and Nevada."[56] In 1930, McDonald sold his controlling interest to the Masons; he had been trying to persuade them to purchase his interest during the previous four years. The bank survived the Depression years but in a somewhat changed form: after the Banking Act of 1933, the bank in 1935 became a private bank that would not loan depositors' money.[57] Even after selling his majority interest, McDonald remained closely aligned with the bank until his death in 1950.

McDonald attained the pinnacle of his financial achievements in the 1930s. In 1930, although he retained one hundred shares, he transferred controlling interest in the Fraternal Bank and Trust Company to the Free and Accepted Masons for the sum of $220,000, to be paid over a ten-year period. He still received a salary of $1,200 per year for acting as president of the bank, and the Masons paid him at least $1,500 a year for his duties as their secretary. He derived income from land he owned in Kaufman and Tarrant Counties, Oklahoma, and Chicago. McDonald also invested in government bonds; according to a story in the Kansas City Call, he owned $105,000 worth of bonds in 1940. Reports circulated that McDonald was a millionaire, one of the wealthiest blacks in the United States. For example, at his death, an article in Ebony stated that McDonald was "the world's richest Negro." He was not, but the size of his estate probably ranged from one-third to one-half of a million dollars at its height. He definitely was one of the richest black men in the Southwest.[58]

However, for a number of reasons, McDonald's estate had dwindled to approximately $100,000 by the time of his death. The Depression, which affected the financial well-being of nearly everyone, hurt McDonald despite his diversification. Some of his tenants were unable to pay rent. Also, the value of property declined during the years of the Depression, and since McDonald owned considerable property, his net worth went down. Financially, McDonald retired during the last years of his life, not adding to his holdings. He lived well in an elaborate house ostensibly modeled after the plantation home where his father was a slave. He hired servants to help care for the house as well as his personal needs. McDonald owned expensive cars and liked to wear diamond rings and other accoutrements of wealth. He spent funds for philanthropy, as did other businessmen later in their lives. A further drain on his estate were two brief marriages and divorces during the 1930s, from which his young wives may have derived substantial benefits in settlements. His illness during the last years of his life also depleted his financial reserves. Even so, McDonald left a valuable estate to his wife when he died on July 4, 1950.[59]

Perhaps it was fitting that William Madison McDonald's life should end on the Fourth of July, since he rose to heights attained by few other black Southerners during the first half of the twentieth century—literally, as one observer declared, "from poverty to banker."[60] Although a black man in white Texas, his life fulfilled the promises set forth by the Declaration of Independence. Not only did McDonald's successes epitomize the American Dream, but he believed in those promises and ideals and accepted the basic tenets of capitalism. Although he was apparently neither a close friend nor a disciple of Booker T. Washington, the prominent Southern black leader, some of McDonald's expressed views appeared reminiscent of the Tuskegee leader's philosophy. In a 1919 speech at Shreveport, McDonald pointed out his devotion to self-help when he said that "we must do all of these things ourselves." He then continued.

> If you want a beautiful home, go build it. If you want concrete sidewalks, go have them put down. . . . Do you wish to have Negro clerks in grocery stores? Go and establish such stores. Do you wish to have Negro bank clerks and cashiers? Go and establish you a bank. . . . Do you wish to have Negroes manage great business concerns and great enterprises? Go and establish them. Treat these as we have the church and lodge-stand by them, support them and feel that you are honored when you support and maintain business enterprises managed and controlled by Negroes for the benefit of our race.[61]

His beliefs, reflecting his status as a successful black businessman and politician, sometimes failed to acknowledge the advantages he possessed for his quests and the obstacles placed in the path of the black majority. At the same time, though, he called for blacks to work together, to support each other, to pursue a policy of self-help—essentially, to acquire what has been referred to as *Green Power*.

McDonald's devotion to self-help and racial solidarity was derived from his experience as a fraternalist, a politician, and a financier. McDonald was no outspoken advocate of race pride and confrontation, as was the Northern leader W. E. B. DuBois; nor was he a devotee of public accommodation, as was Washington. Rather, an independent and successful politician and businessman, his racial views appeared somewhere between the two. August Meier, in *Negro Thought in America, 1880–1915*, declared that "politicians . . . in open expression . . . were, on the whole, the most conservative of the elite group during the age of Washington." But Meier also showed that the conservative politicians were those indebted to Booker T. Washington; other politicians, such as Judson Lyons of Georgia and George H. White of North Carolina, were not nearly so conservative.[62] William Madison McDonald's attitudes and directives were similar to those of Lyons and White; he was not a follower of Washington and was able and willing to speak out strongly on a variety of issues.

McDonald's personal goals—wealth and power—dominated his life and seemed at times to overshadow his racial goals. But he believed that if one succeeded in a world of white power, that individual attainment would also bring racial strength—that for a black to be successful, he must operate within a segregated society but have contact with whites. His early years were devoted to personal aggrandizement. He later became something of a philanthropist, seemingly less concerned with the acquisition of wealth and power—no doubt because he had accomplished his goals. The intriguing aspect of McDonald is that his quest for personal advancement (often supported by, if not at the expense of, fellow blacks) pushed forward the black cause in Texas. He fought for political rights. He spoke out against mob rule, referring to a Fort Worth mob as "deliberate, cruel, insane, unreasonable and revengeful." "In McDonald's opinion," Melvin James Banks argued, the "vicious circle of suppression and denunciation could be broken only by a solid, determined Negro movement that would expose Texas and southern behavior before the court of national and world opinion."[63] McDonald argued for black economic enterprises. He aided black cultural growth, and he called upon whites for equitable justice.

His own racial program, McDonald termed *uplift and justice*. In a speech given to the bishops of the African Methodist Episcopal church, he stated, "We are often confronted with the theory of Bishop Turner, deportation, or of that school of theorists who advocate assimilation, or of the Rev. Dixon class, who preaches annihilation.... Over against that trinity of impossibilities, deportation, assimilation or annihilation, let me offer the simple plan of uplift and justice. Let the superior adopt the policy of uplift by encouraging and teaching the inferior the great lessons of our life's problems.... Let the superior demonstrate its superiority by the manner in which it applies justice to the inferior."[64] But for the majority of blacks, whites gave little justice and produced little encouragement for uplift.

McDonald's path to accomplishment was both similar to and different from that of his black Texas contemporaries who also achieved distinction. As did other black leaders, he participated actively in the fraternal orders; he taught school and indicated an interest in education. He engaged in business, and he argued for a philosophy of self-help among blacks. But he was also a very independent person, one who preferred to operate as a kingmaker rather than hold the titular offices. He operated effectively with whites, using their assets to advance his own interests. And given the social conditions of Texas, he was more successful than most. In politics, no black Texan has outranked him in the twentieth century. Very few were wealthier. In the fraternities, although he had his counterparts in the Pythians and other societies, he controlled one group totally, and he wielded decision-making influence in other organizations. McDonald sought and gained personal wealth and power, and as a black leader in white Texas, he strove for racial advancement.

Glasrud, Bruce A. "William M. McDonald: Business and Fraternal Leader." In Black Leaders: Texans for Their Times, edited by Alwyn Barr and Robert A. Calvert, 82–111. Austin: Texas State Historical Association, 1981. Reprinted by permission of the author, the editor, and the Texas State Historical Association.

NOTES

1. William Oliver Bundy, *Life of William Madison McDonald, Ph.D.* (Fort Worth: Bunker, 1925), 331, 333; Steve D. Gulley, "M. M. Rodgers, the Politician, 1877–1909" (MA thesis, Prairie View Agricultural and Mechanical College, 1955), 36; Thomas Robert Cripps, "The Lily White Republicans: The Negro, the Party, and the South in the Progressive Era" (PhD diss., University of Maryland, 1967), 176; A. Maceo Johnson to L. B. M., June 17, 1958, interview, in Leonard Brewster Murphy, "A History of Negro Segregation Practices in Texas, 1865–1958" (MA thesis, Southern Methodist University, 1958), 264.

2. "From Poverty to Banker: Life Story of William Madison (Gooseneck Bill) McDonald," *Negro Achievements* 5 (December 1951): 3–4, 29–31; *Negro Achievements* 6 (January 1952): 5, 45–47. Other accounts include "Fabulous Bill McDonald," *Christian Science Monitor*, December 3, 1949, magazine section, 20; Richard Bardolph, *The Negro Vanguard* (New York: 1959), 200–201; A. W. Jackson, *A Sure Foundation and a Sketch of Negro Life in Texas* (Houston: 1940), 120–21; Effie Kaye Adams, *Tall Black Texans: Men of Courage, A Relevant Reading Worktext with Comprehension Vocabulary and Study Skills Exercises* (Dubuque, IA: 1972), 151–52; and Walter Prescott Webb, H. Bailey Carroll, and Eldon Stephen Branda, eds., *The Handbook of Texas*, vol. 3 (Austin: 1952), 556.

3. "The Ten Richest Negroes in America," *Ebony* 4 (April 1949): 13–18; "Death Comes to the World's Richest Negro," *Ebony* 5 (October 1950): 66–68, 70. The extremely inflated evaluations of McDonald's wealth in these articles led E. Franklin Frazier to use them as examples of the uncritical reporting of the black press. Frazier caustically remarked that "as in the case of many other wealthy Negroes, when this Negro multimillionaire died, only $100,000 remained of his reputed $3,000,000 fortune." E. Franklin Frazier, *Black Bourgeoisie: The Rise of a New Middle Class in the United States* (New York: 1957), 155.

4. Thomas Yenser, ed., *Who's Who in Colored America: A Biographical Dictionary of Notable Living Persons of African Descent in America* (New York: 1927–50). His death was reported in Jessie Parkhurst Guzman, ed., *Negro Yearbook* (New York: 1952), 382.

5. Bundy, *McDonald*, 281, 332; "Death Comes," 66; Adams, *Tall Black Texans*, 152; Arthur H. Lewis, *The Day They Shook the Plum Tree* (New York: 1963), 81.

6. Bundy, *McDonald*, 112–13; Houston *Informer*, October 31, November 7, 1925; Dallas *Morning News*, September 18, 1949; Lewis, *Day They Shook*, 81.

7. Dallas *Morning News*, September 18, 1949; Houston *Informer*, October 31, November 7, 1925; July 15, 1950; Dallas *Express*, April 19, 1924; July 15, 1950; Fort Worth *Star Telegram*, quoted in Texas Writers' Project, *Fort Worth and Tarrant County, Texas* (Fort Worth: 1941), 19,870; Bundy, *McDonald*, 263–82.

8. Bundy, *McDonald*, 1–15; Fort Worth *Star-Telegram*, July 6, 1950; Lewis, *Day They Shook*, 81–82; McDonald to W. L. Dixon, March 14, 1911, in Bundy, *McDonald*, 202; Houston *Informer*, July 8, 1950.

9. Dallas *Morning News*, September 14, 1949; Kansas City *Call*, February 2,

1940; Lewis, *Day They Shook*, 82;
Douglass Geraldyne Perry, "Black
Populism: The Negro in the People's
Party in Texas" (MA thesis, Prairie
View University, 1945), 29; William
("Gooseneck Bill") McDonald Folder,
Arthur H. Lewis Notes (Free Library
of Philadelphia). A copy of the
materials from the McDonald folder in
the Lewis notes are in the possession
of the author, courtesy of Arthur H.
Lewis and Frances H. Ritchey.
Information on the 1,887-student
strike at Roger Williams University
can be found in James M. McPherson,
"White Liberals and Black Power in
Negro Education, 1865–1915," *American
Historical Review* 75 (June 1970): 1,371.

10. Bundy, *McDonald*, 15, 20–24, 33, 81–90;
Adams, *Tall Black Texans*, 151; Lewis,
Day They Shook, 82; Lawrence D. Rice,
The Negro in Texas, 1874–1900 (Baton
Rouge, LA: 1971), 197.

11. Bundy, *McDonald*, 91–98; Dallas
Express, June 5, 1926; "From Poverty to
Banker," *Negro Achievements* 6 (January
1952): 47; Murphy, "Negro Segregation
Practices," 90; Fort Worth *Star-
Telegram*, July 6, 1950; Lady George
Munchus-Forde, "History of the
Negro in Fort Worth: Syllabus for a
High School Course" (MA thesis, Fisk
University, 1941), 140.

12. Dallas *Express*, May 29, June 5,
1926; July 8, 15, 1950; Texas Writers'
Project, *Fort Worth*, 22,458; Vivienne
McDonald, W. M. McDonald, divorce
granted in District Court, Seventeenth
Judicial District, Tarrant County, Texas
(certified copy in author's files); Jackson,
Sure Foundation, 564–65; Adams, *Tall
Black Texans*, 152; Houston *Informer*,
June 5, 1926; June 29, 1929; April 18 and
October 10, 1936; July 8, 15, 1950.

13. Texas Writers' Project, *Fort Worth*,
22,457.

14. Houston *Informer*, November 14, 1925;
Texas Writers' Project, *Fort Worth*,
22,458.

15. Charles W. Ferguson, *Fifty Million
Brothers: A Panorama of American
Lodges and Clubs* (New York: 1937),
184–202; William A. Muraskin, "The
Social Foundations of the Black
Community: The Fraternities, the
California Masons as a Test Case,"
Midcontinent American Studies Journal
11 (Fall 1970): 12–35; William A.
Muraskin, *Middle-Class Blacks in a
White Society: Prince Hall Freemasonry
in America* (Berkeley, CA: 1975);
Harold Van Buren Voorhis, *Negro
Masonry in the United States* (New
York: 1940); William H. Grimshaw,
*Official History of Freemasonry among
the Colored People in North America*
(New York: 1969).

16. Lewis, *Day They Shook*, 83; Houston
Informer, October 31, 1925.

17. Bundy, *McDonald*, 17–20, 23–24.

18. Ibid., 37–39, 65, 78; Houston *Informer*,
August 7, 1926; August 6, 1927; August
11, 1928; May 4, 1929; Texas Writers'
Project, *Fort Worth*, 22,456.

19. Houston *Informer*, August 18, 1928;
June 29, 1929; Bundy, *McDonald*, 37,
101; Rice, *Negro in Texas*, 269; Dallas
Express, July 23, 1921.

20. Bundy, *McDonald*, 101; Dallas *Morning
News*, August 3, 1901; February 1, 1903;
Houston *Informer*, August 18, 1928;
Rice, *Negro in Texas*, 195.

21. Bundy, *McDonald*, 37–38; Lewis, *Day
They Shook*, 83; Texas Writers' Project,
Fort Worth, 21,664; Neil Gary Sapper,
"A Survey of the History of the Black
People of Texas, 1930–1954" (PhD
diss., Texas Tech University, 1972), 510;

Houston *Informer*, November 14, 1925; June 29, 1929.

22. Bundy, *McDonald*, 38–39; Muraskin, *Middle-Class Blacks*, 170, 225; Houston *Informer*, June 29, 1929; July 15, 1950; Dallas *Express*, July 15, 1950; Fort Worth *Press*, July 5, 1950; Dallas *Morning News*, September 18, 1949.

23. Bundy, *McDonald*, 38–39; Houston *Informer*, June 29, 1929.

24. Houston *Informer*, June 29, 1929.

25. Houston *Informer*, December 12, 1925, October 16, November 27, December 18, 25, 1926, June 16, 1928, June 8, 22, 29, 1929.

26. Bundy, *McDonald*, 100, 215–16, 233–34; Kansas City *Call*, February 2, 1940; Perry, "Black Populism," 29; "From Poverty to Banker," *Negro Achievements* 5 (December 1951): 29.

27. Bundy, *McDonald*, 235; Houston *Informer*, January 19, 1931; November 24, 1934; June 6, 1936; Dallas *Express*, November 17, 1934.

28. Lewis, *Day They Shook*, 83. The background of black political participation in Texas can be found in the relevant chapters of Rice, *Negro in Texas*; Bruce Alden Glasrud, "Black Texans, 1900–1930: A History" (PhD diss., Texas Tech University, 1969); and Sapper, "Black People of Texas." Rice, Glasrud, and Sapper wrote dissertations under the direction of Lawrence L. Graves, professor of history at Texas Tech University. See also Alwyn Barr, *Black Texans: A History of Negroes in Texas, 1528–1971* (Austin: 1973); Lamar L. Kirven, "A Century of Warfare: Black Texans" (PhD diss., Indiana University, 1974); and William Joseph Brophy, "The Black Texan, 1900–1950: A Quantitative History" (PhD diss., Vanderbilt University, 1974).

29. Rice, *Negro in Texas*, 50–51; Dallas *Morning News*, July 6, 1950.

30. Houston *Informer*, July 8, 1950; Bundy, *McDonald*, 104–6, 111–12; William M. Ellison Jr., "Negro Suffrage in Texas and Its Exercise" (MA thesis, Colorado State College of Education, 1943), 56–57; William ("Gooseneck Bill") McDonald Folder, Lewis Notes. Studies of Cuney include Paul Douglas Casdorph, "Norris Wright Cuney and Texas Republican Politics, 1883–1896," *Southwestern Historical Quarterly* 68 (April 1965): 455–64; Virginia Neal Hinze, "Norris Wright Cuney" (MA thesis, Rice University, 1965); Maud Cuney Hare, *Norm Wright Cuney: A Tribune of the Black People* (New York: 1913); and Carter G. Woodson, "The Cuney Family," *Negro History Bulletin* 11 (March 5, 1948): 123–25, 143.

31. Lewis, *Day They Shook*, 85–91; Bundy, *McDonald*, 143; Texas Writers' Project, Fort Worth, 20,692–93, 22,458; Oliver Knight, *Fort Worth: Outpost on the Trinity* (Norman, OK: 1953), 148; Paul Casdorph, *A History of the Republican Party in Texas, 1865–1965* (Austin: 1965), 70–71; Dallas *Morning News*, September 18, 1949; July 6, 1950; Estate of E. H. R. Green, in William ("Gooseneck Bill") McDonald Folder, Lewis Notes; Murphy, "Negro Segregation Practices," 89.

32. Dallas *Express*, July 15, 1950.

33. For an example, see Bundy, *McDonald*, 143–44; Gulley, "M. M. Rodgers," 36.

34. Casdorph, *Republican Party in Texas*, 252–59; Houston *Informer*, March 13, 1920.

35. Bundy, *McDonald*, 113–26; Lewis, *Day They Shook*, 85–91; Casdorph, *Republican Party in Texas*, 70–72; Alwyn Barr, *Reconstruction to Reform:*

Texas Politics, 1876–1906 (Austin: 1971), 186–90; Dallas *Morning News*, July 10, 1950; Henry Lee Moon, *Balance of Power: The Negro Vote* (Garden City, NY: 1948), 106.

36. Casdorph, *Republican Party in Texas*, 252–59; Dallas *Morning News*, January 28, 1903.

37. San Antonio *Express*, August 15, 1912; Gulley, "M. M. Rodgers," 56–58; Casdorph, *Republican Party in Texas*, 98–108; Glasrud, "Black Texans," 60–63; William F. Nowlin, *The Negro in American National Politics* (New York: 1931), 53–55.

38. San Antonio *Express*, August 12, 1914; Dallas *Morning News*, August 3, 1916; Casdorph, *Republican Party in Texas*, 108–17, 256; Glasrud, "Black Texans," 63–65; Ernest Winkler, ed., *Platforms of Political Parties in Texas*, Bulletin of the University of Texas, no. 53, Austin, September 20, 1916, 616–17.

39. Houston *Informer*, March 13, 1920; Austin *Statesman*, May 26, 1920; Dallas *Morning News*, August 11, 1920; September 18, 1949; Casdorph, *Republican Party in Texas*, 118–24; *Christian Science Monitor*, December 3, 1949; Fort Worth *Star-Telegram*, June 9, 17, 1920.

40. *Christian Science Monitor*, December 3, 1949; Houston *Informer*, May 26, 1928.

41. Dallas *Morning News*, October 2, 1896; Rice, *Negro in Texas*, 83–84; Barr, *Reconstruction to Reform*, 170; Perry, "Black Populism," 29; Roscoe C. Martin, *The People's Party in Texas: A Study in Third Party Politics*, Bulletin of the University of Texas, no. 3308, Bureau of Research in the Social Sciences Study No. 4, Austin, February 22, 1933, 243–45.

42. Glasrud, "Black Texans," 77–78; Dallas *Express*, September 18, 1920; May 29,

1926; Houston *Informer*, November 21, 1925; April 21, 1928.

43. Dallas *Express*, August 16; September 6 and 27; October 11 and 25; and November 1, 1924; William ("Gooseneck Bill") McDonald Folder, Lewis Notes.

44. Dallas *Morning News*, July 17, 1928; New York *Times*, July 17, 1928; Houston *Informer*, August 25, September 22, and November 3, 1928; Casdorph, *Republican Party in Texas*, 122; John Hope Franklin, *From Slavery to Freedom: A History of Negro Americans*, 3rd ed. (New York: 1969), 524; Frances Jerome Woods, "Negro Suffrage under the Texas Direct Primary System" (MA thesis, Catholic University of America, 1945), 54; Paul Lewinson, *Race, Class, and Party: A History of Negro Suffrage and White Politics in the South* (New York: 1932), 158–73; McDonald to R. Hawkins, in Houston *Informer*, September 22, 1928. See also "An Open Letter from Wm. M. 'Goose-Neck Bill' McDonald to Hon. J. R. Hawkins," *Fraternal Review* 7 (October 1928): 4–5.

45. Bundy, *McDonald*, 144; Houston *Informer*, August 7, 1926; December 24, 1927; August 25, 1928; Dallas *Morning News*, July 17, 1928; New York *Times*, July 17, 1928.

46. Houston *Informer*, October 19, 1940; Dallas *Morning News*, September 18, 1949; Sapper, "Black People of Texas," 114–15; Murphy, "Negro Segregation Practices," 88–90; Perry, "Black Populism," 29; Fort Worth *Press*, July 5, 1950; William ("Gooseneck Bill") McDonald Folder, Lewis Notes.

47. Bundy, *McDonald*, 113–14, 249–53; Lewis, *Day They Shook*, 86–87; Dallas *Morning News*, January 28, 1903; Munchus-Forde, "History of the Negro," 121; New York *Times*, July 17,

1928; Kansas City *Call*, February 2, 1940; Houston *Informer*, February 7, 1920; October 31 and November 7, 1925; September 8, 1928; June 29, 1929.

48. Lewis, *Day They Shook*, 90; Fort Worth *Press*, July 5, 1950; Texas Writers' Project, *Fort Worth*, 20,693, 22,458; Woods, "Negro Suffrage," 53–54. The case involved the estate of E. H. R. Green, who died on June 8, 1936. The US Supreme Court eventually settled the matter of Green's residence in *Texas v. Florida*, 306 US. 398 (1939). See also information in William ("Gooseneck Bill") McDonald Folder, Lewis Notes; and Truman O'Quinn, "Texas, Taxes, and Where Did Colonel Green Live?," *Texas Bar Journal* 24 (September 22, 1961): 827–28, 884, 886–93.

49. Woods, "Negro Suffrage," 53–54; Fort Worth *Star-Telegram*, cited in Texas Writers' Project, *Fort Worth*, 19,870. See also Gulley, "M. M. Rodgers," 36.

50. Dallas *Express*, July 15, 1950; Texas Writers' Project, *Fort Worth*, 22,455; Kansas City *Call*, February 2, 1940; Fort Worth *Star-Telegram*, July 12, 1950.

51. Bundy, *McDonald*, 13–14, 103, 209–11; "From Poverty to Banker," *Negro Achievements* 5: 45–47; Houston *Informer*, July 8, 1950; Kansas City *Call*, February 2, 1940; Bardolph, *Negro Vanguard*, 201; Dallas *Express*, July 15, 1950; Texas Writers' Project, *Fort Worth*, 20,692, 22,455, 22,459; "Death Comes," 68.

52. Bundy, *McDonald*, 13–15, 20–24, 81–90, 126; Houston *Informer*, July 8, 1950; Adams, *Tall Black Texans*, 151; Lewis, *Day They Shook*, 82; William ("Gooseneck Bill") McDonald Folder, Lewis Notes; Texas Writers' Project, *Fort Worth*, 21,907–8, 22,457.

53. Texas Writers' Project, *Fort Worth*, 20,692.

54. Fort Worth *Star-Telegram*, July 12, 1950; Kansas City *Call*, February 2, 1940; Texas Writers' Project, *Fort Worth*, 20,692, 21,907–8, 22,457–58; Bundy, *McDonald*, 39; Lewinson, *Race, Class, and Party*, 173.

55. Bundy, *McDonald*, 209–13; Kansas City *Call*, February 2, 1940; Fort Worth *Press*, July 5, 1950; Houston *Informer*, October 18, 1930; July 15, 1950; Dallas *Express*, July 15, 1950; Dallas *Morning News*, September 18, 1949; Texas Writers' Project, *Fort Worth*, 19,285–86; Arnett G. Lindsay, "The Negro in Banking," *Journal of Negro History* 14 (April 1929), 183; Muraskin, *Middle-Class Blacks*, 141–43.

56. Kansas City *Call*, February 2, 1940; Texas Writers' Project, *Fort Worth*, 20,690, 22,455; Houston *Informer*, January 29, 1927.

57. Houston *Informer*, October 18, 1930; Texas Writers' Project, *Fort Worth*, 19,285–86; Dallas *Express*, June 26, 1926; July 2, 1927.

58. Houston *Informer*, June 29, 1929; October 18, 1930; and July 8, 1950; Kansas City *Call*, February 2, 1940. According to "Ten Richest Negroes," 13, he also owned land in Dallas and Houston. Texas Writers' Project, *Fort Worth*, 20,689, 20,691, 22,455, 22,457; Dallas *Express*, July 15, 1950; *Negro Yearbook*, 382; "Death Comes," 66–68, 70.

59. Johnson to L. B. M., June 17, 1958, interview, in Murphy, "Negro Segregation Practices," 264; *Christian Science Monitor*, December 3, 1949; Dallas *Morning News*, September 18, 1949; July 6, 1950; Kansas City *Call*, February 2, 1940; Texas Writers' Project, *Fort Worth*, 20,691–92; Bundy, *McDonald*, 98–100; Murphy, "Negro Segregation Practices," 90; Munchus-Forde, "History of the Negro," 140;

Houston *Informer*, April 18, 1936; July 8, 1950; Fort Worth *Star-Telegram*, July 6 and 12, 1950. According to "Death Comes," 67, McDonald's financial decline came about thusly: "but generous to himself, to charity as well as to his numerous wives (he had five), he doled out his money liberally rather than have his heirs pay tremendous inheritance taxes." On the same page, the article argued, "Legend has distorted much of 'Gooseneck's' amazing career, but it is an admitted fact that in later years he acquired a penchant for young brides '20 or under.' On each he lavished $3,000 fur coats, automobiles, jewelry and divorce settlements of $10,000. His marriage bargains were struck with only one pre-agreed requisite: each had to return his first wife's jewels when she decided to leave him." There is no other evidence to support these statements that I have located.

60. "From Poverty to Banker," *Negro Achievements* 5: 3.

61. William M. McDonald, speech at Shreveport, Louisiana, January 1, 1919, cited in Bundy, *McDonald*, 292–93. On McDonald's racial views, see also William Madison McDonald, "Letter in Answer to Questionnaire: Group Tactics and Ideals," *Messenger* 9 (January 1927): 11, 13–14.

62. August Meier, *Negro Thought in America, 1880–1915: Racial Ideologies in the Age of Booker T. Washington* (Ann Arbor, MI: 1966), 248, 255.

63. McDonald to W. L. Dixon, March 14, 1911, in Bundy, *McDonald*, 201; Melvin James Banks, "The Pursuit of Equality: The Movement for First Class Citizenship in Texas, 1920–1950" (SScD diss., Syracuse University, 1962), 138. The Rev. Mr. S. R. Prince declared at McDonald's funeral that "he was a racial patriot and did all he could for his race that he knew was an infant race." William ("Gooseneck Bill") McDonald Folder, Lewis Notes.

64. McDonald, speech at Dallas, Texas, in 1921, in Bundy, *McDonald*, 240.

10

The "Waco Horror"

The Lynching of Jesse Washington

James M. SoRelle

As noted in the introduction to African Americans in Central Texas, *one of the more atrocious race incidents in Texas history was the 1916 lynching in Waco of an illiterate black youth, Jesse Washington. In this gruesome episode, Washington, likely not guilty of his alleged crime, was tortured, beaten, and lynched by burning, with parts of his body sold as souvenirs. This incident is well depicted by James M. SoRelle, professor of history at Baylor University; among SoRelle's other publications is the critical two-volume set* Taking Sides: Clashing Views on Controversial Issues of United States History; *his multi-edition study was coedited with Larry Madaras.*

★

During the years from 1889 to 1918, the United States experienced 3,224 lynchings within its borders, or roughly one every three days. Nearly 80 percent of the victims were Negroes, and the vast majority of the incidents occurred in the South. Georgia, for example, held the dubious distinction of leading all states, with a total of 386 lynchings, while Mississippi and Texas followed closely with 373 and 335, respectively. These statistics furnish an irrefutable record of mob violence and seem to corroborate Mr. Dooley's characterization of the racial climate confronting black Americans in the early twentieth century: "Th' black has manny fine qualities," the bartender-sage told his friend, Hennessey. "He is joyous, light-hearted, an' aisily lynched."[1]

For some white Americans, lynching apparently represented a justifiable means of punishing alleged black criminals and of providing a vivid reminder that white supremacy still reigned in the land. "The white man in lynching a Negro does it as an indirect act of self-defense against the Negro criminal as a race," one apologist argued. "When the abnormally criminal Negro race . . . puts himself [*sic*] in harmony with our civilization, if ever, through assimilating our culture and making our ideals its own, then may it be hoped that his [*sic*] crimes will be reduced to normal and lynching will cease, the cause being removed." Such a statement reveals the climate of opinion that no doubt led J. W. Bailey, editor of the *Biblical Recorder*, to observe, "Lynching, mob-spirit, lawlessness, are in the blood of our people." Many other whites, simply preferring to ignore the problem, would have agreed with the reader of the *Crisis*, the official organ of the National Association for the Advancement of Colored People (NAACP), who expressed his dissatisfaction with "so much talk about the lynching of Negroes" in the pages of that journal.[2]

On the other hand, a vocal minority of Americans, by publicly denouncing the trend toward mob violence in the country, refused to support a conspiracy of silence with respect to lynching. Bishop Charles B. Galloway of the Methodist Episcopal Church, South, proclaimed that "every Christian patriot in America needs to lift up his voice in loud and eternal protest against the mob-spirit that is threatening the integrity of this Republic." Similarly, the NAACP from its inception considered lynching (which the *Crisis* identified as "the standard American industry") one of the most important problems in the country and the eradication of lynching one of the most important planks in its program for racial advancement. Of particular concern to individuals and organizations determined to halt episodes of mob-inflicted violence was the fact that while the frequency of lynchings began to decline after 1900, those incidents that did occur were often characterized by extreme barbarity. Few examples of lynch law in twentieth-century America demonstrate this more graphically than the mutilation and burning of Jesse Washington at the hands of a white mob in Waco, Texas, on May 15, 1916—an episode dubbed the "Waco Horror."[3]

Located on the banks of the Brazos River in the fertile blackland region of Central Texas, Waco was a thriving community in 1916. Local boosters described the Lone Star State's eighth-largest urban area (estimated population 33,670)[4] as the "Wonder City" and emphasized the "progressiveness" of the town. Economic opportunities reportedly abounded, particularly in businesses associated with the cotton culture of the surrounding agricultural districts. In addition, city fathers depicted Waco as a center for wholesale dealers and for the rapidly expanding insurance business. One publication of the Young Men's Business League described Waco in 1912 as "a true Southern city which is possessed of all the business possibilities of the metropolitan cities of the nation." Wacoans also expressed pride in their religious and educational institutions, which included sixty-three churches of various denominations and Baptist-affiliated Baylor University, the state's oldest college. The influence exerted by these institutions probably explains the message on a large electric sign that spanned one of the principal street intersections, proclaiming Waco to be "The City With a Soul."[5]

Despite Waco's aura of middle-class respectability in 1916, the city's history had been interspersed with episodes of violence, thus earning the town the sobriquet "Six Shooter Junction." This frontier tradition of lawlessness, though less evident after the turn of the century, surfaced on numerous occasions and shattered the idyllic image so carefully crafted and defended by Waco's community leaders. The lynching of Jesse Washington for the murder of a white woman was one of those occasions.

Early in the evening on May 8, 1916, Chris Simons was walking toward his home on the outskirts of Robinson, a small farming community seven miles south of Waco, when he heard screams coming from the direction of George Fryer's place, some five to six hundred yards down the road. Simons ran to the Fryer home, where he encountered the hysterical twenty-two-year-old Ruby Fryer and her fourteen-year-old brother, George Jr., who were staring at the lifeless form of their mother, fifty-three-year-old Lucy Fryer, sprawled across the doorway of the seed shed. Upon learning from the children that their father was working in the fields, Simons hurried to find the elder Fryer. Informed of the tragic news delivered by his neighbor, Fryer drove to Waco, the county seat of McLennan County, where he reported the crime to Sheriff Samuel S. Fleming. Fleming swiftly assembled an investigative team composed of his deputies, local constables, and a number of Waco policemen and departed for Robinson.[6]

The report of Lucy Fryer's murder spread rapidly through the Robinson community, and several local men banded together to offer their assistance to Sheriff Fleming and his contingent of law enforcement officials. Meanwhile, Dr. J. H. Maynard, a physician from nearby Rosenthal, arrived to examine the dead woman's body. Maynard discovered several deep gashes in Lucy Fryer's head, including two massive wounds penetrating the brain cavity. These blows, the doctor determined, had been delivered by an assailant who used a heavy, blunt instrument.[7]

Suspicion fell almost immediately upon Jesse Washington, an illiterate seventeen-year-old Negro who, with his brother, William, had worked as a hired hand on the Fryer farm since January. Shortly after 9 p.m., an entourage of peace officers drove to the Washington place, where they discovered the young suspect (wearing a blood-stained pair of overalls and undershirt) sitting outside whittling on a piece of wood. Following a few routine questions, Deputy Sheriffs Lee Jenkins and Barney Goldberg took the Washington family into custody and escorted them to Waco for further interrogation, after which William and his parents were released. During this questioning in Waco, Jesse Washington offered several conflicting statements but consistently denied any knowledge of the circumstances surrounding Lucy Fryer's death.[8]

The arrest of Jesse Washington produced a volatile climate in Robinson. One Waco paper reported that local law enforcement officials quickly "realized that the enormity of the crime would cause the hot blood of the Robinson countrymen to flame and cry for protection of their women and homes against the lust of the brute." Aware of the potential for mob violence, Sheriff Fleming decided to remove the black suspect beyond the reach of a lynching party. During the predawn hours on Tuesday, May 9, Fleming transferred his prisoner to Hillsboro, a small town thirty-five miles north of Waco. Once in Hillsboro, Fleming resumed his questioning of the accused in the presence of Hill County Sheriff Fred Long, an interrogation that climaxed with Jesse Washington's confession that he indeed had killed Lucy Fryer. Washington identified the murder weapon as a medium-sized blacksmith's hammer and told his interrogators that he had hidden the hammer in a field on the Fryer place. With this information in hand, Sheriff Fleming returned to Waco, while Sheriff Long escorted the confessed killer to Dallas, where Washington dictated a confession to Dallas County Attorney Mike T. Lively in which he admitted to raping and murdering the wife of his employer. The black youth signed this confession with an X in lieu of his name, which he was incapable of writing. Lively then had Washington locked in the Dallas County jail to await trial and, presumably, to protect him from possible mob assault.[9]

Meanwhile, Sheriff Fleming arrived back in Waco and, accompanied by Deputies Lee Jenkins and Joe Roberts and County Prosecutor John B. McNamara, drove to the Fryer farm. There the search party discovered a blood-caked blacksmith's hammer under a pile of hackberry brush adjacent to the field in which Jesse Washington had been working the previous day—and precisely in the location the black youth had described as the hiding place for the murder weapon.[10]

The discovery of the hammer allegedly used to kill Lucy Fryer, coinciding with the publication of the black suspect's confession in the Waco newspapers, inflamed passions among Robinson's citizenry still further and led some to insist upon drastic action. Shortly after 10 p.m. that evening, Sheriff Fleming encountered a procession of some five hundred citizens from Robinson, Rosenthal, and several smaller communities in southern McLennan County headed toward Waco along the Lorena road. The ringleaders of the group demanded that Fleming release Jesse Washington to them so that swift "justice" might be carried out, and one of the men reportedly declared, "When we left home tonight our wives, daughters and sisters kissed us good bye and told us to do our duty, and we're trying to do it as citizens." When Fleming informed them that the suspect had been removed from the city for safekeeping pending his trial, several of the men refused to believe him and requested to search the jail. Fleming acquiesced, and the caravan of automobiles, buggies, and horses carrying the vigilantes proceeded toward Waco. Upon their arrival at the county jail, the men conducted a meticulous search of the cells, including close scrutiny of every black prisoner. Having satisfied themselves that Washington was not there, the men left quietly and returned to their homes. Following this initial attempt to circumvent the judicial process, community leaders in Robinson assured Waco law enforcement authorities that no further mob action would be planned as long as the legal system operated swiftly in convicting and punishing the confessed rapist and murderer.[11]

Officials in Waco needed little encouragement to resolve the case quickly. On Thursday, May 11, a McLennan County grand jury convened and required only thirty minutes to return a murder indictment against Jesse Washington. District Judge Richard I. Munroe appointed six young Waco attorneys to defend the accused and set the trial date for the following Monday. The *Morning News*, noting these preliminary maneuvers, predicted that "justice will move on swift feet in the case."[12]

The trial of Jesse Washington commenced at 10 a.m. Monday, May 15, in the Fifty-Fourth District Court of McLennan County, with Judge Munroe presiding over a courtroom filled to capacity. Spectators packed the balcony, and some stood on railings and benches to obtain a better view. On several occasions, prospective jurors had to be lifted over the crowd to reach the front of the courtroom. Judge Munroe periodically sought to preserve decorum by gaveling for silence and reminding several of the male onlookers to remove their hats. Those who could not get inside congregated around the courthouse, lining the sidewalks on all sides. Among this crowd of bystanders (described as the largest ever seen in the city) were several African Americans whom one Waco paper characterized as "quiet and seemingly not much excited."[13]

Among some of the white spectators, however, the mood was ugly. Trouble was narrowly averted before the trial when Jesse Washington, whom Sheriff Fleming had brought back to Waco the previous evening, was escorted into the courtroom by sheriff's deputies. At the sight of the defendant, an unidentified white man pulled a revolver and declared, "Might as well get him now." Violence was prevented by another white spectator, who overpowered and disarmed the gunman and proclaimed, "Let them have the trial. We'll get him before sundown, and you might hurt some innocent man." At another point early in the proceedings, an anonymous voice called out, "Don't need no court."[14]

The trial proceeded rapidly. Jury selection required a mere thirty-five minutes, as the defense counsel, headed by Joseph W. Taylor Jr., offered no peremptory challenges to prospective jurors. Once the jury was empaneled, Judge Munroe read the indictment and asked the defendant to state his plea. When Washington seemed puzzled by the request, the judge asked the black youth whether or not he had committed the crime for which he was being prosecuted. Munroe explained that a guilty plea would result in hanging or a sentence of from five years to life in the state penitentiary. The defendant's response consisted of a muttered "Yeah," which the court translated as "Guilty."[15]

Upon the completion of these preliminary matters, the prosecuting attorney, John B. McNamara, opened the case for the state. Dr. Maynard took the witness stand to describe the wounds inflicted upon Lucy Fryer but, curiously, made no mention of evidence of a sexual assault. Following this medical testimony, Mike Lively, Fred Long, and W. J. Davis, a legal investigator and former Dallas policeman, related the details of Jesse Washington's confession in Dallas and identified the defendant as the person who, in their presence, had admitted to raping and murdering Mrs. Fryer. Sheriff Fleming and his deputy, Lee Jenkins, described to the court their roles in the arrest of the defendant and the successful search for the murder weapon. Finally, Chris Simons and Constable Leslie Stegall offered testimony pertaining to their discovery of the dead woman's body on the evening of May 8. Attorney McNamara then read Washington's confession into the court record and rested his case.[16]

The counsel for the defense, which chose to ask only one question during cross-examination of the state's witnesses, opened and closed its case by calling a single witness—Jesse Washington. Joe Taylor asked his client if he had anything to say to the jury on his own behalf. The black man replied, "I ain't going to tell them nothing more than what I said—that's what I done." Washington's subsequent remark was unintelligible to the courtroom. Taylor told the jury, "He says he is sorry he did it." The young counselor then asked the defendant if he had something more to add. Washington remained silent, at which point the defense rested.[17]

In his summation, Prosecutor McNamara praised Joe Taylor and the other young Waco attorneys for complying with their legal duty to defend their client. Furthermore, he lauded the fairness of the trial, proclaiming, "The prisoner has been given a fair trial, as fair as any ever given in this court room." This statement produced a round of applause culminating in "a mighty yell" among courtroom spectators, after which the jury retired to consider the fate of the accused.[18]

The deliberations did not take long. The jury returned after only four minutes, and Foreman William B. Brazleton, a prominent Waco businessman, read the verdict: "We, the jury, find the defendant guilty of murder as charged in the indictment and assess his penalty at death." Following a second reading of the jury's decision, Judge Munroe began writing the verdict into the docket book and law officers were preparing to remove Jesse Washington from the courtroom when pandemonium erupted. An unidentified white spectator yelled, "Get the nigger," and a group of men surged forward, seized the convicted youth, and hustled him down the stairs at the rear of the courthouse, where a crowd of about four hundred persons waited in the alley. A chain was thrown around Washington's neck, and he was dragged in the direction of the river, where, someone suggested, he could be hanged from the city's historic suspension bridge, the site of the lynching of another black man, Sank Majors, in 1935. Instead of continuing to the bridge, however, the mob turned on Second Street and marched toward city hall, where another group of vigilantes had gathered to build a bonfire. As the crowd pushed forward to this destination, several individuals attacked the struggling Washington, tearing the clothes from his body, stabbing him with knives, and battering him with bricks, clubs, and shovels.[19]

By the time the procession reached the city-hall grounds, Jesse Washington was semiconscious and bleeding profusely. The leaders of the mob picked up their victim, tossed him onto a pile of dry-goods boxes that had been gathered under a tree, and doused his body with coal oil. The chain wrapped around Washington's neck was thrown over a sturdy limb of the tree, and several men united to jerk their victim into the air for all to see. "When the negro was first hoisted into the air," the Waco *Times-Herald* reported, "his tongue protruded from his mouth and his face was besmeared with blood." Then Washington's body was lowered onto the pile of combustibles, and several whites advanced to cut off his fingers, ears, and toes. One eyewitness reported that the mob also emasculated the black youth. Many spectators of this grim affair also seemed eager to assist in burning the convicted slayer. According to the *Times-Herald*, "People pressed forward, each eager to be the first to light the fire, matches were touched to the inflammable material and as smoke rapidly rose in the air, such a demonstration as of people gone mad was never heard before." The flames swiftly engulfed Jesse Washington.[20]

As news of the lynching spread through the city, a large crowd consisting of men, women, and children assembled to watch the grisly spectacle. Many Waco business-men left their places of employment downtown to witness the events on the city-hall lawn. Mayor John R. Dollins and Chief of Police Guy McNamara viewed the event from the mayor's office in city hall, while local photographer Fred A. Gildersleeve, forewarned that Washington would be lynched at the conclusion of the trial, had set up his camera to take pictures of the incident. Of the female bystanders, one local paper reported, "As matters progressed . . . they seemed to get accustomed to what was taking place, and some of them were soon laughing, and chatting, albeit their faces were in some cases still blanched." One well-dressed woman applauded gleefully "when a way was cleared so that she could see the writhing, naked form of the fast dying black." A large number of children, including students from nearby Waco High School who had rushed to the scene during their lunch hour, also witnessed this exhibition of horror. Other spectators leaned out of the windows of nearby buildings to get a better look.[21]

As the body continued to burn, some onlookers searched the ground for bits of bone, broken links of the chain noose, and pieces of the hanging tree—items that presumably could be kept or sold as souvenirs. Within two hours, the smoldering remains of Jesse Washington consisted of little more than a charred skull and torso. In midafternoon, a horseman approached, lassoed the burned corpse, and dragged it through the main streets of downtown Waco. At one point during this macabre procession, the skull bounced off and was retrieved by a group of young boys who extracted the teeth and sold them for five dollars apiece. Finally, several men placed the victim's remains in a cloth bag and pulled the bundle behind an automobile to Robinson, where they hung the sack from a pole in front of a blacksmith's shop for the community's residents to see. Later that afternoon, Constable Les Stegall retrieved the body and turned it over to a Waco undertaker for burial.[22]

Thus ended an episode that most Wacoans probably preferred to forget. Reper-cussions on the state and national level, however, kept the lynching in the public eye for several months and brought condemnation upon Waco, the state of Texas, and the nation as a whole for permitting a climate of race relations to exist that tolerated such an atrocity.

In the wake of the events of May 15, the response by local whites to the lynch-ing of Jesse Washington varied from vigorous approval to public condemnation of the mob's actions. Glenn Bruck, whose brother Earle had served on the jury that had convicted Washington, proclaimed that his only regret was not having been present to assist the vigilantes. The typical white Wacoan, according to the *Morning News*, either seemed satisfied with what had transpired or refused to comment on the incident. For its own part, the *Morning News* expressed regret over the mob's actions but also voiced resentment over the "wholesale denunciation of the south and of the people of Waco" that followed. The *Times-Herald* refrained from editorial comment entirely, noting on the day following the lynching, "Yesterday's exciting occurrence is a closed incident." NAACP investigator Elizabeth Freeman reported to Royal Nash, the executive secretary of the association, "I find very few who really condone all that was done—but when they make it personal they feel that they would have done likewise." On a later occasion, she informed Nash, "The feeling amongst the best people is one of shame for the whole happening. They realize it could have been stopped if they had had a leader—now they think they are right in trying to forget it and fancy the world will do so too." When Freeman questioned Judge Munroe about his failure to halt the mob by using the pistol he kept hidden in a drawer at the bench, the judge responded, "Do you want to spill innocent blood for a nigger?" The apparent failure of Waco's religious leaders to condemn publicly the affair particularly distressed the NAACP investigator. "Cannot get the ministers to aid," she told her superiors in New York. "They simply say it is deplorable." On May 21, she reported, "So far I have not found a Christian (?) minister who has protested against the action of the Waco folk."[23]

Some whites in McLennan County seemed disturbed not so much by the lynching per se but rather by the mob's treatment of Jesse Washington's burned corpse. John Strauss, one of Robinson's educational leaders, claimed that the people in his community unanimously condemned the dragging of the black victim's body through the streets of Waco. "If only they had just hung [*sic*] him," wrote Elizabeth Freeman in attempting to characterize local white opinion, "they felt that would have been all right, but the burning—the dragging of the charred torso through the streets is so much worse than his crime."[24]

Not all local whites, however, shared the opinion that silence and inaction were the most appropriate responses to the lynching. Several leading Wacoans, including the jury foreman, William Brazleton, and local newspaperman Edward M. Ainsworth, argued that some public protest should be made. Moreover, they were especially critical of the city's law enforcement officials for not intervening to prevent mob violence. In addition to the opposition voiced by a few individual citizens, a special committee of the faculty at Baylor University issued a series of resolutions condemning the mob's actions and expressing concern that the incident "will evoke from the outside world reproaches unmerited by the majority of the people of our fair city and county." These efforts to challenge the legitimacy of the mob in taking Jesse Washington's life, however, clearly represented a minority course of action among white residents of Waco and McLennan County.[25]

Blacks living in Robinson and Waco generally reacted to the events surrounding the murders of Lucy Fryer and Jesse Washington either by keeping their thoughts to themselves or by taking a conciliatory stance. One of the few blacks to offer his opinions publicly was C. H. Dorsey, a Robinson school teacher, who characterized

Mrs. Fryer's murder as a "most horrible outrage." Dorsey gave assurances that all respectable black Robinsonians deplored Washington's crime and proclaimed that the incident had produced no pernicious repercussions in the community. "The white people of Robinson," he wrote prior to Washington's trial, "have shown the negroes here the same sympathetic and helpful spirit that they had always shown before." In Waco, the Rev. John W. Strong, dean of the all-black Central Texas College, and the Rev. I. Newton Jenkins, pastor of the New Hope Baptist Church, expressed their regret with respect to the crime that had taken Lucy Fryer's life, but in a confidential statement to Elizabeth Freeman, they noted their disappointment that Waco's white clergymen had not been more outspoken in denouncing the brutal and extralegal execution of Jesse Washington. After interviewing several local blacks concerning their views of the events that had transpired between May 8 and May 15, Freeman concluded, "The feeling of the colored people was that while they had one rotten member of their race the whites had 15,000."[26]

While most local blacks were reluctant to condemn the lynching, at least one black man in Waco refused to curb his outrage. A. T. Smith, managing editor of the *Paul Quinn Weekly*, the school paper at all-black Paul Quinn College, published several articles denouncing the incident. Richard D. Evans, a black attorney in Waco, commented that the Smith articles "took this city to task harder than any I have read on this lynching." In fact, one of the editorials included an unfounded charge (reprinted from the Chicago *Defender*, one of the nation's leading black weeklies) that George Fryer Sr., not Jesse Washington, had murdered Lucy Fryer. This charge led to Smith's arrest and conviction on charges of criminal libel. Attorney Evans informed the NAACP that the Smith case had produced additional racial tensions in Waco and that, despite Evans's decision to defend the embattled editor, "the colored people here were afraid to help him [Smith] and afraid for me to do so."[27]

Elsewhere in Texas, newspapers published a report of the lynching distributed by the Associated Press wire service. A few white dailies in the larger cities offered editorials condemning the brutality of the incident and bemoaning the fact that public opinion everywhere would blame the entire state for the affair. The San Antonio *Express*, for example, called for a halt to lynching in the South, adding, "The Waco disgrace is the disgrace of Texas." The Austin *American Statesman* admitted that Jesse Washington deserved to die for his crime (a common sentiment in the state press) but not at the hands of a band of vigilantes. Particularly distressing to the *American Statesman* was the occurrence of such a barbaric event "in one of [the state's] great centers of learning, of boasted civilization. . . . A city of good people, of fine homes, of refinement." The two major white dailies in Houston published criticisms of the lynching that resembled each other in tone. "Not a word of defense is there to offer; not an extenuating circumstance to plead," the *Chronicle* proclaimed in its editorial. "Bestial cruelty, though seemingly sanctioned by religious indignation, never did, and never will, strengthen those customs, institutions and standards which make society respectable and the individual's life safe." The

Post agreed that "from no angle viewed, can there be the least excuse, much less justification, offered for" the lynching and asked in a tone of rhetorical indignation, "Oh Shame! Where is thy blush?" In Dallas, the white dailies remained editorially silent. Nor was the Dallas *Express*, a black weekly, substantially more forceful. Usually known for its hard-hitting attacks against all forms of discrimination against African Americans, the *Express* assumed a restrained position and maintained that no mob would have wreaked vengeance in Waco had Lucy Fryer not been murdered. "There is a time to talk and a time not to talk," the *Express* informed its readers. "To our mind, here is a time for thought."[28]

Outside the state, reaction to the lynching was generally harsh. "Waco did more than burn a Negro," one California newspaper explained. "She burned her own courage, decency and character, outraged the imaginations of her young people, and smeared a foul disgrace across her civic life." The New York *Times* objected to the mob's refusal to permit the law to take its full course in punishing Jesse Washington and emphasized the boldness of the vigilantes in acting in broad daylight. Waxing hyperbolic, the *Times* concluded that the lynching had been carried out "apparently by the whole population of the place."[29]

Several progressive journals added their voices to the wave of indignation produced by the Waco affair. The *Independent* characterized the lynching as "an orgy of mob brutality and savage lust" and, in a subsequent issue, proclaimed, "Waco is indelibly disgraced. Texas is indelibly disgraced. The United States is indelibly disgraced. . . . Nothing in the reports of the atrocities in Belgium, East Prussia, Serbia or Armenia shows a more hideous state of public opinion than that manifested by the people of Waco in participating in such a degrading display of wanton savagery." The *New Republic* called the lynching in Waco "a filthy crime" and expressed dismay that Fred Gildersleeve's photographs of the incident "showed a typical straw-hatted summer crowd gazing gleefully at the hideous crisp of what was once a Negro youth." Oswald Garrison Villard's *Nation* castigated the faculty of Baylor University for failing to condemn publicly the episode. This uninformed assertion elicited a prompt response from Dean John L. Kesler, the University's acting president, who apprised Villard of the faculty resolutions deploring the action of the mob. Kesler further reported that he had "condemned [mob law] in as strong words as the English language would permit without violating the ten commandments [*sic*]" in the presence of eight hundred students assembled for chapel services. Finally, Dean Kesler claimed that the lynching had been denounced from the city's leading pulpits in sermons delivered by the Revs. Frank P. Culver of Austin Avenue Methodist Church, Charles T. Caldwell of the First Presbyterian Church, Frank S. Groner of Columbus Street Baptist Church, and Joseph Martin Dawson of First Baptist Church. Villard noted the correction to his earlier charge but maintained that "Waco cannot hold up its head until the criminals are punished."[30]

At the same time that the editors of several major newspapers and journals condemned the Waco lynching, their comments produced rebuttals from a number of whites who attempted to justify the mob's action or, at least, to place the blame elsewhere. One Northern-born Texas resident complained that the *Nation* should direct its editorial venom against the crime of rape rather than lynching. "It may be bad to lynch," he admitted, "but is it not far worse for a dehumanized fiend, swelling with bestial lust, to lay his cursed hands on a pure, defenceless woman to satisfy his animal nature?" A white Floridian added the oft-repeated reminder that Northerners could not possibly understand race relations in the South and, therefore, could not react objectively to the lynching of blacks. The only preventive for black crime, he concluded, lay in "a sure, swift punishment as was meted out by the Ku Klux Clansmen [*sic*] in the days of reconstruction." The editors of the *Outlook* condemned the failure of Waco officials to prevent the incident. "Political, moral, and physical cowardice are written all over the story," the journal charged. At the same time, the *Outlook* offered a unique (though highly questionable) interpretation to account, at least in part, for the recurrence of lynchings in the United States by blaming "a small group of Negro leaders who have been preaching covetousness and envy as virtues, and who have tended to dull the minds of some of their followers to a sense of duty and to the importance of self-control."[31]

The public responses by blacks on the national level to the Waco lynching fell into two categories—either one of conciliation or one of condemnation. Even when not compelled to silence by geographical proximity to McLennan County, a few took a conservative stance. For example, a black Georgian asked that the race as a whole not be judged by the acts of "troublesome and insolent" African Americans like Jesse Washington. "Our beloved neighbors will attest," he continued, "that the negro is the last one in general to harbor a desire to defend from just punishment any sort of criminal."[32]

In contrast, the black press outside Texas almost uniformly denounced the mob's actions in Waco. The Savannah *Tribune*, referring to lynching as the "popular life-taking game in the southland," characterized the Waco incident as "about as barbarous a deed as can be committed." In an editorial for the New York *Age*, James Weldon Johnson declared that the details of Jesse Washington's death were "enough to make the devil gasp in astonishment." Johnson called upon Pres. Woodrow Wilson to condemn such lawless incidents in a public statement and asserted that nowhere else in the world "could be found a people so close to the brute but they would have done such a deed. In comparison with them [the Waco vigilantes], a crowd of Mexican bandits is a company of high-souled, chivalrous gentlemen." Perhaps the most outraged protest in the black press, however, emanated from the offices of the Chicago *Defender*. Edited by Robert S. Abbott, the *Defender* immediately announced its belief in Jesse Washington's innocence, arguing that the black youth had been railroaded by the Waco judicial system. Several of the *Defender's* reports of the lynching were sensationalist in nature, including the previously cited publication of the unfounded rumor that George Fryer Sr. had been arrested and charged with murdering his wife.[33]

Of all the national attention devoted to the Waco lynching, however, the most far-reaching demonstration of outrage generated by the affair occurred within the ranks of the National Association for the Advancement of Colored People. Reports of the incident stirred the NAACP to launch a full-scale investigation of the lynching. The association contacted Elizabeth Freeman, who was attending a women's suffrage convention in Dallas, and asked her to travel to Waco to collect data relating to Jesse Washington's death. Freeman's findings appeared (as previously noted) in a supplement to the July 1916 issue of the *Crisis*, entitled "The Waco Horror." The journal's editor, W. E. B. Du Bois, sermonized, "To other persons we say as we have said before: any talk of the triumph of Christianity, or the spread of human culture, is idle twaddle so long as the Waco lynching is possible in the United States of America."[34]

Several NAACP officials saw in the "Waco Horror" a powerful cause célèbre upon which the association might expand its antilynching crusade to include a federal law prohibiting the crime of lynching. In late July, Joel E. Spingarn, chairman of the NAACP's board of directors, and Oswald Garrison Villard, the organization's treasurer, issued a joint appeal for contributions to an antilynching fund to finance "the first nation-wide campaign against the ancient American institution of lynching that ever gave promise of wiping the blot once [and] for all from our escutcheon." The following month, Spingarn informed Philip G. Peabody, a prominent Boston attorney who had expressed interest in financing an antilynching campaign, that "the publicity we gave Waco has roused a fighting spirit we must not let die." Meanwhile, Villard, in an appeal for financial assistance for the NAACP's Anti-Lynching Fund, proclaimed, "The crime at Waco is a challenge to our American civilization, yes, to every American."[35]

Invigorated by the national attention devoted to the lynching of Jesse Washington, the NAACP's antilynching crusade proceeded at such a furious pace during the remainder of 1916 that Joel Spingarn optimistically declared the campaign "the most striking achievement" of the year. By early 1917, however, international events dominated the nation's attention to such an extent that little interest could be generated for reforms in the realm of race relations. With the entrance of the United States into World War I in April, NAACP leaders probably realized that they had little hope of winning support for such a politically divisive issue as a federal antilynching law. Consequently, while NAACP antilynching efforts continued on several fronts during the war, the "Waco Horror" was relegated to an anonymous position among thousands of instances of mob violence inflicted upon black Americans in the pre–World War I era.[36]

In many respects, the events surrounding the lynching of Jesse Washington differed little from other episodes of mob violence in the United States. The incident occurred in the South, and the victim was a black male who had confessed to crimes that in the eyes of some white Southerners made lynch law justifiable, even necessary. Nor was the barbarity of the mob particularly unusual for the time. Moreover, the refusal of Waco officials to seek indictments against the ringleaders, even though their identities were known throughout the city, indicates that this incident followed a pattern generally adopted by local officials dealing with similar acts of violence.[37]

Significantly, however, in lynching Jesse Washington, the mob in Waco unwittingly provided the NAACP with a cause célèbre that the national association could utilize to invoke support for a systematic campaign to halt lynchings. To capitalize upon Philip Peabody's offer to fund an antilynching crusade, the NAACP needed a particularly sensational incident to demonstrate to the American people the urgency of a federal antilynching bill. The burning and mutilation of an illiterate black farmhand, graphically documented by Fred Gildersleeve's camera, packed the necessary emotional punch to dramatize the exigency of federal action. In addition, the fact that this incident occurred in a city reputed to be an enlightened, respectable, middle-class community supplied the NAACP further evidence of the breadth of a lynching mentality in the United States. And yet, despite the seemingly advantageous timing of the "Waco Horror," the campaign fell victim to the inopportune entrance of the nation into the First World War, thereby forcing the NAACP to postpone its federal antilynching crusade until 1919.

"What's goin' to happen to th' naygur?" Hennessy asked Mr. Dooley in a conversation over the "Negro problem" in the United States. "Well," said Dooley, "he'll ayther have to go to th' north an' be a subjick race, or stay in th' south an' be an objick lesson."[38] While the NAACP had hoped to exploit the "Waco Horror" to further its antilynching program, Jesse Washington's death unfortunately became but another "objick lesson" reminding blacks of the dire consequences awaiting those who stepped outside their "place" in American society.

Originally published as SoRelle, James M. "The Waco Horror: The Lynching of Jesse Washington." Southwestern Historical Quarterly 86 (1983): 517–36. Reprinted by permission of the author and the editor of the Southwestern Historical Quarterly.

NOTES

1. National Association for the Advancement of Colored People, *Thirty Years of Lynching in the United States, 1889–1918* (New York: 1919), 7; Finley Peter Dunne, "The Booker Washington Incident," *Mr. Dooley's Opinions* (New York: 1901), 210 (quotation).

2. Winfield H. Collins, *The Truth about Lynching and the Negro in the South* (New York: 1918), 70–71 (first quotation); "Some Thoughts on Lynching," *South Atlantic Quarterly* 5 (October 1906): 353 (second quotation); J. H. T. to the Editor, *Crisis* 7 (November 1913): 348 (third quotation).

3. "Some Thoughts on Lynching," 353 (first quotation); James Weldon Johnson, *Along This Way: The Autobiography of James Weldon Johnson* (New York: 1933), 310; *Crisis* 9 (March 1915): 196 (second quotation); Walter

White, *Rope and Faggot: A Biography of Judge Lynch*, reprint ed. (New York: 1969), 19–20. The specific title "Waco Horror" seems to have originated with the editors of the *Crisis*, who published an account of this incident as an eight-page supplement to their July issue. Prior to the appearance of this report, however, the Houston *Chronicle* expressed its editorial opinion of "The Horror at Waco," and a New York *Times* editorial stated that the mob in Waco had "Punished a Horror Horribly." See "The Waco Horror," supplement to the *Crisis* 12 (July 1916): 1–8; Houston *Chronicle*, May 16, 1916; and New York *Times*, May 17, 1916. Previous discussions of this affair include brief accounts in Charles F. Kellogg, *NAACP: A History of the National Association for the Advancement of Colored People, 1909–1920* (Baltimore, MD: 1967), 218; and Robert L. Zangrando, *The NAACP Crusade against Lynching, 1909–1950* (Philadelphia, PA: 198), 29–30; and a more thorough exploration in Rogers M. Smith, "The Waco Lynching of 1916: Perspective and Analysis" (MA thesis, Baylor University, 1971).

4. US Department of Commerce, Bureau of the Census, *Fourteenth Census of the United States Taken in the Year 1920*, vol. 3 (Washington, DC: 1921–23), *Population, 1920, Composition and Characteristics*, 1,015. The census bureau set Waco's population in 1910 at 26,425; ten years later, the figure stood at 38,500. The town's population in 1916 can be estimated by computing the percent of increase between 1910 and 1920 and assuming that the increase occurred evenly over the decade. Although no certain degree of accuracy can be claimed for this figure, it undoubtedly is more accurate than the Waco city directory's estimate of 45,237. See R. L. Polk et al., comp., *Waco City Directory, 1916* (Houston: 1916), 21.

5. Polk, *Waco City Directory*, 21 (first quotation), 51–54; Charles E. Gilbert Jr., comp., *Waco* (Waco, TX: 1912), 63 (second quotation); William H. Curry, *A History of Early Waco with Allusions to Six Shooter Junction* (Waco, TX: 1968), front flyleaf (third quotation).

6. Testimony of Chris Simons in *State of Texas v. Jesse Washington*, District Court of McLennan County, Texas, Fifty-Fourth Judicial District, March Term, 1916, Case No. 4141, 6; Elizabeth Freeman, "The Waco Lynching," National Association for the Advancement of Colored People Archives, Manuscript Division, Library of Congress, Washington, DC (hereafter cited as NAACP Archives), 8.

7. Waco *Morning News*, May 9, 1916; Waco *Times-Herald*, May 9, 1916; testimony of Dr. J. H. Maynard in *Texas v. Washington*, 1–2.

8. Waco *Morning News*, May 9, 1916; Waco *Times-Herald*, May 9, 1916.

9. Waco *Morning News*, May 10, 1916 (quotation); testimony of Fred Long, Mike T. Lively, and W. J. Davis in *Texas v. Washington*, 2–4.

10. Testimony of S. S. Fleming in *Texas v. Washington*, 4–5.

11. Waco *Morning News*, May 10, 1916; Waco *Times-Herald*, May 10, 1916 (quotation).

12. Waco *Morning News*, May 11, 12, 14 (quotation), 1916. In Texas, the common practice in cases involving murder and criminal assault, where the guilt of the accused was beyond doubt, was to ensure the defendant a

speedy jury trial and, following a guilty verdict, to carry out the death sentence at the end of a thirty-day waiting period. "This has had the effect," the *Morning News* reported, "of stopping many of the lawless demonstrations which formerly characterized the commission of the diabolical crime of which Washington stands accused and to which he has confessed." Ibid., May 13, 1916.

13. Ibid., May 16, 1916 (quotation); Waco *Times-Herald*, May 15, 1916.

14. Waco *Morning News*, May 16, 1916.

15. Ibid.

16. *Texas v. Washington*, 1–9.

17. Ibid., 10.

18. Waco *Morning News*, May 16, 1916.

19. Ibid. (quotations); Waco *Times-Herald*, May 15 and 16, 1916.

20. Waco *Times-Herald*, May 15, 1916 (quotations); Waco *Morning News*, May 16, 1916; Freeman, "Waco Lynching," 14.

21. Estimates of the size of the crowd varied widely. Waco's afternoon newspaper set the figure at ten thousand, while the morning paper claimed that fifteen thousand persons had witnessed the burning. Elizabeth Freeman, an English suffragist who investigated the lynching for the NAACP, reported that during her early interviews concerning the incident, most citizens admitted to the larger number, but as they became more suspicious of her motives, subsequent witnesses stated that only five hundred bystanders had gathered on the city-hall lawn. A popular account of the episode published a half-century later claimed that one thousand persons had watched the execution. Waco *Times-Herald*, May 15, 1916; Waco *Morning News*, May 16, 1916 (quotations);

Freeman, "Waco Lynching," 15, 20, 21; Curry, *History of Early Waco*, 90.

22. Waco *Times-Herald*, May 15, 1916; Waco *Morning News*, May 16, 1916; Freeman, "Waco Lynching," 15–16.

23. Waco *Morning News*, May 16, 19, and 24 (first quotation), 1916; Waco *Times-Herald*, May 16, 1916 (second quotation); Elizabeth Freeman to Roy Nash, May 20, 1916, NAACP Archives (third and sixth quotations); Freeman to Nash, May 24, 1916, NAACP Archives (fourth quotation); Freeman to Nash, May 21, 1916, NAACP Archives (seventh quotation); Freeman, "Waco Lynching," 11 (fifth quotation), 17.

24. Waco *Morning News*, May 16, 1916; Freeman to Nash, May 20, 1916 (quotation), NAACP Archives.

25. Freeman, "Waco Lynching," 18–19, 23; Waco *Morning News*, May 28, 1916 (quotation).

26. Waco *Morning News*, May 14, 1916 (first and second quotations); Freeman, "Waco Lynching," 2 (third quotation), 3.

27. R. D. Evans to the Editor, *Crisis* 13 (January 1917): 122 (quotations), 123; Memorandum from Roy Nash to Joel Spingarn, August 11, 1916, NAACP Archives. After waiving his right to a jury trial, Smith was sentenced to one year of hard labor on a county convict labor gang.

28. San Antonio *Express*, May 17, 1916 (first quotation); Austin *American Statesman*, May 17, 1916 (second quotation); Houston *Chronicle*, May 16, 1916 (third quotation); Houston *Post*, May 17, 1916 (fourth and fifth quotations); Dallas *Express*, May 20, 1916 (sixth quotation).

29. San Francisco *Bulletin*, May 16, 1916, reprinted in *Crisis* 12 (August 1916):

189 (first quotation); New York *Times*, May 17, 1916 (second quotation).

30. "A Terrible Crime in Texas," *Independent* 86 (May 29, 1916): 325 (first quotation); "An American Atrocity," *Independent* 87 (July 31, 1916): 146 (second quotation); editorial, *New Republic* 8 (June 3, 1916): 102 (third quotation); "The Will-to-Lynch," *New Republic* 8 (October 14, 1916): 261 (fourth quotation); "Moving against Lynching," *Nation* 103 (August 3, 1916): 101; editorial comment, *Nation* 103 (October 5, 1916): 322; J. L. Kesler to the Editor, October 15, 1916, *Nation* 103 (December 28, 1916): 609 (fifth quotation); editorial comment, ibid. (sixth quotation).

31. J. T. Winston to the Editor, May 26, 1916, *Nation* 102 (June 22, 1916): 671 (first quotation); Elliott G. Barrow to the Editor, June 22, 1916, *Nation* 102 (July 6, 1916): 11 (second quotation); "To Lynch or Not to Lynch?," *Outlook* 115 (January 24, 1917): 138 (third and fourth quotations).

32. Robert F. Gibson to the Editor, June 23, 1916, *Nation* 103 (July 13, 1916): 35.

33. Savannah *Tribune*, July 8, 1916 (first and second quotations); New York *Age*, May 25, 1916 (third and fourth quotations); Chicago *Defender*, May 20, 27, June 3, 10, 1916.

34. Roy Nash to Elizabeth Freeman, May 16, 1916, NAACP Archives; "Waco Horror," 1–8; W. E. B. Du Bois, "Lynching," *Crisis* 12 (July 1916): 135 (quotation).

35. Cleveland *Advocate*, July 22, 1916 (first quotation); Joel E. Spingarn to Philip

G. Peabody, August 4, 1916 (second quotation), NAACP Archives; *Crisis* 12 (August 1916): 168 (third quotation).

36. *Crisis* 13 (February 1917), 166 (quotation); Kellogg, *NAACP*, 220, 227–31. The "Waco Horror," however, was not completely forgotten following America's entrance into World War I. Among the literature distributed for the NAACP-sponsored "Negro Silent Protest Parade" in New York City on July 28, 1917—a demonstration against mob violence held in the wake of the East St. Louis race riot—was the following statement: "We march because we want to make impossible a repetition of Waco, Memphis, and East St. Louis, by arousing the conscience of the country and bringing the murders of our brothers, sisters, and innocent children to justice." Zangrando, *NAACP Crusade*, 37, 38 (quotation).

37. Freeman, "Waco Lynching," 13. After several days of talking to local citizens about the lynching, Elizabeth Freeman had acquired the names of six men who represented "the disreputable bunch of Waco" and who had participated in the mob's activities. Ibid., 19. The pattern adopted by local officials in the United States of refusing to seek prosecution of known mob participants is noted in Arthur F. Raper, *The Tragedy of Lynching* (Chapel Hill, NC: 1932), 2, 13–17; and Zangrando, *NAACP Crusade*, 4, 8.

38. Finley Peter Dunne, "The Negro Problem," in *Mr. Dooley's Philosophy* (New York: Harper and Brothers, 1906), 217.

PART 3

Striving for Success
and Civil Rights

The Life and Work of
Dr. Beadie Eugene Conner

An African American Physician in Jim Crow Texas

Keith Volanto

When we think of segregated, Jim Crow Texas, one frequently considers the difficulties of existing in a white-dominated and racist society for the poorer and less well-educated members of the African American community. What author Keith Volanto depicts so well in this article is the type of problems faced by a black man who struggled to become a medical doctor, to establish himself in the practice of medicine, and the especial importance of having black doctors for the black community, notwithstanding any service to the white community. Volanto is a professor of history at Collin College and the author of the valuable study Texas, Cotton, and the New Deal *as well as* Texas Voices: Beyond Myths and Legends—A Narrative History of Texas *and* The American Challenge: A New History of the United States.

★

On a bright, sunny day in late May 1980, commencement exercises were under way at Meharry Medical College in Nashville, Tennessee. Over 250 physicians, dentists, nurses, candidates in health administration, dental hygienists, and medical technicians prepared to receive their certifications from the second-oldest historically black medical school in the country. Wearing a brown gabardine suit, Dr. Beadie Eugene Conner prepared to be called up to the podium along with some former classmates of Meharry's class of 1930 to receive a plaque commemorating fifty years of public service. As he proudly made his way up to the podium, tears began to well up in his eyes as he thought about his mother who would be so proud of him; his deceased wife, Willie Ruel; their daughter Georgia; and the many years that had transpired since he received his medical degree. The event contributed to the retired doctor's desire to write an autobiography. Though never completed, rough drafts of the manuscript's early chapters (along with other existing personal documents) provide an invaluable window into the interesting life of an important African American physician in twentieth-century Texas.[1]

The Conner family's emphasis on education started long before Beadie was born. The earliest relatives of Dr. Conner so far identified are William Conner and Rachel Sterling Conner of Blount County in eastern Tennessee. Family records indicate that William was born a slave in Knox County, Tennessee, sometime in 1814. He had already purchased his freedom by 1843, when he married Rachel Sterling, a woman born in 1829 into a free black family. William and Rachel lived on a Blount County farm through the Civil War years, raising six boys and one girl. Beadie Conner's father, David Alexander Conner, was the fourth-oldest son, born in 1859. After William died in 1866, Rachel moved the family to Louisville in Blount County, where she kept house while David and his two youngest brothers attended school. By the late 1870s, the family had relocated to Knoxville before breaking up and going their separate ways. Among David's siblings, his sister became a schoolteacher, two brothers served as ministers, one brother became a successful mortician, and his youngest brother, George Sherman Conner (destined to become a role model for young Beadie), started out as a teacher in Paris, Texas, before becoming a physician and important community leader in Waco.[2]

Much had transpired in David Alexander Conner's life by the time his twin children, Beadie and Beatrice, were born on July 8, 1902, in Miller County, Arkansas, on a farm along the banks of the Red River. A widower living with six kids from his previous marriage, he had met Queen Fowler Newlin, a short, beautiful woman of French and Choctaw extraction, while attending a Baptist convention in Hope, Arkansas, in 1900. After a brief correspondence and courtship, the two married in 1901. Queen had five children from her previous marriage, thus Beadie and Beatrice became the youngest additions to a family already containing eleven brothers and sisters. (In 1905, another child, named Cleopatra, would be added to the mix.) Beadie noted in his autobiography that it was a tight-knit group. "My sister and I were the pride and joy of the family being the youngest," he wrote. "We were spoiled to no end by them."[3]

The Conners sharecropped until repeated flooding of the Red River forced them to relocate to nearby Texarkana in 1906. At the turn of the twentieth century, Texarkana was a bustling town along the Texas-Arkansas border with ten thousand residents, about 40 percent of them African American. Lumber mills, plus railroad yards and repair shops, provided the basis for a growing manufacturing base. Soon after arriving, David Conner arranged to go into a boarding business with a man who had a two-story frame house, but a fire of unknown origin gutted the place, forcing the family out on the street. He soon established contact with Howell Frank Smith, a prosperous black farmer who owned three brick buildings on Broad Street, Texarkana's main downtown street on the Texas side of the Red River. Perhaps feeling sorry for David, and recognizing the man's determined efforts to provide for his family, Smith granted him permission to open a rooming house and restaurant in one of his unoccupied buildings. This act of generosity not only marked the beginning of a business partnership between David Conner and Howell Smith but created the circumstances by which Beadie Conner would establish a close childhood friendship with one of Smith's sons, the future civil rights activist A. Maceo Smith.[4]

In his memoir, Conner noted that his childhood in Texarkana was rather uneventful. He remembered playing marbles and getting into trouble with Maceo, working as a lead-out boy for a livery stable, earning his mother's wrath for habitually coming home late from school, selling newspapers and cracked pecans while shining shoes in front of his father's boarding house, and developing a strong interest in playing the drums. By the age of fifteen, young Beadie was in business for himself cleaning and pressing clothes in a vacant barber shop. With his mother helping him with the cleaning and his father lending his horse and buggy to deliver finished items to his customers, Conner was able to earn enough money over the next two years to attend Bishop College in Marshall, Texas, with Maceo. While attending Bishop Academic School—the school's college-preparatory program established to aid those students who lacked a high school education—he found employment at a local laundry and also organized a band to perform gigs for spending money. After a year, however, Beadie and Maceo desired a greater academic challenge than the college provided. "While Bishop was a good school, Maceo and I both felt we could do better academically. Fisk [University] represented that chance," Conner noted. Located in Nashville, Tennessee, Fisk was founded in 1866 by the American Missionary Association with help from the Freedman's Bureau. By 1920, the school had earned the reputation of being among the top black colleges in the country. Upon being accepted, seventeen-year-old Beadie joined his friend in the fall of 1919 for a new scholastic adventure. Showing up with a suitcase, drum set, and youthful enthusiasm, he took up residence at Bennett Hall to begin the first of three years attending Fisk's Academic School to prepare him for formal collegiate work.[5]

Just as he was getting started, Beadie found out that his father had died, and he was given permission to return home to be with his family. After the funeral, he talked with his uncle George, the Waco physician, and told him about his desire to be a doctor. His uncle then lifted the young man's spirits by inviting him to share his practice upon completion of his medical education. During a depressing time in his life, Conner recalled, "I was more determined than ever to succeed."[6]

Conner worked hard during these college-prep years, both in and out of the classroom. He remembered spending a lot of time at night playing the drums to help pay for his schooling. Bennett Hall had a curfew, but he established a regular routine of sneaking out on certain nights, picking up his drums at an outside spot where he had left them earlier, heading off to perform, and then returning to the dorm late in the evening through a first-floor window that he had prearranged with someone to leave open. During the summers, Conner would come home to Texarkana and reopen his clean-and-press store to earn money for the next school year. Entering his third year at Fisk Academic School, Conner believed that he had caught up to the other students academically. Although playing music at night cut into his studying time, he completed his academic work. After a hometown friend contacted him about a job opportunity, Conner spent the next summer in Detroit, Michigan, playing music at night with his pal in a hotel lounge. During the day, he made extra money shining shoes, selling newspapers, and working as a porter at a private hospital.[7]

With enough money earned to pay for his school year, Conner returned to Nashville to begin his first year at Fisk University. He also formed a nine-piece band called Beadie Conner and His Tennesseans, which could be broken down to a six-piece ensemble for smaller club dates under the name Beadie Conner and His Harmoniacs. They received some local airplay in Nashville and during the summer traveled as far east as New Jersey. Among the members of Conner's band was the future great jazz orchestra leader Jimmie Lunceford (who played saxophone, trombone, and guitar for the group) as well as legendary saxophonist Willie Smith and piano player Edwin Wilcox, who both later received notoriety in Lunceford's ensemble. While music historians have discussed Lunceford's beginnings as a bandleader upon his graduation from Fisk, none have written extensively about his early days at Fisk with Conner's band. In a well-received recent biography, for example, music journalist Eddy Determeyer makes passing reference to Lunceford's campus-band days, noting that Smith and Wilcox were members, and mentions their travel to New Jersey, but the author simply assumed that Lunceford, rather than Conner, was the group's leader. Conner wrote clearly about their roles in his autobiography: "Jimmy trained many of the members of the band; however, I led the band from my drums while we played. I'd asked Jimmy if he wanted to lead the band, but Jimmy said if he ever led a band it would be his own, so I led it. Jimmy's dream of wanting to lead his own band eventually came true. The band was composed of many of the same members that were in my band."[8]

At the end of Conner's first year at Fisk University, Jimmie's girlfriend, Yolande DuBois (daughter of the famed civil rights leader W. E. B. DuBois and a Fisk student), invited Lunceford and Conner to spend the summer in New York City. They accepted, hoping to make enough money playing music to return to Fisk in the fall. The two buddies arrived at the train station looking like "two country bumpkins," Conner recalled. The taller Jimmie wore a cap and an old army coat cut off and dyed black, carrying two instruments, while the much-shorter Beadie wore a velour hat and a chinchilla coat, struggling to haul a bass drum under one arm and a big case of musical equipment under the other. The pair checked in at a local YMCA, then hit the streets of Harlem looking for work. Eventually, Conner and Lunceford found promoter Deacon Johnson, who arranged many gigs for them.[9]

The two friends did not return to Fisk in the fall as planned because of a student strike that shut down the institution for an entire school year. The strike came as the result of a commencement speech delivered to the class of 1924 by W. E. B. DuBois that was highly critical of the school's white president, Fayette McKenzie, for censoring the school newspaper and student council, stifling student speech, and demanding a rigid dress code. Conner and Lunceford decided to apply for admission to the City College of New York. Once admitted, Conner continued the traditional work pattern he established at Fisk—playing music half the night, studying the other half, and going to class at 8 a.m. while trying to find some sleep during the afternoon before starting it all over again.[10]

Conner returned to Fisk the next year, continued playing music, and graduated after the 1926 spring quarter. The accomplishment filled him with pride. He was also elated because he had been accepted into Nashville's prominent Meharry Medical College. Most of all, he had fallen in love with a young lady named Willie Ruel Kneeland, the "love of his life," whose family members were patients of his uncle George as well as fellow parishioners at the New Hope Baptist Church in Waco. George Conner served as the church's longtime orchestra leader while numerous members of the Kneeland family played in the group. Beadie first met Willie Ruel on a trip to Waco to visit his uncle, and the two began to correspond. Whenever he went home to Texarkana, Beadie always took a trip to Waco to visit Willie Ruel, who he admired as a beautiful, well-educated woman from a respected family (her father, Emanuel Kneeland, was a local blacksmith who played violin in the church orchestra). During that summer of 1926, he asked Willie Ruel to marry him, and she accepted. They were soon married by the local judge and returned together to Nashville.[11]

Beadie Conner was about to receive medical training from an institution with a fine academic reputation. Founded in 1876 as the medical department of Central Tennessee College through financial aid provided by a Scots-Irish immigrant named Samuel Meharry and the Methodist Church, Meharry Medical College was the first school established in the South to train black medical professionals. Thirteen other colleges in the North and South, with varying degrees of competency and success, also emerged after the Civil War to provide medical education for African Americans, but only Meharry and Howard University's College of Medicine in Washington, DC, existed by 1920.[12]

When the Conners returned to Nashville, the young couple rented a five-room brick house near the Meharry campus and tried to get by with scanty resources. Beadie rented some furniture to make the bedroom look nice, but in the kitchen, he had to nail some orange crates to the wall for cabinets to hold the dishes he had bought at a five-and-dime store, used a large wooden box with legs on it for a dining room table, made stools from barrels using handmade cushions for the seats, and purchased a cheap secondhand gas stove for cooking. Willie Ruel's reaction to all this is unknown, but Beadie wrote blissfully of these early days at Meharry, commenting how he would be late for class because he would just "hang around the house looking at my beautiful bride."[13]

Conner wrote in his autobiography that during his second year at Meharry (1928), "my wife suddenly developed a craving for shrimp, and I had to do everything but beg, borrow, or steal to get it." Indeed, Willie Ruel was pregnant. She was sent home to Waco to be properly cared for by her family and delivered by George Conner. While the birth was taking place, one of Willie Ruel's sisters overheard Dr. Conner say that the child's head was bald. Overly excited, she called Beadie to tell him that he was the father of a baby boy. Shortly thereafter, however, he received another call with the correction—the baby was, indeed, a girl, Beadie and Willie Ruel's only child, who they named Georgia.[14]

In May 1930, Conner graduated from Meharry and crammed for the state medical board examinations. After a grueling two days of tests, he eagerly awaited the results and eventually found out that he had passed. He then made preparations to begin a yearlong internship at Kansas City General Hospital #2 (a new facility constructed to serve the city's African American population) and arranged to have Willie Ruel and Georgia stay with family in Waco. Conner sold his musical instruments for a mere $25 to have enough fare for the train ride to Kansas City. "As I looked at those drums," he wrote, "I cried because I realized that this would mark the end of my musical career. I tapped on the drums slowly just to hear that sound for the last time. I never played the drums again, dedicating my life to medicine, though I still loved music."[15]

By 1930, internships had become a standard element of American medical education. But while more than enough internships were available for white doctors, black doctors had far fewer opportunities. Excluded from white hospitals in the South, many young black doctors found that all-black hospitals in the North and South also refused to offer hospital training to them. A survey of over a thousand Southern black physicians conducted by Carter Woodson between 1928 and 1934 found that only 60 percent had been able to serve an internship, thus Conner must have impressed his teachers and administrators to receive the benefit of this important aspect of postgraduate education that was denied to many others.[16]

While in Kansas City, Conner had a routine of working very hard all day, coming home to take a bath, and then dressing well and hanging out with the cab drivers on Vine Street until midnight. He would return to the hospital to check with the nurses concerning patients and then study a bit before going to bed. On some nights, he made a point of going out and listening to the Bennie Moten Orchestra and remembered listening to a young Count Basie playing the piano. Saturday nights at the emergency room proved to be the true testing time of his medical education. The young doctor grew up fast, learning to make split-second decisions and taking responsibility for his actions as he dealt with an array of drunks, attempted suicides, accidents of all kinds, and critically ill patients seeking relief.[17]

During his internship, Conner corresponded frequently with his uncle George. Though George Conner painted a gloomy economic picture in Waco due to the arrival of the Great Depression, Beadie asserted strongly that he still wished to come. When he arrived, the two doctors hammered out an arrangement. Beadie would rent an office next to his uncle's for $25 per month, they would share a common lobby and reception-ist, and Beadie could borrow his uncle's examination and treatment rooms when not in use. This aid from George Conner was indispensable. Indeed, inadequate funds for the establishment of a functioning office with proper medical equipment proved to be among the most salient difficulties for young black doctors wishing to start a practice. He was about to become one of only 205 black physicians in the entire state. By com-parison, there were 5,892 white doctors practicing in Texas at the time.[18]

Beadie Conner had high hopes when he arrived to set up his first medical practice in his wife's hometown. African Americans made up approximately one-quarter of Waco's 52,848 residents. Race relations remained strained in the aftermath of a series of well-publicized lynchings of black men by white mobs during the first quarter of the twentieth century. With segregation firmly entrenched, African American social and economic life centered around Bridge Street and adjacent avenues between the Brazos River and the Waco City Hall. In this section of town, many doctors, such as George Conner, along with dentists, lawyers, pharmacists, barbers, grocers, hotelkeepers, restaurateurs, theater owners, and other members of the black professional middle class thrived while providing valuable services to the local community. Beadie's uncle's office was housed in the three-story Conner and Willis Building located at 131 South Second Street, which the elder doctor had purchased as a business investment.[19]

Conner wrote in his memoirs that he was very excited to get started but "nearly starved to death." Many potential patients decided to forego formal medical attention during the Depression, preferring instead to self-medicate or visit folk healers. The town's ten black doctors also had to compete with Waco's numerous white doctors. Many African Americans gave white physicians their business because they believed that the white doctors had better training and possessed superior equipment and facilities than their black counterparts. Despite the persistence of segregation, many white doctors readily took on black patients who could pay on the spot and were willing to accept the indignity of segregated waiting rooms and being seen after all white patients had been attended. When some patients finally did arrive at the Conner's office, Beadie discovered that they usually wished to see his uncle, who had years of experience and was well trusted among Waco's black community. As he wrote of his early woes, "I sat in my office just above Second and Franklin Streets and looked down in disgust so many times. I was hungry, depressed, and broken-hearted, and wondered when I would ever get a break." With his pride hurt, he would eat at the home of his uncle and his second wife, the accomplished extension service agent Jeffie Conner, who came to see Beadie as a burden to her husband. Meanwhile, his wife's family, the Kneelands, did what they could to help the young couple get by.[20]

Dr. Conner's career really took off once he became mobile. A local car dealer allowed him, through his uncle's good credit, to borrow a used car to make house calls. This opportunity greatly expanded his ability to practice medicine in Waco, plus, as Conner stated, "When I drove away from the office, I looked and acted like a doctor." He drove all over town, servicing impoverished citizens and places of ill repute where his uncle and other local physicians refused to go. The young doctor contacted the local health department to let them know that he was available for emergency and night calls. During the cotton-growing season, he also made visits to the nearby town of Mart, located fifteen miles away. While not thriving, Conner was able to make ends meet for the first time.[21]

Conner's fortunes turned for the better again when his uncle introduced him to an old friend, a Methodist minister from Cameron, Texas, who invited Beadie to come to his town and practice medicine there. African American leaders in the rural South like the minister often used their contacts to recruit medical practitioners for their isolated and neglected communities. The preacher told Conner that he would receive a lot of business because the black residents in Cameron and the surrounding area were in desperate need of a physician. Conner jumped at the opportunity, so the minister and his wife made arrangements for the young doctor to set up an office in a small frame building that they owned. Leaving his wife and Georgia in Waco until he was established, Conner brought his belongings and lodged with a local teacher and her husband. The next day, he went to check out his office. On his way, he encountered a man named Joe hanging outside a beer joint and asked him if he wanted to make a few bucks helping him out. The man agreed, and the two cleaned up the place, used some old furniture, created some make-shift furniture of their own, and borrowed some linen from his landlady to finish the setup. Joe agreed to stay on for a while as the receptionist.[22]

Conner remained in Cameron for the next seven years, serving as the town's only black physician while also servicing African American residents within a twenty-mile radius. For mobility, he financed an old Dodge Coupe that would frequently get its tires beat up on the poor country roads. As he became well known in the community, Conner's practice grew exponentially. Soon, he was able to exchange the Dodge for a nice Model A Ford Coupe and proudly returned to Waco to receive accolades from his family and retrieve his wife and daughter. He eventually bought a home in Waco and had it torn down, with the lumber sent to Cameron to be rebuilt on a plot of land that he purchased outside of town. This house would serve as his new home as well as his office. In the midst of the Great Depression, Beadie Conner was finally successful and justifiably proud that his hard work and perseverance were paying off. As George Conner reported to his wife in early 1936 concerning his nephew's progress, "Beadie has a very nice situation. I think he is to be commended for what he has done in less than 5 yrs."[23]

Conner wrote approvingly of his time as a country doctor in Cameron. Some of the stories that he related are somewhat comical, such as his reaction to being paid in chickens so often by his impoverished patients for services rendered. Another time, he tended to an escaped horse that had been hit by a car on the road near his home. After quickly stabilizing the animal's broken leg with bandages and splints, Conner's "first lesson and last attempt at veterinary medicine" ended when the stable owner arrived on the scene, assessed the situation, and then took out a revolver and shot the horse in the head to put it out of its misery.[24]

Conner also devoted four pages of his autobiography to describe an episode that he considered the worst experience of his entire medical career. One night, he was awakened at 2 a.m. to deliver a child for a nineteen-year-old woman in labor who had received no prenatal care. She lived with her husband in a dilapidated, roach-infested shack outside of town. The child was a breach, coming out feetfirst, and it was too late to try to turn it around. One leg came out fine, then the other, then the buttocks, abdomen, and upper torso. But the child's head was too big to come through the woman's pelvis. The husband tried to comfort his wife, who was in agony. Conner remembered the man looking at him desperately with hope and despair in his eyes. "I was his salvation and he had total faith in me," Conner wrote. "I did not want to fail him nor his wife, but I felt the head and knew it was too large for the small pelvis. . . . I tried and tried and with tears in my eyes I tried, but I was unable to deliver the head past the pelvis. I prayed to God to please let me deliver this child, but I was unable to do it." Conner bemoaned the state of health care at the time, noting that the patient should have been hospitalized, and when it was recognized that she had an abnormally small pelvis, a simple Caesarean section could have been performed when the time came to deliver the baby. But "this was not the case," he wrote, "and I had done all I could do." The child lay lifeless between the legs of her mother, who continued to bleed, so Conner told the husband they had to focus on saving his wife, but they needed help. He hopped into his car and sped to the house of a white physician who lived nearby, pounded on the door, and quickly explained the situation. The doctor got his bag and jumped into the auto. After arriving back at the shack, it took two hours for the doctors to finally extract the lifeless child completely from the woman's body, but she was dead by then too. The husband lay across his wife's body crying uncontrollably and begging God not to take her from him. Conner wrote that it was one of the most horrifying events of his entire life, and fifty years later, he would still wake up occasionally with nightmares from the experience.[25]

While working to improve the quality of life for the people in his community, Conner experimented with contract medicine, forming an organization called the American Benevolent Health Society that provided day care for the children of working mothers and low-cost health care for citizens who would not otherwise have access to a doctor. Running on donations from black and white residents of Cameron, the day-care facility was supervised by a local widow out of a large house across from Conner's home. To receive free doctor's visits and necessary medications under the health care plan, each family was asked to pay one dollar to join and fifty cents per month. Often receiving canned food as payment, Conner would exchange them for cash at one of the black-owned grocery stores in town. He also coordinated with the state health department to sponsor health education programs of various types. Though most medical groups at the time (including the American Medical Association) denounced contract medicine as socialism, many Southern black doctors used various forms of the system to stabilize their incomes while providing health services to their communities. Conner estimated that close to a thousand members eventually benefited from the society's efforts.[26]

In 1937, Conner received a call one day from Dr. Charles Henry Christian, an old friend of his uncle who informed him that he wanted to retire and wished that Beadie would take over his practice in Austin. Despite flourishing in Cameron, Conner thought seriously about the offer. Though he and his family had strong community ties, he believed that Austin would provide enormous opportunities for growth and culture for his wife and especially his bright and beautiful daughter, Georgia, who was now ten years old. After discussing the possibilities with his wife, they decided to make the move.[27]

Beadie Conner and his family arrived at a noteworthy time in the history of Austin's African American community. Until the 1930s, Austin's black population resided in many different neighborhoods scattered around town and also in various freedmen's colonies established on the outskirts of the city limits. In 1928, the city council accepted a master plan developed by a consulting firm that called for numerous ways to make Austin more efficient. Included among its recommendations for better schools, additional parks, and infrastructure improvements was the goal of inducing black citizens to reside primarily in the east side of town, where many African Americans already dwelled. The report stated that Austin would avoid the extra expenses caused by the duplication of schools, parks, and other facilities that segregation required. Upon approving the plan, the Austin City Council began implementation of its many features during the 1930s. Deed restrictions prohibiting blacks from buying or renting property, coupled with the ending of public services to African Americans, except in East Austin, forced most to gravitate to the four existing black neighborhoods there. These actions also contributed to the decline of the area's remaining freedman's colonies. By the 1930s, 80 percent of the city's African American population lived in the East Austin enclave.[28]

As Bridge Street served for Waco, East Austin's commercial district along East Sixth Street became the social and economic anchor for the town's African American community. A 1936 survey revealed that the area boasted five tire stores, six service stations, seven garages, nine tailoring establishments, three cobblers, two furniture repair shops, two blacksmith shops, two meat markets, seventeen grocery stores, three vegetable stands, a fish market, sixteen cafes, a creamery, two boarding houses, a hotel, three drugstores, a lumber yard, a theater, a print shop, three funeral homes, ten insurance-agent offices, a loan agency, two real estate–agent offices, ten beauty shops, and a beauty college. Dr. Christian's office, which Conner took over, was located at 607 San Jacinto Street, in the heart of this gathering of black-owned businesses. After much cajoling, he convinced the retiring doctor's longtime receptionist to stay and work for him. Her experience and sage advice greatly helped him acclimate not only to his clients but also to the greater neighborhood. Conner became one of only three black physicians to serve East Austin in the late 1930s.[29]

The Conner family settled in nicely to life in East Austin, eventually acquiring a modest two-bedroom home in the new McKinley Heights subdivision on East Thirteenth Street that had a large horseshoe-shaped driveway; a big backyard with floodlights, picnic tables, and a built-in barbeque to entertain guests; large oak trees, and a nice stone fence encircling the entire property. While Conner worked at the office, Willie Ruel took care of the home and helped to supplement young Georgia's schooling by tutoring her from books that the couple acquired to form a solid library for their child. The doctor enjoyed nothing more than coming home from a long day of work to kiss his wife and listen to Georgia relate to him what she learned about various topics that day.[30]

Conner's home not only served as a haven from the rigors of the work week but also became an important meeting place for the town's African American elite, of which the doctor was a member by virtue of his education, profession, and desire to work with Austin's black leaders for the benefit of the community. Conner developed a strong relationship with Rev. Karl Downs, the president of East Austin's Samuel Huston (now Huston-Tillotson) College and hosted honored guests of the school at his home since there were no nice public places in Austin where African Americans were allowed to meet. Over time, the list of guests attending soirees at the Conner home would include W. E. B. DuBois, Langston Hughes, Adam Clayton Powell, and (most proudly of all to the ex-musician Conner) Duke Ellington, who entertained the guests one evening by playing songs on Georgia's piano, including a new tune he had been working on, the future hit "Satin Doll."[31]

In 1947, Huston College invited Jimmie Lunceford to perform on campus. The occasion led to a reunion between the two college friends. Before the show, Conner brought Willie Ruel and Georgia to meet the now-famous bandleader. After some reminiscing, the doctor and his family took their seats to enjoy the performance. At the intermission, Lunceford introduced his band, then told the audience about his early musical exploits with Conner while at Fisk. Conner took great offense, however, when Lunceford began to casually make jokes at his expense, including "I can't understand why a famous doctor like Dr. Conner can't afford a good shirt." During the intermission, the proud physician went backstage to express his outrage at being embarrassed in such a manner in front of his family and friends. Lunceford apologized but Conner would not accept, feeling that the musician's ego had gotten out of control. He left the concert and refused to accept Lunceford's repeated phone calls to his house. The next time Conner heard his old friend's name was a few months later, when a radio announcer reported Lunceford's sudden death while on tour in Seaside, Oregon. Conner wrote that he was very distraught that they had ended on such a sour note. Thereafter, when he thought of Jimmie, he tried to focus on the good times that they once shared together.[32]

During the early twentieth century, practicing medicine was not easy for a "black physician"—a term that Conner resented, he said, because when he passed his medical exams, he became a doctor, not a "black doctor." Though racial segregation in

Austin greatly disturbed him, at least he expected that reality, given the current social climate. What he did not foresee were divisions within the black community based on class. As experienced by other African American physicians elsewhere in the South, Conner found that many black businessmen, teachers, and ministers often preferred white doctors to treat them and members of their families, believing them to be superior—not to mention the increased status imparted by being attended to by a white doctor. Conner expressed great annoyance in his autobiography at those ministers who expected him to attend regular church services and businessmen who desired him to patronize their stores, yet they would rather suffer the indignity of slipping through the back door and sitting in a corner of a white doctor's office to wait until all the white patients were seen rather than visit Dr. Conner's clinic. Black physicians like Conner were often seen as caretakers of the poor—those who could afford to see a white doctor went to one. Such pretensions led Conner to go out of his way to help "the little guy" more—he would give extra service and consideration to those who not only needed it more but also "appreciated it the most."[33]

Another significant barrier for African American physicians was the denial of public hospital privileges. At city-owned Brackenridge Hospital, black doctors were barred from treating patients because they were not members of the local medical society. As a result of this discriminatory policy, African American doctors had to find a white physician willing to treat their patients, who often received inferior medical care at Brackenridge. In fact, the poor facilities there contributed to the death of Karl Downs in 1948. After undergoing surgery for stomach problems, possibly appendicitis, the thirty-five-year-old minister and college president experienced complications that were ignored by the attending white physician who performed the operation. Rather than leaving Downs in the recovery room for observation, the doctor sent him back to the segregated ward in the basement, where he died. In a 1984 interview with Anthony Orum, Conner stated that Downs's death profoundly affected those who knew him and that believed he would have survived if he had access to the emergency-room resources and postoperative care reserved for white patients. Jackie Robinson was among those who mourned Downs and became outraged at the circumstances of his untimely death. The future baseball great had been counseled by the minister years earlier, while they both lived in Pasadena, California, and Robinson spent some time in early 1945 repaying Downs by agreeing to teach physical education at Huston College. News of Downs's death filled Robinson with an even greater desire to bring down the Jim Crow system.[34]

In 1940, Father Francis Weber of the Holy Cross Church had founded Austin's first independent hospital when he helped organize the use of a long barracks-like structure that accepted doctors and patients of all races. Never fireproofed, the building failed to meet local code requirements as a full hospital, thus service was limited to a small number of patients on a temporary basis—a forty-bed facility for twenty-five thousand black residents of Austin. Later in the decade, Father Weber made a concerted effort to build a new Holy Cross Hospital and enlisted the help of community leaders such as Beadie Conner. A fundraising campaign that included the use of money jars placed at various businesses around East Austin produced enough money to purchase the land, but a sizeable sum was still needed to build the hospital itself.[35]

Fortunately, 1948 was an election year, and Congressman Lyndon Baines Johnson, then a candidate for the US Senate, was looking for friends. Conner and Johnson had first met in 1937 when Johnson successfully ran for his US House seat in a special election to replace the recently deceased Representative James P. Buchanan. Though blacks were systematically excluded from voting in Democratic Party primary elections by virtue of the state's "white primary" law, this barrier did not apply to nonpartisan elections. In a secret meeting held one morning in the basement of the Huston College administration building, Johnson spoke with Conner, local school principal Friendly Rice, and other local black leaders to solicit their support, promising to work on their behalf if elected.[36]

Because the Supreme Court had invalidated the Texas white primary law in the 1944 *Smith v. Allwright* case, blacks capable of paying their poll taxes were legally allowed to vote in the 1948 Democratic primary election for the US Senate seat that Johnson coveted. Remembering Johnson's pledges to help East Austin's residents and correctly surmising that the congressman desired their votes, Conner called Johnson at his home in Washington, DC. Lady Bird Johnson answered the phone and told him that her husband was not available but that he would get the message. When the congressman called him back, Conner explained the situation about the need for a hospital, and Johnson agreed to help. The Beadie Conner Papers, as well as the Lyndon Johnson Presidential Library, house the resulting correspondence detailing the cooperation between Conner, Johnson, the congressman's staff, and the Texas State Department of Health to acquire federal funds for the project. Johnson eventually secured $164,000 in federal dollars through the Hill-Burton Hospital Construction Act of 1946 for a new Holy Cross Hospital, which formally opened on January 7, 1951. Thereafter, Johnson had also secured Conner's gratitude and undying political support.[37]

In 1951, Conner began a long formal association with Samuel Huston College when he became the school's staff physician. For twenty-six years, he worked a couple of days per week at the college, primarily administering physical examinations to the students. The job allowed the doctor to garner additional income while also providing a valuable service to the college.[38]

Since the 1940s, Conner helped the community by leading various efforts to promote economic independence for residents of East Austin. As he wrote, "I felt there were four pillars of foundation which would establish blacks as free and independent people. They were religion, education, economic security, and political influence. In religion and education, I felt we had made great strides, but in the areas of politics and economic security, we were lagging behind considerably. Indeed, it was not possible to establish political influence without a strong economic base and therefore all efforts were made to provide this foundation."[39]

To these ends, in 1940, Conner with other local businessmen cofounded the Austin Negro Chamber of Commerce. Six years later, he created the Young Men's Business Club to acquaint youthful members of the community with principles of entrepreneurship by holding meetings with local businessmen and inviting guest speakers to share their knowledge with the group. In 1952, he worked with other local leaders to attempt to create a credit union in order to provide assistance to low-income members, but the group's charter application was rejected by the Federal Security Agency's Bureau of Federal Credit Unions. A later attempt to consolidate Austin's sixty-three black-owned cabs failed to draw enough interest to be successful.[40]

Conner's autobiography unfortunately ends abruptly at this point in his life's story. Nevertheless, rough drafts of some proposed later chapters, other documents in the Beadie Conner Papers, family oral history, and additional outside sources enable a basic retelling of some important accomplishments during the doctor's later years. During the 1950s, for example, we know that Conner's personal life fluctuated from times of great joy to despair. On the positive side, he took great pride in his daughter going off to college at age fifteen and becoming the first black graduate of New York's Nazareth College. Georgia later worked for a time at Howard University's College of Medicine as a lab technician under the direction of the famous African American doctor Charles Drew before returning to Austin and marrying Theodore Roosevelt Youngblood Jr., an optometrist with whom she would have seven children. Conner wrote nothing in his autobiography, however, about the death of his wife, Willie Ruel, from colon cancer in 1956, perhaps it being too painful a subject to address. Nor did he discuss his brief and unhappy second marriage to the well-known Austin physician Connie Yerwood Conner, a Meharry graduate who gained notoriety as the first African American doctor to work for the Texas Department of Health, serving as a consultant in setting up health clinics offering well-baby clinics and prenatal care to the rural poor of Texas and later as director of maternal and child health services. Conner only mentioned her once in his autobiography, briefly stating that he initially met her in Cameron while she was setting up a rural health-education program for local residents. The only other reference to Dr. Yerwood in the Beadie Conner Papers is a copy of the couple's 1963 Travis County District Court divorce decree.[41]

Despite these personal lows, Conner continued to be active in East Austin community life and to push for social change. Having been denied admittance to local, state, and national medical societies on racial grounds, Conner had become actively involved in the associations organized by black medical professionals for members of their race, including the Southwest Medical Society, the Lone Star State Medical Association, and the National Medical Association. While these groups allowed him to share knowledge and common grievances with other black physicians, Conner desired to tear down the racial barriers that divided the medical profession. Pressure exerted by Conner and sympathetic white doctors and administrators at Brackenridge Hospital (including Dr. Zachary T. Scott, chief of the hospital's medical staff) ultimately led to black physicians serving as members of the facility's professional staff, with Conner becoming the first African American doctor to perform surgery on his own patients there. In 1955, delegates at the Texas Medical Association (TMA) annual meeting voted 102–32 to begin admitting black doctors. Conner became one of the TMA's first African American members when he joined the organization in April 1957.[42]

Regarding race relations outside of the medical profession, Beadie Conner possessed strong feelings against the existing racial prejudice and worked with other established African American leaders in Austin to foment change. In raw notes that he jotted down for a potential chapter in his autobiography, Conner remembered an incident back in 1937 when he first arrived in Austin. Standing on the corner of Congress Avenue and Sixth Street, he found himself urgently in need of using a restroom, yet knew that he would have to walk about five blocks to use a poorly maintained and unsanitary facility at the Santa Fe Railroad Station rather than simply crossing the street to use the bathroom at the Woolworth's. "It was humiliating, bad, and discouraging to think that in this modern day men of all races, nationalities, and religious creeds could not sit down and eat together or use a common restroom," he recalled. "Man was born to be free. He was born with a heart, soul, and mind, and he will never allow anyone to forever crush him."[43]

Never a publicity seeker, most of Conner's efforts to bring down public segregation in Austin appear to have been done quietly and behind the scenes—the preferred approach for many older black urban professionals in the South.[44] Nevertheless, his name appeared in a March 1, 1960, issue of the Austin *American Statesman* as a member of a delegation appearing at a Travis County Commissioners Court meeting demanding that the commissioners remove the signs designating "Negro restrooms" that still remained in the courthouse building even though it had been previously decided that any vestiges of segregated facilities there were supposed to be removed after the building's remodeling. The commissioners agreed to the delegation's request, and the signs, which had been left over from a nonrenovated portion of the building, finally came down.[45]

Conner continued to treat patients in East Austin until October 1978, when he finally decided to retire at age seventy-six. Huston-Tillotson College hosted a banquet to honor the doctor with numerous tributes and presentations from, among others, Mayor Carole Keeton McClellan (now Strayhorn), Huston-Tillotson Pres. John Q. Taylor King, Conner's pastor at the Ebenezer Baptist Church (Rev. Marvin C. Griffin), and his daughter, Georgia.[46]

Over the next fifteen years of his retirement, Conner relaxed by working on his autobiography, visiting Meharry to receive his fifty-year service award, enjoying visits by his daughter and grandchildren, and travelling once to Europe with his grandson Kneeland. He gave occasional interviews to local newspapers, reflecting on his arrival in Austin, the efforts to overcome racial barriers, and the improved state of race relations taking place in his adopted city. "I've seen remarkable changes for

black doctors and all doctors in Austin. Greater opportunities [and] better facilities,"
he stated in 1978. "The South is becoming the mecca of industry [and] residential
development—the climate is fine, and we don't have all the problems we used to have,
thanks to Martin Luther King and his white and black friends." In another interview,
he proudly proclaimed, "I've seen the day when black doctors have been presidents
of the hospital staff and heads of departments at Brackenridge—the same hospital
where they wouldn't let me attend staff meetings."[47]

The retired doctor wrote down similar positive reflections on what he termed
the *New Austin* in notes found among his personal papers: "The race relations in our
city have much improved for all. We are pleased with its progress. Let us not forget
the sacrifice, humiliation, and bravery of the Freedom Fighters during the Martin
Luther King Era . . . and the cooperation of Christian white leaders and workers
[who] helped to fight for justice and equality for all. Their efforts and dedication
will never be forgotten." Conner also characteristically noted that there was still
work to be done and that renewed dedication would be required to meet the challenges ahead: "Minorities are behind and it is hard to catch up after being deprived
for many years. That, however, is not an excuse. . . . Minorities are behind and must
work twice as hard to keep up and in time, catch up. It can be done; it must be done;
and it will be done. . . . Remember, with hard work your day will come and your
satisfaction will be victory."[48]

When he died on August 28, 1994, at the age of ninety-two, Beadie Eugene Conner left many important legacies. To his family, he instilled the benefits of hard work
and the value of education, which he passed on to Georgia. As she excelled in college,
so did every one of her seven children, many graduating with advanced degrees in
medicine and the law. All of her college-aged grandchildren currently attend top
universities across the country. Doctor Conner also contributed valuable services to
every community of which he was a member, leaving all of them much better places
than when he arrived. His story is a testament to his drive for personal success as
well as a desire to contribute to smashing barriers that held back all black physicians
in Texas during the Jim Crow era. In addition, though the system of public segregation allowed Conner and other black professionals to carve a niche for themselves
as an elite class by virtue of their education, occupation, and wealth relative to the
majority of African Americans, he nevertheless demanded equality for all citizens as a
basic right. When interviewed once by his grandson Kneeland about how he wished to
be remembered, Conner first said simply that he "didn't care about that stuff." But when
pressed for an answer, he finally said humbly that he was just an ordinary man trying to
provide for his family and give back to his people. Beadie Conner was certainly more
than just an ordinary man—and without a doubt, he lived an extraordinary life.[49]

Keith Volanto wished to thank his brother-in-law, Kneeland Youngblood, a
grandson of Beadie Conner, for his generosity in making his grandfather's personal
papers available for viewing. He also thanks his wife, Theresa Youngblood, and
his sister-in-law, Julie Youngblood, for their invaluable assistance. The author is

also grateful to Betsy Tyson of the Texas Medical Association Archives and Geoff Hunt at the Texas Collection, Baylor University, for their additional help with this project.

The memoirs (cited hereafter as "Conner Autobiography"), along with Beadie Conner's other preserved records (cited hereafter as the "Beadie Conner Papers"), are in the possession of Kneeland Youngblood.

This article was originally published as Volanto, Keith. "The Life and Work of Dr. Beadie Eugene Conner: An African American Physician in Jim Crow Texas." Southwestern Historical Quarterly 115, no. 3 (January 2012): 259–80. Reprinted by permission of the author and the editor of the Southwestern Historical Quarterly.

NOTES

1. The memoirs (cited hereafter as Conner Autobiography), along with Beadie Conner's other preserved records (cited hereafter as the Beadie Conner Papers), are in the possession of Kneeland Youngblood, one of Dr. Conner's grandsons and the brother-in-law of the author.

2. Biographical Records Folder, George Sherman Conner Papers, Texas Collection, Baylor University, Waco, Texas (cited hereafter as George S. Conner Papers); 1840, 1850, 1860, and 1870 US Census for Blount County, Tennessee; Virginia Lee Spurlin, "The Conners of Waco: Black Professionals in Twentieth-Century Texas" (PhD diss., Texas Tech University, 1991), 7–8, 11–13. Rachel Conner later moved to Waco to live near her son George before her death in 1913. She is buried next to George in Greenwood Cemetery.

3. Conner Autobiography, 6–7 (quotation). The 1900 US Census for Lafayette County, Arkansas, lists David Conner as living with his children on a rented farm near the township of Boyd before his second marriage. Queen Fowler Newlin is enumerated

in the 1900 US Census for Hempstead County, Arkansas. Though Queen had worked as a school teacher in the past, she is listed as a "washerwoman" living in Hope with her children and widowed mother. The census taker also listed her as a divorcée. Despite the additional children coming from her new marriage, Queen must have been especially delighted to have twins—her previous delivery had been twin boys named Miles and Giles. When Giles was a year old, he died from falling into a fireplace. Maude Conner (niece) to Beadie Conner, undated letter, Beadie Conner Papers.

4. Conner Autobiography, 7–8. The 1910 US Census for Little River County, Arkansas, enumerates the Smith family, with seven-year-old Maceo listed as "Macy." For information on Texarkana's economic growth during the early twentieth century, see Walter L. Buenger, *The Path to a Modern South: Northeast Texas between Reconstruction and the Great Depression* (Austin: University of Texas Press, 2004), 43–44, 136–37.

5. Conner Autobiography, 8–18 (quotation); Application for Admission

to Fisk University, July 20, 1919, Beadie
Conner Papers. For information on
the founding and development of Fisk,
see Joe M. Richardson, *A History of
Fisk University, 1865–1946* (Tuscaloosa:
University of Alabama Press, 2002).

6. Conner Autobiography, 19–20
(quotation). Though Conner recalled
that his father died during his second
year at Fisk (which would have been
1920), official Texas state records show
that David Alexander Conner died in
Bowie County on October 26, 1919;
Texas Department of Health, *Texas
Death Indexes, 1903–2000*, Austin,
Texas. Beatrice Conner also confirmed
that her father died in 1919. Transcript
of Oral Interview with Beadie and
Beatrice Conner, Beadie Conner
Papers.

7. Conner Autobiography, 20, 25–28.

8. Ibid., 29–31; Eddy Determeyer, *Rhythm
Is Our Business: Jimmie Lunceford
and the Harlem Express* (Ann Arbor:
University of Michigan Press, 2008),
24. In a 1985 book, music historian
John Chilton includes a reference to
Willie Smith playing with the "Beaty
Conner Quartet" during a summer
vacation tour in Belmar, New Jersey.
John Chilton, *Who's Who of Jazz:
Storyville to Swing Street*, 4th ed. (New
York: Da Capo Press, 1985), 312.

9. Conner Autobiography, 31–34. For
W. E. B. DuBois's negative opinion of
Lunceford, see David Levering Lewis,
*W. E. B. DuBois: The Fight for Equality
and the American Century, 1919–1963*
(New York: Henry Holt, 2000),
107–8, 222.

10. Conner Autobiography, 35. Conner
found it hard to compete with the
other students, who did not work
into the late hours and only studied.
Nevertheless, his school transcripts

show that he passed every course.
Transcript of Record for Beadie E.
Conner, The College of the City of
New York, and Official Transcript of
the Record of Beadie Eugene Conner,
Fisk University, both in the Beadie
Conner Papers. For a discussion of the
student revolt at Fisk, see Richardson,
Fisk University, ch. 7.

11. Conner Autobiography, 38. The United
States Fourteenth Census (1920s) for
McLennan County listed Emanuel
Kneeland as a fifty-eight-year-old
homeowner living with his fifty-one-
year-old wife, Josephine; his twenty-
five-year-old daughter, Susie (a music
teacher who had attended Fisk); and
Willie Ruel. Though the census listed
Willie Ruel as being eighteen years old,
the 1900 census placed her at three, and
the 1910 census stated she was thirteen.
Thus Willie Ruel was probably twenty-
three years old in 1920 and, therefore,
twenty-nine when she married twenty-
four-year-old Beadie in 1926.

12. For information on the founding and
development of Meharry, see James
Summerville, *Educating Black Doctors:
A History of Meharry Medical College*
(Tuscaloosa: University of Alabama
Press, 1983). During the Progressive
Era, a demand for increased
professionalization of the medical
community placed public attention on
the standards of the nation's medical
colleges. Officials with the American
Medical Association (AMA) asked
the Carnegie Foundation to produce
an independent survey of American
and Canadian medical schools to
identify quality programs worthy
of preservation and incompetent
programs in need of discontinuation.
The Carnegie Foundation turned
to educator Abraham Flexner, who

visited more than 150 schools to assess their facilities, academic standards, and quality of faculty and graduates. In 1910, Flexner issued his report *Medical Education in the United States and Canada*, which questioned the value of many American medical schools. Of the country's seven black medical colleges still in existence by 1910, only Meharry and Howard University's College of Medicine in Washington, DC, earned an *A* rating. In the years before widespread public aid to educational institutions, the report's conclusions led to the quick evaporation of philanthropic contributions to the five other black schools, as AMA leaders desired should occur for those schools failing to receive Flexner's approval. For detailed coverage on the rise and fall of black medical colleges from the Reconstruction years through the Progressive Era, see Thomas J. Ward Jr., *Black Physicians in the Jim Crow South* (Fayetteville: University of Arkansas Press, 2003), ch. 1.

13. Conner Autobiography, 38–39.

14. Ibid., 45.

15. Ibid., 46–47 (quotation). In 1930, fifty-three of fifty-seven Meharry graduates passed their state board examinations, a definite improvement from 1910, when 42.7 percent failed. Ward, *Black Physicians*, 104; "State Board Statistics for 1930," *Journal of the American Medical Association* 96, no. 17 (April 15, 1931): 1,389.

16. For an illuminating discussion of internship opportunities for black doctors during this time period, see Ward, *Black Physicians*, 60–67.

17. Conner Autobiography, 47–49.

18. Ibid., 50; George Sherman Conner to Beadie Conner, letters dated January

21, February 28, March 27, and April 13, 1931, Beadie Conner Papers. For information on the difficulties that young black doctors often encountered while starting a practice, see Ward, *Black Physicians*, 97–120. For the statistics on the number of black and white Texas doctors in 1930, see William Joseph Brody, "The Black Texan: A Quantitative History" (PhD diss., Vanderbilt University, 1974), 100.

19. Spurlin, "Conners of Waco," 26–29, 42; US Fifteenth Census (1930) for McLennan County, Texas. For more information on the importance of the Bridge Street area to African American life in Waco, see the online exhibit maintained by Baylor University's Institute for Oral History, http://www.baylor.edu/oralhistory/index.php?id=32155, accessed September, 22, 2011. For coverage of the horrifying lynching of Jesse Washington in 1916 that long resonated in Waco's black community, see James M. SoRelle, "The 'Waco Horror': The Lynching of Jesse Washington," *Southwestern Historical Quarterly* 86 (April 1983): 517–36; and Patricia Bernstein, *The First Waco Horror: The Lynching of Jesse Washington and the Rise of the NAACP* (College Station: Texas A&M University Press, 2005).

20. Conner Autobiography, 50–52 (quotations). For an exceptional chapter-length discussion on the difficulties that African American doctors encountered in seeking to attract patients, see Ward, *Black Physicians*, 121–52. For information on Jeffie Conner, see Spurlin, "Conners of Waco"; Debra A. Reid, *Reaping a Greater Harvest: African Americans, the Extension Service, and Rural Reform in Jim Crow Texas* (College

Station: Texas A&M University Press, 2007); and Ruthe Winegarten, *Black Texas Women: 150 Years of Trial and Triumph* (Austin: University of Texas Press, 1995). In addition to allowing Beadie to share in his practice, George Conner also loaned money to help his nephew attend Fisk and/or Meharry, as evidenced by a later letter to his wife complaining about young Beadie's excuses for not yet paying him back "for money spent on his education." George S. Conner to Jeffie Conner, February 1, 1935, Correspondence—J. O. A. Conner, 1923–35, George S. Conner Papers.

21. Conner Autobiography, 52–54.

22. Ibid., 55–57. On the recruitment of doctors by African American community leaders, see Ward, *Black Physicians*, 100–106.

23. Conner Autobiography, 57–60; George S. Conner to Jeffie Conner, n.d., Correspondence—J. O. A. Conner, 1937–39, George S. Conner Papers. George Conner wrote over three hundred letters to his wife while she was on her many work trips for the Extension Service during the 1930s. The correspondence, which related valuable anecdotes to keep Jeffie Conner informed about what was happening in Waco, provide a valuable portal for viewing aspects of life in Waco's African American community at the time. Though the letter is undated, it is one of only a handful that Dr. Conner wrote to his wife in blue ink, all of which were written from December 1935 to January 1936. He also mentioned going to Cameron to see Beadie because he and his family fell ill soon after returning from a recent Christmas trip to Waco, thus the assessment of his nephew's progress

was probably written in early January 1936.

24. Conner Autobiography, 60–62.

25. Ibid., 65–68.

26. Ibid., 71–74. For a discussion of the importance of contract medicine for African American doctors during the early twentieth century, see Ward, *Black Physicians*, 138–47.

27. Conner Autobiography, 75–81.

28. David C. Humphrey, *Austin: A History of the Capital City* (Austin: Texas State Historical Association, 1987), 35–46; Michelle M. Mears, *And Grace Will Lead Me Home: African American Freedmen Communities of Austin, Texas, 1865–1928* (Lubbock: Texas Tech University Press, 2009), 137–53. East Avenue served as the traditional line of demarcation between West and East Austin. After being enlarged to accommodate heavier traffic, the thoroughfare became Interstate 35 in 1962.

29. Conner Autobiography, 77–78; J. Mason Brewer, *An Historical Outline of the Negro in Travis County* (Austin: Samuel Huston College, 1940), 58, 63, 75.

30. Conner Autobiography, 80–81.

31. Ibid., 81–84. In 1997, the National Park Service added Conner's home to the National Register of Historic Places in recognition of the home's significance to Austin's cultural heritage. Unfortunately, the house no longer exists. A duplex now sits on the site at 3111 E. Thirteenth Street.

32. Ibid., 84–86. Though Lunceford's death was announced as a heart attack, there is some evidence to suggest that a fish-restaurant owner who despised blacks poisoned the band's food after their leader demanded service at the establishment. Some of the musicians

reported feeling sick afterward, though none suffered the extreme reaction experienced by Lunceford, who was only forty-five years old at the time. See Determeyer, *Rhythm Is Our Business*, ch. 15.

33. Conner Autobiography, 100–101 (quotation); Ward, *Black Physicians*, 124–26.

34. Conner Autobiography, 92–93; Anthony M. Orum, *Power, Money, and the People: The Making of Modern Austin* (Austin: Texas Monthly Press, 1987), 190. For the impact of Karl Downs's death on Jackie Robinson, see his autobiography, *I Never Had It Made* (New York: Putnam, 1972), 82–83; and Arnold Rampersad, *Jackie Robinson: A Biography* (New York: Alfred A. Knopf, 1997), 193. For a good summary of segregated public hospitals in the South and the ultimately successful efforts to grant hospital privileges to African American doctors, see Ward, *Black Physicians*, ch. 6.

35. Conner Autobiography, 92–94; Austin *American*, January 8, 1951.

36. Conner Autobiography, 94–95. Conner later related some details about the encounter in an interview with Ronnie Dugger for the journalist's biography of Lyndon B. Johnson (LBJ). See Ronnie Dugger, *The Politician: The Life and Times of Lyndon Johnson* (New York: W. W. Norton, 1982), 197, 434n3. See also Robert A. Caro's description of the meeting in *The Years of Lyndon Johnson: The Master of the Senate* (New York: Alfred A. Knopf, 2002), 735.

37. Conner Autobiography, 95–96. LBJ to Beadie Conner, undated letter and letter dated May 4, 1948; LBJ to Norman Roberts (Director, Hospital Survey and Construction Division, Texas State Department of Public Health), May 4, 1948; May 13, 1948; Beadie Conner to Walter Jenkins (LBJ assistant), May 19, 1948; Beadie Conner to LBJ, May 29, 1948; July 3, 1948, Beadie Conner Papers as well as the Holy Cross Hospital Folder, Box 19, Lyndon Baines Johnson Archives, Lyndon Baines Johnson Presidential Library, Austin, Texas. For an excellent study of Johnson's efforts to woo Texas black leaders during the 1948 election, which includes a discussion of Conner's dealings with Johnson, see Patrick Cox, "'Nearly a Statesman': LBJ and Texas Blacks in the 1948 Election," *Social Science Quarterly* 74, no. 2 (June 1993): 241–63.

38. In 1995, Huston-Tillotson University renamed a renovated two-story wooden frame building "Conner-Washington Hall" in honor of the distinguished service that Conner and Dr. M. J. Washington provided the school. *Huston-Tillotson University Fact Book 2009–2010* (Austin: Huston-Tillotson University Office of Institutional Research and Assessment, 2010), 69–70.

39. Conner Autobiography, 102–3.

40. Ibid., 103–7; Buford B. Lankford (Regional Representative, Bureau of Federal Credit Unions) to Dr. B. E. Conner, March 26, 1953, Beadie Conner Papers.

41. *B. E. Conner v. Connie Conner*, Case No. 129,109, 126th Judicial District, Court of Travis County, Texas. For short descriptions of Connie Yerwood Conner's professional career, see Ruthe Winegarten and Sharon Kahn, *Brave Black Women: From Slavery to the Space Shuttle* (Austin: University of Texas Press, 1997), 62–63; and Kharen Monsho, "Connor [*sic*], Connie Yerwood," *Handbook of Texas Online*,

accessed December 27, 2010, http://
www.tshaonline.org/handbook/online/
articles/fconp.

42. Application for Membership, dated
December 3, 1956, Texas Medical
Association Archives, Austin, Texas;
Marilyn Baker, "A Tumultuous 50
Years for Medicine and TMA," *Texas
Medicine* 99 (January 2003): 33; Austin
American-Statesman, November 29,
1978; July 10, 1980; Dr. Ira Bell and
Dr. John King to Karen D. Riles of
the Texas Historical Commission,
May 8, 1997, phone interviews,
National Register of Historic Places
Registration Form for the Dr. Beadie
E. and Willie R. Conner House,
section 8, 11 (in possession of the
author). For parallel efforts by black
doctors to receive hospital privileges
in Texas, see Randolph Campbell,
"Black Physicians Broke Color Barrier
at Dallas Hospitals," *Dallas Morning
News*, July 12, 2010; and the fine
website maintained by the University
of Houston's History Department, *To
Bear Fruit for Our Race: A History of
African American Physicians in Houston*,
accessed September 22, 2011, http://
www.history.uh.edu/cph/tobearfruit/
index.html. Thomas Ward surveys the
efforts to desegregate local, state, and
national medical associations in *Black
Physicians*, ch. 7.

43. Proposed chapter 8 of the Conner
Autobiography (quotation), 17.

44. For other Texas examples, see Brian
D. Behnken, "The 'Dallas Way':
Protest, Response, and the Civil Rights
Experience in Big D and Beyond,"
Southwestern Historical Quarterly 111
(July 2007): 1–29; and *The Strange
Demise of Jim Crow*, directed by David
Berman (San Francisco: California
Newsreel, 1998), DVD.

45. Austin *American-Statesman*, March
1, 1960, 25. The other members of the
delegation were local politician and
newspaperman Arthur DeWitty, Rev.
B. L. McCormick (President of the
Travis County Voters League), and
Mrs. Friendly R. Rice (President of the
Federated Negro Women's Clubs).

46. Program for Recognition Banquet
Honoring Beadie Eugene Conner, MD,
Beadie Conner Papers.

47. Austin *American-Statesman*, November
29, 1978 (first quotation); and July 10,
1980 (second quotation).

48. "The New Austin," notes for a proposed
chapter of the Conner Autobiography,
Beadie Conner Papers (quotations).

49. Transcript of undated oral interview,
Beadie Conner Papers.

Aboard the Wrong Ship in the Right Books

Doris Miller and Historical Accuracy

Neil G. Sapper

In the following carefully written article, Neil Sapper reminds us that even historians of repute can make factual errors if they do not do their original research. Black Wacoan Doris Miller was on board the USS West Virginia *and acted heroically during the Japanese attack on that ship and Pearl Harbor on December 7, 1941. However, too many historians, as well as the Navy, continued to, first, not recognize the heroism of this black Texan and, second, place him on the wrong ship, the USS* Arizona. *Eventually, Miller was awarded the Navy Cross, the second-highest award that the navy grants for heroism. Unfortunately, in 1943, Miller and his shipmates were killed in action. Neil Sapper earned his PhD in history at Texas Tech University and for many years was a professor of history at Amarillo College, prior to retiring in Austin, Texas.*

★

Doris Miller, a young black man from Waco, enlisted in the US Navy at the recruiting station in Dallas, Texas, on September 19, 1939.[1] Within four years, his actions—as well as the official reaction to them—revealed the harsh extent of racial discrimination both in the Navy and in the civilian society that it mirrored. And as the case of Doris Miller reveals, racial discrimination can cloud a record of valor.

When he entered the Navy as a mess attendant, third class, Doris Miller became one of slightly more than four thousand black sailors who served exclusively in the Steward's Branch. Recruitment of black messmen to work in the galleys and laundries of the US Navy resumed in 1932, after an interruption of nearly thirteen years. Prior to that time, the Navy virtually excluded blacks in favor of Filipinos for these duties.[2] Unsurprisingly, the black newspaper in Miller's hometown took umbrage at the treatment accorded a Navy recruiting announcement aimed at black Wacoans in the white daily in that city:"Our local daily puts it, presumably ... in forced humor, as giving colored men the opportunity of 'totin' plates instead of cotton sacks. ...' Just think of it, the only way Negroes can die in Uncle Sam's democratic Navy is— slinging hash."[3]

Heightening this irony, within four months, a black Wacoan "slinging hash" aboard the USS *West Virginia* in Pearl Harbor became the first US hero of World War II.

According to accounts of events at Pearl Harbor on December 7, 1941, Doris Miller was collecting laundry when the alarm for general quarters sounded.[4] Enroute to his battle station during the Japanese air attack, he risked the bombing, strafing, and flame-swept decks to assist the mortally wounded commanding officer, Capt. Mervyn Bennion, to a place of greater safety. Another officer on the bridge of the *West Virginia* ordered Miller to supply ammunition to a pair of inactive machine guns on deck. When that officer, Ens. Victor Delano, next checked the machine guns, he saw Miller firing one of them. It was Miller's first experience with such a weapon because messmen were not given the gunnery training received by white sailors. He was quoted later in a self-deprecatory account of his valor:

"It wasn't hard, just pulled the trigger and she worked fine. I had watched the others with these guns. I guess I fired her for about fifteen minutes. ... They were diving pretty close to us."[5]

Before the heat of the flames on the *West Virginia* forced its crew to leap into the sea, Miller had directed his machine gun so effectively that possibly four Japanese aircraft were shot down as they passed over his station.

The inexact number of planes shot down by Miller is but one of the blurred areas on the historical record of his heroism. According to Navy Department records, Messman Miller shot down one enemy airplane, but according to Miller and some witnesses, the number of hits was at least four and perhaps as high as six.[6] Unfortunately, no immediate account of the action at Pearl Harbor was given because Frank Knox, the Secretary of the Navy, imposed a news blackout that lasted for ten days.[7] In the incredible confusion following the attack, Secretary Knox reported his findings following a personal inspection tour in Hawaii. Seeking to assuage a battered national morale, Knox made vague reference to a "seaman aboard a battleship" who "single-handedly manned a machine gun and blasted an attacking torpedo plane as it leveled against his ship."[8] Unfortunately, the Navy secretary failed to identify the heroic sailor.

As more news was released from Pearl Harbor, an anonymous officer who supposedly served on the USS *Arizona* (the hardest-hit warship at Pearl Harbor) was quoted in this eyewitness account:"A Negro mess attendant who never before had fired a gun manned a machine gun on the bridge until the ammunition was exhausted."[9]

At this point, the number of Japanese aircraft shot down by the heroic unidentified sailor was designated vaguely, and the ship being defended was identified mistakenly as the *Arizona*. In the same time span, the armed forces of the United States were already recognizing and validating the valor of other heroes. For example, Capt. Colin P. Kelly Jr. was posthumously praised as the first US hero in World War II. Kelly, a white aviator, was acclaimed for sinking a Japanese battleship three days after the attack on Pearl Harbor.[10] Unfortunately, it was later learned that the "battleship" was, in reality, a much smaller cruiser and that it was not even sunk as first believed.[11] In addition, the War Department publicly cited six white aviators for air action during the attack on Pearl Harbor. But the "Negro mess attendant" remained unidentified for three months.

During those months, the National Association for the Advancement of Colored People (NAACP) grew restive over the discrepancy in the ability of the Navy to identify white heroes while it seemed unable to identify the "Negro mess attendant" who had performed so gallantly at Pearl Harbor. Joining the NAACP on this issue was the outspoken black newspaper, the Pittsburgh *Courier*, which was edited by Robert L. Vann.[12] In response to this pressure, the Navy Department, in February 1942, announced "that the colored messman . . . and two Negro workmen, along with four white men who labored heroically under fire during the vicious Japanese attack . . . may receive Naval awards."[13]

Finally, after concerted effort by civil rights organizations (e.g., the NAACP), the black press (e.g., the Pittsburgh *Courier*), and public figures (e.g., Congressman Vito Marcantonio of New York and Republican presidential-aspirant Wendell Willkie), the Navy revealed in March 1942 that the "Negro mess attendant" was Doris Miller of Waco, Texas.[14] This revelation was accompanied by a standard letter of citation from Navy Secretary Frank Knox that recognized Miller's actions.

However, the mere letter of citation seemed to stir the various organizations and individuals to seek an award more commensurate with the valor exhibited by the first US hero of the war. By comparison, the Navy awarded the second-highest award available to its personnel, the Navy Cross, to a white sailor who had aided in the rescue of nine aviators who were adrift on life rafts after their plane was shot down off Oahu during the attack on Pearl Harbor.[15] The Pittsburgh *Courier* editorialized, "We would like to know why it required so long to identify Mr. Miller, and why to date he has received no reward for his heroism."[16] The black press took the lead in the movement that sought to have the Navy confer a suitably higher award upon Miller. To that end, Congressman John D. Dingell (D-MI) and Senator James M. Mead (D-NY) introduced concurrent legislation to authorize Pres. Franklin Roosevelt to award the Congressional Medal of Honor, the nation's highest military award, to Doris Miller.[17]

The movement to gain more suitable recognition of the heroic messman included such groups as the Fraternal Council of Churches, the Southern Negro Youth Council, the National Negro Congress, leading black fraternities and sororities, and the national black press, as well as thousands of individuals.[18] However, the Navy proved immediately unresponsive. The Pittsburgh *Courier* reported that Navy Secretary Knox had indicated opposition to the legislation pending in Congress to award the Medal of Honor to Miller. In reply to an inquiry by Edgar G. Browne, president of the National Negro Congress, Knox wrote that he already had provided a letter of commendation to Miller and that "in view of the recommendations of the Pacific Coast Fleet Board of Awards and CINCPAC [Commander in Chief of the Pacific Fleet], the recognition already awarded is deemed sufficient and appropriate."[19]

Despite the adamant stance adopted by the Navy secretary, the force of black public opinion had some impact. Earlier, in 1941, black leaders of national stature had threatened to organize a march on Washington, DC. The leaders of the March on Washington Movement envisioned a massive demonstration by one hundred thousand black people in protest over white resistance to black employment in the rapidly growing defense industries stimulated by federal contracts. To avert the damaging image of black protest over undemocratic hiring practices in the arsenal of democracy, President Roosevelt issued Executive Order No. 8802, which opened many defense industries to black job seekers. Now that the United States was at war seeking to defend democracy, the implications of the protest over the Navy's treatment of Doris Miller had great potential to damage morale among black people. At that time, some black leaders began calling for a double victory in the war—a victory for democracy both abroad and at home.

In an obvious attempt to circumvent this growing protest, the Navy Department announced that the heroic messman from Waco would receive the Navy Cross in an appropriate award ceremony on May 27, 1942. Because of unrelenting pressure, in one week's time, Secretary Knox moved from his original sentiment that a mere letter of citation was "sufficient and appropriate" to reconsider Miller's valor as deserving of the second-highest award available to Navy personnel.[20] By his action rescinding the original letter of commendation and ordering the conferral of the Navy Cross, Knox made Doris Miller the first black recipient of the Navy Cross.[21]

On May 27, 1942, aboard an unidentified ship in Pearl Harbor, the Commander-in-Chief of the Pacific Fleet—Adm. Chester Nimitz of Fredricksburg, Texas—conferred the Navy Cross upon his fellow Texan, Doris Miller. As the only black sailor among the nine honorees at the ceremony, Miller was singled out by the crusty admiral, who remarked, "This marks the first time in the present conflict that such high tribute has been made in the Pacific Fleet to a member of his race, and I am sure that the future will see others similarly honored."[22]

And certainly, he was not the last, as a significant number of black sailors matched Miller's heroism, but Miller did not live to see their deeds.

Following a Christmas leave in 1942, when he saw his home and family in Waco for the last time, Doris Miller reported to duty aboard the aircraft carrier *Liscome Bay* as a mess attendant, first class. During the battle of the Gilbert Islands in November 1943, his ship was torpedoed and sunk in the Pacific Ocean. All 655 men aboard the stricken vessel were lost. At that time, Doris Miller had been promoted to cook, third class, and probably worked in the ship's galley at the time of his death.[23]

On June 3, 1972, the USS *Miller* was launched at Avondale Shipyards in Louisiana. Named in honor of Doris Miller, the new destroyer escort commemorated the black sailor's heroism during World War II. The launching was reported by the nation's press, and most newspaper accounts included a reprise of Miller's brave deeds on December 7, 1941. While those news stories correctly placed Miller aboard the USS *West Virginia* at Pearl Harbor, most historical accounts inexplicably have described Miller's activities as having taken place nearby aboard the USS *Arizona* during the surprise attack.

Because of a combination of incredible confusion, both at Pearl Harbor and in Washington, and a curious reticence about a black naval hero by his own white superiors, some of the most respected secondary works dealing with black history during World War II have echoed inaccuracies that confuse the record of the first US hero of the war. In 1944, *The Negro Handbook*, a reference work published annually, proclaimed Miller's heroism and erroneously designated his ship as the *Arizona*.[24] This error was compounded in April 1947, when the *Journal of Negro History* published an essay by Lawrence D. Reddick that discussed the heroism of Doris Miller. Reddick's account was faithful to Miller's testimony in the aftermath of the attack, but the messman was described as collecting laundry aboard the *Arizona* at the time of the attack.[25] This postwar essay, which makes a strong case for Miller as this country's first hero in the war, greatly influenced other writers.

Another important study that also appeared in 1947 and gave evidence of the influence of Reddick's essay was John Hope Franklin's survey of the history of black people in the United States, *From Slavery to Freedom*. Not only did Franklin credit Reddick's assistance in his preface and in his bibliographic notes, but his study also repeated the erroneous statement that Doris Miller was aboard the *Arizona* at Pearl Harbor.[26] Unfortunately, this influential work has gone through four editions, and the erroneous information concerning Doris Miller remains uncorrected.[27] Even more unfortunately, this historiographical error has not been confined to these important scholarly publications.

In 1951, a monograph that surveyed the integration of blacks into the US Navy also repeated the error.[28] Based on his master's thesis written at Howard University in 1947—the same year as the publication of the works of both Reddick and Franklin—Dennis D. Nelson's study gained credibility from the fact that the author was both black and a commissioned officer in the US Navy.[29] By 1954, the inaccuracy was repeated in another historical work, William Z. Foster's study of the black experience in the United States.[30] From that point, the erroneous designation of Doris Miller's ship at Pearl Harbor has appeared in numerous reference books dealing with black history.[31] A more recent repetition of the error came to light, ironically enough, in Miller's hometown. *The Ethnic Cultural Studies Handbook*, published by the Waco (Texas) Independent School District, places the black Wacoan on the deck of the *Arizona*.[32]

The historical facts of Doris Miller's bravery have been published in their correct form in only four instances. The earliest of the four books, written by Langston Hughes for juvenile readers, is entitled *Famous Negro Heroes of America*.[33] An unofficial naval biographical dictionary sets the facts accurately.[34] The third correct account was provided by Phillip T. Drotning in a book also aimed at juvenile readers.[35] And finally, Jack D. Foner has written accurately of Miller in his recent study of the black military experience in the United States.[36] Despite these four exceptions to the erroneous treatment of Miller's exploits at Pearl Harbor, the greater mass of literature dealing with his heroism also reinforces the original error.

Long before the Navy named a ship for Miller, a black newspaper in Houston commented upon the meaning of his sacrifice and the most effective homage that the Navy might pay a dead hero: "Now that Doris Miller's dead, our Navy might very well, instead of naming a ship for him and nothing more, set up as a testimonial to him a new era of justice and fair play to Negroes . . . in the . . . US Navy."[37]

The Navy has made progress in race relations and equal opportunity since Doris Miller's brave actions at Pearl Harbor.

The keepers of the historical record have done less well for this country's first hero of World War II. There is an old adage that history does not repeat itself—only historians do that. Unfortunately for Miller, too many historians have not only repeated themselves, but they have repeated the same error by placing the Texan hero of Pearl Harbor aboard the *Arizona*. Just as the Navy was charged to give Doris Miller a fitting memorial, historians should honor his valor with historical accuracy.

This article was originally published as Sapper, Neil G. "Aboard the Wrong Ship in the Right Books: Doris Miller and Historical Accuracy." East Texas Historical Journal 18 (January 1980): 3–11. Reprinted by permission of the author and the director and editor at the East Texas Historical Association.

NOTES

1. Henrietta Miller, private interview with the author, Waco, Texas, October 12, 1973; US Department of the Navy, Bureau of Naval Personnel, Transcript of Service of Doris Miller, September 16, 1939–November 25, 1944.

2. Dennis D. Nelson, "The Integration of the Negro into the US Navy, 1776–1947" (unpublished MA thesis, Howard University, 1947), 1–2; Houston *Informer*, April 11, 1942, 1.

3. Editorial, Waco *Messenger*, September 26, 1941, 2.

4. Account provided by V. Adm. (Ret.) Edwin B. Hooper in a letter to the author, June 29, 1972. Hooper was

the director of naval history in the Department of the Navy at that time.

5. Waco *Messenger*, January 1, 1943, 1, 6; Dallas *Express*, January 2, 1943, 1.

6. Pittsburg *Courier*, January 2, 1943, 1.

7. New York *Times*, December 16, 1941, 1.

8. Ibid., 1, 7.

9. Ibid., December 22, 1941, 1, 4; Pittsburgh *Courier*, January 3, 1942, 1.

10. New York *Times*, December 13, 1941, 6.

11. Lawrence D. Reddick, "The Negro in the United States Navy during World War II," *Journal of Negro History* 32 (1947): 205; New York *Times*, October 27, 1946, 46.

12. Pittsburgh *Courier*, January 3, 1942, 2, 6.

13. Ibid., February 14, 1942, 1.

14. Ibid., March 13, 1942, 7; Waco *Messenger*, December 10, 1943, 1.

15. New York *Times*, January 6, 1942, 2.

16. Pittsburgh *Courier*, March 21, 1942, 6.

17. Ibid., 1, 4.

18. Ibid., May 9, 1942, 1; "Doris Miller: First US Hero of World War II," *Ebony*, December 1969, 133; Doris Miller, private interview, October 12, 1973.

19. Pittsburgh *Courier*, May 11, 1942, 3.

20. Ibid., May 16, 1942, 1; M. H. Barns, letter to the author, September 19, 1973. Barns was the head of the Decorations and Medals Branch in the Department of the Navy at that time.

21. Dallas *Morning News*, February 12, 1970, AA-5; Waco *News-Tribune*, November 6, 1971, 1; Thomas Turner, "A Man Named Doris," *Texas Star*, May 21, 1972, 4.

22. New York *Times*, May 28, 1942, 8; ibid., June 10, 1942, 3; Pittsburgh *Courier*, June 6, 1942, 1.

23. Transcript of Service of Doris Miller.

24. Florence Murray, ed., *The Negro Handbook*, 1944 (New York: Current Reference Publications, 1944), 5.

25. Reddick, "Negro in the Navy," 204. Reddick's essay contained no citations of sources consulted.

26. John Hope Franklin, *From Slavery to Freedom* (New York: Alfred A. Knopf, 1947), 573.

27. Ibid., 2nd ed. (New York: Alfred A. Knopf, 1956), 576; ibid., 3rd ed. (New York: Alfred A. Knopf, 1967), 591; ibid., 4th ed. (New York: Alfred A. Knopf, 1974), 449.

28. Dennis D. Nelson, *The Integration of the Negro into the US Navy* (New York: Octagon, 1951), 24–25.

29. See note 2 prior.

30. William Z. Foster, *The Negro People in American History* (New York: 1954), 511.

31. John P. Davis, ed., *The American Negro Reference Book* (Englewood Cliffs, NJ: 1966), 632; Peter M. Bergman, *The Chronological History of the Negro in America* (New York: 1969), 494; *Ebony Pictorial History of Black America* (Chicago: 1971); *Reconstruction to Court Decision, 1954*, vol. 2, 252; Harry A. Polski and Ernest Kaiser, eds., *The Negro Almanac* (New York: 1971), 610–11.

32. Walter A. Meeks, "The Black American in Texas after the Civil War," *Negro History Bulletin* 37:242. This essay was excerpted from a chapter in the *Ethnic Cultural Studies Handbook*, published by the Waco Independent School District.

33. Langston Hughes, *Famous Negro Heroes of America* (New York: 1958), 183–86.

34. Karl Schuon, *US Navy Biographical Dictionary* (New York: 1964), 172.

35. Phillip T. Drotning, *Black Heroes in Our Nation's History* (New York: 1969), 177–80. Drotning makes brief note of the inaccuracy in the contention that Miller served on the *Arizona*.

36. Jack D. Foner, *Blacks and the Military in American History* (New York: 1974), 172. Foner cites both Franklin and Nelson in his bibliographic essay, but he inexplicably refrained from repeating their error in this case.

37. Editorial, Houston *Informer*, January 1, 1944, 15.

To Leave or Not to Leave?

The "Boomerang Migration" of Lillian B. Horace (1880–1965)

Karen Kossie-Chernyshev

In this pivotal chapter, Karen Kossie-Chernyshev focuses on an essentially overlooked albeit important black Central Texas woman from Fort Worth, Lillian B. Jones Horace. From Dr. Kossie-Chernyshev we learn about Lillian Jones Horace's publications, contributions, lifestyle, and as Kossie-Chernyshev puts it, her "boomerang migration." This latter phrase points to a black woman who leaves her birthplace yet returns on a number of occasions. What we also learn is that Horace was a gifted writer and teacher who remained overlooked, perhaps due to her race, her gender, and her migrations. For discovering and introducing us to this remarkable woman, we owe Kossie-Chernyshev a debt of gratitude. Kossie-Chernyshev is a professor of history at Texas Southern University; among her publications is Recovering Five Generations Hence: The Life and Writing of Lillian Jones Horace.

★

> *I don't like this old cheap pen. I want a genuine good fountain pen.*
> *I like a heavier pen than this.[1]*

Lillian Bertha Jones Horace, a gifted Texas educator whose greatest desire was to write, paused to comment on her desire for a writing instrument that honored her appreciation for the printed word. Her rich private reflections, in tandem with her overlooked creative and nonfiction works—even those she planned to write, such as her autobiography and a book on "Negro public education over [a] period of 40 years"[2]—now provide scholars of African American women's history with a fresh opportunity to reexamine migration and its impact on black Southern women and their relationships. Horace's life and work also shed light on our understanding of the effects of the patterns of migration on black Southern women educators of the Jim Crow era.

Horace's extraordinary 175-page diary is the catalyst for this study. It is a singular document, dashed down hastily—much of it retrospective, and none of it meant for publication as it stood; it reads more like notes for a work to be written later. It covers the years from about 1942 to 1950, an eight-year period during most of which Horace claimed two places of residence: 9 East Humbolt Street, Fort Worth, Texas, the address of the home she bought with her teacher's pay; and 1717 Benson Avenue, Evanston, Illinois, the parish address of the historic Second Baptist Church (SBC), where she began writing the diary. The migration pattern reflected in Horace's diary affirms and broadens the history of black Southern migration. As historians have pointed out, black Southern migration during the Great Migration was more than a collective centrifugal experience of flight from deadly epicenters of racial violence, poverty, and discrimination. Rather than an exodus from dearth or stasis to prosperity and positive change, Lillian Bertha Jones Horace's many migrations to, from, or within Southern, Western, and Eastern spaces—including Texas, California, Colorado, Kentucky, Illinois, and New York—attest that migration might encompass a complex range of motivations, destinations, durations, and outcomes. The trajectory of Horace's personal life in Chicago reveals a unique migration pattern shared by black Southern female educators for whom teaching was a "calling" and the US South, a mission field. Thus Horace's mission-minded migration pattern, which began and ended in Texas, suggests the need to examine what I call *boomerang migration*.

The word *boomerang* as a noun denotes planned aggression: a weapon or missile constructed specifically to return to the user. As a verb, it suggests an unexpected consequence: the backfiring of an action on the person who undertook it. For the purposes of my study, *boomerang migration* combines elements of both definitions and connotes the movement pattern demonstrated by mission-minded black Southerners, particularly of the Jim Crow period, who departed from and returned to the US South over the courses of their lives, chiefly for the benefit of the communities they served. Lillian Horace's example and the examples of other black Southern boomerang migrants, from Mary McCleod Bethune to Coretta Scott King, contrast with the migrations of Southern-born blacks who left the South for better opportunities and who worked out their senses of social or political obligation in other regions, including the Northeast. This other group of migrants included native Southerners Anna Julia Cooper, Mary Church Terrell, and Nannie Helen Burroughs and, in the far west, selected descendants of the T. McCants Stewart family, "whose social efforts unfolded in Portland, San Francisco, and Hawaii."[3] Additionally, the black Southern educators, the vanguard of the boomerang migrants, were distinguished from Southern peers who changed professions when they migrated north, where most black Southern teachers were denied the opportunity to teach for fear that their "Southern accent . . . would be damaging to the children."[4]

Recent scholarship on black Southern women, education, and migration during the Jim Crow era inform the background of Horace's story.[5] Scholarship elucidating the particular case of black Southern women has been particularly instructive.[6] Also key to this study on Horace are works treating black migration, black life, and activism in the many urban and rural places Horace frequented over the course of her life.[7] Diaries, personal papers, and interviews with a broad spectrum of well- and lesser-known African American women from various regions and with different vocations provided important comparative models for understanding Horace's experience, particularly her life in the African American South.[8] Examined within this context, Horace's contributions and those of various other black women educators and professionals attest that each developed her unique approach to matters of race, class, and gender and that they made their contributions to black advancement with varying degrees of commitment to individual and community uplift.

BECOMING A BOOMERANG MIGRANT

Horace's emergence as a boomerang migrant no doubt stemmed from her family's unique experience with Southern versions of what Patricia Hill Collins has called "matrices of domination" and "interlocking systems of oppression."[9] For most black Southerners, Reconstruction was an anticlimactic epoch of broken promises, dreams deferred, and, most poignantly, loss. Horace noted in her diary, a portable, private space in which she reflected on her family's history in the South, "Grandfather dead died of pneumonia brought on by exposure as he slept around in the woods, fields fleeing from the Ku Klux Klan. He sought to stand up for his citizenship—the masters shot— grandfather saved by a tree—the master wanted to keep wife and children on the farm."[10] Small wonder that Horace felt a need to go out and improve the world—and to go to Thomas Amstead and Macey Matthews in Jefferson, Texas, on April 29, 1880. Lillian observed about the occasion that "nothing auspicious mark[ed] the birth of a little colored baby." Notwithstanding the experience of her grandfather, she would recall later that relations between blacks and whites in Jefferson were not hostile but "quiet following readjustments," her term for "Reconstruction." Racial lines were blurred in unexpected public spaces; blacks and whites "rode together on trains" and were even "buried in the same cemetery."[11] But *Plessy v. Ferguson* (1896) effectively erased such gray areas and affirmed the triumph of white supremacy in the US South.

Equally key to Lillian's development as a boomerang migrant were the intellectual journeys she took in her formative years. Her first ambition was to read, and her second, to write, a desire she cherished as early as second grade. Her childhood fantasies were nonetheless tempered by a reality full of contradictions, injustice, suffering, pain, and financial distress. Even though she was "dreamy-yes-mystical," like many young black children, she had to grow up fast. Census records from 1890 to 1930 show that black children worked at a much earlier age than their white counterparts.[12] Given her father's "failure to safely provide," Lillian was determined to help her mother make ends meet. "I bartered with folks over work my mother did—I asked for advance in pay to pay the rent—met the creditor," she writes, in the frequently elliptical style of the diary.[13] Her mother's financial struggles nurtured Lillian's penchant for philanthropy and self-sacrifice. She developed a "love to lend—a sort of passion with [her]." She "never refuse[d] a loan (unless [she had] had a striking lesson from would be borrower)" and "would have loved to act the role of 'Lady Bountiful,' to spread gifts that brought joy."[14]

Given her mother's struggles, Lillian could not help noticing, even on her childhood journeys to the store, the impact of race and class: "West side of the city—Prairie land—homes of the rich to the west; the valley; gas house; homes of the poor, of Negroes." Her experiences with race in the South prodded her to pose such existential questions as "Who am I—what am I—where is God—do I make any difference in the world—would that bird be flying here had I never been born."[15] Because of her many observations and ruminations, her ambitions were clear by the time she emerged from adolescence. She wanted "to read—to unite—to teach to possess abiding faith in God—to possess no fear of death."[16] The dynamics of race that she observed later as an adult at various secondary and postsecondary institutions within and without the South prompted her conclusion that "in the South if you can wear badge of humiliation—accept inferior place all OK."[17] She and other young black educators were reminded repeatedly of the message, and they were certain that education provided their surest defense against the deleterious effects of racism and structural inequality.

Lillian's introduction to the effects of Jim Crow on the education of black children started at the very beginning of public education for blacks in Texas. Because schools were initially established in rented or donated buildings and were segregated by race, two black churches were rented for the education of Fort Worth's children of African descent. Lillian attended the East Ninth Street Colored School, founded in 1882. It was the first free public school established in Fort Worth.[18] She witnessed firsthand the school's evolution and its various relocations and name changes. It was eventually renamed I. M. Terrell Colored High School in 1921 to honor Isaiah Milligan Terrell's early contributions as its first principal and as a proponent of black education throughout the state. Terrell enjoyed an excellent reputation, one buoyed by his service as Sunday school superintendent at Mt. Gilead Baptist Church,[19] which, incidentally, young Lillian attended. As suggested by the school's very existence, she was fortunate to be in Texas. Despite the state's social shortcomings, Texas led the South in the number of schools available to African American children. Most of these schools were located in the largest cities in Texas, including San Antonio (until 1920, the largest city in the state), Houston (the largest from 1920 on), Dallas, and Fort Worth. None of these cities' black populations matched those of the Northern and Midwestern cities to which black Southerners had begun to migrate in the early to mid-twentieth century, including New York, Washington, Chicago, Cleveland, and St. Louis. But they had bustling black communities that were generally divided along the often rigid theological and cultural lines drawn by members of the nation's largest predominantly black independent religious denominations—including the African Methodist Episcopal Church, the African Methodist Episcopal Church Zion, the Christian Methodist Episcopal Church, the National Baptist Convention (NBC), and the newly established Church of God in Christ—as well as the educational and social institutions that emerged from them.

Having migrated from Jefferson, Texas, to Fort Worth with her parents and her sister Etta, Lillian entered Terrell with new clothes and "a slate, pencil, and reader" that her aunt Betty had bought in honor of her enrollment.[20] Lillian soon discovered, however, that the facilities and materials at Terrell needed serious upgrading, a problem common among underfunded black schools throughout the South. The school had "no gymnasium, cafeteria, or running water," and "children relieved themselves in outhouses."[21] Teachers taught several grades in a limited number of rooms, students used texts passed down from white schools in the area, and there was no library. Reflecting boomerang migrants' typical commitment to uplift, Lillian returned to Terrell to teach years later. She solved the library problem by having children and parents donate books to establish the first library at Terrell.[22]

JOURNEYS WITHIN THE SOUTH

After graduating from Terrell, Lillian enrolled in undergraduate and, later, post-graduate courses at various historically black colleges and universities, including Bishop College, Prairie View A&M, and Simmons University. She was part of a "critical mass of black collegiate women" who obtained degrees between 1910 and 1954.[23] The graduation rate of black college women was evenly balanced between Northern and Southern states in 1890,[24] but most black women in the early to mid-twentieth century obtained their undergraduate degrees in the South. A total of 514 black women had graduated from Southern colleges by 1910 and only 144 from white Northern or Midwestern colleges.[25] By 1936, Texas claimed more black college graduates than any other state—2,758, with 2,477 others completing some college-level work.[26] At predominantly black institutions, Lillian and other students were immersed in a doctrine of self-help and community service, with which in keeping, they established various organizations and programs to meet the needs of African Americans, especially in the South.[27]

Lillian began her career in higher education at Bishop College, where she "learn[ed] to study," was "spiritually awakened," and "learn[ed] more of people" over the course of her sojourn, from 1898 to 1899.[28] Located in the cultural center of East Texas and established by the Baptist Home Mission Society in 1881, Bishop College was one of twelve historically black colleges operating in Texas at the time. Although Lillian's stay at Bishop was brief, its impact on her beliefs was clearly evident in her lifelong commitment to the Baptist faith and its institutions and leaders. The year after she completed her studies at Bishop was a critical one. Lillian married David Jones, the son of Rev. Prince Jones, the pastor of Mt. Gilead and Lillian's pastor since early childhood. Her mother died. The order of events is not entirely clear, but the diary suggests that Macey Amstead's death followed Lillian's marriage. Notwithstanding which happened first, it is certain that both life-changing events catapulted Lillian into an adulthood that would be accompanied by vicissitudes.

Lillian would have known David from his father's church, but she probably also knew him through work. A "Lillian Amistead" was listed as a worker for "Prince Jones & Son" in Morrison and Fourmy's General Directory of the City of Fort Worth, 1899–1900, and David was listed as a laborer on the US Census of 1900. Perhaps father and son performed a variety of odd jobs together. The service Lillian rendered was not described.

Needing time to get on their feet, the newlyweds at first lived in Denton, Texas, with David's family—his parents, Prince Jones and Mary A. Jones, and his younger siblings, Prince, Eva, and Lafayette—all Louisiana natives. It was a young family: Prince Jones was only forty-two, and his wife was five years younger. The siblings were thirteen, nine, and six. Lillian learned firsthand the importance of adaptation and change as she assumed multiple roles. She would almost certainly have pitched in with cooking and cleaning and laundry and probably with child care. But despite the Joneses' bustling household, she managed to study for her teaching exams.

By the time Lillian Jones began teaching in 1901, education "had become a special province of African American women,"[29] with rural appointments being common at the beginning of a new teacher's career. Lillian's first teaching position was at a school in Parvin, Denton County, Texas, where she remained for one year. She recorded her memories of Parvin in the short, impressionistic, evocative phrases characteristic of the diary: "The husband's coming—wild horse—dusk seen over horizon on the prairie land—small pox—reading—hog killing—pigeons—acres of cotton—mother just died—the books I bought—the study I did—the horse we bought that went blind the first night." She regretted that she did not find male students with "serious minded ambitions to grow up in [the teaching] profession."[30]

Lillian relocated to Handley (now a part of Fort Worth), where she was "elected principal of Handley Colored School." As principal, she focused on the school's appearance and became more involved in the community. The school was a one-room building, ten feet square, and student benches were arranged along the walls. Lillian taught all the ages and grades in that one room, and she may have served as janitor, too, unless she impressed some of the students into that service. "Bad days" occurred when "parents kept children home."[31] One student in particular stood out for the young teacher: "the girl who knew arithmetic" and whom Lillian "later . . . saw with many babies." In the spare time she managed to find, she fulfilled two of her "secret" ambitions—to sing and to perform philanthropic acts. A pioneer in the dramatic arts in Fort Worth's African American community at the turn of the century, she sang the role of Queen Esther in a cantata staged in the city hall under the supervision of I. M. Terrell. It was deemed "an excellent entertainment" that "would have done credit to amateur singers anywhere."[32] And she lent her hand to fundraising for the library.

As she traveled to and from work on the crowded interurban connecting Dallas to outlying areas, Lillian was confronted with the social trials stemming from race and gender. On one occasion, when she boarded the interurban car, the conductor stopped the vehicle and forced her to get off. When she protested, saying, "But I must go to work," the men on the car laughed: "We must go too." Chivalry for black women traveling in the South was rarely the exception and never the rule.

Matters of race and class were again at issue when Lillian fell ill a day after an interurban car hit a buggy in which she was riding. When her friends went to the school where she worked to report the incident, they saw the inadequate facility to which she had been assigned and "laugh[ed] at [her] 'University.'"[33] Clearly, it was not one of the Rosenwald Schools, which in East Texas were, according to one observer, "the only Negro school buildings . . . that might be considered adequate for school purposes."[34]

The summer breaks provided little respite from social inequality. Texas teachers attended summer normal institutes to ensure that they remain abreast, but black and white teachers gathered separately, in accordance with segregationist customs. Lillian attended the Dallas Summer Normal Institute, which convened June 22, 1905, one of twenty normal institutes designated for black teachers.[35] An additional twenty normal institutes for black Texas teachers convened on or near the same date in the counties of Austin, Bay City, Bonham, Bryan, Calvert, Colmesneil, Hempstead, Gonzales, La Grange, Luling, Corrigan, Mount Pleasant, Oakwoods, Paris, Port Lavaca, San Marcos, Tyler, Waco, Wharton, Valley View, and Yoakum.[36] The following year, in 1906, Lillian attended a black-only summer normal in Fort Worth at I. M. Terrell, which convened, ironically enough, on June 19—"Juneteenth," the holiday commemorating the date slaves in Texas learned of their freedom.[37] Segregated summer normal institutes reminded Lillian and other black teachers that for them, true freedom did not yet exist.[38]

Lillian reflected extensively on race and its impact on her black students and their families. The gross injustices she observed, experienced, and read about no doubt drove her to write her first novel, *Five Generations Hence*, a 122-page work composed as she taught in rural East Texas schools. Determined to see the book in print, in 1916, the year she turned thirty-six, she self-published it with Dotson-Jones Printing Company, a company that she co-owned with J. Dotson. Lillian and her novel were buried in obscurity for the greater part of the twentieth century until an excerpt of it appeared in Carol Kessler's *Daring to Dream* (1984), and my fortuitous encounter with the Lillian Bertha Horace Papers in 2003 allowed reuniting "Horace" with her earlier identity as "Jones." Research confirms *Five Generations Hence* as the only utopian novel by a black woman before 1950 and the earliest novel on record by a black woman from Texas. A migration narrative in which a black woman teacher and a missionary are heroines, *Five Generations Hence* offers emigration to Africa as a plausible solution to the obstacles facing blacks (especially black men) in the South, despite Lillian's tendency, like that of her contemporaries, to undermine her commitment to uplift by focusing on black pathology.[39]

Lillian's Africa-centered musings had been inspired by attending various predominantly black institutions of higher learning throughout the South, including Prairie View Normal and Industrial College (founded in 1876, the second-oldest institution of higher learning in Texas).[40] While Prairie View and other historically black schools may have buffered students and faculty against immediate confrontations with race, they also acquainted them with the importance of education to black advancement. Lillian was overjoyed to attend Prairie View and "could not believe [she] was going."[41] Looking back years later, Lillian would note in her diary that at Prairie View, she had been valedictorian of a class of seventy-four students. "I had worked hard in great hardships," she wrote, "a small achievement but the effort had been great."[42]

As Lillian moved forward with her teaching career and her studies, her relationship with her husband slowly fell apart. She and David were divorced in 1919, the year she turned thirty-nine. Perhaps finding a constructive way to deal with the dissolution of her nineteen-year marriage, Lillian traveled to Louisville, Kentucky, in 1920, to teach at Simmons College, established by black Baptists in 1879.[43] In its university bulletin for the academic year 1921–22, Simmons described itself as "an institute for the training of colored young men and young women";[44] there, students were reminded that "there is no excuse for anybody to be without an education these days."[45] According to the bulletin, Lillian was a "graduate of Prairie View State Normal School of Texas" with "special work at the University of Chicago and the University of Colorado," a "high school teacher of many years' experience," a "social worker,"[46] and the recipient of an AB from Simmons in 1922.[47] Given the trajectory of her training as an educator and social worker, Lillian qualified as what Francille Rusan Wilson has called the *Shields generation* of social scientists, named for Emma L. Shields Penn, whose exemplars began as teachers, served for a short period as social workers during the Great Migration, and eventually returned to teaching.[48]

When Lillian arrived in Louisville, she encountered a vibrant black community. African American natives were proud to have established the first library for blacks in the United States, as well as churches, black-owned hospitals, banks, social clubs, and settlement houses.[49] But as in most Southern cities, black women in Louisville were largely confined to domestic work, although local black newspapers affirmed the presence of black women entrepreneurs—namely, hairstylists and sellers of hair-care products. Black women were nonetheless engaged in helping improve the lives of African Americans. And members of the National Baptist Women's Convention were busy raising funds to support the educational activities of the church, particularly the operations of Simmons College.[50]

Black women educators taught in one of two high schools established for black children, or they taught at Simmons College, where gender distinctions were clear in professors' assignments. Women faculty members were concentrated in the high school departments of the college, where they taught a variety of preparatory and vocational courses, including arithmetic, foreign languages, grammar, geography, homemaking, millinery, music, and US history. Lillian's colleague Jane Alice Browne Bond, a graduate of Oberlin College (1893) and the mother of eminent scholar Horace Mann Bond,[51] taught Latin and French. Men on the faculty taught university-level and seminary courses, including mathematics, history, physics, chemistry, the Bible, church history, homiletics, and missions. Lillian nonetheless distinguished herself as a leader. She served as dean of women, taught English as an assistant, and worked with the drama department. Apart from the cattiness she encountered from some of the young women at Simmons, Lillian commented little on her experience there.[52] Once she completed her year at Simmons, she returned again to Texas, where she continued her teaching mission.

JOURNEYS OUTSIDE THE SOUTH

Lillian's experiences with education and race in the Jim Crow South helped precipitate her journeys to the Midwest, North, and West, where she studied for the first time with whites. She and other black Southerners who wanted advanced liberal-arts education or graduate degrees were forced to leave the South because the historically black colleges and universities to which they were limited did not have graduate or summer study programs with the course offerings sought by progressive black Southern educators. Lillian's decision to take summer courses outside the segregated South confirmed that she, like many of her black Southern contemporaries, had no desire to enroll in the Jeanes teacher education programs offered during the summers at Hampton and funded by Northern philanthropists who supported the institutionalization of industrial education for rural Southern blacks.[53] Accordingly, she and other black Southern teachers enrolled in summer extension courses at the University of Chicago, where institutionalized summer study had begun in 1894, and at Columbia, the second-most popular non-Southern university among black Southern educators. While Lillian registered for only one summer session at Columbia (1924), she enrolled in five of them at the University of Chicago (in 1917, 1918, 1919, 1920, and 1940)—a clear indication that she appreciated the progressive vision of the first president of the University of Chicago, Pres. William Rainey Harper, who argued that good college training should not be withheld from those who taught during the year and could not afford to leave their jobs to go back to school. By 1910, the University of Chicago offered twelve weeks of summer school and enrolled approximately 3,370 students; Columbia enrolled 2,629.[54] As neither university listed students by race, it is difficult to know the exact number of African Americans enrolled.

Lillian's experience with educational institutions outside the South varied. At the University of Colorado at Boulder and the University of Chicago, she appreciated the libraries and had "a grand time feeling one of them,'"—whites; and she "just had to see" Columbia, where she took coursework until her sister Etta's illness and financial difficulties forced her withdrawal.[55] At the same time, subtle differences reminded her of her marginality as a black woman. "White colleges," she wrote, "the hush at your presence. Your own clumsiness—Some say I don't feel the difference—I'm sorry but I do even when they're extremely nice. Seating advantage of whites even in study—grouping—my experience."[56] She expressed sustained discontent over the lack of respect shown black women regardless of their age, educational preparation, or social standing.

Despite the ubiquitous nature of racism, regional differences were particularly obvious when trains left the far Western and Midwestern states and crossed into Texas, underscoring what she labeled "Negro women's two major handicaps": "being a woman" and being a "Negro."[57] One telling experience—the very first recorded in her diary—reflects both problems and also demonstrates the reputation Texas had, among both races, as a state where blacks had better observe their place: "Returning from Colo[rado]; very cold. At state line,—Whites gleefully: 'This is Texas!' I sort of hide myself, I didn't move. To one another: 'Do you know this is Texas' for my benefit. I'm too ill to move. Later the conductor has me moved—I'm ill. Later, Negro porter ignores my very apparent illness—he carried away by 'gay young things."[58]

Lillian's experience with Jim Crow while traveling was not unique; nor were the affronts she suffered reserved for adults. Mary Church Terrell's first experience with racism occurred when she was but five years old and traveling with her father, who could pass for white; her fair complexion notwithstanding, she could not, and she suffered the usual consequence—expulsion.[59] Lillian's own experiences with race and gender may have affected her decision not to leave the Jim Crow South permanently, particularly given her ties of family and friendship, and the respect she had earned in her community. She, like hundreds of other black Southern women educators, chose to use her intellectual gifts—namely, her abilities to teach and write—to help liberate the minds of young black Southerners, for she understood their plight; it mirrored her own.

THE JOURNEY TO EVANSTON, ILLINOIS

Among the most important journeys Lillian took was the one to Evanston, Illinois, where her second husband, Joseph Gentry Horace, a native of Groveton, Texas, had received a ministerial call to the Second Baptist Church. This was a historic church established on November 17, 1882, by formerly enslaved blacks who had migrated to Evanston in the late nineteenth century.[60] Prior to enacting the quest for autonomy that often led blacks to leave predominantly white religious bodies, some members had joined the First Baptist Church by baptism and others through letters of transference from the historic Olivet Baptist Church, where Lacey Kirk Williams eventually served as pastor.[61] But then, according to an Evanston *Index* item dated July 29, 1882, a "number of the colored people of Evanston ... unified to form a religious organization to hold union services. They ... secured a large room over the post-office." Richard Day, a Second Baptist Church founder, chaired the meeting, which may have been "the first reference to an exclusively black religious gathering in Evanston; social organizations already existed."[62]

J. Gentry Horace's tenure at the Second Baptist Church spanned the period from February 1938 to August 1946.[63] The church address, the same as that of the parsonage where the Horaces lived, figures prominently on the front page of Lillian Horace's diary, like a title marking the setting of an intriguing saga: 1717 Benson Avenue, Evanston, Illinois. Lillian did not indicate how she had met the engaging preacher, but data suggest it may have been at Mt. Gilead Baptist Church in Fort Worth, where Lillian, then still "Jones," had been a faithful member since adolescence and where Horace, whose interest in church work predated his move to Fort Worth, had distinguished himself as a leader through his involvement with the various social and political organizations affiliated with Mt. Gilead.

J. Gentry came from a large and deeply religious Baptist family; he was one of eleven children. The family was well known in Groveton for its commitment to church work. J. Gentry's father, J. H. Horace, had served as a deacon for fifty years by the time of his death in 1924, and his mother, Katie Horace, had "made her home the headquarters of church workers and ministers" for that entire half century. She continued to serve the church until her death in 1947.[64]

By September 12, 1918, when he was about thirty-one, J. Gentry had married Mattie Judson, moved to Fort Worth, and secured a job as a laborer in the meat industry with Swift and Company.[65] By 1920, at thirty-three, he was working as a mail clerk on trains, and by forty-two, as an insurance salesman, but he clearly wanted more. He and Mattie owned a home valued at $10,000, no small sum at the time, but based on Mattie's census description, she was not ambitious; her occupation was listed as "none" on both the 1920 and 1930 census reports. On January 13, 1930, the date census workers visited, J. Gentry and Mattie Horace had been married for more than ten years; by October 1, Mattie was dead.[66] And by the close of the same year, newly widowed J. Gentry Horace—perhaps the "J. H." referenced in the "J. H. affair" of 1928 recorded in Lillian's diary[67]—had married divorcee Lillian Jones, a well-educated, well-traveled, and well-connected teacher and writer several years his senior.

Lillian Jones had undoubtedly recognized J. Gentry's potential as a gifted leader, for he was deeply involved in Mt. Gilead, one of the largest black Baptist churches in Texas and a nexus for religious and social activities at the local, state, and national levels. Among the organizations whose conventions Mt. Gilead hosted in the 1930s were the City Federation; the Masons of Fort Worth, including Eastern Star and Heroines of Jericho; the State Teachers Associations;[68] and the National Association of Colored Women's Clubs. J. Gentry's penchant for leadership was clearly evident by August 1931 when the "Hon. J. L. Webb, national president of the national laymen movement of the United States . . . commissioned the Hon. J. Gentry Horace, Esq., as president of the state laymen movement." The organization was directly linked to Mt. Gilead Baptist Church, where B. W. Horace, perhaps a relative of J. Gentry's, was elected "president of the laymen movement board of Mt. Gilead Baptist Church."[69] By December 19, 1931, J. Gentry had moved into the presidency.[70] He was also referred to as a teacher from "Texarkana, Arkansas," in a news article detailing a car accident in which he and another passenger were involved while heading to a meeting of the State Teachers Association.[71] Despite the generous titles J. Gentry was accorded by writers for the Chicago *Defender*, including "esquire" and "professor," the US census identified him as a mail clerk and an insurance salesman, and he did not begin his advanced education until he married Lillian Jones, who was almost certainly instrumental in it.

Lillian was well positioned to complement her husband's ascension within Texas' black Baptist community, with its historic commitment to social uplift. She knew personally the celebrated Rev. Lacey Kirk Williams, a major religious figure in the region, who had served as pastor of Macedonia Baptist Church in Dallas and had assumed the pastorate of Mt. Gilead Baptist Church in 1909, the year of Pastor Prince Jones's demise.[72] Williams had further distinguished himself by becoming president of the National Baptist Convention and being named pastor of Olivet Baptist Church, Chicago, in 1916. Moreover, Lillian had begun her pursuit of advanced education many years before J. Gentry Horace began his. She had taught and served in administrative positions at the university and secondary levels. By the time she and J. Gentry married, she owned her own home and was well established in the community. All this, in addition to her training as a writer, put her in an excellent position to support her new husband's quests for upward social mobility and intellectual fulfillment. Not long after his marriage to Lillian, J. Gentry began solidifying his plans to enter the professional ministry by preaching while he was earning divinity degrees. In 1935, he enrolled in classes at Bishop College in Marshall, Texas, and he ministered in Texarkana, approximately one hour northeast of Marshall. By 1938, he had been called to Evanston, where he served as pastor of the Second Baptist Church and put his leadership skills to immediate use by engaging the members in various programs, helping marshal the church through the Great Depression, and nurturing a congregation that remained socially engaged enough to enroll seventy-six new NAACP members even after his departure.[73] He also began studying at Northern Seminary on September 10, 1940, as a transfer student from Garrett Biblical Institute, now Garrett Theological Seminary, earning his bachelor of divinity on May 22, 1942, and his master of theology on May 21, 1943.[74]

When J. Gentry Horace was called to his pulpit in Evanston in the late 1930s, the town's population stood at 58,334, with 4,940 blacks constituting 7.8 percent of the population. Small enclaves of blacks lived in some predominantly white residential areas, but most lived in the Fifth Ward, later referred to by locals as the Black Triangle. Lillian and her husband had a spacious church parish within the church proper; it was situated behind the choir loft and pulpit area, and a door leading from it opened onto the sanctuary, which comfortably seated five hundred.

When Lillian took up her life in Evanston (which was limited by her work in Fort Worth), she would have found that beyond the church, Evanston bore the familiar vestiges of racial discrimination and social inequality, particularly as more Southern blacks migrated to the region. The work available to most black women in Evanston was limited to domestic service, and the few black women teachers who found positions in the 1940s and 1950s were assigned to Old District 75's Foster School, where the black population stood at 99 percent, as the school was situated near the Black Triangle. Separate YMCA facilities were maintained for blacks and whites, and some restaurants refused to serve blacks. Black and white high school girls could not shower in the same stalls after physical education classes. Black and white students held separate proms, and African American students at nearby Northwestern University College were forbidden to compete in intercollegiate athletics.[75]

The Horaces encountered pioneering African American men and women who were working to improve the lives of blacks in Evanston, like the Revs. William H. Twiggs, editor, and Jesse S. Woods, editor and proprietor, of the *Afro-American Budget*, one of Illinois's first monthly African American periodicals.[76] The Horaces also met Isabella Garnett, MD, whose address appears in Lillian's diary along with the addresses of thirty-two other Evanstonians. Garnett, daughter of Daniel F. Garnett, one of the founding members of the Second Baptist Church, had earned her medical degree from the College of Physicians and Surgeons, now the University of Illinois College of Medicine, in 1901, making her one of the first black women doctors in Illinois.[77] When hospitals in the region stopped admitting black patients, she and her husband, Arthur Butler, MD, a 1903 graduate of Northwestern School of Medicine, converted their home at 1918 Asbury Avenue into a fourteen-bed hospital for blacks in 1914, naming it the Evanston Sanitarium, the only facility of its kind between Chicago and Milwaukee.[78] The couple lived in a small cottage behind the hospital.

The Horaces' commuter marriage seemed to work well at first. Lillian and J. Gentry's professional activities, personal engagements, and some of their excursions in Alabama, Illinois, Ohio, Texas, and California continued to find their way into the society pages of the Chicago *Defender*. The pair spent time together in Evanston but intermittently. Notwithstanding her husband's relocation, during the academic year, Lillian continued teaching at I. M. Terrell High School in Fort Worth, where in 1942, she was honored for twenty-five years of service. Fort Worth was her primary residence. She had begun her library studies at Prairie View A&M in 1937—a fact not disclosed in her diary but confirmed by archival records at Prairie View—and in the summer of 1940, she resumed graduate studies in library science at the University of Chicago.[79] Her husband, too, was fulfilling academic ambitions. Between 1940 and 1942, he earned a BA in divinity from Northern Seminary, and in 1943, an MA in theology.

Lillian and J. Gentry's hard push between 1937 and 1943 to secure their academic credentials must have been motivated to some extent by the press of time; in 1940, Lillian turned sixty, and J. Gentry, fifty-three. The strain on their marriage must have been great. Both worked; both studied; and Lillian, in addition to traveling back and forth between Fort Worth and Evanston, also continued writing and struggling to get her work published. And she continued to maintain affiliations with various clubs and professional organizations.

Such affiliations were not new to Lillian's agenda. She had participated in the 1933 meeting of the Texas Library Association and the 1936 gathering of Parents and Leaders of Parent-Teacher Associations. In 1937, she attended the annual convention of the National Association of Colored Women (NACW), which met in her hometown, Fort Worth, and was hosted by her home church, Mt. Gilead Baptist.[80] While attending the 1939 NACW convention in Boston,[81] she began work on an ambitious biography of Dr. Lacey Kirk Williams, whose Olivet Baptist Church in Chicago, with its twelve thousand members, was the largest Baptist church in the country. Lillian continued work on the book while she was studying at the University of Chicago in 1940, but it suffered a serious blow when Williams died tragically in a plane crash. Given the power struggle that ensued within the National Baptist Convention, she could not persuade convention leaders to publish the biography the next year. She listed publishing the work, *Sun Crown* (its tentative title), among the twenty goals she "really want[ed]" to accomplish, "not just for [her] but for Dr. Williams' name."[82] But her earnest effort was ultimately blocked by the fight for control of the NBC publishing board,[83] which ended with a denominational split that endures to this day. During this time, she also wrote her article titled "The Education of the Out of School Negro," which underscored her unrelenting commitment to the intellectual development of African Americans.

Given the flurry of all these many activities, as well as her professional commitment to Terrell High School in Fort Worth, the affairs of the Second Baptist Church in Evanston were not Lillian's highest priority, a fact that did not sit well with some of its members. However, in Lillian's absence, J. Gentry's popularity soared. He was a popular speaker not only in his own church but in other venues as well, and when he spoke, his church choirs accompanied him. He was almost certainly a magnetic speaker, and the Evanston *Newsette* observed that he had been "long noted for his fiery, plain-spoken delivery" (March 5, 1946). When he retired his church's debt, he celebrated with a mortgage burning, and in a church bulletin, he reminded his congregation that they had called him from "Deep in the Heart of Texas" (although, technically speaking, they had called him from Canaan Baptist Church in Texarkana).[84] He was evidently a natural leader and a man of marked abilities.

In addition to that, he also had direct blood ties to the NBC political hierarchy in Illinois. His brother James L. Horace, one of three Horace brothers who were ministers,[85] was president of the Illinois State Convention,[86] and another brother, P. H. Horace, was also a minister in the Illinois region. The prominence of the triumvirate natives of Groveton confirmed the professional opportunity available to black male ministers as black Southern members of the National Baptist Convention migrated to Chicago—and simultaneously confirmed that a comparable professional opportunity through migration was not necessarily available to pastors' wives. The workforce at large did not rush to greet professional black women, and pastors' wives, regardless of the level of involvement that different congregations might expect of them, were not paid and were often not even appreciated.

This was certainly the case for Lillian, given that key leaders within the NBC rejected her contribution to the history of the organization through her biography of Lacey Kirk Williams, for which she might have received remuneration had the book been published during her lifetime. One member of the church, who chose to remain anonymous, suggested that Lillian disregarded the traditional manner in which preachers' wives were expected to engage church work "until she knew her husband had a girlfriend." The involvement implied would have included Lillian's devoting significant time to the myriad social and philanthropic undertakings occupying thousands of black Baptist women's auxiliaries in the Chicago region during the Great Migration. But Lillian Horace was a professional woman with a career she loved. To be sure, she was "plodding" financially, especially at the beginning of her career.[87] And certainly, inflation countered what appeared to be increases in her pay. But her modest, steady income and her profession placed her in Fort Worth's black middle class and provided her with prestige in the community. Her role as "the preacher's wife" was accompanied by a certain amount of pomp and circumstance, but it came with no direct financial compensation or access thereto. This may indicate that the role of "first lady" was too limiting for Lillian, especially given that her husband's salary was far from munificent.

On June 2, 1942, Lillian made, she said, the discovery that she was sixty-two years old, not fifty-seven. A birth certificate had revealed her birth date as 1880. The mechanics of how seven years might have been lost from her life is puzzling, but lost she insisted they were; she entered finding them in a list of "Embarrassing Moments" in the diary and, again, in a list of "Moments of Strong Emotion," in close company with the deaths of her mother and sister. And indeed such a discovery, if it was real, must have seemed a kind of death: "What a strange emotion," she wrote, "that I'm old. Strange—others advance—I retreat." But "I shall not be bitter," she resolved. "O for genuine peace in my soul—to wind up work gracefully—I shall."[88]

Militating against the possibility that the loss of those years was deliberate is the fact that all her life, Lillian was around people from Mt. Gilead Baptist Church who had known her since childhood. And the diary entry is genuinely affecting. But then Lillian was a genuinely affecting writer, and it must be acknowledged that the twin evils of ageism and sexism might have induced her to lose the seven years deliberately, perhaps around the time of her divorce from Jones, perhaps when she and J. Gentry were courting—he was, interestingly, seven years younger than she was—or perhaps when she was applying somewhere for a job or even to study. In *Five Generations*

Hence, she has Grace, who is in many ways an alter ego or idealized self, reflect on the one-year difference between Lemuel's age and her own and ask, "What man want[s] a sweetheart older than himself?"[89] In any case, whether J. Gentry became privy to her real age at this time is unknown, but that it had any significant part in the breakup of their marriage is unlikely. Their living arrangements, the infrequency with which they were together, the busyness and pace of their lives, and the fact that J. Gentry's affair was evidently one of long standing are sufficient to explain the rift.

As Lillian learned painfully, her husband had fallen in love with one Portia Cooke, whom he married several years later, on April 11, 1951.[90] The relationship was confirmed to Lillian by Cooke's husband, who discovered the affair while on furlough from the US army, and it was later confirmed by J. Gentry himself.[91] Church and organizational records were reticent about J. Gentry's infidelity, but local newspapers acknowledged his resignation and relocation to Calvary Baptist Church in Chicago Heights, Illinois.[92]

No doubt Lillian restrained her distress in public, but she expressed it in her diary, where in a section titled "Reflections Dec. 22, 1943," she recounted the visit of Portia's husband, who had brought with him a letter between the lovers that made everything clear. He had made photocopies of it, one of which he had that same night delivered to the chairman of the board of deacons of J. Gentry's church.[93]

The impact of the dissolution of her marriage was devastating for Lillian, "the greatest sorrow."[94] She was also deeply hurt that her husband appeared to be more concerned about the effect of his improprieties on his career than on her or their marriage. She braced herself to face the embarrassment of being the deserted wife of a popular preacher—a preacher with considerable influence in the ever-expanding National Baptist Convention.

By 1946, the year the Horaces' divorce was finalized, staying at the SBC parish even in the summers was no longer an option. When Lillian visited Evanston that year, she relied on the hospitality of David McKinley Lindsay and his wife, Florence, of 2012 Darrow Avenue.[95] Lindsay, who had migrated from Abbeville, South Carolina, to Evanston in 1922, was "one of the more industrious Evanston residents." At the close of her stay with the Lindsays, Lillian was ready to bid adieu to Evanston, where she had lost the social status that came with being a preacher's wife, the first lady of a historic congregation. With a second failed marriage added to her list of her life's disappointments, no family in Evanston, and little respite from racial discrimination in housing, education, or employment, Lillian packed her bags and left, apparently finding refuge and healing in traveling, writing, visiting with friends in California, and ultimately returning to Fort Worth. But she did not forget the Lindsays. A Thanksgiving Day telegram sent to their address from Fort Worth on November 28, 1946, confirmed her appreciation for their kindness: "IM GRATEFUL TO YOU TODAY DARLING LOADS OF LOVE=BABE."[96]

In 1947, a year after the divorce, Lillian headed west to California, where she spent six months with friends and "practically decide[d] to marry" a third time.[97] But because "affairs with J. E. were always uncertain," she remained committed to "leaving developments to God—begging his guidance."[98] She journeyed southeast to Florida and Atlanta,[99] and in January 1948, she returned to California, where she spent time in Bakersfield, Berkeley, and San Francisco, the cultural, social, and economic capital of black California. It was at this time that she also wrote the bulk of her second novel, *Angie Brown*. Her consecutive trips to California were not her first. She had traveled to the Golden State in 1926, with her sister Etta, and in August 1934, when she had been listed first in the Chicago *Defender* among "the many interesting vacationists and visitors" and was a house guest of Mrs. E. E. Ealey,[100] whose address appears in her diary. Now approaching her seventies, Horace was clearly in a different place experientially and professionally in terms of creative writing when she wrote *Angie Brown*. She had traveled more extensively and gained greater insight into race and gender through both observation and experience, and in this second novel, she produced a more nuanced narrative than in her first effort, published some forty years earlier.

California was not a Jim Crow state, but race relations were not perfect, and they deteriorated with an increase in black Southern migration to the region. Black students had nonetheless acquired a high school education as early as 1889 at San Jose High School,[101] and Maysfield Grammar School had an integrated class of African American and white students in 1922.[102] By 1952, San Francisco's Westminster Presbyterian Church had become an ethnically diverse congregation when the white congregation from Westminster Church and blacks from Hope Church unified.[103] Familiar indicators of discrimination against black professionals, particularly teachers, were nonetheless prevalent. It was not until 1926 that Ida Louise Jackson, a native of Vicksburg, Mississippi, became the first African American teacher in Oakland Public Schools.[104] The San Francisco Bay area did not welcome its first African American high school teacher until 1948, when Josephine Cole was offered a position at Balboa High School.

But Lillian had journeyed to California not to focus on the social conditions of black Californians, which she understood well from her Southern perspective, but rather to construct a thoughtful narrative on a subject dear to her—the economic advancement of black Southerners, particularly black Southern women, through education and migration, the theme of *Angie Brown*. In this novel, as in her first one, black women intellectuals play a key role, although Lillian's take on migration and race relations moved beyond separatism to the universality of women's suffering and to imagined interracial cooperation between black and white women. In *Five Generations Hence*, the main character has to choose whether her efforts should unfold in Africa or the US South; in *Angie Brown*, her choice is between the Midwest and the South.[105] In both novels, the heroines choose migration, but black Southern women intellectuals, their many travels notwithstanding, remained faithful to the South, where they continued the important collective work of liberating the masses through the printed and spoken word, as well as through direct involvement in the community. Like Betty Yates, the heroine teacher in *Angie Brown*, Lillian, too, returned home.

THE RETURN HOME

Perhaps to an even greater degree than the black Southern expatriates examined in Glenda Gilmore's *Defying Dixie*,[106] boomerang migrants like Lillian often experienced negative repercussions for their efforts. As they lived and worked in the lion's mouth, the consequences they suffered included but were not limited to disruption of their personal lives, marginalization, expulsion, or even death, depending on the nature of their missions and the degree to which they agitated the Southern social order. And of course, black boomerang migrant women had the problems common to most working wives. Lillian's marriages both suffered from her many educational and professional endeavors. As she chose not to leave Texas for good, her married life remained "fragmented and incomplete."

Despite her efforts to "write a book worth the reading by an intelligent person— not necessarily [her] friend,"[107] Lillian's three book-length works have remained largely unknown until now, and none figures prominently in the annals of African American literature or historiography. Although she had to self-publish her first novel and did not live to see *Angie Brown* published, and although her definitive biography of Lacey Kirk Williams was blocked by the power struggle in the National Baptist Convention, at least the biography was a resounding success some twenty years later, at the Progressive National Baptist Convention of September 1964 in Atlanta, where it attracted the attention of young black Baptist ministers, among them Martin Luther King Jr.[108] L. Vencheal Booth, a leader in the newly formed convention, eventually published the work in 1978, thirteen years after Lillian's death. Lillian had tried in 1949 to persuade Lemuel L. Foster of New York to publish *Angie Brown*, but the effort had led nowhere despite the novel's celebration of education and economic self-sufficiency and its incorporation of a contemporary theme— interracial cooperation between black and white women.

Though scholarly recognition of Lillian's life and works was delayed, the individuals and communities that she returned to Texas to serve celebrated her contributions. A pioneering teacher whose intellectual development began with the birth of the Fort Worth public school system, Lillian clearly helped I. M. Terrell High School earn its "separate but superior" reputation before the fall of Jim Crow.[109] Her various educational, professional, and personal journeys within and beyond the South expressed her vision and commitment. When she retired, she was showered with accolades from students and colleagues and was the subject of at least two news articles lauding her accomplishments, especially her dedication to young women. Her direct and indirect impact on I. M. Terrell graduates over the years must have been great; it certainly figured in the molding of Lulu B. White, civil rights activist, and celebrated Texas educator Hazel Harvey Peace. But Lillian was most warmly celebrated by those who knew her best. A letter dated October 27, 1964, from George O. Jackson, a former student who became a public accountant in Washington, DC, attests to the service she rendered her students. Jackson's letter of appreciation for his favorite teacher and her early contributions to his success was timely; within a year of receiving it, Lillian died. She was buried on Monday, August 9, 1965, at two o'clock in the afternoon, with all the fanfare expected at what black Southerners call a good funeral. Among the organizations escorting her casket were the Women's Council of Mt. Gilead Baptist Church; the Psi Zeta Chapter of Zeta Phi Beta Sorority; the Alphin Charity and Art Club; the Progressive Women's Club; the Heroines of Jericho, Viola Court No. 250; and the Eula Elizabeth Chapter, No. 200, Order of the Eastern Star, Prince Hall Affiliation—organizations to which she had been committed throughout her life. They demonstrated by their collective presence that Lillian Bertha Jones Horace had made a respectable mark worth memorializing, one that has posthumously given rise to a new concept, that of boomerang migration—a term that accommodates the contributions of black Southern women educators of the Jim Crow period, who, like Lillian Horace, chose to leave and not to leave and in so doing helped transform a peculiar region in spite of itself, even as they themselves were transformed.

An earlier version of this essay was published in Black Women, Gender and Families *4 (November 2010): 57–87. Related presentations were given at the annual meeting of the Association for the Study of African American Life and History in Atlanta, Georgia, September 28, 2006, and at the symposium "Celebrating Lillian B. Jones Horace and Other Extraordinary Women of the Jim Crow Era" at Texas Southern University, Houston, March 6–7, 2009. This article was originally published as Kossie-Chernyshev, Karen. "The 'Boomerang Migration' of Lillian B. Horace (1880–1963)." In* Recovering Five Generations Hence: The Life and Writing of Lillian Jones Horace, *edited by Karen Kossie-Chernyshev, 105–38. College Station: Texas A&M University Press, 2013. Reprinted by permission of the author and Texas A&M University Press.*

NOTES

1. Lillian Horace, *The Diary of Lillian B. Horace,* ed. Karen Kossie-Chernyshev (Boston: Pearson, 2007), A7. Cited hereafter as *Diary.*

2. Ibid., 46, 141.

3. Albert Broussard, *African-American Odyssey: The Stewarts, 1853–1963* (Lawrence: University Press of Kansas, 1998); Joe William Trotter Jr., ed., *The Great Migration in Historical Perspective: New Dimensions of Race,* Class, and Gender (Bloomington: Indiana University Press, 1991); Milton C. Sernett, *Bound for the Promised Land: African American Religion and the Great Migration* (Durham, NC: Duke University Press, 1997); Bernadette Pruitt, "For the Advancement of the Race: The Great Migration to Houston, Texas, 1914–1941," *Journal of Urban History* 31, no. 4 (May 2005): 435–78; Karen

Kossie-Chernyshev, "Constructing Good Success: The Church of God in Christ and Social Uplift in East Texas, 1910–1935," in *Blacks in East Texas History*, eds. Bruce Glasrud and Archie P. McDonald (College Station: Texas A&M University Press, 2008).

4. Sarah L. Delany and A. Elizabeth Delany with Amy Hill Hearth, *Having Our Say: The Delany Sisters' First 100 Years* (New York: Dell, 1993), 168. See also Francille Rusan Wilson, *The Segregated Scholars: Black Scholars and the Creation of Black Labor Studies, 1890–1950* (Charlottesville: University of Virginia Press, 2006), 181.

5. The following works were useful: William H. Watkins, *The White Architects of Black Education: Ideology and Power in America, 1865–1954* (New York: Teachers College Press, 2001); Wilson, *Segregated Scholars*; Adam Fairclough, *Teacher Equality: Black Schools in the Age of Jim Crow* (Athens: University of Georgia Press, 2001); and Fairclough's extensive study *A Class of Their Own: Black Teachers in the Segregated South* (Cambridge: Belknap, Harvard University Press, 2007); and James D. Anders, *The Education of Blacks in the South, 1860–1935* (Chapel Hill: University of North Carolina Press, 1988).

6. Jacqueline Jones, *Labor of Love, Labor of Sorrow: Black Women, Work, and the Family from Slavery to the Present* (New York: Basic, 1985); Stephanie Shaw, *What a Woman Ought to Be and to Do: Black Professional Women Workers during the Jim Crow Era* (Chicago: University of Chicago Press, 1996); Tera Hunter, *To 'Joy My Freedom: Southern Black Women's Lives and Labors after the Civil War* (Cambridge, MA: Harvard University Press, 1997);

Stephanie Evans, *Black Women in the Ivory Tower, 1850–1954: An Intellectual History* (Gainesville: University Press of Florida, 2007); and Sonya Y. Ramsey, *Reading, Writing, and Segregation: A Century of Black Women Teachers in Nashville* (Chicago: University of Illinois Press, 2008). Works focusing on African American women in Texas shed important light on Horace's regional peers, including Merline Pitre, *In Struggle against Jim Crow: Lula B. White and the NAACP, 1900–1957* (College Station: Texas A&M University Press, 1999); and Merline Pitre and Bruce Glasrud, eds., *Black Women in Texas History* (College Station: Texas A&M University Press, 2008).

7. George C. Wright, *Life behind a Veil: Blacks in Louisville, Kentucky, 1865–1930* (Baton Rouge: Louisiana State University Press, 1985); Albert Broussard, *Black San Francisco: The Struggle for Racial Equality in the West, 1900–1954* (Lawrence: University Press of Kansas, 1994); and his *African-American Odyssey: The Stewarts, 1853–1963* (Lawrence: University Press of Kansas, 1998); and Anne Meis Knupfer, *The Chicago Black Renaissance and Women's Activism* (Chicago: University of Illinois Press, 2005).

8. The papers of Shirley Graham Du Bois and Ozeline Barrett (Pearson) Wise (1903–88), Schlesinger Library, Radcliffe Institute, Harvard University, Cambridge, Massachusetts; Evanston Reference Files, Evanston Public Library, Evanston, Illinois; Simmons University Papers, University of Louisville Library, Kentucky; interviews with teachers from Birmingham and Tuskegee, Alabama, who participated in "Behind the Veil: Documenting African American Life in

the Jim Crow South," Duke University Special Collections, Durham, North Carolina; diaries of Jennie Elizabeth Mustafa (1898–1992) and Layle Lane (1893–1976), Moorland-Spingarn Research Center, Manuscript Division, Processed Collections, Howard University, Washington, DC; Zeta Phi Beta Scrapbook, Schomburg Center for Research in Black Culture, New York; Viola Hill Papers, Amistad Research Center, New Orleans, Louisiana; Special Collections Research Center, University of Chicago Library; and Heartman Collection, Texas Southern University, Houston.

9. Patricia Hill Collins, *Black Feminist Thought: Knowledge, Consciousness, and the Politics of Empowerment* (New York: Routledge, 1990), 95.

10. Horace, *Diary*, 7.

11. Ibid., 13.

12. US Census, 1890, 1900, 1910, 1920, 1930.

13. Horace, *Diary*, 5.

14. Ibid., 6.

15. Ibid., 5.

16. Ibid., 9.

17. Ibid., 45.

18. "Historic Preservation of Schools," *Historical Markers of Tarrant County*, http://www.fortworthgov.org/, 9.

19. *Morrison and Fourmy's General Directory of the City of Fort Worth 1899–1900* (Galveston, TX: Morrison and Fourmy, 1899).

20. Horace, *Diary*, 22.

21. Merline Pitre, *Struggle against Jim Crow*, 8.

22. *Terrelife* (newspaper), Lillian B. Horace Papers, Fort Worth Public Library, Fort Worth, Texas (cited hereafter as Horace Papers).

23. Evans, *Ivory Tower*.

24. Ibid., 40.

25. Ibid.

26. Ibid., 49.

27. Shaw, *What a Woman Ought*, 13–40.

28. Horace, *Diary*, 36.

29. Adam Fairclough, *A Class of Their Own: Black Teachers in the Segregated South* (Cambridge, MA: Harvard University Press, 2007), 226.

30. Horace, *Diary*, 18.

31. Ibid., 19.

32. Ibid., 14. The review is cited in Jan L. Jones, *Renegades, Showmen and Angels: A Theatrical History of Fort Worth from 1873–2001* (Fort Worth: Texas Christian University Press, 2006), 285.

33. Horace, *Diary*, 19.

34. Cited in Mary S. Hoffschwelle, *The Rosenwald Schools of the American South* (Gainesville: University Press of Florida, 2006), 254.

35. "Dallas County Summer Normal," Dallas *Morning News*, June 6, 1922.

36. "Summer Normals in Texas," Dallas *Morning News*, May 8, 1905.

37. "Summer Normal List," Dallas *Morning News*, April 11, 1906.

38. Horace, *Diary*, 107.

39. Kevin Kelly Gaines, *Uplifting the Race: Black Leadership, Politics, and Culture in the Twentieth Century* (Chapel Hill: University of North Carolina Press, 1996).

40. "About PVAMU," *PVAMU*, http://www.pvamu.edu/pages/n9.asp.

41. Horace, *Diary*, 36.

42. Ibid., 38.

43. Simmons Bible College Records, 1869–1971, Simmons University Papers, University of Louisville, Kentucky (cited hereafter as Simmons Papers).

44. Simmons University Bulletin, Academic Year 1921–22, 43rd Annual Catalogue, American Baptist Press, Simmons Papers.

45. Simmons Bible College Records, 1869–1971, Simmons Papers.

46. Horace noted serving as a "Girl Protective Worker" during World War I. *Diary*, 145.

47. Simmons Bible College Records, 1869–1971. Simmons Papers.

48. Wilson, *Segregated Scholars*, 200.

49. Wright, *Life behind a Veil*, 123–55, 167.

50. Evelyn Brooks Higginbotham, *Righteous Discontent: The Women's Movement in the Black Baptist Church: 1880–1920* (Cambridge, MA: Harvard University Press, 1993).

51. *Africana: The Encyclopedia of the African and African American Experience* (New York: Perseus, 2003), s.v. "Bond, Horace Mann."

52. Simmons College was closed in the 1950s and officially reopened on June 28, 2007, as Simmons College of Kentucky, "a biblical institution of higher learning."

53. James D. Anderson, "Northern Foundations and the Shaping of Southern Black Rural Education, 1902–1935," *History of Education Quarterly* 18, no. 4 (Winter 1978): 371–96.

54. H. E. Slaught, "The Teaching of Mathematics in Summer Sessions of Universities and Normal Schools," *American Mathematical Monthly* 18, no. 8 and 9 (2011): 147–57.

55. Horace, *Diary*, 23.

56. Ibid., 59.

57. Ibid., 5.

58. Ibid., 3.

59. Mary Church Terrell, *A Colored Woman in a White World*, ed. Henry Louis Gates (New York: Simon and Schuster Macmillan, 1996), 15–16.

60. The Church History Committee of Second Baptist Church has affirmed November 17, 1882, as the date of the church's establishment.

61. Rhonda Craven, email to Karen Kossie-Chernyshev, October 22, 2009.

62. Ibid.

63. Ibid.

64. "Mother of Three Ministers Dies at Groveton, Tex.," Chicago *Defender*, March 8, 1947, http://www.ancestry.com.

65. Joseph Gentry Horace, World War I Draft Registration Card, 1917–18, Horace Papers.

66. Texas Death Index, 1903–40, Ancestry.com, accessed September, 11, 2018, https://search.ancestry.com/search/db.aspx?dbid=4876.

67. Horace, *Diary*, 44.

68. "Texas State News," Chicago *Defender*, December 10, 1932.

69. Chicago *Defender*, August 29, 1931.

70. Ibid., December 19, 1931.

71. Ibid., December 10, 1932.

72. Horace, *Diary*, 44.

73. Evanston *Newsette*, December 5, 1946. The *Newsette* was published by Melvin Smith.

74. Marilyn R. Mast Hewitt, Registrar and Director of Student Services, Northern Seminary, Lombard, Illinois, email to Rhonda Craven, April 15, 2009.

75. Patricia Grice, Lloyd W. Shepard, and Kenneth A. Whitney, "Certain Aspects of the History of Evanston and Its Public Schools from an African-American Perspective," Ad-Hoc Committee on African-American History, May 8, 1992, Evanston Reference Files, Evanston Public Library, Evanston, Illinois, 1–18.

76. Irvine Garland Penn, *The Afro-American Press and Its Editors* (Springfield, MA: Willey, 1891), 124.

77. Andrew Leslie, "History of Evanston's Blacks—1850–1930," Evanston *Review*, February 17, 1983, 22, Evanston

Reference Files, Evanston Public Library, Evanston, Illinois.

78. "Dr. Isabella G. Butler" (obituary), Chicago *Daily Tribune*, August 25, 1948. See also "Founder of Evanston Medical Center Buried," Chicago *Defender*, September 4, 1948.

79. Prairie View was one of four historically black colleges and universities, including Atlanta University (now Clark-Atlanta), Fisk University, and Hampton Normal and Agricultural Institute (now Hampton University), participating in the Negro Teacher-Librarian Education Program, which trained approximately two hundred African American teacher-librarians from sixteen Southern states during the Jim Crow period. See Allison M. Sutton, "Bridging the Gap in Early Library Education History for African Americans: The Negro Teacher-Librarian Training Program (1936–1939)," *Journal of Negro Education* 74, no. 2 (Spring 2005): 139.

80. Minutes of the National Association of Colored Women, July 25–30, 1937, Fort Worth, Texas (microfilm, Fondren Library, Rice University).

81. Credential Committee, National Association of Colored Women, Conference Program, 1939, Boston, Massachusetts (microfilm, Fondren Library, Rice University), 125.

82. Horace, *Diary*, 35.

83. Ibid., 35, 38.

84. Illinois *Baptist Messenger*, March 15, 1940 (Horace file, Northern Baptist Seminary, Lombard, Illinois).

85. "Mother of Three Ministers."

86. Illinois *Baptist Messenger*, May 15, 1940.

87. Horace, *Diary*, 44.

88. Ibid., 50–51.

89. Lillian B. Jones [Horace], *Five Generations Hence* (Fort Worth: Dotson-Jones, 1916), 33.

90. Cooke County Genealogical Records, Chicago. Found at www.ancestry.com.

91. Horace, *Diary*, 38.

92. Evanston *News*, August 29, 1946.

93. Horace, *Diary*, 38.

94. Ibid., 39.

95. Evanston *Newsette*, December 12, 1946.

96. Mrs. L. B. Horace to 2012 Darrow Street, Western Union telegram, November 28, 12:21 p.m., Horace Papers.

97. Horace, *Diary*, 28.

98. Ibid.

99. Ibid., 46.

100. D. G. Gibson, "Berkeley, Calif.," Chicago *Defender*, August 11, 1934, 18.

101. See Calisphere, an online digital archive of California, at http://content.cdlib.org.

102. Ibid.

103. Ibid.

104. Ibid.

105. Karen Kossie-Chernyshev, "'What Is Africa to Me?': Visions of Africa in Lillian Bertha Jones's *Five Generations Hence* (1916)—A Gendered Means to a Political End," *East Texas Historical Journal* 49, no. 1 (Spring 2011): 135–46; Kossie-Chernyshev, introduction to Lillian B. Horace, *Angie Brown* (Acton, MA: Copley Custom, 2008).

106. Glenda Gilmore, *Defying Dixie: The Radical Roots of Civil Rights, 1919–1950* (New York: Norton, 2008).

107. Horace, *Diary*, 22.

108. "New Book on Life of L. K. Williams," Chicago *Defender*, September 5, 1964.

109. Tim Madigan, "A Tale of Two Schools: The Challenge," Fort Worth *Star Telegram*, October 7, 2002.

Sepia Record as a Forum for Negotiating Women's Roles

Sherilyn Brandenstein

Sherilyn Brandenstein discovered that African American working women were portrayed positively and realistically in the Fort Worth–based magazine Sepia Record *during post–World War II years. The magazine began publication in 1947 under the name* Negro Achievements *but underwent a name change soon after. Eventually known as* Sepia, *the magazine focused on various aspects of African American culture, including women's activities and civil rights. It is important to realize that this vital publication was published in Central Texas. Sherilyn Brandenstein earned a master's degree at the University of Texas at Austin; her thesis title was "Prominent Roles of Black Womanhood in* Sepia Record, *1952–1954."*

★

About five years ago, I was conducting research on R. C. Hickman, a Dallas photographer, when I came upon a magazine for African Americans published in the 1950s. Early issues carried the title *Negro Achievements*, then the name changed to *Sepia Record* late in 1953. I was struck by the number of prominent articles on women, especially career women, in a magazine not intended specifically for women.

Around this time, I had a growing interest in the images in print media and how magazine graphics serve as arenas for negotiating ideas. One of the most significant of these negotiations in our century has had to do with gender roles.

I learned that several scholars already had analyzed the leading national magazines to find out how women were portrayed—that is, how the Victorian ideals of white, middle-class womanhood were either endorsed or challenged. They had addressed how general-circulation magazines had portrayed women according to age and marital status. Only a few investigated whether and how black women were presented in mainstream magazines.

As I read this literature on gendered portrayals, I found little evidence of research on gender as portrayed in major African American periodicals. While a minority of white Americans read such publications, blacks, especially urban blacks, are the targeted audience for these periodicals and have easy access to them. I assumed that if African Americans have had role expectations for women different from the white, middle-class standard, a black magazine would be a good medium to examine for challenges and negotiations about women's proper place.

This article summarizes key conclusions from my investigation of *Sepia Record* (and *Negro Achievements*, its predecessor), developed more fully in my thesis, "Prominent Roles of Black Womanhood in *Sepia Record*, 1952–1954." First, the article discusses existing research on general-circulation magazine coverage of women and whether it matched the actual roles North American women were taking on in the decade after World War II. Then, it describes *Sepia Record*, a Texas-based magazine for blacks, and provides highlights of its presentation of black women in the early 1950s.[1]

A review of the scholarship on portrayals of women in the major general-circulation magazines in the 1950s suggests that the dominant postwar concept of women's lives involved two mutually exclusive scenarios: the devoted wife and mother, whose unpaid work centered on home life and/or community service, or the single woman or childless married woman employed in entertainment or in "female" service jobs. Typically, such jobs were conducive to finding a husband or fulfilling women's presumed needs to nurture. Women choosing professional, technical, or business careers after male veterans had returned from World War II tended to be presented as exceptional. Some magazines went so far as to imply that they were frustrated or incompetent in jobs "better suited" to men.[2]

Betty Friedan, in her 1963 book *The Feminine Mystique*, accused the major US magazines of using a pejorative tone in their coverage of women who sought or held jobs traditionally considered male. She also criticized the advertising industry for consistently promoting a housewife identity for female consumers in American magazines. Friedan identified the key role that industry assigned to women as home-makers to intensify consumerism after the war.[3]

Presumably, editorial content more accurately reflects women's status than advertising content. However, Matthews reportedly studied a sampling of *Time* and *Newsweek* issues from 1940, 1960, and 1980 and found that "women were infrequently pictured ... in all roles except those of 'artist/entertainer' and 'spouse,'" typically in the "Entertainment" or "People" section. This pattern hardly changed across four decades.[4]

Belkaoui and Belkaoui gathered a sampling of general-circulation magazine advertisements from 1958 and the 1970s to learn how women were portrayed across fourteen years. In the 1958 group, they encountered familiar postwar stereotypes: (1) "Most women were shown in nonworking roles, often in the home"; (2) nearly all women portrayed in employed situations were presented as clerical, secretarial, or blue-collar workers (i.e., low-income wage-earners); and (3) in leisure-time situations, female models, unlike their male counterparts, were shown as "decorative features" or "wrappings" for products.[5]

Analyzing female imagery in popular culture, Weibel traced the origins of portraying (white) American women as "housewifely, passive, wholesome and pretty" to nineteenth-century North American practices. She also stated that a sexy image of women in magazine content became increasingly prevalent after World War II, complicating traditional female ideals of "wholesomeness." Married or single, women shown as erotic icons were at peak childbearing age, Weibel noted.[6]

Banta's study of "the American girl" in popular culture concluded that "sexuality was clearly a marketable product by the 1890s, both as an item for direct sale and as a come-on for readers of the tabloid press." She labeled a new turn-of-the-century ideal of young womanhood *provocative winsomeness*, a more subdued version of female sensuality than prevailed after 1945.[7]

By mid-century, the sexual persona was well entrenched in magazine representations of American women. Hartmann has noted the increased emphasis on female (hetero) sexual appeal during World War II in periodicals targeted specifically to men or to women. A study cited by Butler and Paisley found that more than 30 percent of the cigarette, beverage, automobile, and airline advertisements drawn from a two-decade sampling of general magazines (1950–71) presented women as physically alluring.[8]

This practice was so pervasive in the urban publishing industry that it cut across racial categories of marketing and magazine editing.[9] The findings of Jones and of Joseph and Lewis indicate that black women frequently have been portrayed as erotic icons in postwar African American magazines, aligning these periodicals with a dominant ideology promoting women's sexual role.[10]

For example, the obviously greater proportion of female popular entertainers than other employed women highlighted in Johnson Publications' *Ebony* magazine articles fit into the twentieth-century North American pattern of eroticized female imagery. Featuring African American celebrities already familiar to most readers— singers, dancers, and actresses who appeared in television and film—contributed to *Ebony*'s formula for maintaining steady sales nationwide through most of the post– World War II era. By the early 1960s, it had become the highest-circulation secular magazine among African Americans. Yet African American magazines' portrayals of women in the 1950s cannot be characterized as unidimensionally erotic.[11]

Analyzing African American women's roles and activities in the first decade after World War II, Jones examined the coverage of black women in Johnson Publications' *Ebony Magazine*, which became the best-selling magazine written for African Americans.[12] She stated that *Ebony* generally combined messages about various roles for women. Most issues carried imagery of bathing beauties and glamorous female celebrities but also paid tribute to women achievers in the professions, skilled trades, business, and arts. Those who became the first or only black women in the United States to obtain prestigious positions received coverage, as did celebrities who spoke out advocating civil rights for members of their race.[13]

Jones admitted that, while *Ebony* did not accurately reflect the reality most black working women experienced, it did promote examples of a "superwoman"—a well-paid and competent working wife and mother—two decades before the white press did so. She notes the political significance of a magazine in the 1950s conveying the ideas that "civil rights and good jobs went together, and that black women were equally entitled to both."[14]

In contrast to the dominant white-owned magazines, *Ebony* sometimes presented women in activist roles. Female celebrities and "famous wives" were credited for their opinions or actions on public issues as well as their ideas about fashions or homemaking. White Americans, especially women, typically focused on the private, domestic sphere rather than public affairs just after World War II. Meanwhile, *Ebony's* featured subjects who had campaigned for racial integration and equal rights received respectful coverage. By showing African American women's participation, the magazine promoted both ideologies of gender equality and racial equality. Overall, its portrayals of female leaders probably put *Ebony* ahead of its time compared with most white-oriented general-circulation magazines.[15]

Still, as Goodman has noted, Johnson Publications' business strategy from 1945 to 1965 encouraged an editorial policy of minimizing overt social criticism. Indeed, in matters of gender, the magazine's disproportionate emphasis on entertainers and wives of famous men in the coverage of women complicated its role as a trailblazer.[16]

Moving beyond magazines' characterizations of women's lives in the 1950s, what do demographers say *real* American women were doing then? It's worth backing up a bit to assess the impact of World War II on American women's roles.

The biggest changes for women during World War II involved new waves of married and older women entering nonfarm employment. Only about one-fifth of American wives were in the paid labor force by 1944, but they made up 75 percent of the female new hires. For the first time in US history, the number of married women exceeded the number of single women in the total female workforce.[17]

Another change was the substantial addition of older women to the ranks of the employed. Noting their long-term influence, Campbell has written, "By 1945, half of all women workers were over thirty-five; slightly more than one in four was forty-five or older. The typical female worker had changed, from one who was younger and single to one who was older and married. This new pattern maintained itself through the post-war period."[18]

As I mentioned earlier, the overall percentage of African American women in the workforce had not changed that drastically during the war. The nature of the work shifted for some but not most. The war years brought a drop in the number of black women in agriculture (down from 16 percent to 8 percent) and in domestic service, decreasing from three-fifths to roughly half of all black women employed.

Meanwhile, the percentage who were machine operators climbed to 16 percent. Even more took jobs in commercial service.[19]

When the United States converted to peacetime production, men took priority in the higher-paying industrial and business jobs. Many wives and mothers who had been new hires returned to homemaking full-time. The consensus among North Americans during the postwar decade was that any woman who became a wife and mother already had a valid full-time career.[20]

Despite a dip in women's workforce participation in the first year after World War II, women soon returned to work by the thousands, but usually as part-timers. By the time the Korean War erupted in June 1950, spot labor shortages had developed in secretarial, nursing, teaching, and social-work positions. Of course, these vocations, typically filled by women, white *and* black, tended to provide lower wages than traditionally male positions. Yet a growing minority of families had to have the wife and mother working to be able to meet family expenses. In 1950, nearly one-third of all adult women worked for wages, and roughly half of them were married.[21]

Proportionately, more black women than white had wage-earning jobs. Furthermore, black working women were concentrated in domestic and institutional service positions.[22] By contrast, the profile of white American womanhood that emerges from the early 1950s is one of lives typically centered on home life, especially among married and older women. Even when women participated in school, church, and community affairs as volunteers, they generally performed extensions of the same functions women generally had at home.[23] Meanwhile, an increasing female minority within all races worked for wages away from home. For most of them, womanhood involved negotiations over competing family and employment roles.[24]

Comparing the images of American women in the leading adult magazines of the 1950s with the actual roles women had, then, some but not all of the portrayals correlated. Showing women predominantly as wives and mothers in print seems to have reflected the majority of North American women's lives. Subscription magazines, as links between major advertisers and consumers, emphasized women's roles as purchasers of home furnishings, food, and fashions. Despite the steady rise in female employment, women were portrayed far less often than men as employed or in community leadership roles, except in such black magazines as *Ebony*.

General-circulation magazines promoted the ideology of young women, especially attractive single women, as erotic icons. Consequently, young female entertainers and models were presented in magazines in much greater proportion than their actual numbers in the population. It is worth noting that white-oriented American magazines began running profiles on selected African American performers, including women, during the 1940s and 1950s.[25]

By the time the major national magazines started featuring African American celebrities, most of these individuals already had received national publicity in national black magazines, periodicals about which many white Americans had only a vague awareness. *Ebony*, a large-format pictorial, and *Jet*, a pocket-size news digest also from Johnson Publications, were the most familiar examples of the national African American magazines to emerge after World War II. The field also included pictorials such as *Color* and *Our World*.

A publisher based in Fort Worth developed two regional African American magazines, *The World's Messenger* and *Negro Achievements*, in the mid-1940s. By the 1970s, his successor had spun off four more magazines, all distributed nationally. These included a teen magazine, confessions and crime magazines, and a periodical about black entertainers, as well as *Sepia*, a monthly pictorial. *Sepia's* editors strove to make this magazine similar to *Ebony*, but it never had as many corporate advertisements or subscriptions. Like other periodicals from the same publisher, *Sepia* mostly sold on newsstands.[26]

It is difficult now to locate early issues of *Sepia* magazine. The Good Publishing Company, which had produced it, folded in the early 1980s. North Texas State University (NTSU) did not begin acquiring issues of the magazine until 1961. As for those published in the 1950s, all I could find was a two-year run of *Sepia* prototypes: *Negro Achievements* and *Sepia Record*, a transitional form that developed into *Sepia*. The Center for American History at the University of Texas at Austin owns issues dated from 1951 through 1953. My study was based on articles from these and from 1954 issues of *Sepia Record* at Fisk University in Nashville.[27]

Negro Achievements, the predecessor to *Sepia Record*, was born in the closing months of World War II. Horace J. Blackwell, an African. American entrepreneur and Texas Negro Baseball League officer, created *Negro Achievements* as a showcase for amateur writers of autobiographical stories, typically imbued with religious convictions. The magazine employed a true-confessions formula. Shorter features included African American church and social news from the South-Central United States.[28]

When Blackwell died in December 1949, his assistant Adelle Conner Jackson, also black, sought investors to take on the indebted publishing firm. For months, she encountered discouraging responses. Finally, she persuaded a white businessman to assume the company's debts. He agreed to this only if he could have full ownership and direction. Within one year, George Levitan, the new publisher, hired a young white couple to edit the magazines. In the meantime, he retained several black women from the original staff and brought in college instructors to teach them journalism skills.[29]

Seth and Anne Kantor, the new editors, came to the Fort Worth company from Dell Publishing's Modern Magazine Division in New York. The Kantors' strategy was to reshape Levitan's magazines to appeal to young urban blacks and to broaden their market beyond the South. The couple engineered the change of *Negro Achievements* to *Sepia Record* in 1953, emphasizing graphics with a bright, open layout in the new format.[30]

Following trends in celebrity fan magazines and black newspapers such as the Chicago *Defender*, *Sepia Record* carried an increasing quotient of personality feature stories. Confessional stories were moved to another of Levitan's magazines,

Bronze Thrills. Sepia Record, taking cues from *Ebony* and *Jet,* began carrying profiles of African American entertainers, sports celebrities, and pioneers in business and the professions. Levitan named his operation the Good Publishing Company and contracted with an established distribution firm in Chicago to expand magazine sales nationally.[31]

My research on portrayals of black womanhood spans issues from 1952, when the magazine was still under the title *Negro Achievements,* through 1954, following the changes in the name and format. I sought out feature stories about individuals or families, since these predominated in *Sepia Record*'s content. The study analyzed articles focused on an identified woman or women in text and pictures and consisting of two or more pages. Graphic elements, such as photographs and headlines, as well as the copy were noted carefully. I read the interplay of images and text for evidence of gesture, activity, expressive attitude, dress, and relationships—all potential clues to gender and social roles.

If *Sepia Record* accurately represented a range of African American perspectives on women's roles, then it was a wider range than those promoted in general-circulation magazines in the early 1950s. This magazine's sparse coverage of women in full-time mothering and homemaking scenarios allowed for, but downplayed, the likelihood of that sole option for black women.[32]

More central to the imagery of women was work, paid or voluntary, *outside* the home. The work that warranted a particular woman's inclusion in the magazine generally was exceptional, for white women or for blacks of either gender. Most women were not entertainers or professional athletes, but most African American women who made the news in the 1950s *were.* In this latter aspect, *Sepia Record* followed the standard magazine formulas of the time. Like other black magazines, it emphasized stories on African American professionals, countering their low visibility in mainstream media.[33]

Generally, stories about particular women (or families of women) focused on one or several of the following roles:

1. Career woman as mother and/or wife
2. Unmarried, childless career woman
3. Race and gender "pioneer"
4. Career woman as civic or social organizer[34]

Some articles, when describing a woman's multiple roles, emphasized one far more than another. Whatever the emphasis, African American women overall were shown to have varied choices and to live multifaceted lives.[35]

Stressing the theme of the black "superwoman," an October 1953 issue of *Sepia Record* carried a story titled "Concert Singer and Housewife." The subheading said, "Everybody told pretty Darwin Walton she couldn't mix a career with domestic duties—she proved them wrong." Imagery concentrated on Walton as an individual but included a picture of her with husband Claude Walton. Near the end of the article, the writer quoted Darwin Walton: "Claude and I felt that we could have each other and still leave some area in our lives for individual expression. . . . It has worked out wonderfully." These are the words of a middle- or upper-class wife who apparently considers her work to be more a means of self-fulfillment than a financial necessity. Equally revealing was her statement that "marriage and a family represent the greatest opportunities any woman can have. But this doesn't mean the cancellation of other opportunities that have to do with a career—not if a girl is willing to face life realistically."[36]

At the time of her interview, Walton was fitting time with her nine-month-old daughter in between rehearsals for a ten-city concert tour. The article did not include a picture of the baby; it did contain an image of her mother posing in a bathing suit.

Walton was no exception in this magazine's coverage of female achievers. Numerous articles on career women, especially performing artists and medical professionals, included references to their successes as wives and mothers.[37]

Of course, juggling work, marriage, and/or mothering is not every woman's ideal. Even though the prevailing sentiment in American culture encouraged women to marry and have children, Negro Achievements and Sepia Record routinely provided examples of women who had chosen careers over marriage and motherhood.[38]

Gospel singer Clara Ward exemplified the single career woman as Sepia Record presented her. In the summer of 1953, this twenty-eight-year-old had just won awards in a national poll of jazz fans, bringing her increased media attention. Photographic imagery in this article portrayed her singing ecstatically in performance, posing with sheet music from her publishing firm, and reading at home. The text emphasized her devotion to gospel music and penchant for fashionable attire. A rigorous national touring schedule reportedly fueled her $150,000 annual income. As for marriage plans, Ward said that she had not "found the 'man in her life' and that her schedule permits little time for romance." The magazine profile described a woman more committed to her vocation and religious leadings than to launching a family.[39]

Although the war years represented a watershed period for African American men to break into formerly segregated work arenas, some women were able to do the same. When one's race and gender made her a sufficiently rare "double minority" in a high-profile or lucrative occupation, her story landed in the pages of African American magazines. Black female pioneers in sports received special coverage when they moved into Olympic or professional ranks.[40] Issues of Sepia Record and Negro Achievements also ran articles on a Connecticut policewoman and the manager of a five-hundred-unit luxury apartment complex.[41]

From the June 1952 Negro Achievements came a story on Texas State Board of Health physician Connie Yerwood Odom of Austin. It emphasized her work in preventive medicine, especially as it benefitted black women and children. Also mentioned was the growing number of women attending Meharry Medical School, an African American institution from which Odom graduated. The writer specifically noted the community-service activities that Odom managed to work into her schedule.[42]

If the 1950s seemed a decade of hyperdomesticity for whites, African Americans found it a time of compelling social awareness and activism. Black individuals received credit in black magazines for voluntary efforts to benefit their communities. The black press acknowledged blacks' civic achievements when daily newspapers rarely covered them.[43]

In a May 1954 article, Blanche Calloway's former musical career came to the attention of *Sepia Record*'s readers. Most of the imagery and text described the high-energy dancer and bandleader she had been in her youth. In an update, the writer noted that Callaway recently had defeated five male candidates to become the committeewoman in her Philadelphia political ward. She was also serving on a citywide committee to address juvenile delinquency. She posed for the photographer at the Boys and Girls Club and at a reception honoring her community work. Award in hand, she flashed the "famous Calloway smile."[44]

Calloway was not necessarily outdoing middle-class white women in her dedication to civic efforts. Many *were* involved in lobbying and organizing. The difference was that a black woman of Calloway's notoriety received as much credit for her community activism as for her artistic achievements when covered in African American pictorial magazines such as *Sepia Record*.[45]

How do we account for the varied models of womanhood in marriage, careers, and community work that *Sepia Record* presented? First, there was the precedent of most African American women having worked for wages at some time, whether married, parenting, or neither. They and their relatives were the magazine's consumers. Second, consider the principals in the Good Publishing Company during the early 1950s. Adelle Conner Jackson had been in the workforce all her adult life, whether single, divorced, or married. She was raising a son during her tenure at the company. Seth and Anne Kantor both worked as editors. George Levitan, the publisher, comanaged a wholesale business with his wife. These personal experiences of the management, added to the example of black wives and mothers in their employ, supported a positive model of women in the workforce. As Patricia Hill Collins has stated, African American women have survived in a society that denigrates them and their characteristics through their commitment to maintaining positive self-images. The black women at Good Publishing apparently continued that legacy of positive self-definition.[46]

As noted earlier, alluring female imagery in *Sepia Record* and *Negro Achievements* placed these magazines in step with the postwar ideology of women as erotic symbols. They differed from other magazines by acknowledging that women, including older women, could enjoy being sexual.[47]

That women could be portrayed as simultaneously alluring and strong, nurturing and smart, working for wages while also caring for family and community, might have posed an obvious contradiction to some white middle-class readers, and editors, in the 1950s. Yet these multiple roles and strategies had become standard for most black women (and many black men) in the century after emancipation. Their external lives involved challenging complexity, but they did not necessarily see their own *identities* as internally contradictory.[48]

In *Sepia Record*'s complex portrayals of black womanhood, we are reminded of Janice Radway's warning not to assume that patriarchy is monolithic or wholly successful. Instead, she calls it "a set of practices . . . riven by conflicts, slippages, and imperfect joinings." Indeed, *Sepia Record* testified that American womanhood was not as unidimensional in the 1950s as the white mainstream press led readers to believe. Black, brown, or beige, married or single, African American women had "a whole lot goin' on."[49]

Brandenstein, Sherilyn. "Sepia Record as a Forum for Negotiating Women's Roles." In Women and Texas History. *Edited by Fane Downs and Nancy Baker Jones, 143–57. Austin: Texas State Historical Association, 1993. Reprinted by permission of the author's siblings and the Texas State Historical Association.*

NOTES

1. I have labeled periodicals directed toward a predominantly African American readership as either "black" or "African American," regardless of who published or edited them. I assume that a publication's identity is primarily determined by its target audience. Notwithstanding letters to the editors from white readers, *Sepia Record*'s primary audience comprised black adults.

2. Betty Friedan, *The Feminine Mystique*, 20th anniversary ed. (New York: W. W. Norton, 1983), 34–36, 42–44, 52–54, 67.

3. Ibid., 58–59, 206.

4. Frances Coins Wilhoit, ed., *Journalism Abstracts* 20 (1982): 86.

5. Ahmed Belkaoui and Janice M. Belkaoui, "A Comparative Analysis of the Roles Portrayed by Women in Print Advertisements: 1958, 1970, 1977," *Journal of Marketing Research* 13 (May 1976): 170.

6. Kathryn Weibel, *Mirror Mirror: Images of Women Reflected in Popular Culture* (Garden City, NY: Anchor, 1977), 166, 168–69.

7. Martha Banta, *Imaging American Women: Idea and Ideals in Cultural History* (New York: Columbia University Press, 1987), 620–22.

8. Susan M. Hartmann, *The Home Front and Beyond: American Women in the 1940s* (Boston: Twayne, 1982), 198; Matilda Butler and William Paisley, *Women and the Mass Media: Sourcebook for Research and Action* (New York: Human Sciences Press, 1980), 99–101.

9. Joseph and Lewis, as well as Carby, have noted that mainstream-press portrayals of black women as explicitly sexual were hardly a new phenomenon. In fact, white writers historically have stereotyped people of color as sexually provocative, especially relative to whites. The change brought on by wartime conditions and by the mass media was to eroticize *white* middle-class women. The point is that this new mass-media trend influenced nearly all commercial magazines. See Hazel Carby, *Reconstructing Womanhood: The Emergence of the Afro American Woman Novelist* (New York: Oxford University Press, 1987), 37, 39; and Gloria L. Joseph and Jill Lewis, *Common Differences: Conflicts in Black and White Feminist Perspectives* (New York: Anchor Press, 1981), 163.

10. Jacqueline Jones, *Labor of Love, Labor of Sorrow: Black Women, Work, and the Family from Slavery to the Present* (New York: Basic, 1985), 270; Joseph and Lewis, *Common Differences*, 157, 159.

11. Jones, *Labor of Love*, 270–72; Roland Edgar Wolseley, *The Black Press, U.S.A.* (Ames: Iowa State University Press, 1971), 63–64, 118.

12. Jones's observations are qualitative, as she drew on only a few issues from an entire decade to survey.

13. Jones, *Labor of Love*, 270–74.

14. Ibid., 269, 272–74.

15. Ibid., 272–74.

16. Walter Goodman, "*Ebony*: Biggest Negro Magazine," *Dissent* 15 (1968): 404; Jones, *Labor of Love*, 272.

17. D'Ann Campbell, *Women at War with America: Private Live in a Patriotic Era* (Cambridge, MA: Harvard University Press, 1984), 180–82; Hartmann, *Home Front*, 92–93; Ruth Milkman, *Gender at Work: The Dynamics of Job Segregation*

by *Sex during World War II* (Urbana: University of Illinois Press, 1987), 63.

18. Alice Kessler-Harris, *Out to Work: A History of Wage-Earning Women in the United States* (New York: Oxford University Press, 1982), 278; Campbell, *Women at War*, 78.

19. Campbell, *Women at War*, 174; Hartmann, *Home Front*, 86; Jones, *Labor of Love*, 234.

20. Campbell, *Women at War*, 232; Douglas T. Miller and Marion Novak, *The Fifties: The Way We Really Were* (Garden City, NY: Doubleday, 1977), 155; Norman L. Rosenberg, Emily S. Rosenberg, and James R. Moore, *In Our Times: America since World War II* (Englewood Cliffs, NJ: Prentice-Hall, 1976), 64.

21. Hartmann, *Home Front*, 93–94; Susan Estabrook Kennedy, *If All We Did Was to Weep at Home: A History of White Working-Class Women in America* (Bloomington: Indiana University Press, 1979), 204; Kessler-Harris, *Out to Work*, 303.

22. Jones, *Labor of Love*, 234–35, 269.

23. William Henry Chafe, *The American Woman: Her Changing Social Economic and Political Roles, 1920–1970* (New York: Oxford University Press, 1972), 217–18; Eugenia Kaledin, *Mothers and More: American Women in the 1950s* (Boston: Twayne, 1984), 32–33.

24. Kennedy, *If All We Did*, 183–219; Annie Mae Hunt and Ruthe Winegarten, *I Am Annie Mae: An Extraordinary Black Texas Woman in Her Own Words* (Austin: Rosegarden Press, 1983), 67–70.

25. On Dorothy Dandridge, see "Shy No More," *Life* 31 (November 5, 1951): 65–70. *Look* ran "Portrait of an Actress," an Earths Kin profile, in vol. 17 (October 6, 1953): 72–73. For

Newsweek stories on Marian Anderson and Harry Belafonte, see vol. 33 (April 25, 1949): 84–86; and vol. 43 (March 29, 1954): 84–85; respectively.

26. Sherilyn Brandenstein, "Prominent Roles of Black Womanhood in *Sepia Record* 1952–1954" (MA thesis, University of Texas at Austin, 1989), 77–78, 87, 96.

27. The African-American Museum of Life and Culture in Dallas has acquired a collection of *Sepia* photographs obtained from the files of the Good Publishing Company, and museum staff hope to have them catalogued by 1995. I have located no library in or near Texas that has a full run of the magazine from the years 1953 through 1961.

28. Brandenstein, "Prominent Roles," 76–80.

29. Ibid., 80–86.

30. Ibid., 67, 86–87.

31. Ibid., 86–89, 92.

32. Ibid., 111.

33. Ibid., 110–12; Wolseley, *Black Press, U.S.A.*, 118.

34. This study does not include stories about institutions or social issues involving women. Such a survey certainly would turn up images from *Sepia Record* of black women in more routine jobs such as clerks, operatives, and farmworkers.

35. Brandenstein, "Prominent Roles," 111–12.

36. *Sepia Record*, October 1953, 44.

37. "Best Spook Woman in Show Business," *Sepia Record*, July 1953, 1–4; "A Day in the Life of a Nurse," *Negro Achievements* 6 (November 1952): 24–26; "Married in Harmony," *Negro Achievements* 7 (January 1953): 25–27; "'Real Gone' Nellie," *Sepia Record*, November 1953, 14–16; "Two Can

Practice as Cheaply as One," *Negro Achievements* 6 (August 1952): 28, 46.

38. "Angel of Mercy," *Sepia*, September 1954, 43–44; "No Dumb Dora," *Sepia Record*, June 1953, 14–19; "This Teacher Doesn't Know," *Sepia Record*, July 1953, 14–17.

39. "Queen of Gospel Singers," *Sepia Record*, July 1953, 42–45.

40. See "Althea Gibson," *Ebony* 6 (November 1950): 96–100; "Top Pro Ice Skater," *Ebony* 7 (March 1952): 105–8; "Gal on Second Base," *Our World* 8 (July 1853): 8–11.

41. "First Lady of the Olympics," *Negro Achievements* 6 (October 1952): 37–38; "The Team with the Toni," *Sepia Record*, August 1953, 32–33; "Travis Wilburn, America's Toughest Lady," *Negro Achievements* 5 (November 1952): 24–25; "Pistol Packin' Ella," *Sepia Record*, August 1953, 16–19; "Washington's Hotel for Society," *Negro Achievements* 7 (January 1953): 12–13.

42. "She Chose Medicine for a Career," *Negro Achievements* 6 (June 1952): 16, 56.

43. Wolesley, *Black Press, U.S.A.*, 118–20. Also see "Pistol Packin' Ella," 16–19.

44. "What Has Happened to Blanche Calloway?," *Sepia Record*, May, 1954, 20–23.

45. Chafe, *American Woman*, 217–18. For another example of an African American celebrity's community service, see "First Lady of the Stage," *Negro Achievements* 6 (November 1952): 10–11.

46. Brandenstein, "Prominent Roles," 1, 81–91; Patricia Hill Collins, *Black Feminist Thought: Knowledge, Consciousness, and the Politics of Empowerment* (London: HarperCollins Academic, 1990), 22–23.

47. Brandenstein, "Prominent Roles," 130–31. One of the few studies of

magazine coverage of older Americans
indicates that elderly persons are
depicted in negative tones in at least
50 percent of the samples and their
sexual interest is not even mentioned
as a possibility. See James D. Robinson,
"Mass Media and the Elderly: A Uses
and Dependency Interpretation," in
*Life-Span Communication: Normative
Processes*, ed. Jon F. Nussbaum
(Hillsdale, NJ: Lawrence Erlbaum,
1989), 319–37.

48. Bonnie Thornton Dill, "The Dialectics
of Black Womanhood," *Signs* 4 (Spring
1979): 542, 553; Roger Abrahams,
"Negotiating Respect: Patterns of
Presentation among Black Women,"
Journal of American Folklore 88
(January 1975): 64; Collins, *Black
Feminist Thought*, 94.

49. Janice Rodway, "Identifying Ideological
Seams: Mass Culture, Analytical
Method and Political Practice,"
Communication 9 (1982): 10.

Reluctance versus Reality

The Desegregation of North Texas State College, 1954–1956

Ronald E. Marcello

At the distance of sixty-plus years since the efforts of African Americans to enroll in formerly all-white universities, it is difficult to recall the pressures, tactics, and turmoil of those years. Perhaps even some of the black and white leaders who played a part in the process are forgotten. In this well-researched and well-written article, Ronald E. Marcello provides us with a much-needed remembrance of those events connected with the integration of a Central Texas university, now called the University of North Texas. We learn about the courage from black activists such as Irma Sephas and Joe Atkins as well as white administrators like James C. Matthews. Ronald E. Marcello, a specialist in oral history, earned his PhD in history from Duke University and served as the Director of the Oral History Program at the University of North Texas. He is the author of several books, including Small Town America in World War II: War Stories from Wrightsville, Pennsylvania.

★

On February 3, 1956, Miss Autherine Lucy and Mrs. Irma Sephas enrolled at the University of Alabama and North Texas State College, respectively. They were the first African American undergraduates to attend those institutions. Lucy's career at Alabama was short-lived. Accompanied by a police officer who was assigned to protect her, she sat in a row of seats occupied by no other students, and university officials refused to allow her to live in the college dormitories or eat at its dining facilities. Some campus students and outsiders verbally abused her, while others threatened her with physical harm. The president of the university, Oliver Cromwell Carmichael, with the backing of the board of trustees and Gov. James E. Folsom, who opposed desegregation, encouraged turmoil within the student body, faculty, and the campus in general by standing aside as segregationists invaded the grounds to demonstrate and riot. His actions emboldened the mob to defy the federal courts and consequently prevented an orderly adjustment to desegregation. After Lucy had attended classes for just three days, the board suspended her "until further notice" and "for her safety," alleging that she had publicly charged the board with conspiring with the mob.[1]

On the same day Lucy was having problems in Tuscaloosa, the first African American undergraduate to attend North Texas State College, Irma E. L. Sephas, enrolled with no difficulty. A resident of Fort Worth, Sephas planned to commute between her home and the campus in Denton and major in business with a minor in music. She was a woman of varied interests. In addition to operating a small bookkeeping service and teaching piano out of her home, she was also an apprentice mortician, a notary public, and a church organist. Sephas was forty-one years old when she enrolled at North Texas and had previously attended all-black Huston-Tillotson College in Austin in 1931–32. When she entered classes at North Texas the day after her enrollment, few members of the media were present. She encountered no verbal abuse or threats of physical violence. Thus began the peaceful desegregation of North Texas State College.[2]

The administration at North Texas was proud that desegregation of the college had been free of violence. Pragmatic, decisive leadership and fortuitous circumstances in Denton prevented a repetition of the scene in Tuscaloosa. Yet North Texas never encouraged African American enrollment. College officials hesitatingly accepted the first black graduate student, Tennyson Miller, in the summer of 1954, after the Supreme Court's decisions in the *Sipuel v. Board of Regents of the University of Oklahoma* (1948) and *Sweatt v. Painter* (1950) cases. And when Joe L. Atkins, the first African American undergraduate applicant, sought admission for the fall 1955 session, the president of North Texas, James Carl Matthews, in clear violation of the *Brown v. Board of Education* decision of 1954, rejected his application. Litigation through a federal district court forced the college to comply with the law of the land. Although North Texas was one of the earliest state institutions of higher learning in the old Confederacy to desegregate, it did so only in the face of legal reality and then only with reluctance.[3]

To gain a fuller understanding of the events surrounding the desegregation of North Texas, I have had to rely on oral interviews where the pertinent documents were not available. Interviews obviously have certain limitations. Recollections from the period 1954–56 were not always accurate, so wherever possible, I have used multiple oral sources for corroboration. In other instances, I have taken particular care and used sparingly direct quotes allegedly made by individuals at the times some of the events took place. Nevertheless, I have faithfully retained the interviewees' intentions in relating attitudes, opinions, and beliefs.

North Texas, although not directly targeted by the NAACP, eventually became one of the colleges in Texas to be scrutinized by that organization in its attack on segregation in higher education. A pivotal case in the NAACP's assault was *Sweatt v. Painter* in June 1950. In a landmark decision, the Supreme Court ruled in favor of Heman Sweatt, an African American, in his effort to gain admission to the University of Texas Law School. The court declared unanimously that the hastily established law school created by the Texas legislature for African Americans was in no way equal to the one on the Austin campus. By denying Sweatt the opportunity to obtain a legal education while granting it to others, the justices said, the state had deprived him of equal protection under the law as guaranteed by the Fourteenth Amendment. *Sweatt* was another step in undermining the "separate-but-equal" argument established by *Plessy v. Ferguson* (1896) and thus opened doors for the admission of African Americans to professional and graduate schools in general. Equally important, *Sweatt* served as a precedent for later cases challenging segregated undergraduate education.[4]

Within weeks after the *Sweatt* decision, Thurgood Marshall, who was at that time the general counsel for the NAACP's Legal Defense and Education Fund, announced an all-out attack on segregated public education at all levels, "from law school to kindergarten." Segregated colleges, Marshall believed, were particularly vulnerable. He knew that providing equal educational opportunities within the context of "separate but equal" for medical, law, engineering, and graduate schools was financially impossible for Southern states. Marshall was convinced that the NAACP could demonstrate to the federal courts that Southern states were unable to provide separate and equal educational facilities for African Americans and that with extended litigation by his organization, these states would have to capitulate.[5] As a result of *Sweatt*, therefore, African American postgraduate students soon enrolled in public institutions of higher learning in the seventeen "separate-but-equal" states.[6]

The person who would assume the dominant role in determining the conditions under which African Americans would be admitted to North Texas State College was its president, James Carl ("J. C.") Matthews. Born in 1901 and reared on farms in Grayson County, located in North-Central Texas along the Red River, and Foard County in West Texas near the Panhandle, his acquaintance with African Americans was minimal. He was a product of segregated rural schools, and only during the cotton-picking season, when his father hired African American migrant workers from East Texas, did Matthews have contact with them.[7]

Matthews had had a long career at North Texas. In 1920, he enrolled at what was then North Texas State Teachers College. After receiving his teaching certificate, he accepted a position as a teacher and principal at a small rural school for a year. He then returned to Denton, earned his bachelor's degree in 1925, and immediately took a teaching position in the college's Laboratory School. With some periods of leave, he obtained a PhD from George Peabody College for Teachers in 1932. Returning to North Texas, he was named director of the Laboratory School and then later was appointed as the first dean of the newly formed College of Education. In 1948, he became vice president of what had become North Texas State College and then assumed the presidency in 1951. In his professional career to that time, Matthews's only relationship with African Americans came during a period from 1935 to 1937 when he was on leave from North Texas to serve as the director of curriculum and textbooks for the Texas Department of Education, where he did some work in curriculum development with African American teachers and administrators.[8]

As president, Matthews had almost absolute control over this college with a student body of 5,500. He made all major decisions and relied on very few subordinates to carry out his policies. His authority in part stemmed from his close personal friendship with the chair of the board of regents, Dallas banker Ben Wooten, who was also responsible for Matthews's appointment. Faculty and students alike understood the extent of Matthews's power. A staff member commented, "He was a dictator. He knew what the custodians were talking about; he knew what the faculty was talking about. He knew everything."[9] A football coach remembered,

> If you wanted to spend a dollar over what was budgeted, you didn't go to the athletic director, and you didn't go to a vice-president. You went to J. C. Matthews. When you went into his office, you were going to get a "yes" or "no" right there on the spot. And it wasn't going to be referred to a committee because he didn't have any committees; and it wasn't going to be referred to one of the vice-presidents because they didn't make that kind of decision. He was the one who made the decisions on everything that was done. But you knew that. You knew it from day one that he was the boss.[10]

A former student observed, "He was always aloof. He was very businesslike, and he ran a tight ship."[11]

Although Matthews realized that North Texas would eventually have to face the reality of desegregation, particularly after *Sweatt*, he seemed determined to evade the issue as long as possible. When in 1953, an African American woman who was a graduate of Texas Southern sought information about pursuing an EEd at North Texas, his reaction was to ask for an opinion from the attorney general of Texas, John Ben Shepperd. There is no written record of Shepperd's reply, but his public resistance to desegregation in any form was well known. Perhaps emboldened by Shepperd's attitude, Matthews did nothing to encourage the applicant, telling her that "no colored person has enrolled at North Texas to date." As a result, she never applied for admission.[12]

During the second summer session in July 1954, Tennyson Miller, an assistant high school principal in Port Arthur, Texas, became the first African American to enroll at North Texas State College. Miller was forty-one years old when he applied. He had graduated from Prairie View College in 1935 and earned a master's degree from the University of Wisconsin in 1952. Miller was a member of Phi Delta Kappa, a national honor fraternity for men in education. He already had a Denton connection. From 1936 to 1943, before he entered the military, he had taught mathematics and coached football, basketball, and track at Frederick Douglass Colored High School in Denton. From time to time, he attended coaches' clinics offered by the football staff at North Texas, the only African American to do so. Miller continued to maintain a home in Denton after he went to Port Arthur, and his wife had stayed behind to operate her beauty shop. He intended to earn a doctorate in education at North Texas because no black institution in the state offered the EEd.[13]

Matthews continued a policy of procrastination and delay after Miller applied for admission. His attitude became evident during a meeting in his office with Miller and Arthur Sampley, the vice president for academic affairs, on June 21. At the conference, Miller stressed that Matthews's endorsement was "of major importance." To pursue graduate studies without administrative support, Miller believed, would lead to "adverse conditions [and] a waste of time, money, and effort." Miller allegedly told them, "I don't represent the NAACP. I don't represent anything but myself. I just want to go to school." Nevertheless, Matthews and Sampley made no commitment and wanted more time to consider the matter.[14]

That same afternoon, Matthews drove to Dallas to confer with Ben Wooten, who arranged a telephone extension for Matthews, and the two close friends canvassed opinions from the other board members. The consensus was that Matthews should travel to Austin and obtain an informal opinion from the attorney general. He followed through with the board's directive, and the attorney general advised that under the *Sweatt* decision, North Texas had no option but to admit Miller.[15]

These delaying tactics exasperated Miller. After getting no satisfaction from Matthews and Sampley, he, too, went to Austin to seek advice. He received a somewhat different opinion from an assistant attorney general, who stated "with no hesitancy or reservation" that Miller's being admitted to any school offering the doctorate was "soley an administrative decision," although all state schools where doctorate work was being done were legally available to him. As a result of this information, Miller then asked Matthews, "So to me comes the question: since it is an administrative decision, does the [NTSC] administration desire that I not be enrolled at this time? If the answer is 'yes,' then I will direct my efforts toward the University of Texas." In his pursuit of admission to North Texas, Miller made an eloquent plea to Matthews's sense of justice and fair play:

> It is my conviction that my entrance now would contribute much to the successful, inevitable integration of Negroes [at North Texas]. My every effort would be toward the quality of deportment and performance that would dispel much of the apprehension that some are harboring at this time. I understand any caution that may be yours. Yet there are decisions to be made, and we cannot be without the courage to make them. . . . I realize we can easily evade an immediate decision; then we could hardly advise with conviction those whom we supervise to "face up" to new challenges. My entrance at this time should provide a basis for analyzing future reactions when others may be admitted.[16]

Miller's persistence and the attorney general's opinion achieved results. On July 1, Matthews notified Miller that North Texas would accept him for admission to the doctoral program. The decision came none too soon. Miller had lost patience and had planned one last trip to Denton to confer with Matthews and settle the matter, for "time, effort, and money [are] near exhaustion." At last, however, North Texas had committed to accepting its first African American student.[17]

Once Miller was admitted, Matthews took steps to prevent trouble. To head off adverse student reaction, he directed the editor of the college newspaper, the *Campus Chat*, to write nothing about Miller's coming. In addition, press releases from the president's office were designed to assure the public that there would not be a mass enrollment of African Americans at North Texas. Beyond issuing the perfunctory announcements that the college had accepted its first African American student, Matthews emphasized that Miller's admission had nothing to do with the recent decision of the Supreme Court in the *Brown* case: "Our policy on Negro under-graduates or Negroes working on master's degrees has not changed. They will not be admitted at this time." He was still determined to desegregate only as far as he was pushed by the courts.[18]

Miller began classes on July 20 and experienced very little animosity during the six-week summer term. Summer was an ideal time for desegregation to occur. Enrollment consisted mainly of mature individuals, predominantly public school-teachers returning for advanced degrees. James Rogers, director of the North Texas State College news service at the time, observed, "I don't recall that there was any severe controversy in it [Miller's attendance] at all." Matthews also remembered, "The attitude here was as fine as you could have expected to find anywhere in the South. The student body was pretty receptive already to the idea of integration. Not a single problem all summer. Just as routine as any other activity on campus."[19] Miller experienced just one potentially inflammatory incident. On an occasion when he was walking to class, a group of students approached, and one said, "Hey, nigger, how're you doing?" To avoid confrontation, Miller responded, "How're you fellas?" and kept walking. Nothing further happened. He recalled, "Other than that, I had no problem with whites." Thus the fact that Miller maintained a low profile may have partly accounted for the absence of any tense moments. He believed that "by not being too pushy, by not running around with a chip on my shoulder, I was accepted."[20]

Miller attended North Texas for only that semester and never received the doc-torate because his administrative responsibilities at the high school in Port Arthur prevented him from returning. His enrollment was significant, however, for it made it easier for African Americans following him to pursue graduate education. In ret-rospect, Matthews saw Miller as the ideal person to initiate the process of desegre-gation. Without actually using the cliché "credit to his race," the president observed, "We were fortunate that Miller was a good student and that he had a master's degree from a recognized institution [the University of Wisconsin]. If you'd meet him and talk to him, you knew that he knew how to use the English language." Forty years later, Miller reminisced that "I think the administrators wanted me not as a token but as the first to open the doors to other black students."[21]

In limiting the admission of African Americans to doctoral candidates, Matthews followed a policy similar to the one adopted and rigidly held by institutions of higher education in other Southern states, a policy that made these institutions particularly vulnerable to challenges following *Brown*. Up to that time, Southern states had operated on the assumption that, by maintaining separate fair-to-good undergraduate colleges for African Americans, they could hold off desegregation at that level. The Supreme Court's decision in *Brown* and follow-up decisions, however, invariably encouraged future litigation to force the admission of African American undergraduates at previously all-white institutions.[22]

Matthews was well aware of the implications of the *Brown* decision for North Texas, noting that "there was a whole new system as far as the federal government was concerned." In response to *Brown*, he held informal discussions about it with the board of regents. He warned that an African American undergraduate would inevitably apply for admission and that they should adopt a contingency plan. The board did not respond: "We didn't have a specific issue, so we were visiting in the light of principle. There was no debate about how to proceed. The situation was not critical at the moment."[23] James Rogers, a protégé and confidant of the president, was of the opinion that Matthews was more attuned to the ramifications of *Brown* than were the regents. Rogers remembered, "There was a long and arduous process of education and persuasion to the political realities on the part of Matthews with the Regents. There were members who did not wish to capitulate in any way, did not wish to plan for the admission of blacks and thought it was bad." If North Texas were faced with the prospect of a court suit, some members wished to contest it "fully and vigorously."[24] Thus officials were aware of the vulnerability of their segregated institution, but they were unprepared for the challenge when it came.

Matthews and the regents were soon to be targeted by an extraordinary group of African American Texans, who operated out of Dallas, forty miles south of Denton. Due to a massive membership campaign conducted by state organizer Juanita Craft, the NAACP chapter in Dallas had expanded to almost seven thousand members by 1950, making it one of the largest in the country. In addition to its large membership, the Dallas chapter had a group of highly competent and motivated attorneys who, after *Brown*, prepared challenges to undergraduate segregation at state-supported colleges throughout Texas. Due to these advantages, the NAACP established a regional office in Dallas to oversee civil rights activities in the five-state area of Texas, Arkansas, Louisiana, New Mexico, and Oklahoma.[25]

The local coordinator for the legal assault was William J. Durham, who was recognized as the foremost African American attorney in Texas. Durham had had a long career in civil rights litigation and had served as lead counsel in two landmark cases, *Smith v. Allwright* (1944), which abolished the white primary, and *Sweatt v. Painter*. An observer of Durham's career commented, "His legal ability and unparalleled

dedication in his work made him virtually indispensable to the civil rights movement in Texas."[26] A half-dozen other attorneys in the Dallas office assisted Durham,
including C. B. Bunckley, another of Texas' leading African American lawyers, who
worked with Durham in the *Smith* and *Sweatt* cases.[27]

Dallas also had a branch of the NAACP's Legal Defense and Education Fund
because of the large and active membership of the local chapter and the expertise
of its attorneys. The special counsel representing the Legal Defense and Education fund in Dallas was U. Simpson Tate, who reported directly to the head of the
national organization, Thurgood Marshall, in New York. Tate, a graduate of Howard University Law School, came to Dallas in 1948. The advantage of Tate's being
on the local scene was that he could ensure that civil rights cases were initiated in
accordance with national policies.[28] The relationship between the Dallas branch and
Marshall's office was close and harmonious. Dallas NAACP attorney Lewis Bedford
recalled, "When it came to NAACP business or the business of trying to secure civil
rights for blacks, then the focus was on one thing: 'Let's do the best job possible.' And
they would work very well together, and very, very hard, and were very dedicated
to that purpose."[29]

Marshall spent considerable time in Dallas during the 1950s because so much
litigation had been initiated there against racial discrimination in the areas of voting rights, jury service, employment, housing, and public accommodations as well
as education. The Dallas attorneys appreciated Marshall's assistance as well as his
ability to adapt to the scene. Bedford, who was a young NAACP attorney at the
time, fondly remembered,

> I don't think Thurgood came in with the idea that he knew it all. We had a good,
> friendly relationship as well as a professional relationship. I think that made
> for a good, solid team. . . . He was a very easy person to work with. He liked to
> have fun; he liked to joke. But he also knew how to get down to business, and he
> could work long and hard hours briefing, discussing points. He was an extraordi-
> nary person in the sense that he could relax you very easily, and you didn't mind
> working for him. I felt he was very competent, no question about it. I felt highly
> honored to be part of the whole group.[30]

After *Brown*, the full-scale attack on segregated education intensified. Tate commented in October 1954, "The state colleges are ours, if not for the asking most
certainly for the taking."[31]

During the period immediately before and after the arrival of the first African
American undergraduate at North Texas, Matthews also had to consider the strong
and unyielding opposition to desegregation being waged by high state officials, particularly Gov. Allan Shivers and Atty. Gen. John Ben Shepperd. Both men condemned the Supreme Court's decision in *Brown* and attempted various legal ploys to
circumvent it. As an employee of the state, Matthews found himself caught between

the Shivers-Shepperd forces, who chose to defy the courts and fight the NAACP, and the NAACP, which had the courts on its side.[32]

Central to Shivers's opposition to desegregation was his call to the state legislature to invoke the doctrine of interposition. He argued that a state could interpose itself between the people and the Supreme Court and declare a decree of the court to be "null and void" and of no legal effect on the state. The Supreme Court's assertion of authority to invalidate segregation in education by the states, Shivers believed, was a dangerous threat to the rights of states and to powers never surrendered by them to the central government.[33] In February 1956, Shivers called for the state Democratic Party to conduct a referendum on interposition and, if endorsed, to place the doctrine in the party platform. His proposal failed due to the efforts of the moderate Democrats led by Lyndon Johnson and Sam Rayburn. In the primaries of July 1956, however, Texas voters approved referenda favoring interposition and legislation to prevent integration in public schools.[34]

The governor also claimed that the doctrine of interposition gave him the right to call out law-enforcement authorities to defend Texas' rights. In the fall of 1956, he sent Texas Rangers to the Mansfield Independent School District and Texarkana Junior College to prevent violence, maintain order, and prevent the desegregation of both schools. In each instance, Shivers argued, state authority and community hostility superseded judicial authority, thus giving the Rangers the right to turn away the African American students who attempted to enroll.[35]

Atty. Gen. John Ben Shepperd reinforced Shivers's stand. A native of Gladewater in deep East Texas, Shepperd held the racial attitudes of an area one NAACP attorney identified as "the meanest part of the state." In April 1955, he wrote an amicus curiae brief on behalf of the Southern states while the Supreme Court heard arguments on the implementation of *Brown*. Shepperd later refused to use his office to enforce the Court's decision on implementing *Brown*.[36]

Shepperd also championed the cause of the Citizens Council in Texas. This extreme segregationist group organized in East Texas and consisted mainly of reactionary businessmen whose goal was to preserve segregation through legal, political, and economic pressure on African American citizens. His office helped the Citizens Council to obtain a charter after the secretary of state had questions about whether it was an educational or political organization.[37]

The attorney general then launched an all-out campaign against the NAACP, hoping to drive it from the state. In September 1956, he charged the NAACP with violation of the Texas barratry statute. He dispatched assistant attorneys general around the state to investigate the records of local NAACP chapters. Sometimes troopers from the Department of Public Safety accompanied the investigators, and on occasions, the raiders entered private homes as well as offices. Shepperd eventually obtained a temporary restraining order that prohibited the NAACP from doing business in Texas and subpoenaed its leaders. He succeeded in suspending the activities of the NAACP in Texas for eight months, from September 1956 to May 1957.[38]

The attorney general continued to press his attack against desegregation. For the state's colleges and universities, he proposed his personal version of "freedom of choice." He argued that since some state universities had now admitted African Americans, the others should remain segregated. Many white parents, he claimed, wanted to send their children to an all-white institution, and they should have that right.[39]

Shivers's and Shepperd's resistance to school desegregation had a bearing on public attitudes toward the issue. A survey taken in 1956 by noted state pollster Joe Beldon indicated that statewide opposition to racial desegregation of public schools had noticeably increased. Beldon attributed this attitude to public criticism by state officials of the Supreme Court's exercise of power in the *Brown* decision and the opposition of various candidates to desegregation as expressed in the Texas political campaigns in 1955 and 1956. Matthews was certainly aware of these sentiments before and after an African American undergraduate student challenged the segregationist policies of North Texas in the summer of 1955.[40]

On June 13, 1955, Joe Louis Atkins visited the campus with the intention of enrolling for the upcoming fall semester. He came to Denton and conferred with Vice Pres. Arthur Sampley and evidently was encouraged enough to make a formal application for admittance on June 16. A native of Dallas and a graduate of Lincoln High School, Atkins had attended Philander Smith, a small Methodist college for African Americans in Little Rock, Arkansas, from September 1955 to May 1956 and intended to enter North Texas as a sophomore.[41]

As a youth, Atkins had had broad involvement in the civil rights movement in Dallas. His parents, Willie and Mable Atkins, owners of a thriving plumbing business, were active in the local branch of the NAACP. Atkins personally knew civil rights attorney William J. Durham and for a time drove him to meetings and court appearances. In 1952, at the age of sixteen, Atkins joined the NAACP Youth Council in Dallas. The Youth Council served as an auxiliary of the adult branch and enrolled students between the ages of twelve and twenty-one. Although its purpose was primarily social, with emphasis on dances, parties, and travel, the Youth Council also provided a means for the NAACP to educate African American youngsters about the civil rights movement and prepare them for school desegregation after the *Brown* decision.[42]

Juanita Craft, a member of the NAACP since 1935, was a sponsor for the Dallas Youth Council and served as a role model for Atkins and other young African Americans. In the 1940s and 1950s, she had helped organize more than a hundred NAACP chapters in Texas and had been director of the State Youth Council since 1947. Her home became almost a civil rights school for youngsters. The group held monthly meetings there and discussed civil rights issues and planned protest demonstrations. Craft also chaperoned members of the Youth Council on field trips throughout the country and regularly took them to state and national NAACP meetings, where she introduced them to Marshall and other civil rights leaders.

She had a profound influence on Atkins: "Mrs. Craft was a wonderful woman. She helped motivate me and helped me look at issues, especially those dealing with segregation. She made us conscious of discrimination."[43]

Atkins's first direct participation in a civil rights protest occurred in the early 1950s in Dallas during the annual State Fair of Texas. Fair officials traditionally set aside a segregated "Negro Day" as the only time when African Americans were allowed to attend. On that day, they entered the fairgrounds in a parade. At a meeting of the Youth Council at her home, however, Craft asked the group to consider a boycott. Atkins recalled, "She was telling us we needed to go like everybody else, every day it [the fair] was open. As a protest she encouraged us, as students, not to participate in the parade." The boycott created a conflict when administrators at the two black high schools, Booker T. Washington and Lincoln, insisted that the students march in the parade. When the students still refused, school officials retaliated by stripping Atkins and other protesters of their scholastic honors. The episode made a lasting impression: "I learned that people would be punished for standing up for the right thing to do . . . and I learned from Mrs. Craft's courage."[44] The *Brown* decision in May 1954 became the turning point of Atkins's college career. That fall, he entered Philander Smith on an academic scholarship. Philander Smith was about two hundred miles from Dallas, so because of the distance, and after the implications of *Brown* became apparent, Atkins considered transferring to North Texas in Denton. He had previously visited the campus on one of Craft's field trips and liked the school's physical setting. Atkins also hoped to become a teacher, and North Texas had a statewide reputation as a teacher-training institution. Denton was, moreover, just forty miles from his home.[45]

After his freshman year, Atkins returned to Dallas determined to enroll at North Texas. His parents were supportive, although his mother had some misgivings. "It was basically because of all the turmoil going on in the country at the time, so she had a little fear," Atkins later recalled. Craft encouraged him to apply because Denton was essentially a college town—Texas State College for Women (now Texas Woman's University) was also located there—and no widespread racial hostility existed in the community. Atkins was also aware of Tennyson Miller's favorable experience at North Texas.[46]

On June 13, 1955, Atkins, accompanied by his mother and Craft, drove to Denton and went to the registrar's office with the intention of enrolling. The sudden appearance of the three African Americans caught officials by surprise. A flustered clerk summoned the registrar, Alex Dickie, and he in turn suggested that they all should talk to the vice president.[47]

Vice Pres. Arthur Sampley, a soft-spoken, mild-mannered man who at one time was poet laureate of Texas, then met with them and Dickie. Atkins remembered that it was a "long . . . very cordial conversation." Sampley informed them that the college was at that time formulating a plan for gradual integration over a four-year period, starting with senior undergraduate transfers in the first year and finally admitting freshmen in the fourth year. Atkins recalled, "He never told me they would *not* admit me, and he *did* tell me they did not want a test case." Craft made no explicit threats but reminded Sampley of the legal ramifications of *Brown* and advised him not to delay or drag out the process of integration. When she insisted that Atkins be given an application, the registrar came forward with one. On the way back to Dallas, the Atkinses and Craft chuckled over the fact that an undergraduate applicant normally did not have a conversation with the vice president of a college. They had the distinct impression, however, that Sampley and Dickie were very concerned about opening the college to African Americans.[48]

Turmoil continued in the North Texas administrative offices after the African Americans departed. Sampley immediately informed Matthews of the conference and believed that Atkins intended to enroll even if he had to file a suit. Matthews then decided that the best course was to call a meeting of the board of regents to consider a response.[49]

When the board met a few days later, its initial mood was one of defiance. Chair Ben Wooten, a native of Panola County in deep East Texas, opposed Atkins's admission, and none of the other members favored integration at the undergraduate level. One allegedly responded, "Let 'em sue!" The attorneys on the board, Ralph Elliott of Sherman and Berl Godfrey of Fort Worth, advised, however, that the college would lose if a suit were filed.[50]

Matthews and the regents subsequently formulated what they thought was a solution for their dilemma. They decided to deny Atkins admission while accepting the fact that the college would lose a resulting legal challenge. Nevertheless, they could then explain to white parents that the federal courts, not the college, were responsible for the intermingling on campus of African Americans with their sons and daughters. Wooten later recalled, "There were anxieties in the minds of many fathers and mothers. We knew that a court decision would have a better reception than if the Board voluntarily did it." At the same meeting, the board also completed an alternate plan to full and immediate integration that it had been contemplating since the admission of Tennyson Miller. It called for the admission of African American master's candidates in the summer of 1956, senior undergraduate transfers in the fall of 1956, junior transfers in the fall of 1957, sophomore transfers in the fall of 1958, and, finally, the admission of freshmen in the fall of 1959. Thus while shifting responsibility, and blame, for desegregation to the federal courts, college authorities hoped to avoid full integration for at least four years.[51]

Meanwhile, Atkins had forwarded his application for admission and had had Philander Smith send his transcripts to North Texas. On July 18, however, Sampley informed Atkins that the college would not admit him. Sampley based the decision on "the policy of the Board of Regents to admit only those members of your race who are candidates for the doctor's degree."[52]

Atkins and his father took the letter of rejection to the NAACP regional attorney in Dallas, U. Simpson Tate, who recommended that they file suit. Tate also promised that the NAACP would underwrite all financial costs associated with the case. The Atkins family knew Tate and had confidence in his legal expertise, so they agreed to initiate court proceedings against North Texas. Because Joe Atkins was a minor, the father had to file on behalf of the son. Tate also informed them that the federal courts had already ordered Texas Western College in El Paso to desegregate, and he suggested that they consider it as an alternative if they could not obtain a temporary injunction against North Texas. That way Atkins would not lose a semester of schooling if his case bogged down in the courts.[53]

Clearly, the NAACP did not select Joe Atkins, as it had Heman Sweatt, to be its plaintiff in a desegregation suit. As Atkins later confirmed, "We went to the NAACP; they didn't come to us." Nevertheless, Atkins appeared to have the attributes the NAACP sought in a civil rights plaintiff. He was articulate and intelligent but also had the disposition to remain in the background during the litigation process. The NAACP advised litigants not to be aggressive, and for Atkins this created no concern. Regarding President Matthews, for example, Atkins noted, "I had a lot of respect for college administrators and teachers. I felt like with the pressures ... he was doing what was expected of most heads of institutions at that time." In effect, Atkins was to assume the role of a victim of discrimination and at the same time stand as an alternative to a segregated education.[54]

On August 11, 1955, Tate filed a motion for a preliminary injunction with the US District Court in Tyler, Texas. His immediate purpose was to enable Atkins to enroll at North Texas for the fall semester beginning in September. Tate attacked both Texas' segregation laws and the college's rules barring the admission of African American master's and undergraduate candidates. Article VII, section 7 of the state's constitution and the statutes passed by the legislature to implement the constitutional provision stipulated that public schools were to be provided for white and African American students on a separate but impartial basis. Tate argued that these enactments violated the Fourteenth Amendment of the US Constitution as well as certain federal statutes. He further alleged that Atkins and African Americans in general had "suffered irreparable damage" due to the college's rules denying them admission solely on the basis of race and after they had met all enrollment requirements. Tate argued, for example, that under the circumstances then existing, Atkins's only option for an education at a desegregated institution was Texas Western, which meant that Atkins would incur much higher transportation expenses, thus adding to the financial burden of his education.[55]

North Texas clearly intended to fight a delaying action at the hearing scheduled by District Judge Joe Sheehy for September 2. In preparing the college's case, Asst. State Atty. Gen. Billie E. Lee wanted just one witness to represent the college "so that we may call him to put on our limited evidence [since] most of the case is uncontroverted, resolving itself into a question of pure law." Matthews then determined that he and Sampley would attend the hearing but that only Sampley would testify.[56]

The college defended its admissions policies on two grounds. First, it emphasized that student enrollment had increased to the point where North Texas had the highest percentage of classroom-space utilization of all the state's publicly supported colleges. To admit an expected two hundred or three hundred African Americans would, therefore, cause "vast administrative and financial problems in increasing the size and number of classrooms, dormitories, cafeterias, athletic, and recreational facilities to meet the demand caused by this unforeseen source." Sampley said that North Texas currently needed two more dormitories and two additional classroom buildings and that funding for them would require legislative action, which would take time. The college also raised the "separate-but-equal" argument, claiming that Atkins and other African Americans had not suffered irreparable injury by being denied admission because they were free to attend either Texas Southern or Prairie View A&M, "both state institutions of higher learning established exclusively for members of the plaintiff's race and equivalent in facilities and opportunities to North Texas." Sampley, whom Lee described as a "sterling witness," concluded his testimony by outlining the regents' plan for the gradual desegregation of the college.[57]

Judge Sheehy, born in the small town of Saratoga in Hardin County in deep East Texas, denied Atkins's motion. He reminded both sides that in conjunction with *Brown*, the Supreme Court recognized that the transition of school systems from a segregated to a nonsegregated basis presented problems that in some instances required time to solve. While declaring that a start toward desegregation should begin immediately, Sheehy believed that North Texas was making a "bona fide" effort to that end. Noting the college's need for new facilities as well as its plan for gradual desegregation, he said, "I cannot shut my eyes to these facts."[58] Sheehy conceded that Atkins would suffer "some damage" if he had to attend Texas Western, but he noted that the damage would be "no more than the added cost of transportation." The judge concluded that he needed more time to consider all the facts of the case "to be in better position to intelligently … give a final decree," particularly while other desegregation cases were then making their way through the courts. Therefore, he scheduled a full hearing to be held in Sherman, Texas, on December 2.[59]

During the interim between the hearing in Tyler and the trial in Sherman, Atkins enrolled at Texas Western for the fall 1955 semester. He did not want to wait a full term to enroll at North Texas, assuming a favorable outcome from the trial. Consequently, he was not present in Sherman.[60]

Meanwhile, officials at North Texas prepared for the trial. Acting on Lee's advice that they had no legal grounds on which to stand, Matthews and the regents concentrated on the issue of overcrowding and the proposal for gradual desegregation over the period from 1956 to 1959. At a meeting of the regents on October 20, however, Matthews had proudly reported that, because of careful planning, the college could easily absorb, "with no undue disturbance," the 10 percent rise in enrollment for the 1955 fall term. Including the incoming 650 freshmen, enrollment totaled 5,500.[61]

When the trial began on December 2, Tate charged that the college's admissions policies were both illegal and impractical. Failure to admit qualified African Americans, he again said, violated the Fourteenth Amendment, the *Brown* decision, and recent court opinions in similar cases. In attacking North Texas' proposal for gradual desegregation, Tate pointed out that Atkins would not be eligible for admission until his junior year in the fall of 1957, assuming that he remained at Texas Western up to that time. Nevertheless, Texas Western being the only state-supported college that had desegregated, Atkins would have suffered "financial injury" with the additional expenses incurred by having to attend a college six hundred miles from Dallas.[62]

Matthews and Sampley represented North Texas at the trial, but only the president took the stand. He stressed that the college was operating at "102 percent capacity," which created overcrowded conditions at the undergraduate level. Matthews said he hoped to receive a $5 million building appropriation from the legislature in 1957, with construction beginning in 1958. This situation, he explained, was partially responsible for North Texas' refusal to admit African Americans. Tate forced him to admit, however, that the plan for gradual desegregation was just a proposal and not yet a reality.[63]

Not only did Matthews's arguments seem weak, but also a recent court decision in a similar case worked against him. On November 23, 1955, the US Court of Appeals for the Fifth Circuit in New Orleans had reversed a previous decision handed down by Judge Sheehy in which he had denied a request by Tate and Durham for injunctive relief against Texarkana Junior College. In July 1953, African Americans brought suit after the college had refused them admission on account of their race, but Sheehy rejected their motion for an injunction on the grounds that Texarkana had changed its policies after the *Brown* decision. The circuit court thought otherwise, however, declaring that it saw no evidence that school authorities had attempted to desegregate and that Sheehy's argument, "if it ever had any validity," had been rendered "irrelevant" by *Brown*. This reversal evidently influenced Sheehy's thinking in subsequent civil rights trials.[64]

Sheehy in his decision systematically destroyed Matthews's arguments. He pointed out that North Texas had admitted numerous students since Atkins's application, and there was no indication that any had been refused admission because of a lack of facilities. Sheehy also took North Texas to task for its proposed desegregation timetable as a way to cope with a lack of classroom and dormitory space for the assumed influx of two to three hundred African American students. He asked, "Does that fact establish that additional time within which to admit Negro undergraduates to North Texas is necessary in the public interest? In my opinion, it does not." The judge concluded by observing that "violation of the 14th Amendment is no longer an open question. This the defendants seem to concede." On the basis of both legal and practical grounds, therefore, he issued a permanent injunction prohibiting North Texas from refusing admission to Atkins or any other African Americans solely on the basis of race.[65]

For the college, the attempt to exclude African Americans ended. The board of regents decided not to appeal Sheehy's decision. Lee and the attorneys on the board advised that any effort to do so would be futile since the law was such that the courts had no alternative but to enjoin the college to admit African Americans. As his actions would show, Matthews, a man who lived by rules, accepted the judgment literally and made plans to deal with the coming of African Americans.[66]

From that time forward, the board gave Matthews full responsibility and a "free rein" to implement the order to desegregate. He initially chose to interpret literally the court's mandate, which was to admit qualified African Americans. "Our policy," said Matthews, "was to admit them as we admitted everybody else, when they had the 'book documents' that a white person would have. We would not do anything for a person just because he was black. They didn't ask to be treated differently; they asked to be treated equally." Since Sheehy's decision said nothing about the integration of dormitories, cafeterias, athletics, or the student union, Matthews maintained the "Jim Crow" system in those areas. Only gradually did all college facilities become fully integrated.[67]

Matthews followed this "philosophy of gradualism" allegedly "to prevent conflict," according to James Rogers. Rogers believed such a policy was adopted to head off "scuffles" between African American and white students. Matthews rationalized, "What we were trying to do was establish a reasonable policy that reasonable people would realize, and do it for students and faculty and anyone else we were going to work with." Considering Matthews's virtual one-man rule of the college, however, he also took this position in order to remain in complete control of the desegregation process at all times.[68]

The first, and only, African American student to enroll for the spring semester was Irma Sephas, who registered on February 2, the same day that Autherine Lucy was having her problems in Tuscaloosa. Sephas, the mother of a preschool daughter, planned to take a fifteen-hour course load and commute to Denton, which was about forty miles one way from her home. No untoward incidents occurred at the time she registered or when she attended classes on the first day of the new semester.[69]

Matthews took several steps to ensure that order would prevail and that Sephas's coming would be peaceful. He first directed Rogers, who oversaw the operations of the student newspaper, the *Campus Chat*, to meet with the editorial staff and instruct them to play down her arrival. Rogers recalled, "They were essentially pro-integrationists. They wanted to write more than they did. I sat down with them and explained the institutional philosophy: 'We need to make this work; we need to avoid counterreaction and violence. And the best way to do that is not to brag too much.'" According to Rogers, Matthews believed that too much publicity would be like "waving a red flag to potentially antagonistic and violent individuals." As a result, the *Campus Chat* had no banner headlines announcing Sephas's attendance at North Texas.[70] Matthews also instructed Rogers that there would be no public announcements from the news service about Sephas. Rogers recalled that "Matthews's policy was to play down what was happening as much as possible. These were his instructions to me. He said, 'We don't want anything to happen to Mrs. Sephas or to any other student. We do not want to invite rabble-rousing.'" According to Rogers,

Matthews was determined to keep the news media at bay because of his fear that there would be a repetition of what was happening at the University of Alabama, where Autherine Lucy was attempting to enroll at the same time: "He feared that there were enough antagonistic individuals in Dallas and Fort Worth who would read or see what was happening and say, 'Let's go up there and throw rocks at her.' He genuinely believed that that was a probable consequence."[71]

Matthews would not permit the media to follow Sephas into the classroom. He did, "reluctantly," according to Rogers, arrange for a few local television reporters to interview her out on campus. Matthews recollected, "A reporter from a local TV station came on campus, and he wanted to go into class with a microphone and put it in a person's face and say, 'What do you think about having Mrs. Sephas in your class?' Finally, we just had to say, 'You're *not* going to go into class!' And he did not go in. We would not have been doing what one ought to do in the classroom.'" His view," Rogers noted, "was that the classroom was sacrosanct; it was that faculty member's. He would not disrupt the educational process. Nor would Matthews give personal interviews to the media. He did allow them to photograph him, and he did distribute a written statement for information only."[72]

Matthews's strategy for maintaining order generally succeeded. The student body expressed almost no negative reaction. An editorial in the local newspaper commented, "Students at North Texas are to be complimented for their patience and understanding. . . . The college's 'Christian' treatment of a problem that is difficult for most Texans to solve certainly is a direct contrast to the University of Alabama."[73] Matthews observed that students seemed to take Sephas's arrival as a routine event: "We couldn't have hoped for the student body to be any better about it. If you had written a script for them, you wouldn't have been able to do any better. It was a matter of feeling, 'It's coming. Let's make a go of it.' That was the general attitude."[74] Former students corroborated Matthews's assessment. W. C. Brown, who was the sports editor for the *Campus Chat* at the time, remembered that student attitudes were "just sort of matter-of-fact. I don't recall them being apprehensive or anticipating any problems." A Korean War veteran, Charlie Cole, who was an undergraduate at that time, said, "I don't remember any negative talk or any negative gatherings or groups that formed to oppose integration. I think it was just accepted: 'Well, we're integrated.'" In part, this reaction by students occurred because most came from areas within a fifty-mile radius of the campus, areas where African Americans made up a small percentage of the overall population. Most whites, therefore, did not perceive African Americans as social or economic threats. Perhaps the best indication of the calm that prevailed on campus was the fact that throughout February 1956, the African American newspaper in Dallas, the Dallas *Express*, carried very few stories about the desegregation of North Texas.[75]

Nevertheless, scattered incidents did occur on campus from time to time. On two separate occasions, burning crosses appeared on the lawn of the presidential home at the edge of the college grounds. On another evening, a cross was discovered

burning in front of the library. Whether these were acts of pranksters or an organized group was never determined.[76] While walking to his eight o'clock class one
morning, an English professor observed the words "Nigger Go Home" scrawled in
paint on the sidewalk. By the time class was over, however, he noticed that the words
had already been removed by a janitorial crew.[77] This seemed to be the extent of any
overt reaction against the arrival of African Americans.

Matthews also took steps to deal with any faculty who opposed desegregation.
First, he informed all the deans that he expected them to cooperate in implementing
his and the board's policies. At the faculty convocation before the start of the spring
1956 semester, Matthews related the college's policies concerning integration and
presented a "list of things to do or not to do." Described by a faculty member as a
"benevolent dictator ... [whose] administrative style was 'I make the decisions,'" the
president took a blunt approach in handling recalcitrants.[78] On one occasion, when a
couple of faculty members threatened to resign rather than teach African Americans,
he responded, "'That's all right. Go ahead and quit.' They didn't say anymore. That
was the end of the conversation."[79] A member of the English department at the time
aptly summed up Matthews's relationship with the faculty over the issue by observing, "The faculty was not consulted, which was not unusual at that time. The faculty
was never consulted and infrequently informed about anything."[80] Nevertheless, the
faculty was overwhelmingly in favor of desegregation, and most lauded Matthews's
methods in dealing with it.[81]

Meanwhile, Matthews moved to allay the fears of the local townsfolk. To that
end, he had the cooperation of the Denton *Record-Chronicle*. Matthews and the
newspaper's publisher, Riley Cross, were fellow Kiwanians, members of the local
chamber of commerce, and close friends. A civic booster, Cross believed that racial
violence would be detrimental to the Denton business community. At the same time,
Matthews never made any attempt to interfere with the town's Jim Crow policies.
His attitude was that "we were integrated, but they [businesses] were not, and that
was their business. Our jurisdiction ended at the campus boundary." As a result of
his cordial relationship with Matthews, Cross saw to it that the *Record-Chronicle*
downplayed desegregation on campus and never used sensational headlines to
describe events there. Matthews later commented about Cross, "I could not have
had a better teammate."[82]

In line with his policy of gradualism, Matthews continued to interpret the court's
ruling literally when it said only that North Texas had to admit qualified African
Americans. He subsequently ruled that they could not reside in the dormitories or
eat in the college cafeterias. This policy meant that African Americans had to commute from their homes or find accommodations in the black section of Denton.[83]

In the first summer session of 1956, Matthews eased the restrictions by allowing
two African American women, both graduate students, to live in one of the dormitories, and in the fall of that year, he extended the same privileges to undergraduate
women. Nevertheless, he established a quota, never permitting the number to exceed

seven, again using the excuse that physical facilities were overcrowded. The quota remained in effect as late as 1961 and obviously created hardships for African Americans. In August 1957, for instance, a woman complained, "I think it is un-American, undemocratic, and terribly unfair that you are allowing only a small number of Negro girls to live on campus. . . . If there is any fair blood in your body, you will see to it that I am assigned a room in the dormitory for the fall term."[84]

Matthews's modified dormitory and cafeteria policies did not extend to African American men, who were not allowed these privileges until the mid-1960s. His rationale was that he wanted to prevent friction because it was "too easy for boys to get into scuffles."[85] This policy, too, created problems. An undergraduate observed, "It was a hardship not to live on campus. Not isolated, really; frustrating, maybe. You'd pass the dorms and hear the noise and laughing. Then one of those hunger pangs would run across you. You'd say, 'Man, is it worth it?'"[86]

The policy of gradualism also extended to the athletic program. After the first two African Americans, both nonscholarship walk-ons, joined the football team in September 1956, Matthews imposed a quota system under which the coaches were allowed to recruit thereafter two African Americans each year. Head Coach Odus Mitchell remembered, "Dr. Matthews said, 'You get two, but you don't tell anybody you get two.' Nobody knew it. . . . These were his instructions. That's the way it was,' and we didn't question it." An assistant coach commented, "Dr. Matthews thought two was an appropriate number, and that was it." Not until 1960 did the coaches test the dictate, and when they recruited more than two, Matthews said nothing.[87]

Matthews at times, however, adopted different policies for dealing with integration off campus. For instance, when the football team played road games, the coaches, with Matthews's approval, always informed their hosts of the presence of African American players on the squad, while at the same time determining that the team travel, take meals, and lodge together. This approach led to the cancellation of the traditional opening game at Oxford against the University of Mississippi when Ole Miss insisted that North Texas leave its African American players at home. North Texas suffered a real financial loss as a result, for this game usually netted the school about $25,000, which was a large payday for that time. Likewise, when the A Cappella Choir traveled off campus for performances, plans were made to ensure that the members stayed together at all public facilities and accommodations.[88]

Matthews's decision not to immediately integrate the college's dormitories and cafeterias violated a landmark case of the Supreme Court in 1950, *McLaurin v. Oklahoma State Regents*. In 1948, the court ordered the University of Oklahoma to admit George McLaurin to its graduate program. School officials complied, but they prescribed that he should attend on a segregated basis. He was separated from white students in the classroom, studied at a special desk in the library, and was assigned a table and time apart for meals in the union cafeteria. As a result, McLaurin sued again, and the Supreme Court ruled that the university had impaired his ability to study and discuss issues and exchange ideas with his fellow students. Such social isolation, the court found, made McLaurin's education unequal to that of the white students. At North Texas, Matthews's policies placed African Americans in a similar situation.[89]

Still, North Texas, in large part because of the way Matthews handled the process of desegregation and due to the fact that the campus had been violence-free, soon became an attractive choice for African Americans. By the fall of 1957, 181 graduates and undergraduates had enrolled, giving the college the highest proportion of African Americans to the general student body of any formerly all-white school in the state. The number increased to 203 in a total enrollment of 6,700 in 1958, and the following year, 247 undergraduates alone were part of a student body of 7,000. Although campus life for African Americans was limited, one said, "On the whole, the school and the white students are pretty fair." Another commented, "There are no serious conflicts with students and professors. . . . I have a lot of white student friends." Seven years after North Texas accepted Sephas, the Dallas *Morning News* described the college as "an island of integration" surrounded by a segregated town.[90]

Although Denton was segregated, the overall racial climate there contributed to facilitating the desegregation process at North Texas. The town's racism was characterized by moderation and did not take a violent form. This was in part because the African American population was small. In 1960, blacks numbered just 1,950 out of a population of 25,000. Most whites, therefore, did not perceive African Americans as much of a threat to the existing social and economic order. In addition, a coterie of bankers and businessmen ran Denton, and they viewed racial violence as being bad for economic development. Prominent leaders in the black community, men like Principal Fred Moore and Rev. Fred Haynes, worked closely with this white leadership while serving as effective advocates for their people within the confines of the Jim Crow system.[91] African American residents of Denton understood the etiquette of the race relationships under which they were forced to live, but they did not find the constraints to be totally repressive. A leader in the black community, Betty Kimble, remarked, "Whites treated us nice. You could talk to them and feel comfortable, but they kept us in our place." Another African American said, "Denton has always been kind of laid back. Of course, we knew there were restrictions on some things you could do and not do, and you accepted that. Not that you liked it, but you accepted it." Future American Football League football star Abner Haynes, who was born in Denton, moved to Dallas, and then matriculated at North Texas to play football in 1956, in part chose the school because he had fond memories of his youth in the town: "I had good feelings about coming back to Denton. . . . As a boy, I used to walk all over town, and nobody was going to hurt me. . . . So when I came back, I wasn't uncomfortable." Tennyson Miller corroborated Haynes's feelings: "My work in Denton at Fred Douglass was the happiest I had, I'm sure."[92]

Moreover, the business of Denton, with two state-supported colleges, was education. The schools were the town's largest employers, and they, along with a few business enterprises, provided job opportunities for whites and blacks. A county judge during that period observed, "Race relations really get sour when you get white and black people in the low economic brackets competing for jobs." At the same time, a cordial relationship existed between "town and gown," and many professors were active in civic affairs. The generally liberal faculty served as a counterbalance to the rest of the generally conservative community.[93]

Then, too, the first contingent of African Americans who entered North Texas were generally mature individuals seeking, first, an education rather than a confrontation. In addition, Tennyson Miller was well known in the community and had a good reputation, while Sephas was the daughter of Rev. J. L. Loud, a prominent minister in the Dallas-Fort Worth area. The African American athletes who desegregated the football team were outstanding players, particularly Abner Haynes, who later had an excellent professional career. During their playing days at North Texas, the team had successful seasons and on one occasion played in the Sun Bowl. Denton fans as well as students were thus able to suppress whatever racial biases they may have had while the team was winning.[94]

In the final analysis, North Texas State College could be justifiably proud that it was one of the first all-white, state-supported colleges in the state as well as the South to desegregate, and it did so with no violence and little rancor. Strong, decisive leadership as well as the existing racial environment in Denton was responsible for the drastic transition in a way of life. Matthews must be given due credit for defusing a potentially explosive situation. He had spent almost all his adult life at North Texas, and he genuinely loved the college. Violence would embarrass "his" school. Consequently, he maintained firm control over administrators, faculty, and students to see that decorum and order prevailed. Yet the college desegregated reluctantly, only after being confronted by legal realities.[95]

Even then, the administration moved at a cautious, gradual pace in removing the barriers to racial equality in education. Yet to Matthews's credit, he never resorted to demagoguery over the issue. While North Texas was implementing the court's order, the president of Texarkana Junior College was encouraging mob violence to prevent desegregation there. To a gathering of segregationists, he exclaimed, "The federal government cannot make us [desegregate], not unless it sends the militia to force us. . . . It is not only your right but your duty to resist it." Matthews never resorted to such inflammatory rhetoric.[96]

Matthews found himself entangled with certain forces over which he had little control. As the chief administrator of a state university, he had to consider the words and actions of a governor and attorney general who were firmly opposed to desegregation and determined to circumvent it. As president of North Texas, he had to deal with a board of regents, all political appointees, whose sentiments were to resist integration. And at the same time, he had to face a decision of the Supreme Court outlawing the "separate-but-equal" doctrine as well as a powerful local NAACP chapter backed by outstanding civil rights attorneys who were determined to bring down the barriers to segregated education. Finally, Matthews, by upbringing and

education, never questioned the system of Jim Crow until confronted by its oppo-
nents. In the end, he and the regents took what might be considered the easy way by
letting a federal district court determine the course that North Texas should take.

The three African Americans who played significant roles in bringing down Jim
Crow on campus went on to varied careers. As mentioned previously, Tennyson
Miller attended North Texas for just the one summer session and never received his
doctorate. He went back to Port Arthur and finished his career there. Sephas found
commuting from Fort Worth too rigorous and left school after a semester. Joe Atkins
graduated from Texas Western and later returned to North Texas to receive his master's degree in education in 1963. He later revealed, "I was delighted that this [desegre-
gation of North Texas] had happened. I sent a letter to the Dallas Youth Council and
encouraged them to go to North Texas. I was already comfortable at Texas Western
and did not want to go through another readjustment." In looking back, J. C. Matthews acknowledged that he could have, and should have, done things differently: "An
administrator has a role to play concerning the leadership of his Board—to get them
to go in the directions they ought to go. The only thing I would change is the Board's
instructions on Joe L. Atkins. I would have had him come without a contest."[97]

*This article was originally published as Marcello, Ronald E. "Reluctance versus Reality:
The Desegregation of North Texas State College, 1954–1956."* Southwestern Historical
Quarterly *99 (October 1996): 152–85. Reprinted by permission of the author and the
editor of the* Southwestern Historical Quarterly.

NOTES

1. E. Culpepper Clark, *The Schoolhouse
   Door: Segregation's Last Stand at the
   University of Alabama* (New York:
   Oxford University Press, 1993), 53–102;
   Richard Bardolph, *The Civil Rights
   Record: Black Americans and the Law,
   1849–1970* (New York: Thomas Y.
   Crowell, 1970), 474–75; Lewis Jones,
   "Two Years of Desegregation in
   Alabama," *Journal of Negro Education*
   25 (Summer 1956): 206–7; David R.
   Goldfield, *Black, White, and Southern
   Culture* (Baton Rouge: Louisiana State
   University Press, 1990), 115.
2. Denton *Campus Chat*, February 3, 1956;
   Denton *Record-Chronicle*, February
   2, 5, 1956; Fort Worth *Star-Telegram*,
   February 3, 1956.

3. *Sipuel v. Board of Regents of the
   University of Oklahoma*, 332 US 631
   (1948). In *Sipuel*, the court ordered
   the admission of Ada Sipuel, an
   African American, to the University of
   Oklahoma Law School because it was
   the only law school maintained by the
   state at the time of her application. See
   also Bardolph, *Civil Rights Record*, 272.

   North Texas was one of the first ten
   four-year state-supported institutions
   in the former Confederate states to
   offer admission, without reservations,
   to qualified African American
   undergraduate candidates. The others
   were Southwestern Louisiana Institute
   (September 1954), McNeese State
   College (Louisiana, February 1955),

Southwestern Louisiana College (September 1955), University of North Carolina (September 1955), University of Arkansas (September 1955), Arkansas State College (September 1955), Arkansas Polytechnic College (September 1955), Henderson State College (Arkansas, September 1955), Texas Western College (September 1955). See US Commission on Civil Rights, *Equal Protection under the Laws in Public Higher Education* (New York: Greenwood Press, 1968), 66–96.

4. *Sweatt v. Painter*, 339 US 629 (1950); Bardolph, *Civil Rights Record*, 273–75; Darlene Clark Hine, *Black Victory: The Rise and Fall of the White Primary in Texas* (Millwood, NY: KTO Press, 1979), 192; Thurgood Marshall, "An Evaluation of Recent Efforts to Achieve Racial Integration in Education through Resort to the Courts," *Journal of Negro Education* 21 (Summer 1952): 318–20; Charles H. Thompson, "Current Trends and Events of National Importance in Negro Education: Heman Marion Sweatt v. Theophilis Shickel Painter et al.," *Journal of Negro Education* 19 (Fall 1950): 512; Michael Gillette, "The NAACP in Texas" (PhD diss., University of Texas at Austin, 1984), 41, 86–89, 215–16.

5. Marshall, "Evaluation of Recent Efforts," 318–19; quoted in Gillette, "NAACP in Texas," 87; see also ibid., 39, 215–16.

6. Guy B. Johnson, "Racial Integration in Public Education in the South," *Journal of Negro Education* 23 (Summer 1954): 317–18, 320; Gillette, "NAACP in Texas," 216–19.

7. James Carl Matthews, interview by Robert Mangrum, February 18, 1977, transcript, interview OH 360, 1–2,

Oral History Collection, University Archives, Willis Library, University of North Texas, Denton; James Carl Matthews, interview by Floyd Jenkins and Ronald Marcello, April 4, 1984, transcript, interview OH 633, 1–8. All subsequent interviews are found in the Oral History Collection of the Willis Library, University of North Texas, Denton.

8. Matthews, interview by Jenkins and Marcello, OH 633, 10–11; James L. Rogers, *The Story of North Texas* (Denton: University of North Texas Press, 1965), 343–44.

9. Fred McCain, interview by Randy Cummings and Ronald Marcello, April 2, 1984, transcript, interview OH 636, 62.

10. Herbert Ferrill, interview by Randy Cummings and Ronald Marcello, July 20, 1983, transcript, interview OH 605, 35.

11. Abner Haynes, interview by Randy Cummings and Ronald Marcello, May 16, 1984, transcript, interview OH 620, 411–12.

12. Matthews to Shepperd, September 3, 1953, J. C. Matthews Papers, University Archives, Willis Library, University of North Texas, Denton (hereafter cited as Matthews Papers).

13. Matthews to Pastor Grady M. Metcalf, First Baptist Church, Temple, Texas, September 17, 1963, Matthews Papers; Dallas *Express*, August 7, 1954; Dallas *Times Herald*, July 20, 1954; Denton *Record-Chronicle*, July 20, 1954.

14. Quotations from Miller to Matthews, June [no day] 1954, Matthews Papers; Tennyson Miller, interview by Michele Glaze, January 11, 1992, transcript, interview OH 857, 102.

15. Matthews, interview by Mangum, OH 360, 6–7.

16. Miller to Matthews, June [no day] 1954, Matthews Papers.

17. Miller to Matthews, telegram, June 3, 1954, Matthews Papers; Matthews to Miller, July 1, 1954, Matthews Papers.

18. Matthews, interview by Mangrum, OH 360, 7; Matthews, interview by Jenkins and Marcello, OH 633, 22; Dallas *Times Herald*, July 21, 1954; Denton *Record-Chronicle*, July 20, 1954 (quotation).

19. James L. Rogers, interview by Moray Comrie, October 23, 1980, transcript, interview OH 519, 3–5; Miller, interview by Glaze, OH 857, 101–2.

20. Denton *North Texas Daily* (formerly *Campus Chat*), November 4, 1993 (first and second quotations); Miller, interview by Glaze, OH 857, 101–2 (third quotation).

21. Miller, interview by Glaze, OH 857, 102–3; Matthews, interview by Mangrum, OH 360, 7, 41.

22. Johnson, "Racial Integration," 319–21.

23. Matthews, interview by Mangrum, OH 360, 4–5.

24. Rogers, interview by Comrie, OH 519, 12–13.

25. Gillette, "NAACP in Texas," 412; Judge L. A. Bedford, interview by John Bodnar, March 28, 1977, transcript, interview OH 361, 4–5. Bedford was a young attorney who, at that time, researched cases for the other, more experienced civil rights attorneys in the Dallas office. See also William H. Jones, "Desegregation of Public Education in Texas: One Year Afterward," *Journal of Negro Education* 24 (Summer 1955): 348; and William H. Jones, "The Status of Educational Desegregation in Texas," *Journal of Negro Education* 25 (Summer 1956): 335.

26. Gillette, "NAACP in Texas," 402–4 (quotation); Bedford, interview by Bodnar, OH 361, 5–6.

27. Gillette, "NAACP in Texas," 404.

28. Ibid., 137–39, 157; Bedford, interview by Bodnar, OH 361, 6–8.

29. Gillette, "NAACP in Texas," 393; Bedford, interview by Bodnar, OH 361, 12; Hine, *Black Victory*, 206.

30. Bedford, interview by Bodnar, OH 361, 8–11, 14–15 (quotation); Jones, "Educational Desegregation," 342.

31. Gillette, "NAACP in Texas," 206, 235 (quotation), 416.

32. Jones, "Educational Desegregation," 336; Jones, "Public Education in Texas," 352–53.

33. Herbert O. Reid, "The Supreme Court Decision and Interposition," *Journal of Negro Education* 25 (Spring 1956): 109, 111–14 (quotation); Numan V. Bartley, *The Rise of Massive Resistance* (Baton Rouge: Louisiana State University Press, 1969), 126–37; Gillette, "NAACP in Texas," 258.

34. Dallas *Morning News*, February 24, 1956; Bartley, *Massive Resistance*, 138–40; Jones, "Public Education in Texas," 354–56.

35. Dallas *Express*, September 15, 1956; Dallas *Morning News*, August 31 and September 1, 6, and 7, 1956; Bartley, *Massive Resistance*, 156; Earl Black, *Southern Governors and Civil Rights* (Cambridge, MA: Harvard University Press, 1976), 125.

36. Gillette, "NAACP in Texas," 219 (quotation); see also ibid., 216–17, 274–77, 282.

37. Ibid., 276–77; Jones, "Educational Desegregation," 337–38.

38. Gillette, "NAACP in Texas," 289–93; W. Marvin Dulaney, "Whatever Happened to the Civil Rights Movement in Dallas, Texas?," in *Essays on the American Civil Rights Movement*, eds. John Dittmer,

George C. Wright, and W. Marvin Dulaney (College Station: Texas A&M University Press, 1993), 76–77. See also Dallas *Express*, September 22 and 29; October 6, 13, 20 and 27; November 3 and 17, 1956; April 27 and May 25, 1957. The Texas barratry statute, a provision of the Texas Penal Code since 1879, made it a criminal offense to solicit lawsuits for profit where one had no interest.

39. Gillette, "NAACP in Texas," 237; Dallas *Morning News*, August 4, 1956.

40. Jones, "Educational Desegregation," 337.

41. Atkins to Sampley, June 16, 1955; and Sampley to Atkins, June 22, 1955, Matthews Papers; Denton *Record-Chronicle*, August 11 and September 4, 1955; Dallas *Morning News*, August 11, 1955.

42. Joe L. Atkins, interview by Ronald Marcello, June 20, 1995, transcript, interview OH 1057, 2–3, 13; Gillette, "NAACP in Texas," 141–42.

43. Atkins, interview by Marcello, OH 1057, 3, 4 (quotation), 5; Gillette, "NAACP in Texas," 142–43; Dallas *Morning News*, April 20, 1994.

44. Dallas *Morning News*, April 20, 1994.

45. Atkins, interview by Marcello, OH 1057, 5–7.

46. Ibid., 6 (quotation), 7–8.

47. Ibid., 8–10.

48. Ibid., 8–10; Matthews, interview by Mangrum, OH 360, 8.

49. Matthews, interview by Mangrum, OH 360, 8.

50. Ibid., 8 (quotation), 51–52; Grace Cartwright (member of the board of regents), interview by Ronald Marcello, November 15, 1989, transcript, interview OH 789, 62.

51. Matthews, interview by Mangrum, OH 360, 52–53; Ben Wooten, interview by

Ronald Marcello, November 10, 1969, transcript, interview OH 29, 15.

52. Atkins, interview by Marcello, OH 1057, 11; Sampley to Atkins, July 18, 1955, Matthews Papers.

53. Atkins, interview by Marcello, OH 1057, 11–12, 14–16. On July 25, 1955, the US District Court for the Western District, Texas, in *White v. Smith*, ruled that African American students were entitled to enroll at Texas Western College. See US Commission on Civil Rights, *Equal Protection*, 65.

54. Atkins, interview by Marcello, OH 1057, 18 (second quotation); Gillette, "NAACP in Texas," 94–95; telephone interview with Atkins, June 6, 1996 (first quotation). There are no records in the Juanita Craft Papers to indicate that the NAACP had formulated a concerted effort on behalf of Atkins. See Juanita Craft Collection, Dallas Public Library, Dallas, Texas.

55. Denton *Campus Chat*, August 12, 1955; Denton *Record-Chronicle*, August 11, 14, 1955; First Amended Complaint, *Atkins v. Matthews et al.*, Civil Action No. 1104, District Court of the US for Eastern District of Texas, August 11, 1955, Matthews Papers (quotation). The Texas Legislature enacted legislation that stated, "All available school funds shall be appropriated . . . for education alike of white and colored children, and impartial provision shall be made for both races. No white child shall attend schools supported for colored children, nor shall colored children attend schools supported for white children." See Acts of 1905, Article 2900, *Revised Civil Statutes of Texas* (1948), 263.

56. Lee to Matthews, August 25 (quotation), September 19, 1955,

Matthews Papers; Denton *Record-Chronicle*, September 4, 1955.

57. Defendant's Original Answer and Defendant's Motion to Strike Motion of Plaintiff for Preliminary Injunction, *Atkins v. Matthews*, Civil Action No. 1104, September 2, 1955 (first quotation); Atkins, interview by Marcello, OH 1057, 16–17; Lee to Matthews, September 19, 1955 (second quotation), Matthews Papers.

58. Memorandum Decision and Order Overruling Motion for Preliminary Injunction, *Atkins v. Matthews*, Civil Action No. 1104, September 10, 1955 (quotations); Harold Chase et al., *Dictionary of the Federal Judiciary* (Detroit, MI: Gale Research, 1976), 249–50.

59. Memorandum and Decision, *Atkins v. Matthews*, Civil Action No. 1104, September 10, 1955.

60. Atkins, interview by Marcello, OH 1057, 18–19.

61. Lee to Matthews, September 19, October 13, 1955, Matthews Papers; Matthews, interview by Mangrum, OH 360, 46–48; "President's Report," Minutes of NTSC Board of Regents, October 20, 1955, University Archives, Willis Library, University of North Texas, Denton.

62. Plaintiff's Trial Brief, *Atkins v. Matthews*, Civil Action No. 1104, December 2, 1955.

63. Matthews to Lee, November 15, 1955, Matthews Papers; Memorandum, Registrar Alex Dickie to Sampley, September 9, 1955, Mathews Papers; Denton *Campus Chat*, December 7, 1955; Dallas *Express*, December 10, 1955; Denton *Record-Chronicle*, December 2, 1955.

64. Federal Reporter, 2nd Series, 206 F. 2d., *Bruce v. Stilwell* (St. Paul, MN: West

Publishing, 1953), 554–57 (quotations); *Texas Jurisprudence*, 2nd. ed., vol. 41 (San Francisco: Bancroft-Whitney Co., 1963), 7; Dallas *Express*, December 3, 1955.

65. Memorandum Opinion, *Atkins v. Matthews*, Civil Action No. 1104, December 8, 1955.

66. Matthews to Board of Regents, December 2, 1955; Godfrey to Matthews, December 7, 1955; Horace Wimberly (Asst. Atty. Gen.) to Matthews, December 12, 1955; Lee to Sheehy, December 13, 1955; Lee to Matthews, December 15, 1955; and Matthews to Lee, December 17, 1955, Matthews Papers.

67. Matthews, interview by Mangrum, OH 360, 15–18, 42–43 (quotations); Rogers, interview by Comrie, OH 519, 32; Arthur Sampley, interview by Marguerite Haggard, April 5, 1955, transcript, interview OH 252, 103–4.

68. Rogers, interview by Comrie, OH 519, 31; Matthews, interview by Mangrum, OH 360, 22.

69. Denton *Record-Chronicle*, February 2, 5, 1956; Denton *Campus Chat*, February 3, 1956; Fort Worth *Star-Telegram*, February 3, 1956; Rogers, interview by Comrie, OH 519, 14–15.

70. Rogers, interview by Comrie, OH 519, 22–23; Matthews, interview by Mangrum, OH 360, 9.

71. Rogers, interview by Comrie, OH 519, 15–17.

72. Ibid., 17–19 (second quotation); Matthews, interview by Mangrum, OH 360, 10–11 (first quotation); Matthews to Pastor Metcalf, September 17, 1963, Matthews Papers.

73. Denton *Record-Chronicle*, February 7, 1956.

74. Matthews, interview by Mangrum, OH 360, 11–12.

75. W. C. Brown, interview by Randy Cummings and Ronald Marcello, June 6, 1984, transcript, interview OH 652, 18–19; Charlie Cole, interview by Randy Cummings and Ronald Marcello, March 5, 1985, transcript, interview OH 653, 12; Matthews, interview by Mangrum, OH 360, 12–13. See Dallas *Express*, February 1, 1956.

76. Matthews, interview by Mangrum, OH 360, 2; Denton *Record-Chronicle*, August 30, 1956.

77. Martin Shockley, interview by Sharon Perry, April 10, 1995, transcript, interview OH 1052, 4.

78. Matthews to Pastor Metcalf, September 17, 1963 (first quotation), Matthews Papers; Cartwright, interview by Marcello, OH 789, 67 (second quotation); Hiram Friedsam, interview by Sharon Perry, April 28, 1995, transcript, interview OH 1054, 18.

79. Matthews, interview by Jenkins and Marcello, OH 633, 44.

80. Shockley, interview by Perry, OH 1052, 6.

81. Ibid., 3–5; Friedsam, interview by Perry, OH 1054, 4–5; Rogers, interview by Comrie, OH 519, 9.

82. Matthews, interview by Mangrum, OH 360, 24, 38–39 (first quotation); Matthews, interview by Jenkins and Marcello, OH 633, 22 (second quotation); William F. Belcher (former professor of English, North Texas State College), interview by Paulette Hasier, September 27, 1995, transcript, interview OH 1089, 26–27.

83. Matthews, interview by Mangrum, OH 360, 16–17.

84. Ibid.; Theodore R. Chatham (Principal, E. O. Smith High School, Houston) to Robert Toulouse (Dean, North Texas State College Graduate School), January (no day) 1961,

Matthews Papers; and Matthews to Chatham, January 11, 1961, Matthews Papers; Rebecca Humphrey to Matthews, August 5, 1959 (first quotation), Matthews Papers.

85. Matthews, interview by Jenkins and Marcello, OH 633, 25; Rogers, interview by Comrie, OH 519, 36.

86. Haynes, interview by Cummings and Marcello, OH 620, 33–34.

87. Odus Mitchell, interview by Randy Cummings and Ronald Marcello, October 19, 1982, transcript, interview OH 566, 35–37, 39–40 (quotation); Herbert Ferrill, interview by Randy Cummings and Ronald Marcello, July 20, 1983, transcript, interview OH 605, 59. See also Ronald E. Marcello, "The Desegregation of Intercollegiate Athletics in Texas: North Texas State College as a Test Case," *Journal of Sport History* 14 (Winter 1987): 286–316. Matthews denied that he had ever imposed any limits on the recruitment of African American players. See Matthews, interview by Jenkins and Marcello, OH 633, 36–37.

88. Matthews, interview by Mangrum, OH 360, 20–21; Bahnsen, interview by Cummings and Marcello, OH 627, 38; Matthews to Pastor Metcalf, September 17, 1963, Matthews Papers; Marcello, "Intercollegiate Athletics."

89. Bardolph, *Civil Rights Record*, 275–76; Mark V. Tushnet, *The NAACP's Legal Strategy against Segregated Education, 1925–1950* (Chapel Hill: University of North Carolina Press, 1987), 125; Richard Kluger, *Simple Justice: The History of Brown v. Board of Education and Black America's Struggle for Equality* (New York: Alfred A. Knopf, 1976), 268; John T. Hubbell, "The Desegregation of the University of Oklahoma, 1946–1950," *Journal*

of Negro History 57 (October 1972): 376–77, 382–84.

90. Denton *Record-Chronicle*, June 7, 1956; Dallas *Morning News*, April 20, 1958, May 19, 1963 (quotation); Matthews to Richard Morehead (Austin Bureau, Dallas *Morning News*), March 17, 1958, Matthews Papers; Matthews to Morehead, November 19, 1959, Matthews Papers; Matthews to Metcalf, September 17, 1963, Matthews Papers.

91. US Bureau of the Census, *US Census Population: 1960*, vol. 1 (Washington, DC: Bureau of the Census, 1960), part 45 (General Population Characteristics), 118, 249; Judge Jack Gray, interview by Randy Cummings and Ronald Marcello, May 30, 1984, transcript, interview OH 650, 4–8; Jones, "Public Education in Texas," 350; Richard F. Pettigrew and M. Richard Cramer, "The Demography of Desegregation," *Journal of Social Issues* 15 (1959): 64–66. For an excellent analysis of racial conflict as reflected by the proportions of whites and blacks in the general population, see Jones, "Educational Desegregation," 334–44.

92. Betty Kimble, interview by Jane Harris, December 8, 1987, transcript, interview OH 709, 13; Billie Mohair, interview by Richard Byrd, February 25, 1988, transcript, interview OH 713, 2–3; Haynes, interview by Cummings and Marcello, OH 620, 18–22, 25 (quotation); Miller, interview by Glaze, OH 857, 7–8. One of the darker sides of Denton's brand of racism occurred between 1921 and 1923, after the town's

white citizens approved a bond issue to build a park on land occupied by African American residents. The people living there, an area known as Quakertown, were forced to sell out at prices well below market value, and their homes were moved across the railroad tracks to land selected by the city. See Denton *Record-Chronicle*, November 17, 1993.

93. Rogers, interview by Comrie, OH 519, 8; Matthews, interview by Jenkins and Marcello, OH 633, 17; Gray, interview by Cummings and Marcello, OH 650, 3–4, 6–7, 9–10 (quotation). For an excellent analysis of the relationship between economics and racial conflict, see Jones, "Public Education in Texas," 348–60.

94. Denton *Record-Chronicle*, February 5, 1956; Fort Worth *Star-Telegram*, February 3, 1956; Marcello, "Intercollegiate Athletics," 218–316.

95. Texas Western was the first four-year state-supported college to desegregate at the undergraduate level, doing so in September 1955. North Texas was the second. See Dallas *Morning News*, July 9, 1955; New York *Times*, July 24, 1955; Richard B. McCaslin, "Steadfast in His Intent: John W. Hargis and the Integration of the University of Texas at Austin," *Southwestern Historical Quarterly* 95 (July 1991): 29–30.

96. Dallas *Express*, December 3, 1955; September 15, 1956 (quotation).

97. Atkins, interview by Marcello, OH 1057, 20–21, 23, 25 (quotation), 27; Miller, interview by Glaze, OH 857, 103; Matthews, interview by Mangrum, OH 360, 52–53.

Texas Voices

The 1963 Civil Rights March on Austin

Martin Kuhlman

In the US civil rights movement, the year 1963 was a critical one. That situation, as Martin Kuhlman points out so well, included Texas. In August, nearly a quarter-million activists marched to Washington, DC; at the same time, as author Kuhlman notes, a thousand Texans marched on the capital city of Austin. We should not forget, either, that in November of that year, the president of the United States, John F. Kennedy, was assassinated in Dallas; he was succeeded by Texan Lyndon Baines Johnson. Martin Kuhlman teaches history at West Texas A&M University; he has written a number of articles appearing in scholarly journals as well as book chapters on topics such as the African American experience and, in particular, the civil rights movement in the Lone Star State.

★

On August 28, 1963, a major event of the African American civil rights movement took place when more than two hundred thousand activists marched on Washington, DC. A number of Texas activists joined the march. Dallas organizations, including the National Association for the Advancement of Colored People (NAACP), the Catholic Interracial Council, the Texas Council of Voters, and the Dall Full Citizenship Committee, planned car pools to Washington. The Houston *Informer* announced that air-conditioned buses would leave Houston for Washington. But both of these cities also announced transportation to a march in Austin.¹ Of course, the distance from Texas to Washington played a factor in having a march in the state capital. However, a number of other conditions specific to Texas were addressed in the march. The Austin march gives an example of some of the grassroots influence on the movement.

In the summer of 1963, there was some opposition to the Democratic Gov. John Connally. The opposition came from liberal Democrats who formed the Democratic

Coalition. The coalition supported civil rights, labor rights, and other liberal causes. Leaders of the organization included W. J. Durham, president of the Texas Council of Voters and a lawyer for the NAACP; Hank Brown, president of the Texas AFL-CIO; Albert Pena, president of the Political Association of Spanish-Speaking Organizations (PASO); and Franklin Jones, spokesman for a group known as liberal loyalist Democrats. African American leaders in the coalition sent Governor Connally a petition calling on the officials of Texas to use every means available to bring about equality in all parts of the state. The petition urged Connally to speed up desegregation by issuing a broad executive order ending segregation in all state facilities and in businesses requiring state licenses. The petition would be similar to orders recently enacted by the governors of Kentucky and North Carolina. Ten subcommittee members of the Texas Council of Voters Executive Committee signed the petition, including Erma and Moses Leroy and Francis Williams of Houston, Rev. C. William Black Jr. and G. J. Sutton of San Antonio, Durham of Dallas, Marion Brooks of Fort Worth, Willie Melton of Kendleton, and Booker T. Bonner of Austin.[2]

Connally gave his indirect answer to the petition in a thirty-minute televised speech on July 19, 1963. The speech directly responded to Pres. John Kennedy's proposed national civil rights bill. Connally especially denounced the section of the bill calling for mandatory desegregation of privately owned public accommodations like restaurants or theaters. The speech epitomized the governor's reliance on the private sector to make progress in desegregation. Connally feared that the federal legislation would attack the freedom and right to manage private property. The proposed civil rights bill, he argued, "would deprive owners of private businesses of the right to decide whom they serve." The governor also objected to the broad powers given to the Attorney General of the United States. The attorney general would be allowed to file injunctions on the behalf of individuals forcing the desegregation of schools and public facilities. Connally asserted that he could not support "the proposition of violating one person's rights to bestow privilege on another person, regardless of the color or race of either."[3]

Connally urged Texans to continue to listen to moderate voices that had allowed their state to "avoid the cold, arbitrary tool of government edict." He maintained that the civil rights issue should be solved locally and that Texas had already made "tremendous" progress in that direction. Although Connally opposed the legislation, he vowed to uphold the law if passed.[4] The governor had adopted the states' rights argument of the Deep South and defended some types of segregation. Connally, however, did identify voluntary desegregation as progress. At governor's conferences in the following months, Connally positioned Texas with the moderate border states.[5]

A number of Texans supported the governor's speech. US Senator John Tower, a Republican, also opposed the public accommodations section of the civil rights bill. He agreed that desegregation should be on a voluntary rather than a compulsory basis.[6] A number of telegrams sent to the governor's office praised Connally for defending the rights of private property owners.[7] A poll of Anglo-Texans reported that 75 percent opposed the public accommodations section of the bill. Some segregationists took heart in Connally's speech. A few days after the governor's speech, segregationists protesting the entrance of African Americans into a Houston recently desegregated drive-in movie theater carried a sign denouncing Kennedy and lauding Connally as "the only one whose [sic] going to stand up for white people's rights."[8]

Opposition to Connally's speech appeared in many black Texans. The *Houston Informer* marveled at the high percentage of hotels, theaters, and restaurants in the state that Connally cited as being desegregated. The editors expressed the hope that African Americans did not "take the governor at his word and show up for such public accommodations" or "someone will go to jail." The editorial also accused Connally of playing a "Cat and Mouse game" with African Americans by promising them a lot while delivering little.[9] Some black Texans, however, supported Connally's speech.

The United Political Organization (UPO), a pro-Connally group consisting of approximately 150 wealthy conservative black leaders, had formed in 1962. The UPO emphasized employment and voting rights and spoke out against civil rights demonstrations. The UPO's endorsement helped Connally win a number of black votes in 1962. Civil rights leader Booker T. Bonner had criticized the UPO for selling out its community and for being "Uncle Toms." The Houston *Informer* accused the UPO leaders of trading political and constitutional rights for a few jobs and political appointments. The UPO officially proclaimed Connally's speech as the "most significant and positive statement on civil rights by a public official in the history of the state."[10]

Connally's speech also had an influence on the national scene. A few days after the speech, Vice Pres. Lyndon Johnson received a staff memorandum concerning his fellow Texan's speech. The memo pointed out the irony of the state having segregation legislation on its books, which affected private property, and Connally denouncing the interference of legislation in desegregating private property. Hobart Taylor Jr., a black resident of Houston and vice chairman of the national Equal Employment Opportunity Committee, wrote Johnson a letter expressing concern over the controversy caused in Texas by Connally's speech.[11] Although the turmoil gained some national attention, Texans continued to lead the struggle in their state.

The state's civil right supporters believed that Connally, with the aid of the UPO, had misrepresented himself to black Texans, but the speech represented the true stance of the governor on racial matters. E. Brice Cunningham, a spokesperson for the Texas Council of Voters, insisted that Connally's stand on civil rights had aligned "Texas with the Old South and others dedicated to blocking progress."[12] Bonner; Houston Wade, an influential leader of the Austin stand-in campaign; and five other civil rights supporters met at the University of Texas YMCA in the days following the speech. There they decided on an action that would spotlight the governor's civil rights policies.[13] Connally's stand on the desegregation of public accommodations led to direct action.

Bonner sent Connally a registered letter asking for a meeting to discuss their disagreements over the public accommodations section of the civil rights bill. When

Connally left Austin without replying, Bonner went to the governor's office in the state capitol on July 29 to demand an appointment for a meeting. He refused to leave until he received an appointment and staged a one-man sit-in as he spent the day in the waiting room and moved to the hall when the waiting room closed for the evening. That night, he temporarily broke his vigil to lead forty biracial picketers, mainly University of Texas students, in a one-hour march around the governor's mansion. Protesters carried leaflets labeling Connally "a Jim Crow governor of the worst kind" who had exploited the trust and hopes of Negroes. Bonner announced that he and other civil rights activists planned large-scale demonstrations in Texas for August 28 to coincide with the march on Washington. Bonner returned to the hall for the rest of the night and waited in the governor's office the next day.[14] The twenty-six-hour sit-in ended when Governor Connally announced from Houston that he would meet with Bonner, although Connally did not believe anything needed to be discussed. A source of conflict appeared when Bonner stated that he would be accompanied to the meeting by at least four civil rights activists. Howard Rose, the governor's executive assistant, insisted that only Bonner could attend the meeting.[15]

Reaction to the sit-in came quickly. The Club Caravan, where Bonner worked and Connally often ate, fired Bonner the next day. The owners said they "laid off" Bonner because his private affairs interfered with his job and because of an accusation of theft. But Bonner did not accept this reasoning. He told reporters that he had been blacklisted by Austin employers and that state and federal authorities had investigated him. Bonner expressed his anger at the lack of rights for African Americans and labeled the NAACP as "too tame" for him. Bonner had served in Korea and felt disturbed about fighting for the United States and finding out he still had few rights at home.[16]

Bonner continued to lead marches around the governor's mansion until the scheduled meeting, hoping to maintain interest in integration activities and inspire others to join future demonstrations. On August 1, seven civil rights supporters marched, and a group of ten segregationists, consisting of youths ranging from twelve to twenty in age and calling themselves the Children of the Confederacy, countermarched. Edmond Jackson, a student from the University of Mississippi and a member of the White Citizen's Council, led the segregationists. No confrontation occurred as the group left ten minutes after the integrationists arrived. Bonner also planned a parade of pickets for the night before the scheduled meeting with Connally "to prove to the governor on Tuesday that we mean business."[17]

Upon reading about Bonner's sit-in, Francis Williams, a member of the Democratic Coalition, searched for other leaders to attend the meeting with Bonner. At 11:30 a.m. on August 6, Bonner arrived in Connally's waiting room flanked by six other civil rights leaders: four African Americans—Dr. Ruth Bellinger and Sutton of San Antonio, Cunningham of Dallas, and James McCoy of the University of Texas—and two Hispanic leaders, Henry Munoz and Lalo Solis of San Antonio. When told the governor would see him, Bonner asked that the other leaders be allowed to attend. After a short consultation with Bonner, Sutton, and Cunningham, the governor canceled the meeting. Connally balked at the presence of the other leaders. Sutton wondered if the governor planned to meet with black Texans "one at a time" while Bonner proclaimed that "one Negro can't speak for all the rest of the Negroes in Texas." Bellinger became extremely agitated at the cancellation of the meeting since she had served as the cochairperson of Connally's 1962 campaign in Bexar County. The minority leaders left behind a petition once again asking Connally to issue an executive order banning segregation in state-owned facilities. The petition also asked for the enactment of at least a $1.25 minimum hourly-wage law, the repeal of all Jim Crow laws in Texas, the immediate integration of all public schools, and access to college and university facilities for all races.[18]

Sam Wood, the state-capital correspondent for the *Austin American Statesman*, labeled Bonner's sit-in as "obviously politically inspired to embarrass Connally." Wood said the liberal Democratic Coalition wanted to fan the flames for "liberal opposition to Gov. Connally in the 1964 election." The sit-in represented a planned strategy to revive the minority coalition. The evidence, however, does not support that conclusion.[19] The Democratic Coalition did not join the sit-in or the planning of further demonstrations. Although members of the coalition, including Bonner and Williams, joined or initiated activities, the coalition never became officially involved.

After the cancellation of the meeting, nearly fifty civil rights supporters renewed the picketing of the mansion. Bonner said that he had given up on the possibility of a personal conference with the governor and picketers would switch their emphasis to the state capitol. He told reporters that "every Negro man in Texas will know the governor definitely is not his friend. . . . The Negro must know his rights are legal or he will never get them." Countermarchers heckled Bonner with chants of "you ran away today" and carried signs proclaiming, "Connally yes, Kennedy no."[20]

There were opposing voices from the black community. Dr. J. J. Seabrook, president of Huston-Tillotson College in Austin, accused Bonner of attempting to create a sensation. Seabrook said, "We don't want outside people coming in and telling us what must be done in Austin. They do not know how much already has been done in this city." But Bonner had grown up in Wallis, Texas, and lived for a number of years in Austin. The fact that Huston-Tillotson received at least some support from the white establishment may have influenced Seabrook's statement.[21] Opposition to Bonner also appeared from other areas of the state. Rev. C. A. Holliday, a Connally appointee as the first African American on the State Board of Corrections in March of 1963, labeled Bonner's actions as "uncalled for at this time." He praised Connally as a progressive in the area of civil rights.[22] Obviously, Holliday had his own motivations for supporting the governor.

When national civil rights groups planned a march on Washington, DC, on August 28 to call for equality, activists in Texas scheduled demonstrations to correspond with the national march. Bonner announced plans to organize a march in Austin to the capitol and the governor's mansion. Civil rights leaders recognized that some black Texans would not be able to make the trip to Washington. Thus a state march would give them an opportunity to vent their frustration. Bonner, Williams, and other leaders met at the YMCA in Houston to discuss strategy for the march.[23] Civil rights supporters sent out over 1,200 mailings to urge groups and individuals across the state to attend. For example, Erma LeRoy sent information sheets to numerous organizations describing the governor's stance on civil rights. She accused Connally of aiding the segregationist argument. LeRoy urged the organizations to help "make it clear that he (Connally) can't be a hero to the East Texas segregationist and Negro citizens at the same time!" She defined the controversy as one of "PROPERTY RIGHTS VS. HUMAN RIGHTS." The governor should be more concerned about protecting the rights of people than property rights.[24] Although Bonner announced the march, Williams did much of the organizing. He worked with groups in cities such as Dallas and Houston. A few days before the march, Bonner and other supporters handed out leaflets in the Austin African American community soliciting participants. Clarence Laws, the Dallas regional secretary of the NAACP, urged black Texans to attend the national march but added that the Austin march would be a good alternative. Organizers expected four thousand activists to join the two-mile "March For Jobs and Freedom" through downtown Austin. Along the route, a committee of five planned to deliver a petition to Connally calling for integration of all state-owned facilities. The Freedom Now Committee received permission for the August 28 march from the Austin City Council.[25]

Dallas organizations, including the NAACP, the Catholic Interracial Council, the Texas Council of Voters, and the Dallas Full Citizenship Committee, planned car pools and buses to Austin and Washington. Civil rights groups in other Texas cities planned to do the same.[26] The Houston *Informer* announced that air-conditioned buses would leave Houston for Washington and Austin. Approximately seventy Houstonians participated in the Austin march.[27]

Labor supported both marches. The AFL-CIO of Houston announced its "whole-hearted support" for the marches. Labor called on the state to abolish the use of race, creed, or color as a basis for employment. The AFL-CIO injected some of its own agenda into the civil rights controversy, such as the repeal of the right-to-work laws and the passage of a minimum-wage law.[28]

Some opposition to the march appeared within the African American community. D. B. Mason, attorney and head of the Dallas County Democratic Progressive Voters League, announced that none of his group would join the march "because we feel that Gov. Connally has done well and advanced our cause as well as could be expected in Texas at this time." He pointed to the appointment of two African Americans to state boards as steps in the right direction. Connally's appointees included Holliday and Charles Jackson Clark to the State Board of Morticians. Mason added, "In Texas we must take things slowly and cannot advance as rapidly as in the East or North."[29]

Governor Connally had offers of "protection" against the Freedom Now marchers. The Indignant White Citizens Council (IWCC), led by Bob Joiner of Grand

View, also asked for a permit to march in Austin on the twenty-eighth. Connally urged the group to postpone their march, however, saying he feared violence if the two groups confronted each other. Joiner expressed displeasure over Connally allowing the integrationists to march while asking the segregationists to stay away. "We are not barbarians," Joiner stated, "we know right from wrong." He added that the IWCC would march if the Freedom Now march went on.[30] Bonner also disagreed with the governor on the attempt to censor the racists: "He's asking those people not to express their constitutional rights." The IWCC planned to hold its march three hours prior to the Freedom Now March, and Joiner expected at least three thousand marchers.[31]

The fear of confrontation between the rival demonstrations increased the anxiety looming over the state capital. A large number of state and local police organized in Austin to prevent instances of violence during the marches. Austin Police Chief R. A. Miles called every available police officer to duty for the day of the marches. He assigned two hundred uniformed and plainclothes police to monitor the protests. The officers received riot equipment, including batons and helmets. Even before the marches had been announced, the Austin police had initiated a stepped-up program in riot control. State police planned to encircle the capitol building to aid local police.[32] Waggoner Carr, the state attorney general, had received a report outlining laws that might be enforced against marchers. The report brought up the possibility of using the state national guard if needed. "The Report on Legality of Sit-Ins and Picketing" was clearly aimed at civil rights activists.[33]

The IWCC parade started out from Congress Avenue at eleven o'clock on the morning of the twenty-eighth. Eleven marchers "swelled" the ranks of the segregationists, most of them carrying Goldwater or prosegregation signs. Joiner told reporters, "One of our aims is to support and protect the governor." When reminded the governor did not want the IWCC's help, Joiner accused Connally of having been around "the Kennedy brothers too long." From his red pickup, which led the marchers, Joiner shouted, "You are either a Communist and a nigger lover, or you will join us. You can't be in the middle." After the march, Joiner expressed his disappointment that "so many gutless Texans have refused to stand up and say they are for segregation."[34]

Ex-Gen. Edwin A. Walker visited Austin as an observer. Walker had rallied segregationists in Oxford, Mississippi, in 1962, attempting to block integration of the University of Mississippi, and was arrested for promoting riots. In a press conference after the first march, Walker stated that "Joiner's group represent, in spirit, millions more Americans over the nation than those to parade this afternoon." Walker added, "I came to see how much interest and support the pro-Kennedy, pro-Communist, pro-social rights program could get in Texas. It will be an obvious flop." Walker accused the Kennedy administration of supporting civil rights demonstrations to "take the spotlight off their biggest flop—Cuba."[35]

A crowd of participants in the Freedom Now march gathered at the Doris Miller Auditorium in East Austin for a premarch rally early that afternoon. Seven black youths led the crowd in freedom chants and songs. One freedom song was

> *In all America, true things are happening*
> *To make the white man try to see,*
> *That we are human, and we are equal*
> *And that we shall, we shall be free.*
> *In all America, true things are happening*
> *To make the black man try to see,*
> *That we must fight here, that we must fight here*
> *If we are ever to be free.*[36]

Approximately six hundred to one thousand civil rights supporters, fifty of whom were white, began the two-mile trek at 2 p.m. in 102-degree weather. High school and college students made up the majority of the marchers. Other marchers included members of the clergy; representatives of liberal groups, including an official delegate of the state AFL-CIO and a staff member of the Democratic Coalition; and professionals. They streamed past the capitol as some marchers chanted and spelled *freedom*, while others sang, "I want to be a free, free man" and "Tell John Connally we shall not be moved." Some of the slogans on the sea of signs included "Jim Crow Must Go," "Gradualism, Tokenism, Connallyism," "Faubus–Wallace–Barnett–Connally," "If Not Now, When?" and "No More 50 cents per hour." The marchers continued on to a rally in Woolridge Park.[37]

A major difference between the national and the state marches appeared in the reactions of the executives. President Kennedy praised the march and met with the leaders, while Connally remained in his office as the marchers passed. At the march in Washington, Martin Luther King Jr. and others curtailed any attacks on Kennedy.[38] No physical violence or arrests of marchers occurred, but police were ready. The Dallas *Morning News* estimated that there were more uniformed police and plainclothes officers than marchers. Highway patrolmen, including Col. Homer Garrison Jr., the director of public safety, waited outside of the governor's office during the day.[39] Connally, however, suffered numerous verbal assaults during the rally in the park.

Williams introduced eight speakers, including Bonner as "the man who started it off." After encouraging the crowd to applaud themselves, Bonner gave the platform to other speakers. Marion Brooks, a Fort Worth physician, told the crowd that the 625,000 eligible African American voters and the eight hundred thousand Hispanic voters, along with the two million liberals and the five hundred thousand labor supporters, would "sweep the state house clean." Rev. Claude Black proclaimed, "We are tired of humiliation. We come here to warn Connally and all other segregationists that their days are numbered." Durham explained to the cheering crowd the reason a petitioned was not delivered to the governor: "I didn't want to see the governor. I wanted the governor to see us go by." He added, "I've got news for Governor Connally. Tell him that each of us Negro voters will remember him on election day." Dr. Ruth Bellinger declared that the governor has "let us down."[40]

Durham also spoke against the UPO due to the group's support for Connally.[41] But the organization did not give unconditional support to the governor. Many members remained upset over Connally's speech and resigned from the group in protest. Rev. H. Rhett James, the UPO executive secretary and a civil rights leader in Dallas, sent a telegram to Don Yarborough, a supporter of the proposed national civil rights bill, hinting that he might be asked to oppose John Connally in the gubernatorial race of 1964. Other members urged Connally to establish a board to recommend state civil rights legislation that would include the establishment of a human relations committee.[42]

The rally included two clerical speakers from Dallas. Rev. William Oliver of the First Community Church, who had brought a bus of twenty-eight marchers to Austin, told the crowd that churches should be aware of their responsibility in the area of race relations. Rev. B. L. McCormick of the St. Paul Methodist Church also spoke.[43]

In his book *Fighting Their Own Battles*, Brian Behnken presents evidence that Mexican Americans did not join the African American struggle for civil rights. One of the few examples of the two groups working together appeared at the rally.[44] Henry Munoz, a representative for PASO, read a statement from Albert Pena, ending with the sentence "Until justice is blind to color, until education is unaware of race, until opportunity is unconcerned with the color of men's skins, we have fallen short of assuring freedom of the free." Durham proclaimed, "They'll never separate Latin Americans and the American Negro any more in politics." But a less-supportive voice appeared from the Mexican American community. A few days before the march, the president of the League of United Latin American Citizens, Paul Andow, denounced public demonstrations as casting "aspersions on our government in the eyes of the rest of the world." He identified "education and self-improvement" as the best means to fight discrimination. The rally ended at 5 p.m. with Durham asserting that civil rights supporters could unseat Connally in 1964.[45] Other marches took place in Texas cities on that day, including a three-hundred-person march in Corpus Christi around the city hall calling for an ordinance banning segregation in all public facilities in the city.[46]

Over two hundred thousand civil rights activists marched in Washington, DC, on August 28, 1963. The crowd in Austin was much smaller, with about one thousand marchers, but a number of conclusions can be made. The grassroots nature of the movement becomes apparent. There were many similarities between the marches. Various liberal groups joined in the Austin march. Both marches spotlighted similar issues such as the need for civil rights legislation. But Texas activists did have their own agenda. The marchers in Austin verbally attacked the executive, John Connally, while marchers in Washington did not need to attack the more sympathetic John Kennedy.

This article was originally published as Kuhlman, Martin. "Texas Voices: The 1963 Civil Rights March on Austin." In Bricks without Straw: A Comprehensive History of African Americans, *edited by David A. Williams, 46–59. Woodway, TX: Eakin Press, 1997. Reprinted with changes by permission of the author and Eakin Press.*

NOTES

1. Houston *Informer*, August 24, 1963.
2. Dallas *Morning News*, July 14, 1963.
3. Ibid.
4. Ibid.
5. James Reston Jr., *The Lone Star: The Life of John Connally* (New York: Harper and Row, 1989), 293–94. Larry Temple, an aide to Governor Connally, had objected to the speech because it would identify the governor with George Wallace. But Temple admitted that the speech gave Connally the image of not being controlled by Kennedy and Johnson as the speech opposed the views of both these national leaders.
6. Dallas *Morning News*, August 2, 1963.
7. Social Change, Race [telegram], Office of Governor John Connally, Lyndon Baines Johnson Library, University of Texas at Austin.
8. Austin *Texas Observer*, August 9, 1963.
9. Houston *Informer*, August 3, 1963.
10. Ibid.
11. Reston, *Lone Star*, 292–93.
12. Dallas *Morning News*, August 3, 1963.
13. Booker T. Bonner, interview by Marty Kuhlman, November 11 and 17, 1992, tape recording in author's possession.
14. Austin *American Statesman*, July 30, 1963.
15. Dallas *Morning News*, July 31, 1963.
16. Dallas *Morning News*, August 1, 1963.
17. Dallas *Morning News*, August 2, 1963.
18. Austin *American Statesman*, August 7, 1963.
19. Austin *American Statesman*, August 7, 1963.
20. Dallas *Morning News*, August 8, 1963.
21. Austin *American Statesman*, August 1, 1963.
22. Dallas *Morning News*, July 31, 1963.
23. Dallas *Morning News*, August 11, 1963.
24. Open letter from Erma LeRoy to civil rights leaders, Moses LeRoy Collection, Houston Metropolitan Research Center, Houston Public Library.
25. Austin *American Statesman*, August 25, 1963.
26. Houston *Informer*, August 24, 1963.
27. Houston *Informer*, August 31, 1963.
28. Dallas *Morning News*, July 19, 1963.
29. Dallas *Morning News*, August 28, 1963.
30. Ibid.
31. Austin *American Statesman*, August 27, 1963.
32. Ibid.
33. "Report on Legality of Sit-Ins and Picketing," August 1, 1963, Waggoner Carr Papers, 1945–85, Southwest Collection, Texas Tech University, Lubbock.
34. Austin *American Statesman*, August 29, 1963.
35. Ibid.
36. Austin *Texas Observer*, September 6, 1963.

37. Austin *American Statesman*, July 29, 1963.

38. David J. Garrow, *Bearing the Cross: Martin Luther King, Jr., and the Southern Christian Leadership Conference* (New York: Random House, 1986), 285.

39. Dallas *Morning News*, August 29, 1963.

40. Austin *American Statesman*, August 29, 1963.

41. Dallas *Morning News*, August 29, 1963.

42. Ann Fear Crawford and Jack Keever, *John B. Connally: Portrait in Power* (Austin: Jenkins, 1973), 223, 224, 228.

43. Dallas *Morning News*, August 29, 1963.

44. Brian D. Behnken, *Fighting Their Own Battles: Mexican Americans, African Americans, and the Struggle for Civil Rights* (Chapel Hill: University of North Carolina Press, 2011), 9.

45. Austin *American Statesman*, August 29, 1963.

46. Dallas *Morning News*, August 29, 1963.

SELECTED BIBLIOGRAPHY

Anderson, Mia L. "African American Life through the *Sepia* Lens: A Chronicle of Fort Worth's *Sepia Magazine* during the Early Civil Rights Movement, 1955–1961." *Journal of South Texas* 31, no. 1 (Fall 2017): 36–49.

Atkinson, Lillie E. "Slavery in the Economy of Colorado County, 1822–1863." Master's thesis, Prairie View Agricultural and Mechanical College, 1954.

Bailey, Edward Lee. "Survey of the Negro Schools in Brazos County, Texas." Master's thesis, Texas Agricultural and Mechanical College, 1931.

Bean, Robin Carlyle. "The Role of the Commercial-Civic Elite in the Desegregation of Public Facilities in Waco, Texas." Master's thesis, Baylor University, 1990.

Bernstein, Patricia. *The First Waco Horror: The Lynching of Jesse Washington and the Rise of the NAACP*. College Station: Texas A&M University Press, 2005.

Brackner, Elmer Joe, Jr. "The Transition from Slave Potter to Free Potter: The Wilson Potteries of Guadalupe County, Texas." In *Texana II: Cultural Heritage of the Plantation South*, edited by Candace

Volz, 39–53. Austin: Texas Historical Commission, 1982.

———. "The Wilson Potteries." Master's thesis, University of Texas at Austin, 1981.

Brandenstein, Sherilyn Ruth. "Prominent Roles and Themes of Black Womanhood in *Sepia Record*." Master's thesis, University of Texas at Austin, 1989.

———. "*Sepia Record* as a Forum for Negotiating Women's Roles." In *Women and Texas History*, edited by Fane Downs and Nancy Baker Jones, 143–57. Austin: Texas State Historical Association, 1993.

Brewer, J. Mason, ed. *An Historical Outline of the Negro in Travis County*. Austin: Samuel Huston College, 1940.

———. *A Pictorial and Historical Souvenir of Negro Life in Austin, Texas: Who's Who and What's What*. Austin: privately printed, 1951.

Brice, Donaly. "Black Trail Drivers of Caldwell County." *Plum Creek Almanac* 33 (Fall 2015): 111–13.

———. "Jerry Thornton." *Plum Creek Almanac* 33 (Fall 2015): 117–18.

———. "Stephen 'Rowe' McClain." *Plum Creek Almanac* 33 (Fall 2015): 114–16.

Brown, Michael K. *The Wilson Potters: An African-American Enterprise in 19th-Century Texas.* Houston: Bayou Bend Collection and Gardens, Museum of Fine Arts, 2002.

Brown, Olive D., and Michael R. Heintze. "Mary Branch: Private College Educator." In *Black Leaders: Texans for Their Times*, edited by Alwyn Barr and Robert A. Calvert, 113–27. Austin: Texas State Historical Association, 1981.

Bundy, William Oliver. *Life of William Madison McDonald.* Fort Worth: Bunker, 1925.

Butler, Jay M. "James Harrison and the Development of Harrison Switch." Master's thesis, Baylor University, 1989.

Carey, Ida, and R. Matt Abigail. "Evans, Richard D." *Handbook of Texas Online*, accessed June 5, 2017, http://www.tshaonline.org/handbook

Carlson, Shawn B., ed. *African American Lifeways in East-Central Texas: The Ned Peterson Farmstead, Brazos County, Texas.* College Station: Center for Environmental Archaeology, Texas A&M University, 1995.

Carrigan, William Dean. *The Making of a Lynching Culture: Violence and Vigilantism in Central Texas, 1836–1916.* Urbana: University of Illinois Press, 2004.

———. "Slavery on the Frontier: The Peculiar Institution in Central Texas." *Slavery and Abolition* 20 (August 1999): 63–86.

Cary, Rebe. *How We Got Over! Update on a Backward Look: A History of Blacks in Fort Worth.* Fort Worth: privately printed, 2005.

———. *Princes Shall Come Out of Egypt, Texas, and Fort Worth.* Pittsburgh, PA: Dorrance, 2012.

Chote, James. "Desegregation of the Austin Independent School District: A Question of Balance." Master's thesis, University of Texas at Austin, 1991.

Corley, Rex Spencer. "A Comparative Study of the Public Schools for Whites and Negroes in the Independent School Districts of Falls County, Texas." Master's thesis, University of Texas at Austin, 1950.

Cutrer, Thomas W., and T. Michael Parrish. *Doris Miller, Pearl Harbor, and the Birth of the Civil Rights Movement.* College Station: Texas A&M University Press, 2018.

Debes, Robert Randolph. "A Sociological Study of Paul Quinn College, Waco, Texas." Master's thesis, Baylor University, 1949.

Doggett, Dorothy Lasseter. "Survey of Fort Worth's Negro Schools." Master's thesis, Texas Christian University, 1927.

Duren, Almetris M., and Louise Iscoe. *Overcoming: A History of Black Integration at the University of Texas at Austin.* Austin: University of Texas Press, 1979.

Fine, Betty, et al. *Clarksville.* Austin: School of Architecture, University of Texas Press, 1969.

Foley, Neil. *The White Scourge: Mexicans, Blacks, and Poor Whites in Texas Cotton Culture.* Berkeley: University of California Press, 1997.

Glasrud, Bruce A. *African Americans in South Texas History.* College Station: Texas A&M University Press, 2011.

———, ed. *Anti-black Violence in Twentieth-Century Texas.* College Station: Texas A&M University Press, 2015.

———, ed. "William M. McDonald: Business and Fraternal Leader." In *Black Leaders: Texans for Their Times*, edited by Alwyn Barr and Robert A. Calvert,

82–111. Austin: Texas State Historical Association, 1981.

Glasrud, Bruce A., and Paul H. Carlson, eds. *Slavery to Integration: Black Americans in West Texas*. Abilene, TX: State House Press, 2007.

Glasrud, Bruce A., and Archie P. McDonald, eds. *Blacks in East Texas History*. College Station: Texas A&M University Press, 2008.

Glasrud, Bruce A., and James M. Smallwood, eds. *The African American Experience in Texas: An Anthology*. Lubbock: Texas Tech University Press, 2007.

Goldstone, Dwonna. *Integrating the 40 Acres: The 50-Year Struggle for Racial Equality at the University of Texas*. Athens: University of Georgia Press, 2000.

Gooch, Augusta. *Life of Lenora Rolla: A Citizen Shapes Her World*. Lexington, KY: privately printed, 2013.

Gordon, John Ramsey. "The Negro in McClennan County." Master's thesis, Baylor University, 1932.

Gould, Lewis L., and Melissa R. Sneed. "Without Pride or Apology: The University of Texas at Austin, Racial Integration, and the Barbara Smith Case." *Southwestern Historical Quarterly* 103 (July 1999): 66–87.

Grant, Boston Philip. "An Evaluation of the Vocational Guidance Program in the San Marcos, Texas, Negro School." Master's thesis, Colorado State College, 1943.

Greene, A. C. "The Durable Society: Austin in the Reconstruction." *Southwestern Historical Quarterly* 72 (April 1969): 492–519.

Griffin, John Howard, and Theodore Freedman. *Mansfield, Texas: A Report of the Crisis Situation Resulting from Efforts to Desegregate the School System*. New York: Anti-Defamation League of B'nai B'rith, 1957.

Hales, Douglas. "Paul Quinn College." In *The New Handbook of Texas*, vol. 5, edited by Ron Tyler et al., 97–98. Austin: Texas State Historical Association, 1996.

Hall, Ida Leggett. "History of the Negro in Waco, Texas." *Waco Heritage and History* 14 (1984): 9, 14, 32–33.

Harvey, McClennon Phillip, ed. *A Brief History of Paul Quinn College, 1872–1965*. Waco, TX: privately printed, 1965.

Henneberger, John. *Clarksville: A Short History and Historic Tour*. Austin: Clarksville Community Development, 1978.

Henry, Willie Ray. "Slavery in the Economy of Brazos County, 1821–1860." Master's thesis, Prairie View Agricultural and Mechanical College, 1954.

Hurd, Michael. *Thursday Night Lights: The Story of Black High School Football in Texas*. Austin: University of Texas Press, 2017.

In Fulfillment of a Dream: African Americans at Texas A&M University. College Station: Texas A&M University Press, 2001.

Jackson, C. Emerson, and Gwendolyn McDonald Jackson. *The History of the Negro, Wichita Falls, Texas, 1880–1982*. Wichita Falls, TX: Humphrey, 1988, 2003.

Jackson, Jacquelyne Johnson. "Suzanne J. Terrell: This Other Kind of Doctors—Traditional Medical Systems in Black Neighborhoods in Austin, Texas." *Contemporary Sociology* 20 (September 1991).

Jackson, Joelie. "Morton, Azie Taylor." *The Black Past: Remembered and Reclaimed*, accessed June 3, 2017, http://www .blackpast.org

Jackson, Robena E. "East Austin: A Socio-historical View of a Segregated Community." Master's thesis, University of Texas at Austin, 1979.

Jefferson, Calvin B. "Tenancy as It Affects the Negro Farmer in Brazos County, Texas." Master's thesis, Prairie View Agricultural and Mechanical College, 1956.

Johnson, Shannon Dorsey. *Found in Black Texiana: Contemporary Poetry, Stories and Notes for Women with Texas and Louisiana Roots.* San Bernardino, CA: privately printed, 2013.

Johnston, O. G. "A Sociological Study of Standards of Living of Families in the Waco Negro Housing Project." Master's thesis, Baylor University, 1951.

Kearney, James C. *Nassau Plantation: The Evolution of a Texas German Slave Plantation.* Denton: University of North Texas Press, 2010.

Keir, Scott S. "Middle-Class Black Families in Austin, Texas: An Exploratory Analysis of Husbands and Wives." PhD dissertation, University of Texas at Austin, 1987.

Kilmer, Rita Kathryn. "Residential Movement of Blacks in Austin, Texas, 1950–1970." Master's thesis, University of Texas at Austin, 1974.

Kossie-Chernyshev, Karen, ed. *Recovering Five Generations Hence: The Life and Writing of Lillian Jones Horace.* College Station: Texas A&M University Press, 2013.

Krawczynski, Keith. "The Agricultural Labor of Black Texans as Slaves and as Freedmen." Master's thesis, Baylor University, 1989.

Kuffner, Cornelia. "Texas Germans Attitudes toward Slavery: Biedermeyer Sentiments and Class-Consciousness in Austin, Colorado, and Fayette Counties." Master's thesis, University of Houston, 1994.

Kuhlman, Martin. "The Civil Rights March on Austin, Texas, 1963." In *Bricks without Straw: A Comprehensive History of African Americans in Texas,* edited by David A. Williams, 153–66. Austin: Eakin Press, 1997.

———. "Direct Action at the University of Texas during the Civil Rights Movement, 1960–1965." *Southwestern Historical Quarterly* 98 (April 1995): 551–66.

Labor, Joanna. "A History of Slavery in Austin and Surrounding Area." In *Lone Star Legacy: African American History in Texas,* edited by Delicia Daniels, 73–79. Houston: Lone Star Legacy, 2011.

Lack, Paul D. "Slavery and Vigilantism in Austin, Texas, 1840–1860." *Southwestern Historical Quarterly* 85 (1981): 1–20.

Ladino, Robyn Duff. *Desegregating Texas Schools: Eisenhower, Shivers, and the Crisis at Mansfield High.* Austin: University of Texas Press, 1996.

Langham, Barbara A. "Azie Taylor Morton." *Handbook of Texas Online,* accessed June 3, 2017, https://tshaonline.org/handbook/online/articles

Leavitt, Urban J. D. "Desegregation and Attendance Zoning in Austin." Master's thesis, University of Texas at Austin, 1956.

Lewis, Oscar. *On the Edge of the Black Waxy: A Cultural Survey of Bell County, Texas.* St. Louis, MO: Washington University Studies, 1948.

Lightfoot, Billy Bob. "The Negro Exodus from Comanche County, Texas." *Southwestern Historical Quarterly* 56 (1953): 407–16.

Liles, Deborah M. "Before Emancipation: Black Cowboys and the Livestock Industry." In *Black Cowboys in the American West: On the Range, On the Stage, Behind the Badge,* edited by Bruce A. Glasrud and Michael N. Searles, 19–30. Norman: University of Oklahoma Press, 2016.

———. "Slavery and Cattle in East and West Texas." *East Texas Historical Journal* 52 (Fall 2014): 29–38.

———. "Southern Roots, Western Foundations: The Peculiar Institution and the Livestock Industry on the Northwestern Frontier of Texas, 1846–1864." PhD dissertation, University of North Texas, 2013.

Liles, Deborah M, and Angela Boswell, eds. *Women in Civil War Texas: Diversity and Dissidence in the Trans-Mississippi.* Denton: University of North Texas Press, 2016.

Manaster, Jane. "The Ethnic Geography of Austin, Texas, 1875–1910." Master's thesis, University of Texas at Austin, 1986.

Marcello, Ronald E. "The Integration of Intercollegiate Athletics in Texas: North Texas State College as a Test Case, 1956." *Journal of Sport History* 14 (Winter 1987): 286–316.

———. "Reluctance versus Reality: The Desegregation of North Texas State College, 1954–1956." *Southwestern Historical Quarterly* 99 (October 1996): 152–85.

Martin, Bonnie, and James F. Brooks, eds. *Linking the Histories of Slavery: North America and Its Borderlands.* Santa Fe, NM: School for Advanced Research Press, 2015.

McCaslin, Richard B. "Steadfast in His Intent: John W. Hargis and the Integration of the University of Texas at Austin." *Southwestern Historical Quarterly* 95 (July 1991): 25–36.

McDonald, Jason. "Confronting Jim Crow in the 'Lone Star' Capital: African-American and Ethnic-Mexican Political Leaders in Austin, Texas, 1910–1930." *Continuity and Change* 22 (May 2007): 143–69.

———. "Marginalising the Marginalised in Wartime: African Americans and Mexican Americans in Austin, Texas during the Era of World War I." *Journal of Ethnic and Migration Studies* 32 (January 2006): 129–44.

———. *Racial Dynamics in Early Twentieth-Century Austin, Texas.* Lanham, MD: Lexington, 2012.

McGowan-Johnson, Cernoria. "A Study in the History and Development of the Urban League Program in Fort Worth, Texas, 1944–1945." Master's thesis, Atlanta University, 1946.

McKey, Nola. "Preserving a Texas Legacy: The H. Wilson and Co." *Texas Highways* 10 (October 2012): 58–60.

McQueen, Clyde. *Black Churches in Texas: A Guide to Historic Congregations.* College Station: Texas A&M University Press, 2000. 23–84.

Mears, Michelle M. *And Grace Will Lead Me Home: African American Freedmen Communities of Austin, Texas, 1865–1928.* Lubbock: Texas Tech University Press, 2009.

Miles, Charles M. "Voting Habits and Political Attitudes of Negroes in Austin, Texas." Master's thesis, North Texas State University, 1963.

Miller, Norman Theodore. "Attitudes of a Selected Group of Black and White Secondary School Students toward White and Black Teachers in a Newly Desegregated High School in Austin, Texas." Master's thesis, University of Houston, 1974.

Miller, Vickie Gail. *Doris Miller: A Silent Medal of Honor Winner.* Austin: Eakin Press, 1997.

Munchus-Forde, Lady George. "History of the Negro in Fort Worth: Syllabus for a High School Course." Master's thesis, Fisk University, 1941.

Nash, Sunny. *Big Mama Didn't Shop at Woolworths*. College Station: Texas A&M University Press, 1996.

Nevels, Cynthia Skove. *Lynching to Belong: Claiming Whiteness through Racial Violence*. College Station: Texas A&M University Press, 2007.

Nieman, Donald G. "African Americans and the Meaning of Freedom: Washington County, Texas, as a Case Study, 1865–1886." *Chicago Kent Law Review* 70 (1994): 541–79.

———. "Black Political Power and Criminal Justice: Washington County, Texas, 1868–1884." *Journal of Southern History* 55 (August 1989): 391–420.

Noe, Minnie Alice. "History of Jarvis Christian College." Master's thesis, Texas Christian University, 1966.

Oliphant, Dave. "Eddie Durham and the Texas Contribution to Jazz History." *Southwestern Historical Quarterly* 96 (1993): 490–525.

O'Neal, Bill. *Doris Miler: Hero of Pearl Harbor*. Waco, TX: Eakin Press, 2007.

Person, Oswell. *African American Bryan Texas: Celebrating the Past*. Charleston, SC: History Press, 2012.

Ponder, Janace Pope. "*Sepia*." Master's thesis, North Texas State University, 1973.

Preuss, Gene. "Within Those Walls: The African American School and Community in Lubbock and New Braunfels, Texas." *Sound Historian* 4 (Fall 1998): 36–43.

Radford, Garry H., Sr. *African American Heritage in Waco, Texas: Life Stories of Those Who Believed They Could Overcome Impediments*. Austin: Eakin Press, 2000.

Reid, Debra A. *Reaping a Greater Harvest: African Americans, the Extension Service, and Rural Reform in Jim Crow Texas*. College Station: Texas A&M University Press, 2007.

Robinson, Dorothy Redus. *The Bell Rings at Four: A Black Teacher's Chronicle of Change*. Austin: Madrona Press, 1978.

Sample, Albert Race. *Race Hoss: Big Emma's Boy*. Austin: Eakin Press, 1984.

Sanders, Bob Ray. *Calvin Littlejohn: Portrait of a Community in Black and White*. Fort Worth: TCU Press, 2009.

Sanders, Drew. *The Garden of Eden: The Story of a Freedmen's Community in Texas*. Fort Worth: TCU Press, 2015.

Sapper, Neil G. "Aboard the Wrong Ship in the Right Books: Doris Miller and Historical Accuracy." *East Texas Historical Journal* 18 (January 1980): 3–11.

Schupak, Charles W. "A Comparative Study of White and Negro Schools in Fayette and Eight Adjoining Counties." Master's thesis, University of Texas at Austin, 1953.

Selcer, Richard F. *A History of Fort Worth in Black and White: 165 Years of African-American Life*. Denton: University of North Texas Press, 2015.

———. "William Madison McDonald: A Man of Wealth and Power." Reprinted in *Lone Star Legacy: Poetry, Prose, and History in Texas*, edited by Delicia Daniels, 29–42. Houston: Lone Star Legacy, 2015.

Shackles, Chrystine I. *Reminiscences of Huston-Tillotson College*. Austin: Best Printing, 1973.

Simond, Ada DeBlanc. *Looking Back*. Austin: Austin Independent School District, 1984.

Sitton, Thad, and James H. Conrad. *Freedom Colonies: Independent Black Texans in the Time of Jim Crow*. Austin: University of Texas Press, 2005.

Smallwood, James. *A Century of Achievement: Blacks in Cooke County, Texas*. Gainesville, TX: Gainesville Printing, 1995.

Smith, Rogers M. "The Waco Lynching of 1916: Perspective and Analysis." Master's thesis, Baylor University, 1971.

Smyrl, Vivian Elizabeth. "Bluff Springs, Texas." *Handbook of Texas Online*, accessed June 26, 2017, www.tshaonline.org/articles

SoRelle, James M. "The Waco Horror: The Lynching of Jesse Washington." *Southwestern Historical Quarterly* 86 (1983): 517–36.

Spurlin, Virginia L. "The Conners of Waco: Black Professionals in Twentieth-Century Texas." PhD dissertation, Texas Tech University, 1991.

Stein, Bill, ed. "The Slave Narratives of Colorado County." *Nesbitt Memorial Library Journal* 3 (January 1993): 3–32.

Terrell, Suzanne J. *This Other Kind of Doctors: Traditional Medical Systems in Black Neighborhoods in Austin, Texas.* New York: AMS Press, 1990.

Tomlinson, Chris. *Tomlinson Hill: The Remarkable Story of Two Families Who Share the Tomlinson Name—One White, One Black.* New York: St. Martin's Press, 2014.

Traynor, Ronald D. "Barrett Station, Texas: Life in a Black Community, 1865–2005." PhD dissertation, University of Houston, 2005.

Ulrich, Ora Emma. "A Study of the Expenditure of Urban Negro Work Relief Families in Travis County, Texas as Compared to an Adequate Diet." Master's thesis, University of Texas at Austin, 1935.

Uzzel, Robert L. *Blind Lemon Jefferson: His Life, His Death, and His Legacy.* Fort Worth: Eakin Press, 2002.

Walters, Katherine K. K. "The Great War in Waco, Texas: African Americans, Race Relations, and the White Primary, 1916–1922." Master's thesis, Southwest Texas State University, 2000.

Wassenich, Paul Green. "A Social Study of the Negro Population of Austin, Texas, 1928–1935." Master's thesis, University of Texas at Austin, 1936.

Williams, David Alvernon. "A History of African American Higher Education in Austin and Travis County, Texas." In *Bricks without Straw: A Comprehensive History of African Americans in Texas,* 279–308. Austin: Eakin Press, 1997.

Williams, J. Allen. "The Effects of Urban Renewal upon a Black Community [Kealing Section of Austin, Texas]: Evaluation and Recommendations." *Social Science Quarterly* 50 (1969): 703–12.

Williams, Joyce E. *Black Community Control: A Study of Transition in a Texas Ghetto.* New York: Praeger, 1973.

Williams, Mabel Crayton. "The History of Tillotson College, 1881–1952." Master's thesis, Texas Southern University, 1967.

Wilson, Anna Victoria. "Forgotten Voices: Remembered Experiences of Cross-over Teachers during Desegregation in Austin, Texas, 1964–1971." PhD dissertation, University of Texas at Austin, 1997.

Wilson, Anna Victoria, and William E. Segall. *Oh, Do I Remember! Experiences of Teachers during the Desegregation of Austin's Schools, 1964–1971.* Albany: State University of New York Press, 2001.

Wilson, Samuel. "Vanished Legacies and the Lost Culture of I. M. Terrell High School in Segregated Fort Worth." Master's thesis, University of Texas at Arlington, 2012.

Xie, Jingling. "The Black Community in Waco, Texas, 1880–1900." Master's thesis, Baylor University, 1988.

Yates, Donald Lee. "Correlates of Attitudes toward the Police: A Comparison of Black and White Citizens in Austin, Texas." PhD dissertation, University of Texas at Austin, 1984.

INDEX